Three Great Air Stories

In the same series

THREE GREAT ESCAPE STORIES
The Wooden Horse
Escape Alone
Return Ticket

THREE GREAT ANIMAL STORIES
Return to the Wild
The New Noah
Sauce for the Mongoose

THREE GREAT WAR STORIES
The Tunnel
The Man Who Saved London
Carve Her Name with Pride

THREE GREAT SEA STORIES
Malta Convoy
Tinkerbelle
Unbroken

THREE GREAT ADVENTURE STORIES
One More River
Airline Detective
The Tartan Pimpernel

Three
Great Air Stories

Reach for the Sky

Skymen

The Man in the Hot Seat

COLLINS

ST JAMES'S PLACE, LONDON

ISBN 0 00 192330 7
Three Great Air Stories was first published 1970
Reprinted 1971

Reach for the Sky was first published 1954
A junior edition was first published 1957
© Paul Brickhill 1954, 1957

Skymen was first published 1961
A junior edition was first published 1964
and this shortened edition 1970
© Larry Forrester 1961, 1964, 1970

The Man in the Hot Seat was first published 1969
© Doddy Hay 1969

Printed in Great Britain
Collins Clear-Type Press
London and Glasgow

Contents

REACH FOR THE SKY
Paul Brickhill

SKYMEN
Larry Forrester

THE MAN IN THE HOT SEAT
Doddy Hay

Reach For The Sky

PAUL BRICKHILL

To Thelma

CONTENTS

I.	YOUNG CHAMPION	*page* 9
II.	PILOT OFFICER, R.A.F.	15
III.	CRASH!	29
IV.	BOTH LEGS LOST	34
V.	FIGHTING BACK	43
VI.	"TIN LEGS"	50
VII.	HE WALKS AGAIN	62
VIII.	HE FLIES AGAIN	71
IX.	OUT OF THE R.A.F.	79
X.	A WIFE AND GOLF	87
XI.	WAR!—BACK IN UNIFORM	97
XII.	SPITFIRE PILOT	106
XIII.	FIRST VICTORY	115
XIV.	SQUADRON LEADER	122
XV.	THE BATTLE BEGINS	129
XVI.	THE THICK OF THE FRAY	136
XVII.	WING LEADER	147
XVIII.	HITLER'S FIRST DEFEAT	155

CONTENTS

XIX. MORE PROMOTION   *page* 158

XX. ON THE ATTACK!   165

XXI. INVINCIBLE?   174

XXII. DOWNFALL   181

XXIII. ESCAPE   193

XXIV. RECAPTURE   206

XXV. PRISON CAMP   217

XXVI. OUT AGAIN—IN AGAIN   226

XXVII. PUNISHMENT CAMP   237

XXVIII. FREEDOM AND VICTORY   242

INTERIM EPILOGUE   252

CHAPTER ONE

YOUNG CHAMPION

IN 1909 the doctor warned Jessie Bader that her second baby might not be born alive and that it would be risky for her to go ahead with it, but she resisted any interference.

Frederick Bader[1] brought his young wife and the other baby, Frederick, or 'Derick, home to England from India on furlough for the birth and they took a house at St. John's Wood. The doctor and midwife arrived on 21st February, 1910, and Fredrick Bader walked restlessly around the house. Jessie's sister, Hazel, and the German nursemaid waited hours outside the bedroom door until a thin but persistent cry broke the quiet; a little later the door opened and the doctor came out.

" The little trouble-maker has arrived," he said benignly. " It's a boy."

They christened the baby Douglas Robert Steuart; and the " Steuart," from his maternal great-grandfather, was not all that the baby inherited from the intractable John Steuart Amos, who drove to the Liverpool docks in the family carriage one day in the 1840's, got out pulling a kitbag after him, and told the coachman, " You may tell the family I will not be returning." He walked on board a windjammer, talked himself into a job as ship's carpenter and worked his passage to India.

In a few years John Amos was an officer in the Indian Naval Service. He married, and later appalled his family

---

[1] Pronounced Bahder.

of daughters by telling them how he watched the ring-leaders of the Mutiny lashed across the cannon's mouth and blown out of this world.

His eldest daughter, Jessie, was least appalled by the story. She had her father's bold eyes and was impervious to fear. In the 'eighties she married a gentle engineer in India called McKenzie, and they had two daughters, Jessie and Hazel. Mr. McKenzie died then, and his wife brought up the two girls with a resourceful hand. Hazel was a pretty girl who had inherited her father's gentleness, but it was becoming clear that her sister, Jessie, had inherited the mettle of John Steuart Amos and her mother.

She was seventeen when she met Frederick Roberts Bader, and she was eighteen when she married him. He was twenty years older, a gruff, heavily moustached, almost confirmed bachelor. They lived comfortably in the hot, dry plains around Sukkur and Kotri, and a year later the first baby was born. Both of them doted on 'Derick and within a year all three were on their way back to England for Jessie to have the second baby.

Three days after Douglas was born in St. John's Wood, both mother and baby caught measles, and as soon as both were better Jessie had to have a major operation. From the start baby and mother were virtually separated. Jessie recovered, and then the family was due back in India. Douglas was only a few months old ; a little young, they thought for India's climate, so they left him with relatives on the Isle of Man.

He was almost two by the time he was taken out to join the family in Sukkur and that may have been the beginning of the loneliness that has been deep within him ever since. He was a stranger in India. 'Derick had been receiving the attention lavished on an only child and the new boy did not fit in.

Then the war came and Frederick Bader was commissioned in the Royal Engineers and went to France. Douglas, now a spirited five-year-old, was ever ready to show his mother and 'Derick that he was no minor underling, and 'Derick, finding he would leap at any challenge, used to dare him to carry out hazardous exploits. Never refusing a dare, Douglas came to be considered as much the naughtier of the two.

Soon Douglas joined 'Derick at Colet Court, a nearby prep. school. Their Aunt Hazel was back from India and usually escorted them to and from school in the bus, a series of nightmare journeys, as they seldom stopped fighting.

At Colet Court he had his first fights and they were always with bigger boys. After a while there were not so many fights because he never lost one.

'Derick went on to prep. school at Temple Grove, near Eastbourne, and there was a little more peace in the house.

The boys seldom saw their father, who was in the thick of it in France. In 1917 shrapnel wounded Major Bader badly in the head. They could not get all the shrapnel out, but he recovered without home leave and went back into the fighting.

Douglas followed 'Derick to Temple Grove, a pleasant school with plenty of playing fields. The régime quickly drew the new boy into organised games and overnight he seemed to flare up like a Roman candle with eagerness. It was the perfect outlet for his mercurial nature and he literally threw himself into rugger. Fast on his feet and fast-thinking, he shone as fly-half, and after the first few games was promoted to more senior teams.

In the gym he limbered up on the parallel bars or the horizontal bar, the vaulting horse or in the boxing ring;

he would try anything, hating to let anything beat him. People lost count of the times he fell off the parallel bars, but he learned to fall without hurting himself; in fact, he lost all fear of falling, and that, as he later discovered, was one of the most important things that ever happened to him.

At home in the holidays, the favoured 'Derick talked his mother into buying them bows and arrows. They started shooting at each other first, and then as they became too accurate for comfort took to ambushing passers-by.

Now the war was over but still they rarely saw their father, who was still in the Army, helping repair war damage.

Meantime Hazel had married an R.A.F. flight lieutenant, Cyril Burge, who had flown most of the war in the Royal Flying Corps. He fascinated Douglas by the wings and ribbons on his tunic and his stories of the war.

Back at school, Douglas shone at cricket too, being miraculously quick as a fieldsman and a batsman who believed that the ball was there to be hit.

Though he always tried to the limit at games he never tried hard in the classroom. He picked up Latin and Greek with ease and was often top of his form, but never worked harder than just enough. Maths and other modern subjects he detested and did the barest minimum of work on them so that his reports usually said, " Very good, but could do better if he tried."

The P.T. instructor, Crease, a retired chief petty officer with a beard, taught him to shoot. Crease drilled it into him to get his bead and shoot quickly before the sight became blurred with concentration, and he became accurate and fast in shooting (which years later cost men their lives).

In 1922 a War Office telegram came to the house in

Kew regretting that Major Bader had died of his wounds in St. Omer—the shrapnel which had wounded him in the head in 1917. Though the boys had seen little of their father, it did not make Douglas feel any more secure. Later, a more practical effect had to be faced. 'Derick had already gone on to King's School at Canterbury. Now there was doubt whether funds were enough to send Douglas to public school too. The one solution was a scholarship, and a very loath boy began studying to prove his reports : " could do better if he tried."

Not for a moment did he slacken his sporting activity. In that year he was captain of cricket, captain of rugger, captain of soccer, and in the school sports in the final term won every senior race he could enter for, then set a new school record for throwing the cricket ball. At term's end the headmaster told him he had also won a scholarship to St. Edward's School, Oxford.

About this time Jessie Bader, dark and vividly good-looking at thirty-two, remarried. The boys' stepfather was the vicar of Sprotborough (Yorkshire), the Reverend Ernest William Hobbs, who had been a gentle bachelor of thirty-seven before his life was so radically stirred up. Jessie was devoted to him but still had her outspoken wilfulness, while the two boys resented going up to Yorkshire to live in the rambling rectory.

The vicar was too mild for his intransigent new family. He suggested that 'Derick and Douglas might like to mow the grass but they flatly refused, and that was that. Jessie was firmer, insisting that the two boys take it in turns to pump the water in the kitchen, and they did so. The vicar tried to institute family prayers after breakfast, but Douglas and 'Derick scuffled and fidgeted so much that he gave it up. Jessie was inclined to blame Douglas, and he began to feel more at home out of doors.

That summer he was packed off for a week with Cyril and Hazel Burge at Cranwell, where Cyril was adjutant of the Royal Air Force College.

From Hazel and Cyril the welcome was warm. Only thirteen, Douglas had never been near aeroplanes before, and when the quiet, good-humoured Cyril sat him in the cockpit of an Avro 504 trainer the thick hair almost vanished as the boy bent over the controls and dials like a terrier. Later he stood for hours in Cyril's garden watching the bellowing Avros taking off over his head as the cadets practised " circuits and bumps." Every morning at 6.30 he joined the cadets in training runs, doggedly trying to keep up.

When Hazel and Cyril were putting him in the train for Sprotborough he said, " Crumbs, I want to come back to Cranwell as a cadet."

CHAPTER TWO

PILOT OFFICER, R.A.F.

A MILE OR TWO along the Woodstock Road outside Oxford, St. Edward's School lay behind a high stone wall. The boys seldom saw much of Oxford. If they went outside the gates in the stone wall it was usually to cross the road to the playing fields. Behind the wall the school buildings stood around the quad, the Warden's house, School House, Big Hall, Big School, and the other houses. And a little apart, Cowell's House, into which the new boy, Bader, in new blue suit and new bowler hat, walked on a late summer morning in 1923. The new boys always arrived a day before school reassembled. A dozen or so were allotted to Cowell's and for a while they and Douglas stood meekly in the lower hall, lonely and strange, waiting for their next directions. Upstairs, the housemaster had some guests for sherry before lunch. Douglas dropped his new bowler hat. He did not like it very much. He gave it a kick to express what he felt.

A voice above said crisply : " Boy ! "

He looked up. A lean face peered over the landing balustrade, cold eyes behind spectacles.

" Stop kicking your hat about. Pick it up and be quiet."

" Yes, sir," said the boy, abashed.

The face vanished. For seconds the hall was quiet. Then Douglas dropped his hat and kicked it once more to establish independent self-respect.

Above, the voice rasped louder : " Boy ! "

In the hall the new boys froze. The face of the house-master peered again over the balustrade. " Come here, boy ! " he said.

The sherry guests were impressed to see the house-master return, excuse himself briefly, draw a cane from behind the grandfather clock and make his resolute exit. They did not witness the six strokes on the tightened trousers seat. Nor for that matter did they hear anything. Douglas never yelped.

Games claimed his interest and absorbed excess energy. He played house cricket down on the canal fields, clouted a punching ball in the gym and swam in the pool. School became his real life, not only the playing fields but the little things in the background—the red blankets on the iron beds in the dormitories, the overgrown patch in the middle of the quad known as " The Jungle," the " San," the " Crystal Palace " (main lavatories), " Hell " (the mysterious base-ment room where the text-books were stored), and Hall, where they clattered in to the long refectory tables. In his second term the rugger season was in. As fly half in the House second team he showed such dash that they promoted him to the House first team.

Back home for the holidays, 'Derick and Douglas bought air-guns, and a reign of terror began in Sprot-borough until the day Douglas saw through a bathroom window the pale form of a noted local lady about to step into the bath. Someone dared him, and a moment later the pellet smashed through the splintering glass, followed by a squeal. The sharpshooter vanished and later had a heated argument with 'Derick about the suffering inflicted by an air-gun pellet. 'Derick demonstrated by shooting Douglas in the shoulder at point-blank range, and that started a scuffle which ended with Jessie confiscating the guns.

The year 1924 was trouble-free at St. Edward's because he was busy on the playing fields. At Christmas time the boys put on a Shakespearian play in the Big School and a youngster called Laurence Olivier outshone the others.

In 1925 Douglas was more games-mad than ever, and more fidgety in class. It was not easy to pin charges on him because with no effort he still shone at Latin and Greek, showed interest in history and absorbed pages of poetry with obvious pleasure. Maths was his weakness: he still hated them and refused to bother, so that several times he was " carpeted " by his new housemaster, A. F. Yorke.

Simple misdemeanours such as indoor rugger and debagging, combining with his academic reluctance, brought him occasionally to the attention of the Warden (headmaster), the Rev. H. E. Kendall.

In the summer holidays 'Derick persuaded Jessie to let them have the air-guns again, and the boys used them for poaching. An accurate snapshooter, Douglas once got a partridge on the wing, a rare feat with an air-gun. Jessie confiscated the guns again and scolded bitterly that their behaviour was undermining her authority as vicar's wife. The two boys were good friends now, making common cause against authority, though they were beginning to have affection for " Bill " Hobbs, the gentle vicar.

Back at school, Douglas was " capped " for cricket, aged only fifteen and the youngest boy in the team. He had finished the season top of both batting and bowling averages for the First Eleven and set up a new school record for throwing the cricket ball.

But it was winter he was waiting for. He liked the rough and tumble of rugger above everything. On the Thursday before the first game the captain pinned the names of the First Fifteen on the board under the cloisters of Big School, and Douglas, looking over the heads of the huddle round it, saw his own name scrawled there as fly-half. A glow flushed through him and he walked away soaked with quiet, fulfilled happiness. It was the warmest moment of life. On the Saturday he played, almost broke his nose in a tackle, had blood drawn from a gashed lip, scored a try and distinguished himself by his fiery vigour.

At Easter his mother told him she did not think they would be able to keep him on at St. Edward's after the new term.

Half-way through the next term, Walter Dingwall, a young history master who also acted as bursar for the school sent for him and said, " I'm sorry, Bader, but we've just had a letter from your mother to say that she does not think you will be able to return here next term. Don't worry. We'll see what we can do about it."

A week later Bader was playing for the First Eleven again, boxing and running for his House, and Yorke had just made him a House prefect. At the end of term he went home for the holidays, but no one said anything about leaving school and after the holidays he went back to St. Edward's again.

The Warden made him a school prefect with the privilege of wielding a cane and of possessing a study in the " Beehive," a quaint little octagonal building where the rooms were tiny triangles just big enough for a boy, a desk and chair and a trunk covered with cushions.

Early in summer he went to the San one day and said he thought he was getting 'flu. They found he had a temperature and put him to bed, and as he lay there he began to feel light-headed and then his heart began to pound. He was drifting away from the room and reality, withdrawing into himself. The nurse found him delirious with rheumatic fever.

For several days he wandered in delirium, close to death. They sent for his mother and she came down from Sprotborough and stayed nearby. In the chapel the whole school prayed for him. Then the fever broke one night and the crisis passed.

Out of the San he began training again, swimming, then gym and running. Soon after the rugger season started the doctor examined him and, a little surprised, found he was fit enough to play. So fit, as it happened, that Arthur Tilley made him captain of the First Fifteen.

This was Bader's first real taste of leadership. He lived for the team, full of a breezy, non-stop enthusiasm both on the field and off that infected everyone else. Every player was a brother (slightly junior) to be exhorted and coached and fired with enthusiasm from dawn till lights out. Douglas lived for them—with one proviso: they must also live for the team, dedicated, tireless and fearless. Tilley noticed that Bader's paternal concern for his team was overshadowing his own ego.

At lunch one day the Warden asked him what he was going to do when he left school, and Bader said simply that he did not know. Lately he had begun asking himself the same question. Go on to Oxford? He could probably win a scholarship, but that would mean hard study. Besides, what would he read at Oxford? Classics? History? Neither appealed. Certainly not maths. 'Derick was talking of going out to South Africa in engineering but that did not appeal either. As he did so often with tedious things like text-books, he put the problem out of his mind.

Shortly before Christmas an old boy, Roy Bartlett, now at Cranwell, visited the school, and Bader remembered his own visit there five years earlier. Flying might be fun. That night he wrote to Uncle Cyril asking what his chances were of getting into Cranwell as a cadet.

Cyril Burge had left Cranwell and was now personal assistant to Air Chief Marshal Sir Hugh Trenchard, Chief of the Air Staff, With the satisfaction of a match-maker, Cyril wrote back saying that Douglas was just the type they wanted and he would do everything he could to help. There was one catch—Cyril pointed out that it would cost Jessie and the vicar about £150 a year[1] to send him to Cranwell, and the course lasted two years. Could they afford it ?

Douglas took the question home and Jessie quickly settled it. (a) She did not like flying, (b) she did not think Douglas should go into the Air Force, and (c) they could not possibly afford £150 a year.

She added, " You wouldn't be at St. Edward's now but for the kindness of Mr. Dingwall."

" What d'you mean ? " He was puzzled.

" I didn't want you to know yet," his mother said, " but Mr. Dingwall has been paying the rest of your fees since 1926."

The news staggered him, more so as he knew his mother had never met Dingwall, who was such a reserved person that he himself hardly knew Dingwall.

Back at school he went to thank Dingwall, and the master shrugged it off with a laugh and got off the subject by asking him what he was going to do when he left. Bader mentioned that he had hoped to get into the R.A.F.

" Something might be arranged," Dingwall said.

Shortly another letter came from Burge saying that six prize cadetships were given every year to Cranwell.

---

[1] In those days Cranwell was like a public school in that it charged fees. Now, no fees are charged ; in fact, cadets are even paid.

Several hundred boys fancied them, there was a stiff eliminating examination and the academic standard was high.

Bader tapped on the housemaster's door. Did Mr. Yorke think he was good enough to win a prize cadetship?

"I think you *could* get one, Bader," Yorke said.

"But I'm no good at maths, sir."

"You're lazy at maths, I know that."

"If I worked hard, sir, and you coached, d'you think I could catch up?"

"If you worked hard," said Yorke, "I *know* you could do it. Are you prepared to?"

Bader took a breath and said, "Yes, sir, I'll have a shot."

He joined the small circle of boys, sometimes known as "the Army Sixth," whom Yorke coached in maths. They were all trying for the Services. After his day's work, duties and games, Bader spent a couple of hours every night "cramming" maths, hating it but sticking to it.

That spring (1928) he became captain of cricket, then early in June a letter called him to London for R.A.F. examination, interview and medical.

He sat for the exam in a comfortless room in Burlington Place. The maths paper, happily, was almost a replica of those that Mr. Yorke had been setting for him, and he finished on time. After lunch he stood to attention in front of a long table while five elderly men in civilian clothes gazed at him. Some of the questions seemed irrelevant: "How often do you brush your teeth?" —"What is the capital of Sweden?"—but all the time the eyes were on him.

"Why do you want to join the Air Force?"

" I think it would suit my temperament, sir . . . and so does my housemaster."

(Satisfied nods).

" What do you do in your holidays ? "

" Oh, games, sir. *Team* games usually. Cricket or rugger."

He came out knowing he had done well. (Out of a maximum of 250 points for the interview he had, in fact, scored 235, a figure which is seldom approached.)

Then to the doctors. They looked down his throat, into his eyes and ears, tapped him all over, made him blow a column of mercury up a fuse and hold it, holding his breath, listened to his heart and took his blood pressure.

About a week later another letter came from Air Ministry and he made himself open it slowly. The unemotional, numbered paragraphs told him he had come fifth in the examinations, had won a prize cadetship and would be required to present himself at Cranwell in September with a change of underclothes, bowler hat and toilet articles.

He was proud when he told Dingwall.

" From what I know of Cranwell, all the chaps there have motor-bikes," Dingwall observed. " I think you'd better have one, too, as a reward for your work."

He pressed the point over the boy's reluctance with discreet insistence, and soon Bader had a second-hand, flat-twin Douglas motor-cycle for which Dingwall had paid £30.

At Sprotborough his mother was still dubious about the Air Force as a career. As 'Derick had gone off to South Africa, Douglas got more attention than usual and responded warmly to it.

In the second week in September, Douglas strapped two small suitcases to the pillion of the motor-cycle, rammed a new bowler hat rakishly over the headlight, kissed his mother, shook the vicar's hand, and pelted with exhaust blaring down the highway towards Cranwell. Two hours later, roaring down the Ancaster straight four miles from Cranwell, he saw a cow wander across the road ahead and swerved; his front wheel hit the grass verge and the motor-cycle kicked over the steep bank and cartwheeled on the other side. Thrown clear on the grass, he got groggily to his feet, shaken and bruised but otherwise unhurt. Watched by the cow, he hauled the motor-cycle upright, wheeled it back to the road and kicked the self-starter. The engine blurted healthily and everything seemed all right till he noticed the headlamp sticking through the top of the bowler hat where the crown had burst and a flap at the top gaped open like a tin lid. Eight minutes later he rode through the gates of Cranwell.

A confused couple of hours then, waiting, coming to attention and saying, " Sir," filling in forms, saying a few brief and guarded words to other new boys, and then a corporal led four of them to a hut, into an end room where four iron cots covered with khaki blankets stood against the wooden wall. Rough bedside tables, four lockers—an impression of bareness.

A couple of days later he reported to the flight hangar with flying kit. A chunky little man came into the cadet pilots' room and introduced himself as Flying Officer Pearson. Bader was to be his pupil. They went out on the tarmac and Pearson led him to a flimsy-looking biplane. It was an Avro 504, the same type he had sat in at Cranwell five years earlier.

" We're going up for half an hour," Pearson said. " You won't touch the controls this time. It's just to get you used to the idea of flying." He explained briefly why and how the machine flew, pointed out the controls, strapped him in the rear cockpit (all open in those days)

23

and slipped into the front cockpit himself. The propeller spun into noisy life, and in a little while they were bouncing across the field. Gently the grass sank below, wing-tips tilted, and Douglas, leaning over the leather-padded rim of the cockpit, wind whipping at his face, looked down on green country, exhilaration bubbling in him. Soon they dipped towards the landing ground.

"How did you like it?" Pearson asked, and found his answer in gleaming eyes.

Next afternoon Flight Cadet D. R. S. Bader took the control column in the air for the first time, gingerly at first, then too tightly, till Pearson's voice nudged at him to relax. Stick gently forward and the nose dipped; gently back and it rose; stick to each side and it tilted. Then feet on the rudder bar and the first co-ordinated turns. Taut concentration for a few minutes: it was strange; one had to think before one could tentatively act. Then the athlete's eye, mind and muscle began to combine in harmony and he had the feel of it. Pearson kept quietly drilling into Bader: "Never be brutal with your aeroplane. Guide it. Don't shove it." And another time: "I never want to hear you call it a plane or a kite. The word is aeroplane or aircraft." (Never since that day has it ever been anything else from Bader's lips. Pearson taught him to look on an aeroplane as a man might regard his favourite horse.)

A fter a landing in October, when the pupil had had only six and a half hours' dual instruction, Pearson got out and said: "D'you think you could take it around on your own?" Douglas grinned and nodded, and Pearson casually waved him off, saying: "All right. Don't bend it." It is always done like that, before a pupil has time to start worrying. Bader did not worry; he opened the throttle and eased the Avro into the air. Gently he turned upwind, slanted her down towards the field, jockeyed her down, flattening, holding off, as the tail sank until the little aeroplane settled in a velvety and somewhat flukey three-pointer.

Now he had gone solo, Flight Cadet Bader wanted to be a fighter pilot, and flying vied with rugger for his devotion. He liked Cranwell exceedingly. Sometimes they could stay out until midnight, they could ride motor-bikes, smoke and be men of the world. After a couple of puffs at a cigarette he had tossed it away with distaste. He tried a pipe, liked it, decided it would not clog his lungs if he did not inhale, and soon was an addict.

The only catch was the schoolroom part. Theory of flight, engines, signals, armaments and such things were reasonably interesting, but the maths! He ignored them. Besides, the rugger season had arrived. He was picked for the First Fifteen, and for the first time Cranwell beat both Sandhurst and the Woolwich Military Academy.

The flight cadets were paid £4 a month pocket money, but every twelve weeks the post brought Bader cheques for a further £12 from Walter Dingwall, with a brief note when the first cheque arrived saying that there was no reason why Bader should have less than the others. He wrote several letters of thanks, deeply touched at Dingwall's generosity, but Dingwall always stayed remotely in the background. Bader never saw him after leaving St. Edward's, but he did discover that Dingwall had intended to pay his fees at Cranwell had he failed to win his prize cadetship.

In the air Pearson was initiating him into aerobatics, teaching him not to throw the Avro about, but to coax her through every antic in the book. Bader began to find the joy of an artist, in a slow roll, for instance, of revolving her evenly about her axis without losing height. Yet not

25

all his flying was copybook. An enterprising fellow-cadet named Hank More evolved a hair-raising trick of climbing out of his rear cockpit in mid-air and crawling forward to tie a handkerchief about the joystick in the empty front cockpit, then getting back into the rear cockpit. One had to take one's parachute off to do it. On his next solo flight, of course, Cadet Bader did it too, finding it diverting to be straddled across the fuselage like a bare-back rider, holding on with the heels while the hands were busy tying the handkerchief.

The fact is that discipline alone was never enough to curb him. They "gated" him for roaring round the district at high speed on his motor-bike, and when he was freed from barracks he did it again, more culpably, by having John Chance or his particular friend, the dark, slight Geoffrey Stephenson, on the pillion (pillion riding was strictly forbidden). Chance bought an old Morris car for £50, and the three of them kept this banned luxury hidden in an old barn about a mile from the camp.

After a year they sat for exams. He struggled with his maths, and afterwards, with Chance, Stepehenson and Denys Field, rattled off to a dance at Grantham in the old Morris. They arrived back at the barn with three minutes to sign in at the guardroom a mile away. Bader alone had his motor-cycle there; all four festooned themselves on it, and two minutes later, after a crazy ride, he was pulling up a hundred yards from the guardhouse to let the others off to walk the rest, when suddenly a torch shone on them, held by an advancing policeman. It was a fair cop. Service police came down from the guardhouse and there was a solemn period of name and note-taking.

In the morning the four of them had a menacing interview with the squadron commander. Bader was fined £2 for being in improper control of his motor-cycle, and next morning the four of them went out in the car again. As they returned a hawk-eyed instructor coming in to land just overhead, spotted them. At this trying moment the results of the exams came out and Cadet Bader, scholarship winner, was nineteenth out of twenty-one.

This time he stood alone on the carpet, and after a crisp homily the squadron commander concluded by saying: "I'm fed up with you. If you don't change considerably I shall take steps to have you and your friends removed from the college."

Bader emerged a disturbed young man and received a message to report to the commandant. Unhappily he went.

Air Vice Marshal Halahan was a former heavyweight boxing champion who spoke in a quiet voice. Bader listened to a dispassionate review of his misdemeanours and winced at the end when Halahan said, "You're young. I can understand your trouble, but the Air Force won't go on understanding. They don't want schoolboys here. They want men."

He almost crept out, feeling he had shrunk to about half size. To have his manhood challenged! After a couple of days' heavy thinking Flight Cadet Bader was a different young man. He even began studying maths. Like any convert, he steered a rigidly straight path, his maths kept improving and his flying, as always, was deft and accurate.

Now the course was flying single-seater Siskins, biplane fighters odd to modern eyes, but they made Bader keener than ever to be a fighter pilot.

He stuck to his studies, but without missing a moment from games, and in both his years at Cranwell got his "blues" for cricket, rugger, hockey and boxing.

Young tyros in the R.A.F. have not always been noted

for temperance, but Bader was. Once he tried beer, and once each sherry and whisky, but never finished any of them. He did not like them; therefore he ignored them. In any case, at a party he had his own spirits to exhilarate him.

Early in 1930 his persistent new virtue was rewarded when he and another outstanding cadet, Paddy Coote, were appointed under-officers of " A " and " B " Training Squadrons. Once again he was a leader with responsibilities.

June they sat for their final exams and this time he had no qualms about his work. The exam results came out, and Paddy Coote just beat him for the Sword of Honour. No one could mind being second to a man like Coote.

In official terms the report on Bader summed him up neatly : " Plucky, capable, headstrong." His flying rating was " above average," which is R.A.F. understatement for a natural pilot. Then the postings :

" P/O Bader, D. R. S., to 23 Squadron, Kenley."

He rode his motor-cycle to London and traded it in for his first car, a second-hand Austin Seven. In this, on an August morning in 1930, he drove to Kenley, brimming with content. No. 23 Squadron flew Gloster Gamecock fighters.

CHAPTER THREE

CRASH!

BEFORE THE AGE of runways Kenley was a large grass
field, and behind the hangars on the rim lay the graces of
a station built in peace for an Air Force that was small
and select. A mess waiter showed Bader to his room, an
austere enough affair with an iron bed, leather chair and
simple furniture. It was home: the life he wanted lay
before him.

In the morning B Flight commander sat him in a
Gamecock and showed him " the taps." She was a tubby
little thing and from the cockpit he felt he could almost
touch the tips of the two braced and strutted wings. Top
speed was 156 m.p.h., but the stumpy fuselage made her
the most agile little aeroplane in the R.A.F. He took her
up that morning, rolled and tumbled her about the sky for
half an hour and joyfully agreed with that.

He slid effortlessly into squadron life, perhaps a shade
too confident for a new boy, but too friendly and vital to
irk anyone. On " dining-in " nights when immaculate,
in mess kit, they passed the port decanter, Douglas, strictly
sober, joined as wildly and hilariously as anyone in the
subsequent games of rugger in the ante-room with a
waste-paper basket for a ball. Life was idyllic, with
flying, games and fellowship, buttressed by the tangible
prestige and comfort of a permanent commission from
Cranwell. Most of all he liked aerobatics in the Gamecock.

That same August he arrived at Kenley he was picked for the R.A.F. cricket team.

A month later, when cricket was finished, the Harlequins, famous amateur rugger club, asked him to play in a trial game. A few weeks later he was picked for the R.A.F. Fifteen. By his twenty-first birthday in February, 1931, his name was becoming widely identified with a sinewy, beautifully-tuned human machine that weighed eleven stone six pounds stripped, and had the temperament of a dynamo.

All other fighter squadrons now had the Bristol Bulldog or the Siskin; only 23 Squadron was left with Gamecocks, and that was partly why they were chosen to do the combined aerobatics at Hendon that year. Woollett picked C Flight Commander, Harry Day, to lead the team, and all the other pilots started training hard for selection. In April, Woollet told Douglas that he was to be second man in the team, with Geoffrey Stephenson as number three, in reserve. Harry Day was a lean, glint-eyed man who had fought as a youngster in the Great War, and now, a hawk-faced thirty, commanded instant obedience.

The Times said that 175,000 were inside Hendon Aerodrome on the day of the display and that " hundreds of thousands of others crowded hillsides and fields outside." They saw " the event of the day " as Day and Bader in the Gamecocks " provided the most thrilling spectacle ever seen in exhibition flying."

The aerobatics team flew to Cramlington for a display, and on the way back, Bader dropped out of the formation to spend an hour skimming over the hedges. When they landed, Day read him an angry lecture on flying discipline.

A couple of weeks later he heard that he was on the " A List," a roster of young officers due for posting overseas. He seemed slated for Iraq, and late in summer, sitting in the pavilion at Aldershot waiting to bat, he mentioned to Squadron Leader Brian Baker, of 32 Squadron, that it would probably be his last game in England for a long time. Baker commented : " I don't think so. You probably won't be going till next year." Bader wanted to know why and Baker said he fancied they were going to keep him at Kenley to give him a chance to get his " cap ". for England at rugger.

At last 23 Squadron was getting Bristol Bulldog fighters to replace Gamecocks. The Bulldog was the last word in fighters. She could do 176 m.p.h. There were minor drawbacks ; she was not as manœuvrable as a Gamecock, being heavier, which gave her a tendency to sink faster on her back in the middle of a slow roll. Low aerobatics were banned, though some people ignored that. Then one of the pilots spun into the ground and killed himself.

Squadron Leader Woollett left the squadron and Harry Day took over command. Another pilot crashed and killed himself. Day called all the others together and read them a lecture on low aerobatics in the Bulldog. It was sound advice. Besides, people were not in the habit of ignoring a warning from Harry Day.

Pilot Officer Bader did. In November a flight commander spotted him doing low aerobatics and " beating up " the airfield. Day had him on the mat and told him crisply to watch his step and not to show off. After a chastened Douglas went out Day wondered whether perhaps he should not have slapped him down harder.

As it happened, Day's remark about " showing off " had given Bader the jolt he had had from Halahan at Cranwell ; he began to watch what he was saying and shy away from ostentatious aerobatics. Also the Springboks had arrived from South Africa for a series of rugger tests

31

against England, and with that goal in front of him he was training harder than ever before.

At the end of November the Combined Services team was named and there it was—" Fly-half : D. R. S. Bader." For days he savoured the prospect, and on the Saturday played with a dashing, high-geared vigour. Just after half-time he flung himself at a huge Springbok who was trampling for the line, brought him down, but broke his own nose at the same time. They'd be picking the England team in about three weeks. Too much at stake : he played on.

The Monday morning, 14th December, 1931, was bright and clear with a nip in the air and a little scattered cumulus about 4,000 feet. About ten o'clock Bader saw two Bulldogs taking off and remembered that two of the pilots, Phillips and Richardson, were flying over to Woodley Aerodrome near Reading to see Phillips' brother, who helped to run the aero club there. Bader tacked on to make a threesome, and half an hour later they settled on the grass in a neat vic at Woodley. In the clubhouse some young pilots asked Douglas, the Hendon star, questions about aerobatics, and then someone suggested he give a demonstration. Bader said, no. The Hendon show had been in a Gamecock and the Bulldog was not quite the same (and uncomfortably he remembered Harry Day's " show-off " remark). The matter was dropped until they were leaving, and a young man suggested it again. Bader again said no, and someone grinned and made some barbed joke about being " windy."

Richardson took off first, and then a tight-lipped, angry Bader. As Phillips left the ground Bader was banking steeply, turning back, and slanting down for a low run across the field. Just above the grass, rocking a little in the thermals, the Bulldog, engine bellowing, swept across

32

the boundary fence, rushing at a spot beside the clubhouse. The nose lifted a fraction and she began rolling to the right.

He had the stick well over . . . a little top rudder to hold the nose up . . . stick forward to keep it up and as she rolled upside down throttle back to keep the engine alive. He felt her starting to drop.

Stick *hard* over now ; the wings were vertical, glinting in the sun, and she was dropping fast. Grimly he was reefing her round and she was rolling out of it fast when the left wing-tip hit the grass and jerked the nose down. As propeller and cowling exploded into the ground the engine tore out, bouncing in a cloud of flying dirt, and the Bulldog seemed to crumple and cartwheel into a tangle very fast. Pinned by his straps, Bader did not feel anything but heard only a terrible noise.

All the airfield was suddenly still, except for the fierce boil of dust around the awkward heap in the middle that looked like crushed brown paper. As the dust began to drift the men by the clubhouse were running.

CHAPTER FOUR

BOTH LEGS LOST

AFTER THE noise everything was suddenly quiet. The cockpit was tilted. It leaned sideways. He must have crashed; but it was only a hazy idea and not very interesting because pain was stabbing his back.

Gently as the mind came into focus he was aware that his knees were buzzing as though he had hit his funnybone. The eyes wandered down and absorbed with curiosity that his legs were in peculiar positions. At least his right leg was. He could not see the left leg. (It had buckled under the collapsed seat so that he was sitting on it.) His right foot was tucked over in the far, right-hand corner and the white overalls were torn at the knee and staining in blood that was pumping in little squirts and spreading in filmy waves. There was his knee through the blood, and something was sticking through it. Very odd. For a while it made no impact until an ugly thought crystallised: "Damn! I won't be able to play rugger on Saturday."

A man in a white coat was standing beside the cockpit. There was a face and a white coat and a hand holding out a glass. A voice said: "Here you are, sir. Have a bit of this brandy. (It was a steward from the clubhouse.)

Automatically, he answered casually: "No, thanks very much. I don't drink."

A young man stood there instead of the man in the white coat, and leaned in and started undoing his harness, saying things in a gentle voice.

34

Jack Cruttenden, the big man, an Australian student pilot at the club, found he could not lift Bader out of the crushed cockpit. He started tearing at bits of the wreckage and other men did the same. Someone brought a hacksaw and cut away a twisted centre-section strut.

Consciousness was lapping and receding in waves. He was lying on the grass. Someone was taking his shoes off. Cruttenden's hands were doing something to his right knee : they felt very strong and were covered in blood. He felt no pain. A little to one side two white doors with red crosses opened and the crosses went out of sight. He supposed he was in an ambulance.

Then he was lying in it on a stretcher and men were bent over his legs. He tried to sit up but could not get very far.

He started struggling up on his elbows and Cruttenden said : " Take it easy. Won't be long now."

Bader said petulantly : " I want to get out now."

He tried to struggle up again, and Cruttenden took one hand from the knee and pressed it gently against his chest to hold him down.

Being held down by a stranger was irritating. He twisted a shoulder off the stretcher, hooked his right fist up and hit Cruttenden on the chin.

Cruttenden, looking at him with a pacifying grin, said : " Ease it up, mate."

The ambulance stopped in front of the Casualty door of the Royal Berkshire Hospital. Within a minute he was on a table with the duty doctor tying the artery and swabbing the pulpy mess in both legs where the bones had torn through. The right leg looked nearly off at the knee and the left shin was broken and badly splintered, the torn flesh full of oil and dirt. The patient's pulse was getting weaker, so that the doctor broke off to give a heart stimulant.

He straightened both legs and put them in box splints, then got Sister Thornhill in Benyon Ward on the house phone.

"There's a young man coming up with multiple injuries, shock and loss of blood from an aeroplane crash. Get him warm in bed to ease the shock." Soon they wheeled Douglas in, now deeply unconscious, and she packed hot-water bottles and blankets round the body, which was very cold.

Thornhill remembered that Leonard Joyce, who was probably the best surgeon in England, was operating at the hospital that day and rang the theatre, but they said he had just left. Hurrying, she found him in the entrance hall putting on his coat to go. She said: "Excuse me, Mr. Joyce, but we've just admitted a young Air Force officer after a bad crash. Could you have a look at him?"

He took his coat off and followed her back to the ward, and shortly was saying that he would wait and see if the patient came out of shock enough to try and operate.

When Harry Day rang the hospital from Kenley they were very guarded and he understood clearly that Bader was dying. He sent a telegram to Jessie, at Sprotborough, and to Cyril Burge, who was at Aldershot.

About two o'clock Sister Thornhill noticed that the patient was breathing more noticeably. Gradually his condition kept improving, and Joyce, surprised, put it down to his physical fitness. At 3.30 he decided to try and operate.

On the operating table Bader came to and lay looking up at a white ceiling, becoming aware of a hospital smell and a man in a long white surgeon's coat and cap standing by his head who said in a quiet voice: "Hallo, old chap. I see you've had a bit of an accident. Don't worry. Just lie back and we'll soon have you fixed up."

Bader looked at him vaguely, and said : " Don't give me an anæsthetic, will you. I can't stand the stuff."

" Don't worry," the man said, " we'll see things are all right."

Afterwards Bader could not remember getting the anæsthetic. As he was going " under " the plates came in from the X-ray room and Joyce held them up, still wet, to the light. First the right leg. He passed it almost instantly to the nurse, saying briefly : " That must come off." He hesitated over the left leg and finally passed it across without comment. The plates of the abdomen and head showed only two ribs broken, though the face was gashed and a tooth had come through the upper lip.

Joyce worked fast. The patient was too shaky for thorough surgery ; there was time only to try and patch things temporarily in a race with the imminence of more shock and fatal collapse. He severed the right leg above the smashed knee, but that did not take long because it was almost off already. When he turned to the left leg the patient was sinking and there was just time to clean the torn mess and seal it, hoping no infection would set in, and inject a saline solution. Bader was close to death when they got him to a private room and started working on him for post-operative shock.

Cyril Burge reached the hospital and waited. By nine o'clock Bader was still alive, but shock was draining him of the last resistance and he was nearly pulseless. Joyce told Burge he was not expected to live till the morning and a matron gave Burge a room to sleep in, promising to call him when the time came.

A nurse woke him out of a doze about 2 a.m. and said softly : " Will you please come down now." He got up and followed her without a word. He put his head in the door and saw two doctors and two nurses bending over a bed doing something to the shape in it. One of the doctors saw him and came over and murmured : " Would you wait outside, please ? "

Half an hour later the doctor came out again and said they might as well go and rest for a while. He would call them if anything happened. Burge went back to his room and was called again an hour later, but when he got there the doctor said the patient had rallied again.

In the morning Bader was still alive but it seemed only a matter of time. His mother, Mrs. Hobbs, arrived but was so overwrought that the matron gave her a room and a sedative. At nightfall Bader was still holding on, but at midnight they called Burge again, then sent him back to rest. By morning the patient still lingered with a fingertip hold on life.

Twenty-four hours later Bader's eyes opened. Sunshine flooded the room. He was conscious of objects that meant nothing for a while but then slowly focused into meaning : a cream ceiling, white sheets and then a tall girl in white with a red cape standing by a window with her back to him. After a while he murmured : " What the hell am I doing here ? "

Sister Thornhill turned and came over smiling. He saw she was about twenty-five, nicely rounded with a strong, capable face, healthily attractive.

" Oh, you're awake, are you ? " Her voice was pleasant and steady. " You've had an accident. You crashed in an aeroplane."

" Oh, did I ? What a silly thing to do."

She laughed and said she must go because Mr. Joyce wanted to see him as soon as he was awake.

He did not know who Mr. Joyce was nor care if he came. He became aware that there was an enormous

mound in the bedclothes. " Must have broken my leg,"
he thought.

The door opened and Joyce came in, but he did not
recognise the pointed, sensitive face.

" Hallo," Joyce said. " Glad to see you're awake."

Bader looked at him composedly but did not speak.
Joyce said : " I'm very sorry, old chap, but I'm afraid
we've had to take off your right leg."

Bader gazed placidly at him. Politely he said : " That's
all right. I hope I haven't been a nuisance."

Thornhill leaned over his body to block his view while
Joyce lifted the bedclothes and started unwrapping the
dressings. Joyce looked at the right stump first. It seemed
all right. He unwrapped the dressing on the left leg and
saw the red puffiness of incipient septicæmia and the dead,
grey signs of gangrene. He wrapped it up again, smiled
at Bader : " I'll see you again soon," and went out to
find Mrs. Hobbs and Cyril Burge.

As soon as the door had closed, Bader lifted the blankets
and looked. Yes, there it was. A short stump of thigh
with a rather bloody bandage round it. Oh, well . . . he
put the blankets down, not even noticing the left leg.

The door opened and Joyce walked into the sick-
room again and said : " We've got to reset your left leg,
old chap. It might hurt a bit, so we'll put you to sleep for
a while."

" That's all right, Doc," Bader murmured.

A burly man came in. He had a big nose, a cheery
face and a breezy manner that made Bader feel like getting
up to shake hands. Commander Parry Price, R.N.R.
(Ret'd.), the anæthetist said : " By Jove, old boy, you
look fine. Now let's see, what do you weigh ? "

" I used to box at eleven stone six."

" That's fine. Just about what I thought you were."

In the operating theatre Joyce worked fast again, taking the left leg off about six inches below the knee. As he lifted it away, Parry Price, who had been watching like a hawk, said quietly : " The heart's stopped."

Joyce looked up, motionless. In dead silence Price jabbed with a needle and took the wrist. The silence lingered on, and then Price felt the little thready flutter start again.

Joyce finished quickly and they wheeled him back to the room. Every ten minutes they kept taking his pulse and it kept palpitating with the thin, fast persistence.

Some time in the night, Bader's eyes opened. Vaguely on the rim of a dim circle of light that played round him a nurse was sitting.

Six hours later he came to again, conscious only of pain. His left leg was hurting with a bitter, steady ache. After a while Sister Thornhill came in and said : " Oh, you're awake."

" My left leg's hurting," he complained. Thornhill gave him a little morphia to ease it, but it seemed to make no difference : the terrible hurting went on, stabbing stronger and stronger. But he had to stand it because it went on and on. For a while he slept under more morphia, but soon awoke to more pain. The following morning he drifted into unconsciousness, but now and then revived for brief spells.

That night they sent for Burge again, but Bader did not die.

Later the young man woke and the pain had gone. He could not feel his body at all, but his mind was perfectly clear. He lay still, looking through the top of a window at a patch of blue sky, and into his mind crept a peaceful thought : " This is pleasant. I've only got to shut my eyes now and lean back and everything's all right." Warm peace was stealing over him, his eyes closing and his head seemed to sink into the pillow. It did not occur to him that he was dying.

Through the slightly open door a woman's disembodied voice slid into the receding clarity : " Sssh! Don't make so much noise. There's a boy dying in there."

The words quivered in him like a little electric shock that sparked a sharp thought : " So that's it. Hell, am I ! " Feeling began flickering out through his body like ripples from a pebble tossed in a pool. He stopped letting go and the mind was clearing. It was the challenge that stirred him.

As he lay thinking, the pain came back to his leg. Somehow he did not mind this time ; it was almost satisfying because he felt he was normal again and had slipped away from the ethereal spirit that had been floating him to Limbo.

That night delayed shock took effect and he sank into unconsciousness that lasted two days. Thornhill kept rolling him over in bed from time to time to avoid lung congestion that would lead to pneumonia.

Slowly the shock subsided and he came out of the coma. Morphia helped deaden the pain of the leg and the face lost some of its greyness. Thornhill changed the dressings that day, and he rose up with a groan of agony as she whipped away the last lint that stuck bloodily to the raw wound. She leaned her body carefully over so that he could not see that he had lost both legs.

The next day he winced as usual when she was changing the dressings and asked : " How are they ? "

Now ! she thought. Do it casually.

In an off-hand way she said : " Well, they took one off the same day and the other came off below the knee a couple of days later when septicæmia set in. Don't worry

41

about it. A man with your guts can overcome that. They've got pretty good artificial legs nowadays."

She waited nervously for the answer and was amazed when he said quite casually : "I suppose so." He was quite calm about it, and after the moment of anti-climax she wondered how he had known.

In fact, Bader had not known, and still did not know. He had heard her words, but they had not registered in his drugged mind because he could still feel his toes, and did not know anything about the phantom sensations that lead a man to feel his foot so realistically after losing his leg that he can waggle his toes in his mind.

It was the following day that the boy found out, and he only discovered it then because in spite of the morphia he was in torment that sharpened the brain into a little clarity. Squadron Leader Woollett had come in to ask how he was, and Bader said : "All right, sir, but my left leg's hurting like hell."

"I expect it's bound to hurt for a bit," Woollett said.

"Well, I wish they'd cut it off like the right leg," he groaned, "that doesn't hurt at all."

Woollett leaned forward, and said quietly, "As a matter of fact, Douglas, they *have* cut it off."

CHAPTER FIVE

FIGHTING BACK

THE IMPACT of losing his legs never hit Bader in one
moment, or even in a day or a week. The realisation
formed slowly in a doped mind. Against the urgency of
the pain it was only a detail, and when the pain ebbed and
allowed other things to matter his feelings were cushioned
by dope.

Next day, Christmas Eve, Joyce had him moved a
hundred yards across a courtyard from the main hospital
to Greenlands, the private nursing home in the hospital
grounds. They put him in a friendly little room on the
ground floor looking out on the lawns. There were gay
curtains, deep chairs and a bookcase to give it warmth of
atmosphere. Nurses kept injecting dope to quell the
outraged nerves in the left leg, and Christmas Day was a
blank to him. So were the next two days. Joyce was still
afraid he would die from either thrombosis or sepsis.

On the fourth morning he was conscious of a new
nurse by his bed saying that she would have to change his
dressings, and he started sweating again, but she brought
hot water and spent twenty minutes soaking them off so
that he did not feel a thing. It endeared him to the new
girl from that moment. Dorothy Brace was petite, with a
friendly laugh and used her hands tenderly.

The pain was under control now, and about this time
he remembered talking to his mother for the first time,

43

though she had been sitting by the bed for days dabbing sweat off the grey face.

Just before New Year Joyce took the stitches out. Suddenly he began to get better. The face filled out and got some colour, and the dark rings went from round the eyes. So did the pain in the left leg and they tapered off the morphia. He felt well and alert, yet still unconcerned about the loss of his legs. He did not—yet—miss his legs. He was comfortably in bed where legs were only remote extensions, and surrounded by attractive girls who brought him anything he wanted like devoted and adoring angels.

On 15th January he got up for the first time—a month and a day after the crash. Dorothy Brace pushed a wheel-chair to the bed and he heaved himself into it and sat there beaming with satisfaction. He wheeled himself to the window and sat looking out, but found he quickly became tired and was put back to bed in a couple of hours. Yet within a week he had the bandages off his stumps and was able to wheel himself down into the garden.

At the end of January, Joyce said he could have a peg-leg on the left stump and try getting about with crutches. Bader wanted to start off with a " real " artificial leg, but Joyce said that would be a waste because the stump would probably shrink later. The real reason was that he had to operate on the stump again to cut more bone away.

A little man in a white coat came into the room next day to take a plaster cast of the stump for the socket into which it would fit on the peg-leg. Bader bared his stump and the man slapped the plaster on. In five minutes it had set, and as the man pulled it off all the hairs of the stump were dragged out by the roots, in a thousand little pin-pricks of torture. Bader's shocked bellows of agony reached to the farthest cranny of the hospital. The little man apologised; he had forgotten to put a thin sock over the stump first.

The little man was back in a couple of days with a short smoothly turned piece of wood, painted black, and with a rubber pad on the bottom. At the top was a leather socket made from the plaster cast and above this two metal arms stuck up on each side, hinged where the knee went and ending in a leather corset to be laced round the thigh.

The stump fitted neatly into the moulded leather, but it felt strange to the unaccustomed skin, and the thigh corset gripped firmly. Sitting on the edge of the bed with the little man, Dorothy Brace and a big Irish nurse watching, he bent his knee to waggle the pylon.

One on each side, they helped him up from the bed. Tentatively he let his weight sink on to the pylon and the knee buckled like a piece of paper. They held him up while he shuffled each crutch forward in turn, and like that they lurched all over the room. After half an hour he was tired out. Later he tried again and again, but it was three days before he was able to hobble a couple of steps without help, with the left knee feeling it would collapse at any moment. Apart from that it did not seem very difficult. He took to new crutches with rings round the elbows instead of pads under the armpits and they were more manageable.

A day or two later came a milestone in his career when he was able to stump down the corridor and take a bath. He had worked out in advance how he would get into it—sit on the edge, unlace the pylon and then lower himself into it with hands on each side. Sinking into the hot water was ecstasy and he lay there a long time.

Soon he was independent of outside help and spent

hours stumping about the garden. It felt really good to be moving round again, and in the limited world of the garden the loss of his legs still did not seem serious, though the skin over each stump was contracting and stretching tightly over the bone-ends that he could clearly feel protruding. Joyce said one day : " We'll have to trim these off a bit soon. Otherwise they might split the skin."

Joyce sawed about two inches off the bone of the right stump, pulled the muscles down over the bevelled edges to make a pad at the base and sewed them underneath. On the left leg he took about an inch off the fibula, the little bone behind the shin. There was no hurry this time; the patient stood it easily.

Bader woke drowsily back in his bed, noted that the blankets were humped with the cradle again, and drifted off to sleep again. Hours later, nagging pain brought him more sharply awake ; this time it was the right stump. The pain grew till it was like sharp teeth gnawing at the raw nerves. Dorothy Brace gave him morphia, but soon the pain cut through the drug.

The patient was going downhill again, losing weight rapidly, the face growing grey and waxy under the sweat and the eyes sinking into the dark sockets. After a while his mind wandered into delirium and they increased the morphia to a maximum until he was unconscious for long stretches until resurgent pain or nightmares brought him out of it.

Night and day had no meaning and the nightmares came even in the stupor. Joyce guessed that internal sutures must be pressing on the sciatic nerve, and it was a question of time until the sutures absorbed and relieved the pressure.

It was nearly a week before the pain began to ease,

and then one day when Joyce looked at the stump he said :
" You've got a bit of hæmatoma here, old chap."

Bader was too weak and exhausted to bother about
what a hæmatoma was.

" Hang on to something," Joyce went on. " This
might hurt a bit." Before Bader was aware of it, he slid
something sharp into the wound, and Bader grabbed the
back of the bed in such a frenzied spasm that he bent the
iron frame. The pool of blood that had been trapped inside
began seeping out, easing further pressure, and from that
moment the last of the pain began to ebb. By that time the
stitches were out and the physical battle was over. Then
the mental battle started.

But gradually the drip-drip of grave but well-meant
encouragement began to have a sinister effect.

" Of *course* you'll be all right," they said. " Of
course . . ." trying just too hard to be convincing . . .
" Of *course* they'll let you stay in the Air Force . . ."
(They'll *let* me stay . . . Charity !)

Dorothy Brace noticed he was getting less cheerful,
and sometimes for hours would lie back with his eyes open,
silent and moody. The first spoken sign came on a day
when he heard that Johnson, a friend on the squadron,
had crashed and was killed.

She said to Douglas : " You're darned lucky you didn't
do that," and he turned his head and said bitterly : " *He's*
the lucky one. He's dead. I'd rather be killed outright
than left like this."

Sometimes he was his cheerful self and at others,
when he thought too much, the moodiness and silence
would settle. Out of the blue he said to Brace one day :
" They won't have me back in the Air Force, you know.
And they won't give me a pension because they'll say it was
my own fault."

To others, his mother, Hilda, Cyril Burge or his squadron friends he always cracked hardy, putting on a brash front, saying that he would rather lose both legs than one hand.

Soon he was up in the wheel-chair again, and a week after that was stumping about the hospital garden on the pylon. Now it was late March and stimulated by the sunshine, he was feeling eager to face the world again. One day he went outside the main gate into Redlands Road, and as he stood on the pavement a peculiar sensation of insecurity welled up. He made himself stump a hundred yards down to the other gate and thankfully went inside again. Trying it again that afternoon, he got the same feeling of exposed vulnerability, and this time it was a shade worse because two people passed him, staring at the peg-leg and the right trouser leg pinned high above the knee.

One day Dorothy Brace and another nurse took him to a cinema in Reading, and he was like a small child bubbling with glee until the taxi pulled up. As he struggled out in a tangle of peg-leg, crutches and helping nurses, people stopped and stared. Clustered faces of pity and vacuous curiosity gave him the feeling of nakedness again, and he hobbled into the foyer shrinking from it. Inside the darkened auditorium he sank into a seat and felt all right again, but later, as he ran the gauntlet across the pavement to a waiting taxi, he heard a woman say: " Oh, look, Jean, he's lost both of them."

Dorothy Brace squeezed his hand in the taxi and said : " Don't worry. You'll get used to it."

After a few more days swinging along Redlands Road he found that he did.

In the middle of April came the time to leave Greenlands. He was still the Air Force's responsibility and they sent a car to take him to their hospital at Uxbridge. The nurses seemed more affected than the patient; most of them gathered on the steps, some in sentimental tears, and he kissed them all with his cheerful enthusiasm and was driven off to face whatever the future held.

CHAPTER SIX

"TIN LEGS"

UXBRIDGE WAS pleasant enough, but different. They were mostly male nurses, respectful but remote. In the ward, however, he was among old chums again : Flying Officer Victor Streatfield with his arm in a cradle, Odbert, who had played rugger with him and was in with a slipped cartilage, and others of his own ilk, all barely mobile "crocks" in some way so that he felt naturally at home among them.

His mother drove down from Yorkshire in the family car for a fortnight and took him for a drive most afternoons. The first time they went out she was driving along a quiet stretch of road in Great Windsor Park when he said : "Stop a minute, Mother, will you ? "

She stopped, and he said : "Now let's change places. I'd like to have a crack at driving."

She looked at him in horror but he bullied her until before she knew what was happening he was in the driver's seat and she was sitting in the passenger's, saying : "But you can't. And what will happen if the police catch you ? "

"We'll have a damn' good argument," he said. "Now, just put your foot on the clutch."

After more vain protests she did so. He selected the gear (the car had a pre-selector gear on the steering wheel) and said : "Right. Now let it up." She lifted her foot slowly, he pressed his peg-leg on the accelerator and off they went. It worked like a charm and as they went along he worked out a drill for changing gear. He'd say, " Mother ! " Her foot would go on the clutch, he would select the new gear, say " Right," her foot would come up and that was all there was to it. After a couple of hours the team-work was quite good and his mother became enthusiastic. " What a pity you can only drive with a partner beside you," she said.

" If only I had something to prod the clutch with."

" Well, dear, would my umbrella do ? "

" Yes ! That's a wonderful idea."

She passed across her short, black umbrella. He took it in his left hand, selected the next gear, held the wheel with his right while he felt for the clutch with the ferrule, pressed it down, let it up again and the car had changed gear smoothly.

Patients at Uxbridge were not supposed to have cars but Peel, a young flying officer with a broken left leg in plaster, had an old Humber parked in a garage a few hundred yards away and he suggested to Bader and Streatfield that they should go for a surreptitious spin. In the safe period after lunch the three cripples clumped down the road to the car. Peel's claim that he could still use his plastered leg on the clutch pedal turned out to be correct and cheerfully they cruised about the district. As the car had a normal gear lever Bader had no ambitions about driving it until he noticed that it had a hand throttle on the steering wheel. It occurred to him that a hand throttle would spare the peg-leg to work the clutch.

" I could drive this car," he said. " Pull up and let's have a go."

Peel did so and left the engine running while Douglas slid behind the wheel. Streatfield in the back started muttering : " If I'm going to have my arm broken again I'd rather have a surgeon do it." Bader pressed the clutch down with his peg, put the gear lever into first, and let the clutch up again, working the hand throttle, and they moved off smoothly. After a while he found that changing gear with two movements of the clutch called for tricky co-ordination but with occasional crashes from the gear box, he managed reasonably well, though in due course they ran into Slough where the traffic was heavy and he began sweating with the concentration of stopping, restarting and slowing as they moved jerkily in the stream. It was easier to try and keep the car moving, even if only slowly in first gear, so he ploughed on, butting, weaving and honking, carving a kind of bow-wave of squealing brakes on other cars and pedestrians jumping like startled springboks out of the way.

In due course, Streatfield said: " How about stopping somewhere for a cuppa ? "

" Good idea," Peel said.

As they came over a little bridge on the outskirts of Bagshot, Streatfield said: " There's the Cricketers pub. Let's stop there."

But the pub was on the other side of the road and just as they neared it a stream of cars came the other way making it too awkward for the unpractised driver to ease up and swing behind them, so he said: " Let's go on a bit. Bound to be another place soon."

Chance hangs on such slender threads. A hundred yards on he saw a sign hanging out on the same side as the car: " The Pantiles." " Morning Coffee. Lunches. Cream Teas." He eased the car and swung off the road on to the gravelled apron in front of an attractive converted barn, surrounded by garden, shrubs and ornamental trees. Outside, people were sitting at little tables in the sun.

No one said a word while the three hobbled to a table, sat down and distributed sticks and crutches around them.

They looked up as a waitress arrived at the table. She was a slim girl with a delicately modelled face and a sensitive, expressive mouth—very good looking. Bader was first off the mark, flashing his glowing smile and saying : " Can we have three teas, please ? "

" Cream or plain ? " asked the girl.

" Cream," Bader said.

The girl came back with the tea and laid it out in a faintly strained silence, conscious of being watched. Later when she came back with the bill Bader made a couple of facetious comments and she permitted herself a faint smile.

As the strange procession stumped back to the car everyone gaped again, especially when the one with the peg-leg got back into the driver's seat. With a grinding of gears the car jerked into motion. The girl watched it go from the serving-hatch, feeling that the bold eyed one with the peg-leg had an arresting personality.

Next day when his mother took him out he artfully contrived that they should arrive at the Pantiles for tea and sit at the same table. The girl came over, looking more attractive than ever, and after some discussion Mrs. Hobbs decided on cream tea.

A day or two later came the moment he had been waiting for. One of the Uxbridge doctors said : " It's time you got your new legs, Bader. We're sending you over to Roehampton for measuring."

Roehampton was a hospital in London where the Ministry of Pensions carried out its obligations. In the grounds were several wooden huts occupied by artificial limb makers. The R.A.F. car took Bader to the hut of the Dessoutter Brothers who used to make aeroplanes until Marcel Dessoutter lost his leg in an early crash and became interested in artificial limbs.

"You *are* an ass getting both of 'em messed up," Dessoutter said. "Let's have a look."

Bader showed the stumps. Dessoutter inspected them professionally and said : "By jove, those are good. Who did them for you ? "

Bader told him about Leonard Joyce and added : ". . . so now if you can trot me out a pair of your pins I'll bung 'em on and get cracking."

"Ha, we don't take 'em off the peg," Dessoutter said. "We tailor 'em to the stumps pretty carefully. It'll take a couple of weeks. How tall used you to be ? "

"Five feet ten and a half in socks."

"I see." Dessoutter did some measuring and then slid thin socks over each stump and slapped plaster over them. Ten minutes later when he slid the casts and socks easily off, not a single hair came away.

"Right," said Dessoutter, "I'll let you know in a couple of weeks when we're ready for a fitting. Send me an old pair of your shoes so I can give you the right-sized feet."

During the next two weeks Bader drove the Humber a lot in defiance of regulations, steering it to the Pantiles for tea till it became a kind of ritual which Peel and Streatfield bore tolerantly. The girl always served him and every day the little chit-chat between them increased.

She was becoming rather important to him and he was beginning to realise that the situation was raising a new mental hurdle. Driving a car with companions in the normal world had lifted him out of the bitter moods of Greenlands but a girl, in the serious sense, was a different thing altogether. The new legs might be his solution. He would drive his own M.G. straight to the Pantiles, walk in with full-length trousers and no crutches and sit at the old table. He wrote to the garage at Kenley where the little

M.G. was stored and told them to change the brake and clutch pedals.

Dessoutter rang one day. He was ready for a fitting. The first things Bader saw when he stumped into the hut were the new metal legs standing up by the wall. Unpainted, they looked shiny and new and covered in little rivets, nuts and screws, and he was amused to see that they wore socks and his own shoes.

" Ah," said Dessoutter : " handsome, aren't they ? Look at those muscular calves. You'll be about an inch shorter than you used to be."

" Why ? " Bader demanded indignantly.

" Gives you better balance. If you want them longer we can always lengthen them."

" As long as I can be as tall as any girl-friend."

" You can marry an Amazon if you like," Dessoutter said. " We can make you seven feet tall."

They went into the fitting-room, a long rectangular place with large mirrors at the end and what looked like parallel bars, but so low that a man could walk between them, holding on to the bars for balance.

" Sit down here." Dessoutter indicated a stool and introduced two of his white-coated assistants, a jovial little man called Charlie Walker, and Tulitt, a big man with glasses. They made him strip to vest and underpants and then Walker, the " below-the-knee " specialist, pulled a woolly " sock " over the left stump and slid it into a leather socket sunk in the calf of his new left leg. Above the calf, metal bars came up on each side like the ones on the peg-leg, hinged at the knee and ending in a lace-up leather corset. Walker laced the corset round the thigh.

" You'll find it a bit different to the pylon," Dessoutter said. " You've got ten inches of fairly rigid foot sticking

55

out at the bottom and you'll have to lift your leg higher to get the toe clear."

"All right," Walker said. "Hups-a-daisy." He put the crutches under Bader's armpits and he and Tulitt helped him up. Bader stood firmly on the leg and it felt fine. Much more solid, somehow, than the pylon. Leaning experimentally on it he felt a slight "give" in the foot and Dessoutter explained that it was hinged at the instep with little rubber pads inset to allow a faint, resilient movement. The toe was jointed with a rubber pad too. Confidently Bader took a pace forward on the crutches and the wooden left toe caught on the mat and he nearly tripped.

He tried again, lifting his leg like a high-stepping horse, and walked up and down the room like a one-legged man with crutches. "Right," he said. "Let's have a go at the right leg."

Tulitt brought it over. The thigh was a shaped metal cylinder that came right up to the groin and strung to it were straps leading up to a thick belt, with more straps looped on the top like a double military Sam Browne. Tulitt pulled a "sock" on the right stump, eased the stump into the deep socket of the thigh and then buckled the belt to which it was attached round Bader's lower abdomen over his underpants. Over each shoulder he buckled the leather braces and then strapped the thigh corset of the left leg to the body-belt.

Bader sat in growing dismay, feeling he was being trussed into a strait-jacket.

Walker and Tulitt took each arm round their shoulders and hauled him to his feet. As his weight came on both, especially the right stump, it was the worst shock he ever had. He felt wildly unbalanced and strange. His right stump was utterly helpless and uncomfortable to the point of hurting and the harness itself seemed to cripple him.

In stung despair he burst out: "Good lord, this is absolutely impossible."

"That's what they all say the first time," Dessoutter said. "You get used to it."

Bader said grimly: "I thought I'd be able to walk out of here and start playing games and things."

"Look," Dessoutter said gently. "I think you ought to face it that you'll never walk again without a stick."

Bader looked at him with dismay, and then as the challenge stirred him he said pugnaciously: "I'll never, *never* walk *with* a stick!"

In his stubborn anger he meant it.

"Try a step or two," Dessoutter suggested.

Feeling he would be more secure staying on the left leg he tried to swing his right leg forward, but it did not move.

"How do I get it to move?" he demanded.

"Try kicking the stump forward," Dessoutter said. "The right knee will bend automatically. Then when it's forward, kick the stump downwards and it'll straighten out on the heel. It's like cracking a whip."

He kicked the stump forward and the metal knee bent as the leg went forward. He jerked the stump down and the knee straightened as the heel hit the mat.

"That's better," Dessoutter said. "Now come forward."

Bader suddenly felt paralysed, unable to move.

"How the devil *do* I?" he asked irritably.

"That's the big lesson you've just learned," Dessoutter said. "You haven't got any toe or ankle muscles now to spring you forward as you used to. That right leg is a firm barrier that you have to push yourself over, on top of, by leaning forward and by your momentum when you're moving."

Bader said to Tulitt and Walker: "Pull me forward over this damn' leg."

They heaved him forward till he was balanced on the weak right stump. Having his own knee, he was able quite easily to swing the left leg forward and then he stuck again.

They pulled and he flicked his right stump forward again and they pulled him on to it and he got his left leg forward once more; so it went on in clumsy, stiff, jerky movements as they pulled him the length of the room. There was no natural automatic movement at all; he had to think each step out in advance and then signal his mind to make the move. Whenever they eased the forward tug he felt the stiff leg out in front would push him over backwards. At the end he lowered himself on to another stool and uttered with grim feeling: "This is—awful."

"It always is the first time," Dessoutter said. "Don't be too depressed. It's learning to walk all over again with an entirely new system and you can only learn it by practice. Don't worry. You'll do it, but it might take you six months."

"Don't be silly. There's a girl I want to see in a couple of days and I want to be walking then."

Dessoutter broke a slightly appalled silence: "You'll find a stick useful in pushing yourself over the leg in front."

Bader stuck his jaw out aggressively. "Not me! Come on, you two. Let's have another go."

They hauled him to his feet again and this time they took his elbows instead of having his arms round their shoulders. "Try taking very short steps,"[1] Walker said.

He tried that and the improvement was immediate. They still had to pull him forward, but he did not get

[1] This is one of the real secrets at the beginning.

quite the feeling of coming to a dead stop whenever he put a leg forward, especially the right leg. They went up and down the room several more times and slowly, subconsciously, he began to get the hang of it, leaning the top of his body well forward so that his unbalanced weight tended to carry him on to the leg placed just in front.

Dessoutter said after a while, " Let's try taking half an inch off that right leg."

Bader sat down and unstrapped it. Walker and Tulitt took it away for half an hour and lowered the thigh about half an inch into the knee socket. Bader put it on again and without so much weight to overcome found that he could transfer his weight with a little less trouble. They helped him up and down the room several more times and then he said : " All right, now let me go." They were too cautious to do so, so he shrugged his elbows to push them away and took his first steps alone, three or four jerky stumbles that ended with him just grabbing the parallel bars before he fell over.

Dessoutter was laughing in genuine delight. " I've never even seen a chap with *one* leg do that before first time," he said. " You've done enough for to-day, you must be feeling pretty tired."

That was true enough. He was hot, and sweaty, beginning to feel exhausted, and the right stump was stiff and sore. As he strapped on the peg-leg again Dessoutter suggested he come back for more practice in a couple of days.

Back at Roehampton in a few days he found the legs painted a smart yellow. " Looks more natural than any other colour through a thick sock," Dessoutter explained.

Walker and Tulitt walked him up and down the room again and it was not quite as bad as the first time he had tried. After a while he made them loosen their grip and with their hands hovering by his elbows he was able to walk the length of the room. Standing facing the wall he found a new problem—he could not turn. In exasperation, hands steadying him against the boards, he said to the wall, "What does a man do now?" The others turned him round and back at the parallel bars the same thing happened. It seemed impossible to turn his feet round. He lurched back to the other wall and this time as he neared it he teetered round in a tight semi-circle, fending himself off against the wall. For two hours he practised that morning until he was almost too tired to stand.

"I honestly think you're incredible," Dessoutter said as he unstrapped the legs. "None of us has ever seen anyone like you before."

It was a glorious spring morning when Bader drove back to Roehampton to take delivery and his spirits were soaring at the prospect. Dessoutter had a set of three shallow wooden steps with banisters in a corner of the room and when he had put the legs on and tried a couple of circuits round the room, he made his first attempt at the steps. With the banister to support him, it turned out to be relatively simple—hand on the rail to steady him, left foot on the first step, bring up the right foot to the same step, and then lift the left foot again. Coming down was the same thing. He called it the "dot-and-carry" system and has never used any other for stairs. That morning he learned how to get up out of a chair without help too—lean forward, a good shove on the seat of the chair with both hands and the left knee took the strain and lifted him.

"Well, there you are," Dessoutter said. "They're all yours. It's a bit soon to let you have them really, but

I suppose you'll only start complaining if you don't take them." He grinned. " Shall I wrap them up for you ? "

" Not on your life," Bader grinned back. " I'm walking out on 'em."

" Now what about a stick," Dessoutter suggested.

" Never ! " he answered crisply. " I'm going to start the way I mean to go on."

For the first time he began putting the rest of his clothes on over the legs and harness, the shirt over the belt and shoulder straps, the trousers over the legs. Ah, here was another catch ! He had to lift the right leg with a hand round the thigh to do it, and then found that with the foot sticking rigidly out he could not point his toes to slide into the trouser leg. The heel and toe caught and he had to ease the foot through the cloth by tugging on each crease alternately.

He put on his tie and jacket, stood up and looked at himself in the mirror. He looked *quite* normal. It was a terrific moment. He was *standing up*—dressed like an ordinary chap—looking like one.

As Walker and Tulitt helped him totter out to the waiting car he became irksomely conscious of the harness. Under his clothes it seemed worse than before, cripplingly uncomfortable, as bad as walking with a stone in one's shoe . . . in the circumstances a ridiculous comparison, he thought wryly.

As they handled him into the car Dessoutter said : " Don't worry if you have a bad time for a while. You've done amazingly well so far, but don't expect it to go on as fast as that. Everyone feels desperate for a while." They shouted " Good luck ! " through the glass and the car moved off. He relaxed, satisfied, on the soft seat and discovered a new catch. He could not cross his legs.

CHAPTER SEVEN

HE WALKS AGAIN

WHEN THE car pulled up just before lunch in front of the Uxbridge hospital doors an orderly helped him out and the wing commander was standing by the door talking to another doctor. Bader pushed away the orderly who was fussing at his elbow and lurched with tense concentration about six paces to the door feeling smugly proud.

The wing commander briefly turned his head, said curtly: "You ought to have a stick, Bader," and turned back to the other doctor. Bader tottered angrily through the door, praying that he would not fall.

In the dining-room the greeting was hearteningly different. There were roars of welcome and ribald remarks. Streatfield bawled: "Long John's got his undercarriage back." He walked across to them, concentrating too much to make any answer and feeling that he was going to spoil his entrance at any moment by making a three-point landing and denting his tail-skid. One of them pulled out a chair and he just made it.

"No doubt any moment now you'll be wanting to dash off to the Pantiles," Streatfield suggested.

"Not on your life," he said. "I'm going to learn to walk on these pins first and the next time I go there I'll be driving my own car."

His ward was on the first floor and after lunch he tottered out to the stairs. They looked appallingly high and steep, but he dragged himself up and was sweating at the top. In the ward he tried to give a demonstration of walking, lurching a precarious way from bed to bed, grabbing each bed-rail as he reached it, and encouraged by cheerful barracking from patients in the beds. But after a few minutes he was so tired he could hardly stand.

At dinner-time he was able to struggle downstairs, but when he went to climb back he just could not do it; the strength was drained out of him and he was aching all over. A burly orderly carried him up with Bader's arms round his neck, body dangling over his back, and lowered him on to his bed.

In the morning as he woke he remembered with satisfaction that he was mobile. Was it worth putting on his legs to walk to the bath, taking them off and putting them on again afterwards? No. He went to the bathroom on his rump and put his legs on afterwards. Clutching the banister rail he dot-and-carried down the stairs to breakfast and after that teetered out into the garden, where he got another shock as he stepped on to a patch of grass and pitched forward—his first fall. He took the shock on his hands. That part was all right, but now he had to get up again. He lay for a while thinking about it. A man came running up and said sympathetically : " Hang on to me, old boy. Soon have you up."

" Go away," he snapped. " I'll do this."

He took his weight on his hands and lowered the rear weight on to his left knee, then pushed hard. In a moment he had fallen back on his hands again. He tried again, pushing up on the left toe, straightening his left knee, and pushing his hands back towards the toe, and came uneasily but without too much difficulty to his feet again. Then he took another step and fell again.

That morning he fell at least twenty times but managed to stumble up and down the grass again and again, arms

63

flailing to keep his balance like a novice on ice skates, but persisting until his legs were aching and trembling with exhaustion again. Worse, the right stump was sore in spots—obviously chafing.

After lunch he got the orderly to carry him upstairs to the ward where he practised from bed-rail to bed-rail again. Soon he was in agony from the chafed right stump and had to struggle to his bed. Unstrapping all the harness and taking off the stump sock he found that the skin round the groin was rubbed raw in a couple of places.

With a sudden idea he called an orderly to bring him some sticking plaster and taped it over the raw parts, put his legs on and tried again. It was a little better, but then the whole stump was so stiff and sore that it was hard to tell which part hurt most. That evening a nurse put some of her cold cream on the raw patches.

In the morning a car drove him back to Roehampton.

"I thought you'd be back about this time," Dessoutter said. "Let's have a look at those stumps." He, Tulitt and Walker spent about two hours adjusting the sockets of the legs.

Bader went back to Uxbridge to try again, but they seemed no better. For two days he stumbled about, continually falling, curtly refusing any help and getting up unaided to lurch and fall again. Mostly he fell forward, sometimes backwards, two or three times sideways, sometime on hard floors, often on the grass. As he did not fall on the stairs where he had a banister to cling to the others kept suggesting he use a stick but he refused tersely.

Hour after hour he doggedly kept at it. Moving the stiff, chafing and aching stumps was torment but he made himself keep on doing so, his face running with sweat that poured all over him, soaking his underclothes and the stump socks too, so that they lost their woolly softness and began chafing again. The good-humoured barracking that had greeted his first efforts died away as people became aware that they were watching a man battling to do something that had never been done successfully before.

Soon, stumps plastered like a quilt, the car took him to Roehampton again where Dessoutter found that the right thigh seemed to have shrunk. In due course, he said, they would rivet the metal a little tighter, and meanwhile he slipped a second stump sock over it. That felt better, and then Dessoutter found a hard muscle developing at the back of the thigh and with a little hammer Tulitt tapped out an almost imperceptible indentation in the metal to accommodate it. To reduce sweat and chafing Dessoutter suggested keeping both stumps well powdered.

But the main problem, the sheer clumsiness, they could not help. Dessoutter, who had noticed the new grimness in Douglas, said : " Look, in this business I've seen that only people who've actually lost a leg can know the shock of awkwardness when they first try an artificial one ; it's just a thing they have to work on till they develop a new skill. Most of them take months to learn. Some never do. Chaps who lose one leg have still got a good one to rest and hop on and an ankle and toe to give them spring when they're walking. You haven't, so you've just got more to learn."

Back at Uxbridge he kept trying but it seemed impossible to acquire balance and natural movement, and still he kept falling. Gradually he found the right stump did not ache so much, as the flabby muscles hardened with use and the chafing came under control, but that eased only the pain ; the legs were as unwieldy as ever, yielding no fraction to practice. Mentally, it was the worst time since the accident. His nature, in any case, rejected defeat and now the menacing implications produced obsession to master the legs.

And then, about ten days after he got his legs, he detected the first hint of automatic control. As though some barrier had been removed, he began walking a little more easily and after that the improvement was rapid. In five days he was lurching about without having to concentrate so hard either on movement or balance; some automatic instinct seemed to have taken over part of the work. He still fell, but not so often.

He telephoned the garage at Kenley and asked them to drive his car over.

" Off to the Pantiles ? " Streatfield asked, and he nodded.

Bader heaved himself into the seat behind the wheel. His feet seemed to fit easily enough over the pedals. He pressed the clutch down with the right leg—it was purely a thigh movement with no feeling in the leg or foot at all but he *could* feel the pressure of the clutch against his thigh with enough sensitivity to control it and let it up slowly. He tried the left foot on brake and accelerator and found there was enough feeling in the shin to switch the foot from one to the other. The whole thing seemed to be easier than he had expected. He started up and drove slowly round the asphalt parade ground. For a quarter of an hour he drove in figure eights, stopping, starting and reversing, and was highly gratified.

Blithely he set off for the Pantiles and pulled into the gravelled apron. This time as he got out and lurched to the usual table hardly anyone looked except the girl. He saw her over by the serving hatch, staring, but he kept looking straight ahead concentrating on appearing casual. She came across to the table looking very bright and he switched on the glowing grin. With a little less reserve than usual she remarked that he had not been there for some time and he was delighted that she was too discreet to mention the legs. He chatted before he ordered and chatted again when she brought the tea, and again when she brought his bill. He paid her, got up, stumped over to the car, praying that he would not fall, turned round—she was still watching—and gave her an enormous wink. As he drove away he wondered what her name was.

Now with the car and able to walk, even if still precariously, life took on a new savour and he drove out every day to sample it. Most days he arrived at the Pantiles for tea and the friendship with the girl progressed decorously with no particular move on either side. He still had to find out where he stood in regard to life.

Kendall, the Warden of St. Edward's School, had been writing to him constantly ever since the accident and Bader wrote to let him know how successful the new legs were.

Several times he went to the Stoops at Hartley Wintney and once stayed the night, scaring the life out of a maid in the morning by bouncing down the stairs on his rump and hands because for some small unremembered errand he could not be bothered to put his legs on.

From time to time the Stoops introduced him to other visitors who were never told, at least till later, that he had no legs. They took him one night to a party where someone started playing a gramophone and couples began dancing. Bader asked a girl to dance; she smiled and got up, and as they started he caught his toe and fell, luckily not dragging her down with him, but as he got clumsily to his feet she said tartly: "You're drunk," and left him. Later she was horrified when she found out, but she need not have worried because the incident did not trouble Bader, who was too practical to have any pity for himself.

About the middle of June he suggested some sick-leave, and drove himself to Kenley and walked into a deserted mess. A waiter he did not recognise said that most of the pilots were away on an air-firing course at Sutton Bridge. Then Harry Day walked in and saved the moment. " Hey, hey," Day said cheerfully. " What've we got here. Good lord, you look like a drunken sailor." Then the mess sergeant came along beaming with pleasure and said he could have his old room back.

He felt a queer moment of pleasure when he looked again at the spartan bed, the lino, rug, chair and the book-shelves. It was even his old batman who answered the bell, and said warmly : " Why, Mr. Bader, sir, it's good to see you back."

Bader shook his hand. " It's good to *be* back," he said. " I'm staying for a while. Have you still got my kit here ? "

" Yes, sir," said the batman. " All safely in store. I'll go and bring it straight up."

Bader rested in the chair while the batman began hanging up the clothes and stowing shirts and things in drawers. There was an awkward moment when he pulled out a pair of rugger boots ; their eyes met and the batman put the boots back in the trunk. A little later Bader said : " Bring up my cricket bag, will you ? "

Next afternoon was hot and Day suggested he join his family for a swim—Day had a lovely home with a swimming pool on a Surrey hill near Kenley. That raised a new problem. He also had three children.

Bader asked awkwardly, " Will the youngsters mind if they—er—see me ? "

" Good lord, no." Day said. " They'll be fascinated."

While the others changed in the house Bader walked across the lawns to the pool, took his legs off and changed under a tree, then rump-walked to the edge of the pool and lay on the grass waiting.

At the deep end the springboard jutted over the water

from a platform on stilts about eight feet high. He rump-walked to it and hauled himself up the short ladder with his hands. Then he stood on his hands and dived in. Spouting water and grinning, he surfaced (right way up), finding himself more buoyant in the water without his legs, though swimming seemed more tiring because he could not kick to help himself along and his rump tended to sag in the water instead of trailing in the normal flat position.

Having tea on the grass afterwards the children stared frankly and with great interest at the stumps, but so innocently and naturally that he was not in the least embarrassed.

Round about seven the family went back to change and Douglas dressed on the lawn. As soon as he started walking back to the house he felt the shoulder straps chafing his shoulders and realised that he was sunburned. By the time he reached the house they were beginning to hurt.

In the morning when he got up the shoulders were red and tender. He strapped the legs on but as soon as he stood up the straps bit into his shoulders like hot bread-knives, and he sat down hurriedly, wincing, and slipped them off with relief. From a little thing like that he was helpless again, unable even to get to the dining-room for breakfast unless he submitted to the unthinkable indignity of the rump-walk in public.

In desperation he unbuckled them from the belly-belt hoping he might be able to struggle out cautiously without them. After pulling the belt fairly tight, he eased himself up from the bed and gingerly took a few steps; to his delight the legs felt better than ever before and just as secure. For several minutes he stumped about the room, and everything he did felt better. After that he tossed the

69

shoulder straps into a corner, dressed and stumped out to breakfast. (He never wore the shoulder straps again.)

A note came to him from the Under Secretary of State for Air, Sir Philip Sassoon, inviting him for a week-end at his house near Lympne. Clearly it would be not only a pleasant week-end but a chance to find out where he stood for his future in the Air Force. Sassoon suggested that he bring a young man from the squadron with him as companion so he drove down in the M.G. with Peter Ross, a lively young pilot officer with whom he had become friendly.

Sassoon was a millionaire and his house was a mellow old mansion on a slope beside Lympne Aerodrome where 601 Auxiliary Squadron was busy flying Hawker Demon two-seater fighters on its annual summer camp.

The Saturday afternoon they spent lying beside the swimming pool with the Demons taking off just over the pool. As one of them roared over Bader said wistfully : "By gosh, I wish I were up there again." He turned to his host and added : "You know, sir, I'm quite sure I could fly perfectly well now."

"Well, they've got an Avro 504 on the aerodrome," Sassoon said. "Would you like to have a shot at it ? "

"I'd *love* to," Bader said, and Sassoon promised to arrange it. Bader spent the rest of the afternoon in nervous hopes that Sassoon would not forget, but at dinner that night Sassoon said : "I've had a word with the C.O. of 601. The Avro will be ready for you in the morning, and Ross can go with you in the other cockpit."

CHAPTER EIGHT

HE FLIES AGAIN

In the morning it felt wonderful just to be putting on overalls, helmet and goggles again.

" Take it as long as you like," Norman, the C.O. of 601 said. " All I ask is bring it back in one piece."

He put his foot into the slot at the side of the rear cockpit and Ross gave him a heave up. Then clutching the leather-padded rim of the cockpit with his left hand it was simple to grab his right calf and swing it over into the seat. He eased himself down, delighting in the familiar smell of an Avro cockpit. Eyeing instruments and crash-pad and taking the stick in his hand, sent a flush of enchantment through him.

Ross climbed into the front and his voice came through the earphones : " Shall I start her up from here, Douglas ? "

" No," he said ; " just turn on your switches."

The Huck starter backed up and turned the propeller ; the warmed-up engine caught smoothly and the aeroplane was quivering with life. He ran up to test magnetos, set the cheese-cutter trim in neutral, waved the chocks away and taxied downwind, jabbing the rudder and finding it easy to steer. Turning at the hedge he saw the grass stretching down to Romney Marsh, pushed the throttle forward and the engine let out a deep, hearty bellow. She started rolling, and as the tail came up and she yawed with the torque he prodded automatically at the rudder and she straightened, gathering speed. Pure joy flooded him at that moment; he knew already he was completely at home. At about 55 m.p.h. he let her come gently off the grass, climbed a little, turned and circled the aerodrome and then steered for Kenley. The old touch was back and as she cruised over the familiar fields he was sublimely happy. A circuit over Kenley and then he was slanting in to land. This was the acid test.

She swayed and dipped docilely as he nursed her with delicate movements of stick and rudder so easily that he did not notice how simple it was to hold her straight. Quite unconscious of the legs he flattened, held back, back, back, and then she touched gently on three points. On the landing run he was conscious of his legs again but held her straight and turned and taxied to the tarmac apron in front of the squadron's hangar.

After an extremely cheery lunch in the mess Bader flew Ross in the Avro back to Lympne and made another neat landing. At the house Sassoon asked how he had got on, and he said: "Absolutely fine, sir. Honestly, no different at all to flying with my old legs." Later he added carefully: "I've got to have a medical board, sir, to see if I can fly again. I was rather hoping you might let them know that I have flown again."

Sassoon said: "You let me know before you go for your board and I'll see to it."

Back at Kenley a telegram arrived telling him to report for his medical board and he drove down to the Central Medical Establishment in Kingsway. He went the rounds of the doctors who examined his eyes, listened to his heart and chest and tapped him here and there. One of them absentmindedly took up a ruler to tap his knees for reflexes and then dropped it with a foolish laugh.

The senior doctor, a wing commander, glanced over

the findings, and said : " Well, you seem to be in pretty good shape so we're passing you out as A2H, which means restricted flying at home. I'm afraid you won't be able to go solo with that, but we'll recommend you for a posting to the Central Flying School at Wittering."

Bader knew he would have no trouble with the flying boys, and while waiting for a posting went back to Uxbridge (the depot, not the hospital, this time) and did normal duties, taking parades, acting as orderly officer and so on. Several times he went to Roehampton for more adjustments to the legs and also kept driving over to the Pantiles for tea as often as he could, though he still did not know the girl's name. Yet he felt the friendship was ripening, so that it came as a shock one day when she mentioned that she was leaving the Pantiles soon and going back to London.

Then the posting arrived, ordering him to the glowing new horizon at the Central Flying School, but his pleasure was tempered by the knowledge that Wittering was far away. One last time he drove to the Pantiles and said to the girl when she arrived : " I'm going away too."

" Oh," she said, sounding politely interested.

" Going up north to Wittering to start flying again." He tried to be offhand about it, but she clearly guessed its importance because she smiled with pleasure and said : " Oh, you'll like that, won't you ? I *am* glad."

This was the moment. He said, trying to sound casual again : " I was wondering if you'd care to come out with me one night in London if I can get down."

" That would be nice. I'd love to," she said, sounding neither too eager nor too cool.

He said blandly : " Would you give me your address and telephone number in London ?"

The girl knowing quite clearly what he was thinking, printed on the back of a tea ticket :

Thelma Edwards,
12 Avonmore Mansions,
Kensington, W.14.

" Oh, thanks awfully," he said, relieved. " My name's Douglas Bader."

(She had known that for weeks. Three of her cousins were Air Force officers and she had asked them questions about the young man who had lost his legs. Bader did not discover that till later, when he also found that her father had been a wing commander, that her step-father was a colonel and that the girl had been a young woman of leisure until her pet dog had died and she had gone to stay with a grandmother at Windlesham and taken the Pantiles job to get her mind off her grief about the dog.)

For a while he was too joyfully occupied at Wittering to get up to London. His very arrival there on a flying course filled him with thrilling content. First they gave him dual in an Avro 504 and he was so competent that on the third morning his instructor took him up in a two-seater Bulldog. When they landed the instructor said, apparently in ignorance of the doctor's ruling, " You might as well take her up by yourself after lunch."

After four years in the Service Bader did not volunteer the information that he was not allowed to go solo, but went smugly into lunch where, by the sheerest chance, the station doctor observed in the hearing of the instructor : " I hear you're doing well, old boy. You must be *very* fed up at the doctors not allowing you to go solo."

As consolation the instructor promised him a week-end's

leave and he wrote to Thelma saying that he would be in London during the week-end. Would she care to go out with him to the Café de Paris on Saturday night? A decorous note came back accepting and asking if he would care to call for tea beforehand.

On the Saturday morning he set out in the M.G. with boiled shirt and tails in a case. Avonmore Mansions was six storeys high. There was no lift. Carrying his case, he dot-and-carried up the stairs, twelve flights, ninety-six steps.

The door opened and a uniformed maid showed him into a sitting-room where the girl, looking very fetching in a green dress, rose from the sofa. She introduced him to her mother who looked young and agreeable and a tall, lean man, her step-father, Lieutenant-Colonel Addison. The girl leaned over the tea things and asked, with a tiny smile : " Cream or plain ? "

Later, feeling debonair in tails for the first time since the crash, he took her to the Café de Paris in a taxi. The dinner was good, the girl was charming, and sitting at the little table for two with his legs tucked safely away beneath, the music lilting away stimulated a mood of glowing zest. On the spur of the moment he leaned over, and said : " Would you like to dance ? "

Just for a moment she looked uncertain and then she smiled and nodded.

It was quite easy—if not especially graceful. He held her a little away to give him space for kicking the right leg forward and for a while he was really only walking, steering round the bends still in a walk. Emboldened he tried a mildly fancy turn and it came off.

After a couple of numbers they were moving round the floor quite impressively until suddenly he collided with her and she came to a dead stop, her face tight with pain.

" What's the matter ? " he asked anxiously.

" You're standing on my left foot."

He jumped off in horror, and they danced on. Soon the music changed to a waltz. He had a stab at it but very nearly tripped, taking her with him, on the first half-step. "Sorry," he said. " Afraid I can't cope with this one. Let's go and sit down."

They went off the floor arm-in-arm and as he dot-and-carried up the two shallow steps to their table his other hand missed the banister and he overbalanced backwards, landing heavily on the floor and nearly bringing her down with him.

She helped him up and they got to the table where he grinned to cover up his mortification—he had never fallen in front of her before. She leaned across and put her hand on his arm. " You know, I think you're amazing," she said. It was the first time she had ever referred to the loss of his legs and she did it so warmly and naturally that it endeared her to him.

They danced several more times and he blissfully ignored the fact that his legs were aching and that patches on the stumps were rubbing raw. About 2 a.m. he took her home, bade her a decorous good-night and drove off to the R.A.F. Club where he had to tape the chafed patches on his stumps before he went to bed. On the Sunday he took her for a drive in the M.G. and she managed to convey to him that she admired the way he drove and got around on his legs.

Next week-end he drove to London again and took her to the Ace of Spades roadhouse near the Kingston By-pass.

On the Sunday he drove her to the Stoops' and Audrey Stoop, who approved very much, invited both of them down for the following week-end.

That week at Wittering he was doing aerobatics again in a Bulldog as well as ever he had, though still irked by the presence of the instructor in the back cockpit. Once or twice he assuaged this affront, by criticising the instructor's own aerobatics and giving him a few tips, though the instructor got his own back when a gust caught the aircraft in a cross-wind precautionary landing and the Bulldog swung in an incipient ground-loop till the instructor quickly corrected with his own foot on the rudder bar. He made a few ribald comments, but Bader's flying was so invariably immaculate that resumption of full flying duties seemed " in the bag."

The Chief Flying Instructor sent for Bader and said : " There's nothing more we can teach you about flying and there's no point in your mucking about not able to go solo."

" That's what I was sent here to find out, sir," Bader said. " Once I'm passed by you the medical board can decide on my flying category."

" All right," said the C.F.I. " I'll write and tell 'em."

The answer came back surprisingly quickly—a call for Bader to appear for another medical. He drove to London savouring the moment that evening when he would see Thelma and tell her he was going back to a squadron. In the Kingsway building the rotund warrant officer receptionist who had seen so many accident cases come up for medical check, welcomed him. " You don't have to see the doctor after all, sir. Only the wing commander."

Good, Bader thought. Only a formality. He went into the wing commander's office and the man with the detached professional air behind the desk said : " Ah, Bader, nice to see you again. Sit down, will you ? "

He sat, waiting for the good news. The wing commander glanced at some papers on his desk. " I've just been reading what the Central Flying School says about you. They say you can fly pretty well."

Bader waited politely.

" Unfortunately," the wing commander went on, " we can't pass you fit for flying because there's nothing in King's Regulations which covers your case."

CHAPTER NINE

OUT OF THE R.A.F.

HE SAT in stunned silence for a few more moments and then found his voice: " But of course there's nothing in King's Regulations, sir. That's why I was sent to C.F.S. To see if I *could* fly. I mean . . . doesn't that fit the case ? "

The wing commander cleared his throat. " I'm very sorry indeed, but I'm afraid not."

Bader flared angrily: " Well, why the hell did you send me there to be tested ? "

Embarrassed, the wing commander said apologetically: " Well, you were keen to have a shot and I'm sorry it turned out like this."

It was then it occurred to Bader that the whole question had probably been decided before he went to Wittering. They had expected him to fail at the flying test. Now they were embarrassed by it.

Too sick with disappointment to argue any longer, he pushed himself to his feet, said stiffly, " Thank you very much, sir," and stumped out.

Tight-lipped he drove to Avonmore Mansions, walked up the ninety-six steps again and found Thelma sewing in the sitting-room. Surprised, she asked what had brought him from Wittering, and he told her. She listened quietly and asked: " What's the situation now ? "

" I haven't the slightest idea," he said moodily. " I suppose they'll offer me a ground job."

79

" Well, you'll still have a career in the R.A.F.," she said consolingly and he burst out violently :

" I'm damned if I'd take the job."

She talked to him for a couple of hours before he promised to wait a while and see what happened. A week later—it was November now—he was posted to Duxford, a fighter station some forty miles north of London in Cambridgeshire, where he found 19 Squadron flying Bulldogs, some instructors training the Cambridge University Air Squadron, and a precise, immaculate wing commander in charge of the station, who said : " Glad to have you here, Bader. You're taking over the motor transport section."

The job was simple enough : not much more than sitting in a little office all day drinking tea, signing chits and giving orders about lorries. Officially he was still classed as " General Duties," the flying branch, and stubbornly he felt there might still be a chance of getting an airborne job—how, he didn't know. They asked if he would like to be reclassified " Administrative " or " Equipment " and he said no.

One week-end on leave Adrian Stoop took him and Thelma to see the Harlequins play Richmond at Twickenham. Bader was very excited until the match started, and then in the first couple of minutes he suddenly became quiet. Stoop knew that he had made a mistake. In that hour Bader felt more bitterly than ever before the loss of his legs. Later that evening he told Thelma that he would never go and see another rugger match.

Towards the end of April he was sent for by Squadron Leader Sanderson, C.O. of 19 Squadron. Sanderson had been adjutant at Kenley before Bader lost his legs, and when the young man walked into his office and saluted, the good-natured Sanderson said : " Douglas, this is the worst thing I've ever had to do in the Air Force. I've just received a letter from Air Ministry . . . here, you'd better read it yourself." He passed the letter across. Bader took it and read :

Subject : Flying Officer D. R. S. Bader.

(1) *The Air Council regrets that in consequence of the results of this officer's final medical board he can no longer be employed in the General Duties Branch of the Royal Air Force.*

(2) *It is suggested therefore that this officer revert to the retired list on the grounds of ill health.*

(3) *A further communication will be sent in respect of the date of his retirement and details concerning his retired pay and disability pension.*

Sanderson said : " I'm terribly sorry, Douglas."

" That's all right, sir," he said, and stumped out.

He drove down to see Thelma and told her.

" But you could still stay in on the ground, couldn't you ? " she asked.

He said bluntly : " I suppose I could, but I won't."

He took her out to dinner at the Indian Restaurant in Swallow Street, just off Piccadilly, and they sat close together over curry. After a silence he said : " I'm not much of a proposition for anyone. No legs. No job. No money."

" Don't worry," she said. " We'll make out."

There was not much more said than that. No blunt question. No blunt answer. Just a delicate understanding that sent him back to Duxford quietly happy, knowing he was not alone.

Shortly another letter came from Air Ministry, impersonal but not unkind, granting him £100 a year total disability pension and £99 10s. a year retired pay.

For a fortnight he was clearing up the ends of his Air Force life, handing over his job to another officer and packing his civilian clothes. His uniforms and cricketing kit he gave to Joe Cox. One day he visited the Officers' Employment Bureau at Air Ministry. A brisk, cheerful man asked him what he would like to do.

"Would you like to go abroad?"

"Not very much. I wouldn't be any good in the tropics with these legs anyway. It's no good when they start to sweat."

The man said at last: "Well, leave it to me and I'll have a look round."

The last few days were trying. Suddenly tired of the whole business, he wanted only to get the final agony over. Then there was only one more signature to get; and that night he took his last uniform off for the last time with no visible sign of emotion. In the morning he dressed in his sports coat and flannels, looked over the Rooms to Let column in the *Daily Telegraph* and marked a few likely ones with a pencil, then dumped his two suitcases in the M.G. and drove to station Headquarters for the final moment of separation. It was quite undramatic. He said to the adjutant: "Here are my clearances, sir. Would you put your mark at the bottom, please?"

The adjutant signed and said: "Well, there you are, old boy. All clear."

He drove straight past the guard-room out of the gates and turned left on the road to London. It was some minutes before he began to think again, and it occurred to him first that now he had no home.

One of the places ticked in the *Telegraph* was 86 Boundary Road, St. John's Wood. Turning into Boundary Road, he pulled up outside a house, a typical three-storied solid affair, and rang the bell. An attractive blonde woman opened the door. Yes, Miss Markham said she had a room for a guinea a week with breakfast, and he followed her up the stairs. She saw his dot-and-carry movement : " Oh, you've hurt your leg ? "

" Well, no," he said. " I haven't got any legs actually."

After an embarrassed pause she said : " Oh, I'm so sorry."

" That's all right. I don't mind a bit."

She said she was sorry the room was two floors up and he said he didn't mind that a bit either.

He liked the look of the room immediately ; it was nicely kept and furnished, with a divan bed and good wash-basin.

He took it on the spot and brought his two suitcases up : their contents, the month's pay in his pocket and the car outside were all he had in the world. After paying Miss Markham for a week in advance he drove off to see Thelma.

The following week brought him for the first time in his life a proper taste of the unsheltered world where there were few rules and fewer privileges and you scrambled with all the others for your share. It was a cold awakening.

On the Monday at the Officers' Employment Bureau the cheerful man said : " Got a few feelers out, old boy, but nothing in sight yet."

On the Tuesday he drove all over London, but not looking for a job ; just driving. On the Wednesday he did the same, not accepting yet the drop in status and the need to scramble. Mixed with this was an attitude, inchoate but stubborn, that he was not going to drop his standards. On the Thursday he drove Thelma down to the Pantiles for cream tea. The place had charm for them both. On Friday he called for her again and she brought out a Thermos of tea and a packet of sandwiches. " We might as well get used to things," she said. "If you won't watch the pennies, I will."

In the mornings now he took to looking at the jobs-vacant column in the *Telegraph*. Then a letter came from the Officers' Employment Bureau suggesting he go along to see the staff managers of Unilevers and the Asiatic Petroleum Co. He went to Unilevers first and they told him about soap and its by-products, and offered him a job starting at £200 a year in London before going out to West Africa. He explained that his legs would bar him from the tropics.

Then the petroleum company, where a scholarly man like a university don also suggested a job that would mean going to the tropics. Depressed, he explained about his legs. The scholarly man thought for a while. "We've got a little aviation section growing up here," he said. "They might have a vacancy. Would that interest you?"

At the word "aviation" Bader was extremely interested.

The man took him along to the office of the aviation department, where the manager said magically, yes, he could do with a smart young man. It would be a job in the office helping sell aviation spirit to airlines and governments. Bader began almost literally praying they would take him on. Then they took him to the home staff manager, who sized him up and then said abruptly: "Well, we'll pay you £200 a year and start on Monday. How's that?"

He drove to tell Thelma he was now employed, and they went on to the Ace of Spades, where, over a more expensive curry, he said with unromantic directness: "I suppose we can start thinking about getting married now."

She looked at him in the odd, half-smiling tolerant way that was coming naturally to her. "How much do you think we'll need?" she asked.

"Oh, I don't know," he said. "I suppose at least £500 a year."

That seemed reasonable enough. They were only twenty-three, and with his job and pension he now had £399 10s. a year. "I'll make sure the pay from the job goes up smartly," he said, rather cockily, and they settled down to an engrossing discussion about costs of flats and food and engagement rings. Thelma suggested that he should forget about an engagement ring and have a secret engagement to preserve domestic content at her home.

When the day came he put on his blue suit and drove hatless to his new office just off Bishopsgate in the City of London. The manager showed him to a desk with a green top and swivel chair backed against another desk. All told there were eight desks and eight pink and shaven young men. One showed him on a map where all the petroleum installations were, and he listened politely while others explained what the organisation did. Then they gave him a mass of documents to read about aviation spirit, prices, marketing and so on, and at the end he was little wiser.

After a couple of weeks he gradually got the hang of things, and was concerned mainly with prices and delivery of aviation spirit and oils to Australia. It was remote and dull, a tenuous, vicarious and somewhat hollow association with flying.

One September week-end he drove Thelma up to Sprotborough and was delighted that his mother liked her. So did Bill Hobbs, the vicar, and later that week the young man and the girl began thinking about getting married if he got his Christmas rise in pay. They could just marry on his present income of a little over £7 10s. a week, but there were two barriers. First, he had to run a car, which was expensive.

There were other practical considerations. He had just £2 in the bank. And what would happen if the car were damaged? It was only insured "third party" because the companies seemed to look dourly on Air Force officers with fast sports cars, especially when they had no legs. However warily they viewed the car, Bader cherished it not only for its usefulness but for its symbolism as fitting for a vital young man who loved flying. On the Saturday morning when he hosed and washed it carefully to take Thelma to the Stoops he was wondering if they dared marry if the rise did not come through.

Soon he forgot that in the joy of driving along the Great West Road at his usual 70 m.p.h. Passing the spot where London Airport is now, a large Humber pulled out ahead on the other side to pass a lorry, and Douglas eased his foot on to the brake to give it time to swing in again. The brakes had not the slightest effect (brake-drums full of water from the hose washing). Suddenly alert to danger, he tried to swing in, but another lorry was parked ahead on the left and the little M.G. darted at uncontrollable speed for the narrow gap left between the lorry and Humber on one side and the lorry on the other, all unfortunately abreast at the same moment. The gap was not wide enough.

CHAPTER TEN

A WIFE AND GOLF

EVEN AS fright alarmed the mind the M.G.'s offside front wheel sliced along the Humber's running-board as they came together at about 100 m.p.h. In a screeching flash the front wheel had gone, the door by Bader's elbow vanished, the rear wheel tore off and the M.G. lurched crazily on to its brake drums and screeched along the bitumen. By some luck it ran straight, slowing up on the drums, and then it was motionless. Thelma relaxed her grip on the seat as Douglas said, " I'm sorry, darling." He got out, surprised to see that his door and two wheels were gone, and realised that he was extremely lucky.

The Humber had pulled in to the other side of the road, apparently all right, about 200 yards away, and in it an admiral's wife was shaken with shock but otherwise unhurt. Two daughters comforted her, and the third daughter, a forthright young woman who had been driving, got out and began striding towards the M.G. Oddly enough she was an acquaintance of Thelma's. She arrived and said stormily to Bader : " Were you the lunatic driving this car ? "

" Yes," he said, " but I should prefer you not to be rude because I shall only be rude back."

The two bristled at each other and then the daughter recognised Thelma sitting on the bank of the road. " Hallo, Thelma," she said, " were you in this ? "

"Hallo, Maisie," Thelma said. "Yes, I was." A big chauffeur-driven car pulled up and a large businessman got out and entered the conversation with a statement that the young man had driven past him a couple of miles back going like a maniac.

The businessman made it clear that he would be delighted to give evidence for the admiral's daughter. Everyone exchanged names and addresses. The businessman drove off and the daughter went back to the Humber. A man brought along one of the M.G. wheels he had found in a field a hundred yards away. They could not find the other wheel (it took a garage man two hours the following day to do that). An agreeable young man gave them a lift back to London.

For the next three weeks he travelled to work by tube or by bus, standing.

The bill for the Humber came in—£10 (an insurance company paid the rest). Then the M.G. was ready and he went to collect it. They gave him the bill at the same time —£68. The friend said sympathetically that it was as low as he could make it, but he could pay it off at £1 a week. He took Thelma to the Ace of Spades for dinner (this time back to scrambled eggs and bacon.) They danced, and as they came off the floor the piano struck into "Stormy Weather."

"Very apt," Thelma said dryly. "How long do you think it will take to pay it all off?"

He said that if he got his rise he might be in the clear by next June.

Thelma said comfortingly: "Never mind, darling. It'll give us good practice for saving for a wedding."

He thought gloomily for a while and then burst out impulsively: "Look, why don't we get married anyway now?"

88

Thelma suggested that there might be a little reluctance from her parents.

" Why tell them ? " Douglas asked.

After a while she said : " All right, darling. Let's do it. When ? "

"" Next Saturday," he said. " I'll hop in and get a licence."

At Hampstead Registry Office he said to the clerk : " I want to get married next Saturday."

The clerk said yes, that would be all right. He could do it with a special licence for twenty-five guineas.

" Good grief," Bader said. " I haven't got twenty-five shillings."

The clerk said that then he would have to wait three weeks and it would cost only thirty shillings. Bader found he actually had just over £2 and settled for that. With a new idea he went back to the office, and got a fortnight's holiday to start in three weeks. Back at Avonmore Mansions that evening, when the others were out of the room he whispered to Thelma : " Zero hour October 5th."

He told her about the honeymoon.

" Oh, my gosh," she said, " what am I going to tell the parents, going away with you ? "

That was another problem. The solution was quite fortuitous. They happened to meet Thelma's uncle just back from a holiday at Porthleven in Cornwall, where he had stayed at a most respectable guest-house.

" I've got some leave coming up," Bader said artlessly. " D'you think I'd like it there ? "

" You'd love it," Uncle said. " So would Thelma. Why don't you both go down for a while ? "

On Wednesday, 4th October, Douglas got the next day off from the office for " urgent private business."

At 10.30 on the Thursday morning Mrs. Addison went out shopping, and Thelma rang Douglas and got into her new dress. By eleven Douglas had arrived and they were off to Hampstead.

In a drab, lino-floored office a strange man muttered from a book and at last looked up and said: " Well, congratulations, Mr. and Mrs. Bader."

That night they announced their engagement to the family. Everyone seemed quite happy; in fact, Mrs. Addison no longer noticed that he had no legs. After he had gone to Boundary Road that night she brought out an old diamond ring and gave it to Thelma, saying: " Look, darling, I don't suppose Douglas has many pennies to buy a ring, but this old one of Granny's has some nice diamonds and he could probably get them re-set."

On the Saturday morning *The Times* announced the engagement and the happy couple drove off towards Porthleven for their honeymoon.

It rained all the way down and nearly all the fortnight they spent in the grey, Cornish stone house where the unsuspecting landlord woke each in their separate rooms at eight o'clock every morning with a cup of tea.

On the last Saturday they drove back to London to start married life. He left her at Avonmore Mansions and went back to Boundary Road. Thereafter he saw her nearly every evening, either having dinner at Avonmore Mansions or taking her out for scrambled eggs to the Ace of Spades. On Christmas Eve, the manager said to Douglas : " We're very satisfied with your work, Bader, and I'm happy to tell you that we are raising your salary by £50 a year."

It helped in paying the car bills, but as winter dragged on he began to feel bogged down in a morass, increasingly frustrated by the dull and undemanding job and the indefinite separation from Thelma. The job offered no challenge and as he was barred from going overseas offered few prospects. There was not even a game he could turn to for relief. His legs still troubled him: he could never walk far without weariness and chafing, and sometimes he had to go back to Roehampton for adjustments.

About that time 'Derick was killed in an accident in South Africa. The Bader family seemed to be out of luck.

On a spring Saturday at Hartley Wintney, Adrian Stoop and Tinny Dean, a Harlequins and England scrum-half, were going to play golf at a local nine-hole course and suggested that Douglas and Thelma go and see them hit off. After they drove off Douglas said he would potter about the fairway until they returned, so Stoop handed him a seven iron and a ball. When Stoop and Dean had gone on he dropped the ball on the grass and took a swing at it, but the club missed the ball by inches and he overbalanced and fell flat on his back. He got up and tried again and the same thing happened.

Again and again he fell until about the twelfth attempt the club hit the ball with a sweet click and, lying on his back a moment later, he could still see it in parabolic flight.

Next day he tried the seven iron again on the Stoops' lawn, this time with Stoop coaching. Several times he hit the ball but still he kept falling over. He had fallen about twenty times again when he tried a shorter and slower swing, hit the ball and just kept his balance. As he looked up with a triumphant grin Thelma said: " Good, now you'll be satisfied."

" Not on your life," he said, got the ball back and kept on trying. Shortly he hit it without falling again.

The following week-end he tried again at the Stoops',

until nine times out of ten he was hitting the ball and not falling.

Next week-end he improved still more, his brain absorbing the instinctive reflexes needed to keep his balance. A couple of week-ends later Tinny Dean took him over to the golf course and handed him a three-wood on the first tee. Acutely aware of the eyes of the usual first-tee onlookers, he desperately wanted to hit the ball, stay on his feet and not let them know he had no legs.

With taut concentration he braced his feet wide apart, took a slow swing and connected. Stumbling, he still kept his feet and saw the ball flight about a hundred yards, fading with a little slice.

He walked down the fairway with Dean, borrowed a couple of clubs and more or less hacked his way to the green. Later he returned to the clubhouse, stumps chafed, glowing with satisfaction and perspiration.

All that week Bader found he was looking forward with longing to the week-end's golf practice. Dean took him to the North Hants course at Fleet and he struggled round the first two holes, falling over only once. Already the muscles of the stumps were developing and he learned the trick of smearing zinc ointment on spots that were likely to chafe, then powdering and taping them. He was hitting drives consistently over a hundred yards, sending them farther and farther as he developed more instinctive balance.

The odd thing was that though he sometimes mis-hit, his good shots sailed dead straight, probably for the simple reason that where normal men tried to " press " with wild and sloppy swings, Bader *had* to keep perfect balance and control—or fall over. After a month he got to the stage of doing three or four holes every Saturday and Sunday, feeling stronger and hitting the ball longer each new week-end.

The club secretary suggested he might become a member. Then he started wondering how he could afford to buy clubs.

" My dear chap," Dean said, " spring along to the Railway Lost Property Office."

He did so and bought six good steel-shafted clubs for 7s. 6d. each and a light bag. Thelma became an enthusiastic caddy and never stopped encouraging him.

Towards the end of August he was playing six holes at a time. In early September he played nine holes for the first time. The following week he did twelve holes.

It was at the beginning of October—nearly the first wedding anniversary—that he played his first straight eighteen holes. Back at the clubhouse, delighted, he said: " You know I feel so fresh I could do another nine."

" No, you don't," Thelma said. " You come and have some tea."

He resolved after that to play eighteen holes every time, and at the end of November he broke 100 for the first time. Even on cold days the sweat ran off him, evidence of the tremendous effort that he had to exert in getting round.

There was one further complication about playing golf with artificial legs : the feet had a little fore and aft movement but no lateral " give," so that when he straddled his legs to play a shot the ankles were stiff and he stood uncomfortably on the inside of each sole. He lamented of this defect at Roehampton, and the ingenious craftsmen there designed and fitted a kind of universal joint in the ankles, allowing lateral " give " against rubber pads, so that he could stand with legs apart and feet flat on the ground.

That Christmas he got a rise of £25 a year. He was out of debt now and it brought his total income to £475 a year, so that they could really start saving for a second wedding. Yet by this time the passionless decorum of the office was reducing him to desperation and he began talking fretfully about trying to get something less stultifying.

One morning (this was 1935) he opened the *Telegraph* and saw a headline : " Royal Air Force To Be Expanded."

All morning he thought about it, and after lunch he wrote to Air Marshal Sir Frederick Bowhill, now Air Member for Personnel, who had been his A.O.C. when he crashed.

An answer came back in a few days, sympathetic and understanding. Sir Frederick said that if it were left to him he would have Bader back in the Service, but there was no chance of persuading others to agree.

Golf was the opiate that made life bearable after that. By late summer he was good enough to start playing competition, his scores ranging between 90 and 110, with a handicap of 18. A few weeks later he won a silver jam spoon in a bogey competition and they dropped his handicap to 16.

As well as golf, North Hants had several tennis courts near the clubhouse, and one day Tinny Dean suggested : " Come and have a shot, Douglas." Bader did not need much persuading.

He partnered Dean in doubles and found it surprisingly easy. When a ball came within reach he was very accurate, with a smashing forehand drive, yet, he felt he could not pull his weight properly. In doubles he could only get to a ball that came reasonably within reach and his partner had to do a tremendous amount of running.

At Christmas he got a rise of £30 a year, bringing total income to £505, and they began planning to be married again as soon as they had £100. By May they were nearly half-way there, when driving back from Hartley Wintney one Sunday he noticed a knock in the engine. It got progressively worse and soon he had to pull into a garage, where a mechanic diagnosed a broken crankshaft.

For a week Bader travelled by bus and tube again. Then the repaired car was ready. He collected the bill at the same time—£30. When he drove away a loud grating came from the back. Smashed crown wheel and bevel!

Eventually, driving back to London with Thelma, they came to an accident at the top of the hill by Virginia Water, where two cars had collided and he stopped to see if he could help. Before he could get out a motor-cycle combination pelted over the top of the hill, swerved to avoid the damaged cars, and the sidecar rammed the M.G. head on. In the jolt Thelma's face jerked against the ignition key, cutting her nose badly, and the front of the car was stove in. Ambulance men bandaged Thelma's face. She was all right in a day or two, apart from a black eye, but Bader was without the car for nearly a month. Luckily the motor-cyclist's insurance covered most of the damage, but it still left Douglas with some £15 to pay taxis, doctors and incidentals.

Then in August (with another friend in the car this time) he was approaching a rise near Rugby at about 70 m.p.h. when the driver of a large Rolls Royce in front waved him on. As he pulled out to pass, a car came over the rise. He braked and pulled in sharply behind the Rolls, but the Rolls was braking, too, and the M.G. rammed its rump very hard. Geoffrey Darlington, the passenger, copied Thelma, cutting his face on the ignition key. Everyone got out of the cars and all were remarkably polite about the affair, but that did not help a great deal towards paying the bill of £30 for the M.G. Thelma was haunted for weeks by the guilty note in her fiancé's voice when he rang up and confessed: "Darling, I've busted the car again."

At Christmas he got a rise of £35 and said: "Come hell or high water we're going to get officially married this year."

CHAPTER ELEVEN

WAR!—BACK IN UNIFORM

IT WAS Thelma's idea that they should get married again on 5th October, fourth anniversary of the uninspiring Hampstead ceremony. She found a flat in a new block going up in West Kensington and at the end of September the fluctuating bank account was drained again, this time to pay for the furniture.

Only one mild hitch happened at the last moment: at a wedding rehearsal at Avonmore Mansions on the evening of 4th October he bent to kneel in the prescribed way and tipped flat on his face. It was a great joke until he said: "What the hell do I do to-morrow?" Geoffrey Darlington, who was to be best man, said he would buttonhole the vicar beforehand and get permission to stand.

Next morning they were re-married, standing, in St. Mary Abbott's Church, Kensington, Douglas looking very dapper in cutaway coat and sponge-bag trousers. All the relatives and friends were so warmly happy to see the couple at last married after so many difficulties.

Settled in their own home, Thelma soon noticed that his depressed moods were becoming rare and brief. Besides, his golf handicap was down to nine and he had started playing squash at the Lensbury Club, a pleasant recreation spot for Shell Company staff near Teddington. Bader lunged furiously about the court, taking some terrible tumbles and with legs thumping and creaking on the protesting floor. Rivets often popped out of the legs under this treatment, and one day the knee bolt of the right leg snapped and, as he fell the right shin and foot, complete with sock and shoe, shot across the court.

Hitler had never meant much to him until Munich ; it was then he realised there was going to be a war. He wrote to Air Ministry asking for a refresher flying course, and a note came back saying that the doctors still thought that the legs made him a permanent accident risk.

About April, 1939, when Hitler was marching into the rest of Czechoslovakia, Geoffrey Stephenson was posted to Air Ministry. Stephenson was friendly with the personal staff officer to the new Air Member for Personnel, Air Marshal Sir Charles Portal, and soon Bader wrote to Portal asking the same old question. He got what looked at first like the same old answer : " I am afraid that during peace time it is not possible for me to permit you to enter a flying class of the reserve." And then he came to the last exciting sentence : " But you can rest assured that if war came we would be only too glad of your services in a flying capacity if the doctors agreed."

Part of him began almost praying for war. Thelma, full of dread both at the idea of war and of Douglas trying to fly in it without legs, tried miserably to get him to give up the dream.

The day after Hitler marched into Poland he sent Thelma away to join her parents in the country for a few days in case masses of bombers came over when the whistle went. (The family had recently taken over half a bungalow attached to the Pantiles.) Next morning, washing up his breakfast things, he heard Chamberlain's tragic voice announcing war. He left the washing up, sat down and wrote to Portal's secretary again.

On the Monday the Shell Company began evacuating

some offices to the Lensbury Club, and Bader's boss told him that he would be based there on the list of indispensable workers debarred from call-up.

Bader immediately said : " Would you mind taking my name off that list, sir. I'm not really indispensable and I'm trying to get back into the R.A.F."

Down at the Lensbury Club he began telephoning and writing notes to Stephenson and another friend at Air Ministry, Hutchinson, to get things moving for him. Then, early in October, a telegram arrived : " Please attend Air Ministry Adastral House Kingsway for selection board Thursday 10.30. Bring this telegram with you."

Eagerly on the Thursday he found the right room. A dozen other men were waiting and he thought they all looked rather old for flying. A corporal called his name and he followed into an inner office where he came face to face with Air Vice Marshal Halahan, his old commandant at Cranwell. Halahan got up from his desk and shook hands. " Good to see you, Douglas. What sort of job would you like ? "

It almost took his breath away.

" General Duties,[1] of course, sir."

Halahan said : " Oh ! " and looked dubious. " I'm very sorry but I'm only dealing with ground jobs here."

His stomach sagged a little. " It's only a flying job I want, sir."

Halahan looked at him steadily for some five seconds and then took a piece of paper and began writing on it. No words were said. He sealed it in an envelope and handed it across.

" Take that across to the medical people," he said.

They shook hands again and Bader stumped out. Dying to know what was in the letter he felt strung up

[1] Flying.

99

with fearful hope. The feeling mounted as he crossed Kingsway and went up in the lift to the bitterly remembered medical unit. Guarding the sanctum was the same stout and kindly Cerberus who had seen so many men broken from crashes come in and try to talk their way back to A.1.B.—full flying category. The warrant officer recognised him :

"'Ullo, sir. I thought you'd be along. What's it this time ? "

"Same again," Bader said. "I think they might pass me this time."

"Not A.1.B., sir. Never."

"We'll see. Would you please give this to the wing commander." He handed over the letter from Halahan.

After a while the warrant officer came back and got out a new file for him. "Come along, sir," he said. "We'll get you done as quickly as possible."

Bader always remembered the sequence of events after that. He wrote them down :

"*I visited the various rooms in turn ; eyes, ears, nose and throat ; blood pressure, heart and lungs—never a shadow of doubt. I asked the last doctor, ' Am I all right for flying?' and he gave a short laugh as though I had been joking. Finally my file was complete and the wing commander sent for me. I could see he was looking at my file as though he were thinking, not reading. Then he looked up and said: ' Apart from your legs you're a hundred per cent.' He pushed a bit of paper across to me, and said : ' Have you seen this? ' It was Halahan's note. I said : ' No, sir.' I looked at it and as far as I remember it read :*

"' *I have known this officer since he was a cadet at Cranwell. He's the type we want. If he is fit, apart from his legs, I suggest you give him A.1.B. category and leave it to the Central Flying School to assess his flying capabilities.'*

" I handed the note back without a word. I think I stopped breathing. I was looking directly at him, willing him to think my way. He said, ' I agree with Air Vice Marshal Halahan. We're giving you A.1.B. and it's up to the flying chaps. I'll recommend they give you a test at C.F.S.' "

His face hardly changed, except that he took a deep breath, said correctly: " Thank you, sir." and walked out, feeling that he was picking up life again from the moment he had crashed.

In that mood he drove to the Pantiles. As he walked in the doorway, Thelma said: " Hallo, what are you doing here? Lost your job? "

" No," he said. " I'm getting my old one back."

It was her turn to feel that the moment was too big to show emotion. The deeper the feeling the less she allowed it to show and she said: " I suppose you'll be very happy now."

On 14th October a telegram came from the Central Flying School at Upavon, " Suggest report for test 18th October." He drove down next morning.

It was over seven years since he had flown—he was bound to be rusty—but only on the way down did the insidious, disturbing thought cross his mind that he might fail the test.

It was odd at first walking into the grey stone mess in flannels and sports coat while everyone else walked about in uniform. He felt awkward and out of place until he came across Joe Cox there, and also the thickset, amusing Rupert Leigh whom he had last known as a junior cadet at Cranwell.

" You're my meat," Leigh said menacingly. " I am

the maestro of the refresher flight and I give you your test. I know you will behave courteously towards me."

After lunch Leigh took him out to a Harvard advanced trainer. This was going to be different from the old Bulldog : the Harvard was a sturdy monoplane. It had all the modern things he had never encountered before, flaps, constant speed propeller, retractable undercarriage and brakes. Brakes ! To his horror, when he got into the cockpit he saw that the Harvard had foot-brakes. Leigh soothed his truculent lament :

" Forget about the brakes. I'll work them. You won't have to worry about them after to-day because the Harvard's the only aircraft in the Service that hasn't got a hand-brake on the stick."

Leigh explained the cockpit, climbed into the back seat and started up. " I'll do a circuit first," he said, " and then you have a stab."

He took the Harvard off and explained what he was doing all the way round. After landing he taxied back to the downwind perimeter and said : " Right. She's yours."

Bader was too busy to feel that This Was The Moment. He went through the cockpit drill, and as she went away with a roar and picked up her tail there was no swing. Soon she tilted, docile in his hands. Just for a minute it felt strange, but as he flew round for a quarter of an hour the " feel " came back, filling him with joy. She was heavier than he realised and he undershot but tickled her over the fence with a bit of engine and flattened, easing back till he cut the throttle, held her off and then cut her tail down as she settled. She touched smoothly and ran without swinging. Surprised that she was so easy to fly, he took her off again and spent an hour doing two more landings, and then climbing for a roll and a loop before landing again, exultant.

When they taxied in and got out Leigh's first words were, "Well, it's damn' silly asking me if you can fly. However, I'll humour them and write recommending that you be re-admitted to the fold and posted here for a full refresher course."

Towards the end of November an Air Ministry envelope arrived. He ripped it open and there it was in official language ; they would take him back as a regular officer re-employed in his former rank and seniority (which meant higher pay). His retired pay would cease but his hundred per cent disability pension would continue. (That was a droll touch—hundred per cent fit and hundred per cent disabled.) If the terms were acceptable would he kindly state when he was prepared to report to C.F.S. for duty. That day was a Friday. He wrote back, naming Sunday, rang his tailor to demand a new uniform within a week, and left his desk for the last time.

That gave him a final day with Thelma at the Pantiles and he could not disguise his glee until, on the Sunday when he was ready to go, Thelma, for the first time since he had known her, gave way, and the tears began trickling down her face as she stood by the car. He drove away greatly sobered, and the mood stayed until he turned in past the guardroom at Upavon : at that moment he felt back in the Air Force again.

At the refresher flight he reported to Leigh with a smart " Good morning, sir," and they both started laughing because Leigh, who had been his junior, was now a squadron leader and Bader was still only a flying officer. After lunch another old friend, Christopher Clarkson, took him up in an Avro Tutor for his first flight as an active officer since the crash. Clarkson handled her for the first " circuit and bump " and then let Bader have the controls. The Tutor was an aeroplane he knew—a biplane. His first landing was workmanlike and his second a neat three-pointer. As he turned downwind again Clarkson hauled himself out of the cockpit and said: " She's all yours, chum."

" *This, then, was the moment. At last I was alone with an aeroplane. 27th November, 1939—almost exactly eight years after my crash.*

" *I turned Tutor K3242 into wind and took off. I remember the afternoon as clear as to-day. It was 3.30, a grey sky with clouds at 1,500 feet and a south-west wind. A number of aeroplanes were flying around. I went a little way from the crowd . . ."*

Shortly the telephone rang in Rupert Leigh's office and Leigh picked it up and heard the cold voice of Wing Commander Pringle, the chief flying instructor: " Leigh ! I have just landed. On my way down I passed a Tutor upside down in the circuit area at 600 feet."

Leigh froze with foreboding.

The frigid voice continued: " I *know* who it was. Be good enough to ask him not to break *all* the flying regulations straight away."

When Bader landed and taxied in he found Leigh beside him, saying: " Don't do it. Please don't do it."

" Do what ? "

Leigh told him what had happened but Bader could not very well explain to him that on his first solo flight he *had* to turn the aeroplane upside down at forbidden height. At the time he did not know himself that it had any connection with his last flight in the Bulldog.

On 4th December for the first time he flew a modern, operational aircraft, the Fairey " Battle," a single-engined, two-seater day bomber. She was heavy to handle, approaching obsolescence and not approved for pupil aerobatics (though after a couple of days he was quietly looping and rolling her away from the aerodrome and prying eyes at 7,000 ft.). He preferred a lighter aircraft, but being put on to the Battle did not bother him.

Time continued to slide by with flying every day and comradeship in the mess at night, often developing into exuberant impromptu parties which revived the old spirit he had missed so much, though still he never took anything stronger than orange squash.

Winter froze hard that year. He got out of the M.G. at the mess steps one night and instantly slipped and fell on the icy ground. He got up and slipped over again, soon finding it impossible to keep his balance on the slippery ground. At last he was forced to crawl to the steps on hands and knees, unfortunately just as two brother officers came out and said : " Good grief, look at Bader ! Bottled as a coot." Everyone pulled his leg about being a secret drinker and his amusement changed to annoyance in the morning when he found the ice still on the ground so that he was marooned in the mess. Joe Cox got a brainwave and suggested he put his socks *over* his shoes.

At the end of January Joe Cox said to him : " Well, *we're* happy about your flying if you are. You might as well crack off to a squadron."

Bader rang Geoffrey Stephenson, who had eased himself out of Air Ministry and was now commanding 19 Squadron at Duxford, where Bader thought he had said good-bye to the Air Force for ever. The squadron had Spitfires and Stephenson set about getting him a posting to it.

On 3rd February Bader drove to the Pantiles for his leave. A telegram ended the waiting : " Posted 19 Squadron, Duxford, w.e.f. February 7." The date was already 7th February. Thelma, the stoic again, packed his kit and within two hours he was on his way in the M.G., feeling happier than he could remember.

CHAPTER TWELVE

SPITFIRE PILOT

DUXFORD WAS different. The guardroom was new and bigger. The mess, too, was new and bigger, but the main change lay in the faces there; they all looked about twenty-one. Bader, sitting alone in the ante-room, became sharply aware that he would be thirty in a fortnight and that it was he who had changed most. Geoffrey Stephenson was away for a couple of days and he felt out of it all.

His only cheerful moment in the mess was meeting again Tubby Mermagen. Years ago he had known Mermagen as a pilot officer, but Mermagen now commanded the other squadron at Duxford, No. 222, which flew Blenheims. It was fun to talk over old times, but when he took off his legs to go to bed he felt again a comparatively elderly flying officer.

Then Stephenson came back and Bader greeted him with a glad cry. Next morning he climbed into a Spitfire and a boy of twenty showed him the cockpit. She started easily and he took off without any nerves, feeling instantly that she was extremely sensitive fore and aft. On the downwind leg he started his drill for landing and found he could not move the undercart selector lever into the " down " position. No tugs, pushes or fiddlings would budge it.[1] Only one thing to do—" ring up " and get advice. He switched on the radio and it crackled and popped

[1] The young lad of twenty had omitted to tell him that the undercarriage always hung on the withdrawal pins and a couple of pumps removed the weight of the wheels and allowed the selector freedom to travel into the " down " position.

106

and buzzed, so that he could not hear a word from the control tower. He tried with the undercart selector lever again and finally got things working. After that the landing was an anti-climax, but neat.

On 13th February his flight commander, an unblooded veteran of twenty-five, led him aloft for his first formation flying in a Spitfire. Like the old days in Gamecocks, he tucked his wing in about three feet behind his leader's and stuck there. It takes quick hands and rapt concentration to do that; you watch your leader, not where you're going. Coming in to land the flight commander dipped low beside a wooden hut. Some instinct made Bader look ahead for a second and he saw the hut and that he could not miss it. Shoving on throttle he yanked back on the stick and the fighter roared up, squashing, engine blaring, and the tail smashed into the inverted-V wooden roof, and ploughed through, losing the tail wheel. The rocking fighter was still flying and he steadied her, brought her round and landed her on the naked rump of the tail.

The flight commander came across laughing, and said : " I'm awfully sorry, ol' boy. D'you know not long ago I landed a chap in a tree just the same way."

He never forgot the blunt details which Bader told him about his character.

At dawn a few days later the new pilot made his first operational flight—a convoy patrol. After take-off he turned the ring of his gun button from " safe " to " fire." It was exciting to feel there were eight loaded machine-guns in the wings, cocked to obey a thumb on the button.

For an hour and a half they flew over a dozen tiny ships crawling over the grey water of the East Coast and saw nothing else in the sky at all.

Most days they spent practising the three officially approved methods of attacking bombers, known as "Fighter Command Attack No. 1, No. 2, and No. 3." In "Attack No. 1" the fighters swung into line astern behind the leader and followed him in an orderly line up to the bomber, took a quick shot when their turn came in the queue and swung away after the leader again, presenting their bellies predictably to the enemy gunner. Long ago the theoreticians at Fighter Command had decided that modern aircraft, especially fighters, were too fast for the dog-fight tactics of World War I. Bader thought that was nonsense.

"There's only one way to do it," he growled to Stephenson, ". . . . that's for everyone to pile in together from each side as close to the Hun as they can. Why use only eight guns at a time when you can use sixteen or twenty-four from different angles."

Stephenson and the others argued : "But you don't *know*, do you ? *No* one knows."

"The boys in the last war knew," he said, "and the basic idea is the same now. No Hun bomber's going to stooge along in a straight line and let a line of chaps queue up behind and squirt at him one after the other. He'd jink all over the place. In any case, it won't be one ; it'll be a lot of bombers sticking together in tight formation. Why d'you think our bombers have got power-operated turrets ? "

Probably after the first pass or two the bomber packs could be split up, he considered. There'd be single bombers around then, but the fighters would be split up too and there'd be dogfights all over the sky.

"The chap who'll control the battle will still be the chap who's got the height and sun, same as the last war," he said.

Some of the other pilots ragged him about being pre-war vintage and old fashioned (especially on his thirtieth birthday), and Stephenson soothed him, saying : " You might be right, Douglas, but we've got to keep on doing what we're told until we find out for ourselves."

So Flying Officer Bader kept dourly following his leader in dummy tracks on Wellington bombers which stooged obligingly in a straight line and never fired back. In those circumstances it was easy enough, until one day, diving in line astern on a hedge-hopping Wellington, one eye on his leader and the other eye on the Wellington, Douglas ploughed into a tree-top at about 250 m.p.h. and the Spitfire shot out the other side in a shower of broken branches with one aileron torn and bent. She was controllable, but veering to the right with one wing low and he had a busy ten minutes nursing her down to firm ground.

That evening, in the privacy of his quarters with Stephenson, he said : " Look, I don't feel happy flying behind some of these young chaps. I'm more experienced and older, although I've not so many hours on Spitfires. Don't forget what we were taught in the old days in 23 Squadron that bad leading always causes trouble. I've had it twice now in a short time. I prefer to be killed in action, not on active service. Isn't it about time . . ."

The name of F/O Bader went up on the squadron readiness board next day as leader of a section of three.

He handled his section with confident pride on convoy and lightship patrols, practice battle climbs and even, conscientiously, in the official Fighter Command follow-my-leader attacks.

Tubby Mermagen's 222 Squadron at Duxford was changing its Blenheims for Spitfires and some of the crews were being posted away. In the mess one night Mermagen buttonholed Bader and casually said : " I want a new flight commander. I don't want to do the dirty on Geoffrey, but if he's agreeable, would you come?"

Beaming, Bader remarked that he would be delighted.

"Good show," said Mermagen. "I'll talk to Geoffrey and then fix it with the A.O.C."[1]

Convoy patrol next day had a new savour. Barring accidents Air Vice Marshal Leigh-Mallory was almost sure to approve. In the morning Bader led his section over to Horsham to await convoy patrol orders, and they had been on the ground only about five minutes, sipping cups of tea, when the operations phone rang and the orderly shouted an urgent order to "scramble" (take off immediately) to cover a convoy. An unidentified aircraft had been plotted near it. Bader put his tea down and lurched after the other running pilots to his Spitfire.

Quickly he clipped his straps and pressed the starter button; the still-hot engine fired and he was still winding his trimming-wheel as the plane went booming across the grass. The other two Spitfires were shooting past him, and he sensed vaguely that his aircraft was lagging. A quick glance at the boost gauge; the needle was quivering on $6\frac{1}{2}$ lb.—maximum power. She must be all right; but she was still bumping over the grass, curiously sluggish, running at a low stone wall on the far side of the field. He hauled desperately on the stick and the nose pulled up as she lurched off at an unnatural angle, not climbing. His right hand snapped down to the undercart lever but almost in the same moment the wheels hit the stone wall and ripped away. At nearly 80 m.p.h. the little fighter slewed and dipped a wing-tip into a ploughed field beyond; the nose smacked down, the tail kicked—she nearly cartwheeled—the tails lapped down again and she slithered and bumped on her belly with a rending noise across the soft earth.

[1] Air Officer Commanding.

She jerked to a stop in a cloud of flying dirt and the perspex hood of the cockpit snapped forward and hit him on the back of the head. The brain started working again and began wondering what had happened as he sat there. Automatically his hand went out and cut the switches and then he was motionless again apart from the eyes wandering round the cockpit looking for the answer. It stared back at him—the black knob of the propeller lever on the throttle quadrant poking accusingly at him, still in the coarse pitch position.

His stomach turned. Oh, not that classic boob! He couldn't have! But he had.

Apart from the crack on the head he seemed to be undamaged and he hauled himself out of the cockpit; he started back across the aerodrome just as the ambulance and fire-truck appeared. They drove him back to the operations hut; another Spitfire was parked there and he stumped over to it, climbed in, and took off to join the other two aircraft.

Over the convoy he found them and circled with them for an hour and a half without seeing any sign of the unidentified plane. By the time he landed at Duxford he had a splitting headache. Geoffrey Stephenson said wonderingly: "Why did you go and do a silly thing like that, taking off in coarse pitch?"

"Because I forgot to put it into fine, you stupid clot," Bader snarled, and stumped off towards his room. He must have hurt himself somewhere—he could hardly walk. In his room he undressed and when he took his trousers off realised why he had been walking so shakily: the shins of both artificial legs were smashed in—deep dents that made both legs bend forward like bows. Sitting on the edge of the bed gazing at them, it occurred to him what would have happened if he had not lost his real legs.

Days passed and no word came from Leigh-Mallory. Then the A.O.C. visited Duxford on a routine inspection and sent for him. Bader walked in, saluted and stood to attention. The thickset square-faced man behind the desk regarded him sombrely.

"Bader," he said. "Squadron Leader Mermagen wants you as a flight commander."

Bader's face stayed expressionless, but inside he was suddenly alert.

"I see you took off in coarse pitch the other day and broke a Spitfire," Leigh-Mallory said.

"Yes, sir."

"That was very silly, wasn't it?"

Another silence. Leigh-Mallory was looking at a piece of paper which Bader recognised as his accident report.

"I'm glad to see you've made no attempt to excuse yourself," Leigh-Mallory remarked.

"There wasn't any excuse, sir."

"No, there's no excuse for that sort of thing," said the A.O.C. A pause. "Anyway, you're going to 222 Squadron as a flight commander."

There were prompt results of Bader's promotion to flight lieutenant.

He brought Thelma from the Pantiles to stay at a pub just outside Duxford.

For some days he led his pilots into the air to do the official Fighter Command attacks. In turn he sent each pilot up as a target aircraft, telling him to turn round in the cockpit and watch each fighter in the approved procession pop up one by one and break away in the same direction, presenting his belly for a sitting shot.

When they came down he said: "Now, you can see what's liable to happen to you." Then he took them up for his own style of fighting, leading two or three at a time, darting down out of the sun one each side of a target plan and breaking sharply away forwards and underneath. After that came hours of dog-fight practice interspersed with routine operations like convoy patrols. He led his men also in a lot of formation aerobatics as the best way to teach them complete control.

Early in May a new squadron arrived at Duxford, No. 66. Its commanding officer cheerfully hailed Bader in the mess.

" Ha." he said ; " fiddled my way out of Training Command."

It was Rupert Leigh. Odd how the old Cranwell chums were getting together—Stephenson, Leigh and Bader.

Yet nothing seemed to happen at Duxford except the same old stuff, practice flying and convoy patrols.

May 22 ended the hiatus but not agreeably. A staff car careered up to dispersals, pulled up with a jerk and Mermagen jumped out yelling : " Squadron's posted to Kirkton-in-Lindsay. Everyone ready to leave by 1500 hours."

" Where's Kirkton-in-Lindsay ? " a young P/O asked Douglas as they scrambled into the flight truck.

" Up north, near Grimsby," Douglas said.

By three-thirty, after busy hours, the eighteen Spitfires were taking off for Kirkton while the ground crews were still packing the lorries to go by road. No one seemed to know what the move was all about, and it was next morning before they found out.

Convoy patrols.

Day after day it was the same, lolling in the sunshine at dispersals while the battle raged across the Channel, waiting for a call that would send them stooging aimlessly in an empty sky over a few small ships.

On the afternoon of the 27th a lorry pulled up at A Flight dispersal and a flight sergeant jumped down and said to Bader: " We've got some armour plate for your aircraft, sir."

Everyone clustered round curiously. Men manhandled the plates of flat steel over to the planes and the pilots helped screw them firmly behind the bucket seats. They had never seen armour plate before and were highly pleased. Bader went early as usual to bed.

In darkness he came up out of sleep. A hand was shaking his shoulder and a voice saying: " Wake up, sir. Wake up ! " The light clicked on and he blinked at the batman who stood there.

" Squadron's got to take off for Martlesham at 4 a.m. sir," said the batman. " It's three o'clock now."

Still half-asleep and irritable he reached out and strapped on his legs, then thumped the other pilots awake. Mermagen arrived and said : " I don't know what it's about but we're heading south and not taking any kit."

CHAPTER THIRTEEN

FIRST VICTORY

DAWN GLOWED as the squadron shook themselves into formation, and half an hour later they were landing through feathers of waist-high mist on Martlesham Aerodrome, near Felixstowe. Another squadron of Spitfires had already arrived, their pilots sipping tea in a group nearby. Bader strolled over and asked " the form " from a slim, handsome flight lieutenant.

" Haven't a clue," said the debonair young man. His name was Bob Tuck.[1]

Mermagen bustled over and said almost casually: " Patrol Dunkirk, chaps, 12,000 feet."

It seems odd now that the word Dunkirk did not mean a thing then. The Army had laid a screen of secrecy over the plans for evacuation and people did not realise that the beaches were filling with exhausted men.

Mermagen led them off in four neat vics of three; they climbed steadily and about 9,000 feet vanished into a layer of fluffy white cloud. At 10,00 feet they popped like porpoises out of the cloud and levelled off at 12,000, still in tidy formation . . . unblooded. A Messerschmitt coming up behind could have shot the whole lot down. Far ahead Bader saw a strange black plume floating through the limitless froth they were riding over. Mermagen's voice crackled over the radio: " That looks like it. Must be

[1] A few months later Tuck was famous as a wing commander with a D.S.O., three D.F.C.s and thirty German planes to his credit.

burning oil tanks." They circled the smoke and ranged over the cloud. They saw nothing else in the sky, and after an hour and a half Mermagen led them away.

On the way back 222 Squadron was told by radio to land at Manston, and after that were told to fly to Duxford, and at Duxford were ordered off again for Hornchurch.

At 3.30 a.m. Bader was shaken awake again.

" Take-off at 4.30, sir," said the batman.

It was getting beyond a joke.

Unbroken cloud lay over the land at about 4,000 feet, but this day they flew at 3,000. Skirting the North Foreland to pass Dover on the right, he looked down on the grey sea with amazement. Out from the Thames estuary, from Dover and the bays little boats were swarming, yachts and tugs, launches, ferries, coasters, lifeboats, paddle steamers, here and there a destroyer or a cruiser. It was unbelievable. Far ahead the black smoke rolled thickly up from the edge of Dunkirk, where the oil tanks lay, and all the way in between the swarm of little boats streamed white tails across the water. Hundreds of them.

Mermagen led them across the dirty sand by Gravelines and swung along the beaches towards Dunkirk. At first the men in the distance looked like a wide stain of ants teeming over a flat nest.

A voice on the R/T said : " Aircraft ahead." Bader saw them in the same moment, about twelve of them, about three miles ahead and a little to the right. He wondered who they were . . . not Spitfires or Hurricanes, and a surprised voice said in his earphones : " They're 110's ! "

They were coming head-on and in seconds he could see the twin-engines and twin fins. The Messerschmitts veered sharply left, climbing for the cloud . . . must be carrying bombs, avoiding a fight. Mermagen in front pulled up his nose and cartridge cases streamed out of his wings as he fired. But he was a long way out of normal range.

One of the 110's suddenly streamed black smoke, dipped out of the formation and went straight down, flaming. She hit and blew up behind Dunkirk. The other Germans had vanished into the cloud and the sky was clear again. It stayed clear for the rest of the patrol, and when they landed back at Hornchurch everyone clustered round Mermagen excitedly.

Next morning out of bed at 3.30 again for Dunkirk, and this time not a sign of enemy aircraft, only the ants on the beach and the little boats nosing bravely into the shore.

Again in the morning up at 3.15, and at 3,000 feet he could no longer see the canals—smoke brooded heavily and drifted across the stone breakwaters of the harbour. But no German planes. They came and bombed and killed just after the squadron had turned for home.

In the morning he felt dog-tired when the batman woke him. Same routine. An odd haze stretched towards London from Dunkirk, and even at 3,000 feet he smelt burning oil and knew what the haze was. Down below the same brave little boats streamed over the water. Dunkirk ahead . . . and over Dunkirk, about three miles away, a gaggle of swift-growing dots. He knew what they were instantly. The 110's wheeled inland without dropping their bombs, but the sky was empty of cloud and the Spitfires leapt after them. No time for thinking, but as he turned his reflector sight on and the gun button to " fire " he knew he was going to shoot. A glance back through the perspex ; the straining Spitfires were stringing out in a ragged line and up to the left four grey shapes were diving at them—Messerschmitt 109's.

He rammed stick and rudder over and the Spitfire wheeled after them. A 109 shot up in front; his thumb jabbed the firing button and the guns in the wings squirted with a shocking noise. The 109 seemed to be filling his windscreen. A puff of white spurted just behind its cockpit as though someone had used a giant flit-gun. The puff was chopped off . . . for a moment nothing . . . then a spurt of orange flame mushroomed round the cockpit and flared back like a blow-torch. The 109 rolled drunkenly, and in the same moment he saw the black cross on its side. Suddenly it was real and the 109 was falling away and behind, flaming.

Turning back towards Dunkirk, he did see a plane. From nowhere it seemed a 110 was tumbling down half a mile in front.

The heady joy of the kill flooded back as he slid out over the water towards England. He had fought a plane and shot at it, impersonally, and longed to get back and tell everyone, but when he taxied in the joy died. Two of the others were missing.

That afternoon, thirsting for more, he flew back to Dunkirk with the squadron and, on the fringe of the little boats off the breakwater saw a shadow diving on a destroyer. Another shock—black crosses on the wings as a Heinkel 111 swept over the funnels. A white core of water erupted just behind the destroyer and her stern kicked up. He was peeling off after the Heinkel, which was swinging back to the coast. Little flashes came from the bomber's glasshouse, and Bader pressed his own gun button and the flashes stopped. Good! Killed the gunner! The Heinkel steep-turned sharply inside him. As he pulled up to swing in again two more Spitfires were closing on the bomber, already a mile away.

The squadron stayed at Hornchurch. Morning after

morning up at 3.15 for the dawn patrol, and other patrols, but always it was the other squadrons that found the enemy. All Bader saw were the rearguards on the beaches, embattled and dwindling. When not flying the squadron sat all day by their planes. Geoffrey Stephenson was missing.

Dunkirk was over and Bader, suddenly exhausted, slept nearly twenty-four hours, waking to find a grim new mood lying over England.

On a week-end pass he drove down to Thelma, who had gone back to the Pantiles. He had to tell her Geoffrey Stephenson was missing, and after that they did not talk about the war.

The fight seemed a long time coming and the days were unexciting with training—formation, dummy attacks, night flying. The squadron moved north again to Kirkton-in-Lindsay and Thelma stayed at the Pantiles.

Towards midnight on the 13th June Bader was 12,000 feet over the Humber looking for an unidentified aircraft that had been tracked in from Germany.

"Red One, Red One," the controller's voice said, "weather closing in. Return to base immediately."

He swung steeply down towards the blacked-out land, but the rain cloud moved in faster. On a homing course he was only a few hundred feet up, and right over the airfield before, dimly, he picked up the flarepath suffused through a veil of rain, and swung tightly round it to keep it in sight through the rain-filmed perspex. He floated past the first flare . . . too high. The second flashed behind . . . and then the third before he touched on the downhill runway. The tail was not down and he knew he had misjudged. Stick hard back in his stomach but still the tail stayed up and the flares flashed by. He knew he was going to overshoot and that it was too late to open up and take off again ; then the tail was down and the brakes were on as hard as he dared.

In front there were no more flares . . . only blackness. An agony of waiting, and then a tearing crash as the plane jolted, slid her belly over the low wall of an aircraft pen, sheering the undercart off, and jarred to a stop.

A car screeched along the perimeter grass. Tubby Mermagen loomed out of the darkness.

" Douglas," he called anxiously, " are you all right ? "

" No," Bader growled. " I'm furious."

In the morning Mermagen greeted him with a significant remark : " Well, Douglas, we're losing you."

Bader stared, and thought with a chill of being grounded. " Where ? " he demanded.

" It's all right," Mermagen said soothingly. " You're getting a squadron."

Bader stared again.

" It's not a joke," Mermagen grinned. " Or perhaps it is. Anyway, L.M. wants to see you."

The surge of joy was cut off a moment later when it occurred to Bader that Leigh-Mallory could not have heard of the latest accident.

He drove to 12 Group Headquarters at Hucknall and stood once more before the A.O.C. Leigh-Mallory said : " I've been hearing of your work as a flight commander. I'm giving you a squadron, No. 242."

Bader said : " Yes, sir . . . Sir, there's one thing I should tell you . . . I broke a Spitfire last night. Overshot landing."

Leigh-Mallory said mildly : " Well, that happens sometimes, you know," Brisk again, the A.O.C. went on : " 242 are a Canadian squadron. They're a tough bunch. They're just back from France, where they got badly mauled and lost quite a few aircraft. They need a bit of decent organisation and some firm handling."

The squadron was at Coltishall, near Norwich, and Squadron Leader Bader was to take over as from that moment.

By evening he had driven a hundred miles back to Kirkton, packed his kit, telephoned Thelma and was steering the M.G. towards Coltishall.

Almost the first man he saw at breakfast in the morning was Rupert Leigh. 66 Squadron, apparently, was now also stationed at Coltishall. Shaking his hand on hearing of the promotion, Leigh said : " Now you won't have to call me ' sir ' any more."

After breakfast the " station master " at Coltishall, the pipe-smoking, phlegmatic Wing Commander Beisiegel,[1] told Bader about his new squadron. The ground crews were about half English, three or four of the pilots were English and the rest were Canadians. Wild Canadians, the least tractable young officers he had ever seen, and most allergic to commanding officers !

The news of his arrival reached the squadron. One of the pilots encountered Bernard West, the squadron " plumber " (engineer officer) and said : " Have you seen the new C.O. ? "

" No, I haven't. What's this one like ? "

" Bit unusual," the pilot said cryptically. " I don't suppose we'll be seeing much of him. He's got no legs."

[1] Known far and wide, naturally, as " Bike."

CHAPTER FOURTEEN

SQUADRON LEADER

WHEN BADER got back the pilots were all down at the dispersals. He had a talk about them with his adjutant, Flight Lieutenant Peter Macdonald. At last Bader said: " Well, let's go down and meet these chaps."

" A Flight " dispersal was a wooden hut on the edge of the airfield, and he pushed the door open and stumped in unheralded, followed by Macdonald. From his lurching walk they knew who he was. A dozen pairs of eyes surveyed him from chairs and the iron beds where pilots slept at night for dawn readiness. No one got up.

At last he said: " Who is in charge here ? "

After a while a thick-set young man rose slowly out of a chair and said in a Canadian accent: " I guess I am."

" What's your name ? "

" Turner." And then, after a distinct pause, " Sir."

Bader surveyed the watchful eyes and turned and walked out. A dozen yards from the door a Hurricane crouched with the hump-backed, bow-legged look of all Hurricanes. He headed for it and pulled himself up on the wing. If they thought the new C.O. was a cripple there was one good way to make them think again.

Right over the airfield for half an hour non-stop he tumbled the Hurricane round the sky, doing the old fluent routines of Hendon, one aerobatic merging into another, two or three loops in a row, rolls off the top, rolls, stall turns, finishing up with a Gamecock speciality in which he pulled up in a loop, flick-rolled into a spin at the top, pulled out of the spin and completed the loop. When he dropped her on to the grass and taxied in all the pilots were standing outside the hut watching, but he climbed out unaided, did not even look at them, got into his car, drove off to his office in a hangar and sent for Bernard West.

He liked the solid, north-country look of West as soon as the veteran warrant officer walked in and saluted.

" What's our equipment state ? " he asked.

" Eighteen Hurricanes, sir," West said. " They're all new."

" Good. I want good serviceability on them."

" I'll keep them flying as long as I can, sir," West said, " but that won't be for long. We have no spares and no tools."

West explained that they had all been lost in France.

Bader, looking grim, asked : " Have you requisitioned for a new issue ? "

West said yes, he had. The indent forms and vouchers and all the duplicates made a pile six inches high, but the station stores officer said they had to go through the normal channels in their turn. West considered that the channels were clogged.

" Well," said the new commanding officer grimly, " we'll unclog them."

In the morning he called all the pilots to his office and they stood there in front of his desk while he eyed them coolly, noting the rumpled uniforms, the preference for roll-neck sweaters instead of shirts and ties, the long hair and general untidy air. At last he spoke : " Look here, it is *not* smart to walk about looking like mechanics who haven't washed the grease off their hands. I want this to be a good squadron and you're a scruffy-looking lot. I don't want to see any more flying boots or roll-neck sweaters in the mess. You will wear shoes, and shirts and ties. Is that perfectly clear ? "

Turner said unemotionally in a deep, slow Canadian voice : " Most of us don't have any shoes or shirts or ties except what we're wearing."

" What d'you mean ? "—agressively.

" We lost everything we had in France." Evenly, with just a trace of cynicism, Turner went on to explain the chaos of the running fight, how they had apparently been deserted by authority, separated from their ground staff, shunted from one place to another, welcome nowhere, till it had been every man for himself. Seven had been killed, two wounded and one had had a nervous breakdown— nearly fifty per cent pilot casualties.

When he had finished Bader said : " I'm sorry. I apologise for my remarks." A brief silence. " Have you claimed an allowance for loss of kit ? "

Apparently they had, and it was assumed, with another tinge of cynicism, that the claim was drifting along one of the proper channels.

" Right," Douglas said. " To-morrow the whole lot of you go into Norwich, to the tailors. Order what you want. I'll guarantee that it's paid. O.K. ? "

A shuffle of assent.

" Meantime, for to-night, beg or borrow shoes and shirts from someone. I've got some shirts and you can borrow all I've got. O.K. ? "

" That's fine, sir," said Turner.

" Right ! Now . . ." (briskly) " Relax and take it easy. What fighting have you had ? "

The next half-hour was a lively discussion on various aspects of the trade, and afterwards Bader interviewed each pilot, finding with one or two exceptions, that he liked them very much. Suddenly, they were keen and co-operative, though one pilot, an Englishman, seemed unhappy and thought he would be more suited to Training Command. After talking to him for a while Bader burst out angrily : " The trouble about you is you don't want to fight. I'll have you posted off this squadron in twenty-four hours." The remaining flight commander he also summed up swiftly as unsuitable, and telephoned Group and asked them to send him the best two flight commanders they could find. For one of them he suggested Eric Ball, of 19 Squadron. Group said that would be fine, and for the second chap they recommended a young man called Powell-Sheddon.

Bader went to Wing Commander Beisiegel and explained that until he got tools and spares and the pilots trained under new flight commanders there was no point in regarding the squadron as operational.

After lunch he began leading the pilots up in twos for formation, and was pleased to see that they knew how to handle their Hurricanes, though their formation was rather ragged. Though they had done more fighting than he had, he had already decided to train them for future fighting according to his own ideas. That night in the mess all of them were neat in shoes and shirts and ties, and he turned his sparkling charm on them.

By the second morning there was already a feeling of direction about the squadron. For the first hour or two the new C.O. was appearing everywhere, at dispersals, in the maintenance hangar, the radio hut, instrument section, armoury. By ten o'clock he was leading sections of Hurricanes into the air again, and this time his voice came snapping crisply over the R/T when any aircraft lagged or waffled a few feet out of position. Later in the dispersals hut he lit his pipe and called them around.

"That formation was better," he said. "Next time I want it better still. It's the best training for co-ordinated flying and air discipline." Then he gave them his first talk on the ideas of fighter tactics which he had been expounding at 19 and 222 Squadrons. "I haven't been able to test them properly yet," he said, "and you chaps have seen more fighting than I have, but I'm certain Bishop and McCudden and the others were right."

In the afternoon Eric Ball and George Powell-Sheddon arrived. Ball was lean and firm-jawed. Already he had something to remember the war by—a scar furrowed through the fair curly hair where a 109 bullet had "creased" him at Dunkirk. Powell-Sheddon was shorter and was solidly built.

Ball took over A Flight and Powell-Sheddon B Flight, and that afternoon both were leading their pilots in formation.

Bader kept trying to get the tools and spares, bickering daily with the stores officer. About the seventh day he sent for West and asked if there was any more word.

"No, sir," West said. "The stores chaps started quoting A.P. 830,[1] volume 1, that says you have to wait three months before you can start the procedure for hastening new tools."

"They say *that* now, do they?" grated the C.O. Shortly after he stamped across to the station commander and said: "Look, sir, the boys are fit for anything now, but we still haven't got our tools and spares. I've sent this signal to Group." He handed across a slip of paper and Beisiegel read the curt message with mounting distress:

"242 *Squadron now operational as regards pilots but non-operational repeat non-operational as regards equipment.*"

[1] Equipment Regulations for the R.A.F.

"Good God," the wing commander was appalled. " Why didn't you show it to me first ? "

After a heated scene there, Bader went back to his office and showed it to West.

With masterly understatement, West observed : " It's . . . a bit unusual, sir."

" I'll take the kicks," the C.O. said.

" There'll be an awful shindig at Group, sir."

" There'll be an awful shindig from Fighter Command, too," said Bader. " I've sent a copy there as well."

The upheaval was immediate. Bader was playing snooker in the mess with his pilots that night when an orderly announced he was wanted on the phone. He picked it up and the voice of a squadron leader (equipment) at Fighter Command Headquarters said coldly :

" Squadron Leader Bader, what is the meaning of this extraordinary signal you sent to-day ? "

" It means exactly what it says," bluntly. " We haven't got any tools or spares."

" But you *must* have *some* tools there surely."

" About two spanners and a screwdriver."

The voice observed with severity that these were difficult times and tools and spares were short. Surely a resourceful squadron commander could borrow things and make do till his requirements could be satisfied. Moreover there was a proper procedure for obtaining new equipment.

" I've carried out the correct procedure and nothing has happened," Bader snapped.

" I'm sure you can operate with what you've got."

" Look, don't you tell *me* what I can do. I'll tell *you* what I want and until I get it this squadron stays non-operational."

"You don't seem to care what trouble you cause," snapped the equipment officer. "Well, I can tell *you* that signal of yours is going to bring you trouble. The Commander-in-Chief is furious about it."

In the morning a communications aeroplane landed on the airfield and Leigh-Mallory got out.

"I dropped in to see how you were getting on," he said to Bader and did not mention the other matter till he had half finished his inspection of the squadron. They were leaving dispersals for the maintenance hangar when he said: "Your non-operational signal caused a mild sensation at Group. What's it all about?"

Bader told him of everything that had been done. Leigh-Mallory himself inspected the miserable little collection of tools they had been able to borrow and had a few words alone with Warrant Officer West. Afterwards he sent for Bader again and said: "Well, you've stuck your neck out but I can see why. I'm afraid you're going to be sent for by the Commander-in-Chief about that signal."

The summons came a day later. Bader flew down to Hendon and drove from there to Bentley Priory, the fine old house at Stanmore that was Fighter Command Headquarters.

CHAPTER FIFTEEN

THE BATTLE BEGINS

BEHIND A desk sat Air Chief Marshal Sir Hugh Dowding. Known as " Stuffy " because he could be very stuffy, he said baldly : " What's all this about equipment and that signal of yours, Bader ? "

Bader explained. Without a word Dowding passed a typewritten report over and Bader saw it was from the equipment officer—an account of the phone conversation. He glanced over it and said :

" I did have an acrimonious conversation with an equipment officer, sir, but it was between two officers of equal rank. He tried to shake me by saying you were furious about my signal and that annoyed me."

" Oh, he said I was furious, did he ? " Dowding pressed his buzzer.

In a minute the equipment squadron leader came in.

" Did you say I was furious about the signal from 242 Squadron ? " Dowding asked.

" Yes, sir," said the squadron leader.

Dowding said coldly : " I will not have any officer taking my name in vain or predicting my emotions. Your job is—or was—to help the squadrons in the field. You will be off this headquarters in twenty-four hours."

After the equipment officer went out Dowding seemed to relax. He pressed another buzzer and shortly a grey-haired air vice marshal walked in—" Daddy " Nichol who looked after all equipment for Fighter Command. He

listened to Bader repeating his story and then said cheerfully :
" All right. Now you come with me and we'll fix this up."

At Coltishall the following day Beisiegel held an
inquiry into the affair of 242 Squadron's equipment, and
next morning the lorries were rolling past the guardroom
and up to the maintenance hangar where West supervised
his fitters unloading crates of spare wheels, spark plugs,
oleo legs, spanners, files, piston rings and about 400 other
assorted bits and pieces.

Bader drove to his office and sent a signal to Group,
with a copy to Fighter Command :

" 242 *Squadron now fully operational.*"

The pilots already thought they were the best squadron
in Fighter Command. Now the Hurricanes were hardly
ever out of the air, climbing on practice interceptions, diving
on air firing and tangling in mock dog-fights.

The first time he did dawn readiness with a section he
slept with the rostered pilots on the iron cots in the dispersals hut, taking his legs off and parking them beside the
cot, complete with shoes, socks and trousers on them.[1] It
was the first time they had seen him with his legs off. No
one made any remark but it was uncanny to see that the
man who was so vital and energetic actually *did* have
artificial legs. The legend was true.

A squadron in war is a sensitive body. The men who
fly find glory and die young. The men on the ground live
long with little acclaim but their work is exacting, and if
they fumble once a pilot is likely to die. There must be
mutual respect and trust, and it is the commander who
must inspire this delicate balance. Within a fortnight
242 Squadron was a cohesive unit, trusting in and loyal to

[1] In this way Bader could dress ready for action before the others could put on
their shoes and socks.

the new C.O., and therefore loyal to their corporate selves.

Now when the 242 pilots went out in the evenings to absorb beer it became a habit to go in a group with the teetotal C.O., who did not mind how many pints they sank so long as they were fit in the morning. He brought Thelma up to a house in Coltishall and her presence helped ensure that the evenings were decorous enough, though not excessively so.

Command now had sublimated the last traces of the frustrated years. He lived for his squadron and expected all his men to do likewise.

On 11th July a blanket of cloud sagged over Coltishall and streamed all morning, grounding the squadron. The telephone rang and Operations said they had a plot of a suspicious aircraft flying down the coast from the north. Could they get a section off ? Bader said : " No, we can't get a section off. The cloud's right on the deck, and I won't send my pilots up in weather like this."

" Isn't there any chance ? It's heading for Cromer and we're pretty sure it's enemy." Ops sounded anxious.

" All right, I'll have a go myself." He dropped the phone and sloshed out through the rain.

It was almost an instrument take-off through rain, and within seconds the cloud closed clammily round him. He called up Ops, but water had leaked into the radio and no sound came back. Climbing on instruments there was not much point in going on unless he broke soon into the clear. The needle was pointing at just over 1000 feet when he came out of the cloud, and down below saw the coast. Without a word from Ops there was little chance of seeing anything in the broken sky, but he swung north towards Cromer, to clear his conscience.

Far head a dot appeared in the sky and began to grow

larger. With a shock he saw the thin body and twin fins.
A Dornier!

Heart thudding he wheeled up towards it. Pinpricks of
light flickered from the rear gun and then Bader was lining
up the luminous bead of his reflector sight. He jabbed his
thumb on the gun button in a long burst, then fired again.
the rear-gunner stopped and then the Dornier fled into the
cloud and the Hurricane lunged after it, still firing. He
saw nothing but milky mist, dropped out below and hedge-
hopped back to base. At dispersals, in a temper, he rang
up Ops and told them what had happened.

Five minutes later the phone rang again.

"You know that Dornier," Ops said, excited and
triumphant. "Well, an Observer Corps chap saw it dive
out of the cloud and go straight into the sea. You got him!"

On 8th August, off the Isle of Wight, sixty Stukas
dived out of the sun on a convoy. Two hours later a
hundred more attacked the same convoy. Fighters swarmed
up from Tangmere and other fields and dived on the enemy.
Aircraft spun smoking into the sea and two ships went
down in flame and smoke. In the afternoon 130 German
aircraft savagely bombed a convoy off Bournemouth. The
storm had burst and in the great crook of hostile airfields
off south and east England, Goering had 4000 aircraft.
Fighter Command's squadrons in the front line had 500
pilots and aircraft and there were not many reserves.

The Stukas swept in again and bombs crashed down
on Portland and Weymouth and convoys off the Thames
Estuary and Harwich. Then eleven waves of two hundred
bombers attacked Dover. Portsmouth was next, and then
Portsmouth again, and now the enemy was sending over
400 aircraft in one day. The fighters of 11 Group around
London and to the south tore into them and the Luftwaffe

had lost over 200 planes. Across the Channel R.A.F. bombers were attacking the gathering invasion barges.

Bader and 242 Squadron saw none of this, though every day they waited " at readiness " by the Hurricanes. Burning for the fight, Bader rang Leigh-Mallory and pleaded to be embroiled but Leigh-Mallory told him : " We can't put all our eggs in one basket, Bader. No doubt the enemy would be delighted to draw our fighter cover away from the Midlands."

Bader was not in dispersals the day the controller scrambled a section to cover a convoy when heavy rain cloud almost on the ground had stopped flying. Young Patterson was in that section and did not return. Someone on the convoy reported seeing a Hurricane dive out of control from the cloud into the sea and Bader, almost berserk, drove over to the controller and for ten minutes flayed the man for sending out his pilots in impossible weather.

Next day (it was 21st August) the weather was better and Bader, bringing a section back over the airfield from a practice flight, had just broken them away by R/T to land when he heard a voice saying : " Rusty Red Leader calling. Rusty Red section airborne."

And then the controller : " Hallo, Rusty Red Leader. Bandit angels seven over Yarmouth. Vector one-one-zero."[1]

Yarmouth lay fifteen miles to the south-east and Rusty was the call sign to Rupert Leigh's 66 Squadron. As soon as it had registered, Bader's throttle was wide open as he streaked for Yarmouth.

He came to the coast north of the town. Rusty section

[1] Enemy aircraft 7,000 feet over Yarmouth. Steer 110 degrees magnetic to intercept.

had not yet arrived. A layer of strato-cumulus cloud covered the sky at 8000 feet. He lifted his nose and lifted out of the grey foam into brilliant sunshine and there in front of his eyes flew a Dornier 17. The Dornier spotted him and dived for the cloud, but Bader was between the cloud and the enemy.

Closing fast, he fired, seeing the tracers flick out. The rear gunner was firing. He was nearly straight behind now and something came suddenly away from the Dornier like a little chain with weights on,[1] and then it had whipped past under him. He had his thumb on the button in a long burst when the Dornier slid into the cloud and he followed, still hosing bullets into the greyness.

Suddenly he shot into the clear beneath. No Dornier. In a rage he returned back to base.

The lull ended on 24th August. That evening 110 German fighters and bombers moved towards London, but were intercepted over Maidstone and fled. Next day they were bombing Portsmouth and Southampton. Then it was Dover, Folkestone, the Thames Estuary and Kent. Time and again the great formations ploughed steadily across the Channel and clashed with the spearheads of 11 Group.

Bader alternately sulked and stormed in the dispersal hut at Coltishall, where he and the pilots sat restlessly at readiness like pining maidens waiting for the phone call that never came.

The intelligence officer buttonholed Bader in the mess, and said: " You know that Dornier you popped off at the other day ? "

" That——! "

" I thought you might like to know," said the I.O. " They've fished a couple of bodies out of the sea off

[1] A new weapon which the Germans threw out of bombers. The " weights " were grenades, to explode on contact with a fighter. They were not effective.

Yarmouth. Their log books show they were in a Dornier on the day in question and their watches had stopped just after the time you said you shot. Obviously you got him. It all clicks."

It was pleasant to be credited with a kill that one had not even claimed.

On the morning of 30th August the phone rang in dispersals and Ops said: " 242 Squadron take off immediately for Duxford ! "

Whooping wildly, the pilots were running for the Hurricanes. Bader, ablaze, bellowing to rouse the ground crews, moved as fast as his legs would go to his Hurricane parked only five yards away from the door.

Half-way to Duxford the controller's voice came over the R/T ordering them back to Coltishall.

Irritated, they flew back to base. An hour later Ops ordered them off to Duxford again, and this time there was no recall. By 10 a.m. the Hurricanes stood scattered round a corner of the Duxford field and Bader and his men waited in a restless knot nearby. From Ops they heard that the Luftwaffe was storming over southern England, but still 11 Group sent out no call. Lunch-time came—and went. They had sandwiches and coffee by the aircraft. Bader sat in the dispersal hut, cold pipe clenched between his teeth, seething. At a quarter to five the phone rang and he grabbed it.

Ops said crisply : " 242 Squadron scramble ! Angels fifteen. North Weald."

CHAPTER SIXTEEN

THE THICK OF THE FRAY

As THE wheels, still spinning, folded into the wings and the rest of the pack thundered behind, he flicked the R/T switch. " Laycock Red Leader calling Steersman. Am airborne."

A cool voice answered : " Hallo, Laycock Red Leader. Steersman answering. Vector one-nine-zero. Buster.[1] Seventy plus bandits approaching North Weald." He recognised the voice of Wing Commander Woodhall, Duxford Station Commander.

Behind him the squadron slid into battle station, four vics line astern, and climbed steeply south through haze. Holding a map on his thigh, he saw that 190 degrees led over North Weald fighter station. The sun hung in the orb of the sky over the starboard wing and he knew what he would do if he were the German leader : come in from the sun ! From the south-west.

This was no good. He wanted to be up-sun himself. Disregarding controller's words, he swung thirty degrees west. Might miss the enemy ! One usually obeyed a controller.

" B-b-blue Leader calling Laycock Leader. Th-th-three aircraft three o'clock below." Powell-Sheddon's voice. Over the rim of the cockpit he saw three dots well to the beam. They might be anything.

" Blue section investigate."

[1] Full throttle.

Powell-Sheddon peeled off to starboard, followed by his two satellites.

South-west of North Weald a glint, then another, and in seconds a mass of little dots grew there ; too many to be British. He shoved his throttle forward and called: " Enemy aircraft ten o'clock level."

The bombers were in lines of four and six abreast, fourteen lines—and above and behind them about thirty more aeroplanes that looked like 110 fighters. Above them still more. Over a hundred. The Hurricanes were above the main swarm now, swinging down on them out of the sun, a good spot to start a fight if the 110's had not been above. The main swarm were Dorniers. Must go for them. Too bad about the Messerschmitts above. Have to risk them. He called : " Green section take on the top lot."

Christie led his vic of three up.

Bader led again : " Red and yellow sections, line astern, line astern." From a thousand feet above he dived in the swarm of seventy followed by the last five Hurricanes, and now among the Dorniers saw more 110 fighters. A gust of rage shook him. " Flying over here like that. It's *our* sky."

Black crosses ! Glinting perspex ! Wings that spread and grew, filling the windscreen. He was on them and suddenly the drilled lines burst in mad turns left and right, out of the way. He swept under and up swinging right. A ripple was running through the great herd, and then it was splitting, scattering. Glimpse of Willie McKnight hunting left, Crowley-Milling lunging ahead, and three 110's wheeling in front. The last was too slow. Just behind, he thumbed the button and, as the bullets squirted, pieces flew off the 110.

Above to the right another 110 was slowly curling out of a stall-turn and he reefed his nose up after it, closing fast. A hundred yards behind, he fired for three seconds; the 110 rocked fore and aft, and he fired again. Pieces flew off the wing near the starboard engine.

In the little mirror above his eyes a 110 poked its nose above the rudder, slanting in. He steep-turned hard and over his shoulder saw the 110 heeling after, white streaks of tracer flicking from its nose past its tail. The Hurricane turned faster and the 110 dived and vanished under his wing. Bader spiralled steeply after, saw the 110 well below, streaking east, and dived and chased it, but the 110 was going for home and it was hopeless. He was startled to see that he was down to 6,000 feet. He pulled steeply up, back to the fight, but the fight was over.

A lone Hurricane appeared on the left, and he ruddered towards it, formating alongside till he saw the big scythe, dripping blood, painted on its side. Willie McKnight! Grinning under his oxygen mask, he raised two fingers to indicate that he had got a couple. McKnight nodded vigorously and then three of his fingers were spread above the cockpit rim. Three! Round the field Hurricanes were coming in.

All the Hurricanes were back, the pilots cheering and yelling to each other. "Did you get one?" Drunk on high spirits they babbled out their versions and bit by bit the battle was pieced together: a Dornier had crashed into a greenhouse, another into a field, a 110 had dived into a reservoir, another Dornier exploded into a ploughed field. Two to Bader, three to McKnight; Turner got one, Crowley-Milling had shot the belly out of a Heinkel, Ball had got one . . . several others. They totted up the score—twelve confirmed and several more damaged.

Later Bader explained to Woodhall why he had disobeyed his R/T instructions. "From all the combat reports I've seen the Huns seem to be using the sun."

He expounded his view with the usual vigour.

" It's no good trying to protect North Weald or other targets over the top of them. In the morning they must be protected from way down south-east and in the afternoon from south-west. We've got to catch them before they get to their target, not when they've got there and are dropping their bombs. If the controller will tell us where they are in time—direction and height—we'll sort out the tactics in the air, get up-sun ourselves and beat hell out of them."

" I'm with you," Woodhall said.

Bader led the squadron back to Coltishall in tight formation at 200 feet.

Leigh-Mallory flew over that evening full of congratulations and Bader took his chance to breach a new idea : " If we'd had more aircraft we could have knocked down a lot more. Other squadrons in the group have been standing by like us. Would it be possible for us all to take off together ? "

" How would you handle them in the air ? "

" It'd be easy to lead, say, three squadrons," Bader said. " I haven't worked it out, sir, but the whole object of flying in formation is to get a number of aeroplanes in the same place together. If I'd had three squadrons this afternoon it would have been just as easy to get them to the enemy, and we'd have been three times more powerful. I think the thing is to dive into these bomber formations and break them up. Then it'll be a free-for-all, and the fighters will have the advantage of eight guns against an isolated gun."

" Sounds splendid," Leigh-Mallory said.

Next day 242 Squadron were scrambled three times to patrol North London again, but each time was an anticlimax—no trace of the enemy. It seemed 242 were only sent up at lunch-time or tea-time to give 11 Group a spell when no German aircraft were about. It was frustrating, but in the evening Bader felt better when Leigh-Mallory phoned and said: "To-morrow I want you to try this large formation scheme. We've got 19 and 310 Squadrons at Duxford."

Bader spent three days practising take-offs with the three squadrons and leading them in the air. 19 Squadron flew the faster Spitfires so he had them flying above and behind as top cover with the 310 Hurricanes staggered behind 242 on the same level. In those days he also led 242 on several more patrols round North London, but again saw no trace of the enemy. Exasperating!

At Group's request he wrote a report on how to break up an enemy formation. "They can be dispersed by shock tactics of the leading section fighters diving into their midst as close as possible . . . risk of collision is there, but the fact remains that the effect of a near collision makes German pilots take violent evasive action which breaks up any tight formation."

He kept on drumming that into the pilots of all three squadrons, and adding: "Another thing—keep one eye in your mirror the whole time the scrap's on and if you see a Hun in your mirror, break off fast!" By 5th September he had the "scramble" time down to a little over three minutes in getting his thirty-six fighters off the ground. In the air, skipping formality, it was, "Hallo, Woodie," and "Hallo, Douglas." Leigh-Mallory flew down to watch them practise, and said: "All right, Bader. Next time 11 Group calls on you, take your whole team."

Next day, Goering, for the first time, turned the Luftwaffe on London.

Since dawn waves of bombers had been battering through the defences to the city and Bader heard the reports coming through and was stamping with impatience. All day he railed at Group, at Ops and Woodhall, demanding to be let off the leash, but it was not until a quarter to five that Ops rang.

In the air Woodhall's calm voice : " Hallo, Douglas. There's some trade heading in over the coast. Orbit North Weald. Angels ten."

They climbed fast and hard, and Bader disobeyed instructions again, going on past 10,000 feet to 15,000.

Nearing North Weald Woodhall again : " Hallo, Douglas. Seventy plus crossing the Thames east of London, heading north."

Far to the south-east a cluster of black dots stained the sky. Somehow they did not look like aircraft but he swung his squadrons towards them. Flak bursts ! That meant only one thing.

He caught the glint and in seconds saw the dots. A good 5,000 feet above. Throttle hard on, he kept climbing and the Hurricane was vibrating and thundering, clawing for height on full power. Soon he saw there were about seventy Dorniers and 110's mixed up. And more glints above—Me 109's. Behind him the squadrons were trailing, unable to keep up ; though the Spitfires were faster they did not climb so well. Only Dickie Cork was near. It was going to be sticky. Attacking in a straggle from below with the 109's on top. No chance to break them up. He closed fast and the flanks of the Dorniers were darting by. A quick burst, but the Dornier had only flashed across his sights. Turning under the tails of the rear section, streams of tracer were streaking at him from the rear gunners. Cork was with him—then " Crow "—the others well back. He lifted his nose and a 110 floated in his sights. A quick squirt. He fired again and his eyes caught the yellow spinner of a 109 in his mirror. One more quick burst at the 110—triumph as smoke streamed from it, and then a jarring shock as cannon shells slammed into the Hurricane and jolted it like a pneumatic drill. Instinctively he broke hard left as fear stabbed him. Crashes and chaos and the cockpit suddenly full of reeking smoke. For a moment he was frozen stiff, then thought and movement switched on— he was on fire and going down! His hands shot up, grabbed the twin handles of the cockpit hood and hauled it back. Must get out! Straps first! He yanked the pin of his straps and suddenly the cockpit was clear of smoke— sucked out by the noisy slip-stream. No fire. Must have been only cordite smoke.

His Hurricane was crabbing awkwardly, left wing dropping, and he had the stick hard to starboard, to keep her level. He saw out on the wing that the left aileron was tattered and hanging almost off and there were holes on the right of the cockpit. His Sidcot flying-suit was gashed across the right hip, spilling chewing-gum out of the pocket. Near thing!

After nursing the aircraft back to Coltishall he taxied straight in to the maintenance hangar and climbed out, yelling brusquely : " West, I want this aircraft ready again in half an hour."

West had a quick look at it, and said : " Sorry, sir, but this job won't be flying again for a couple of days."

" That's no damn' good, I want it in half an hour."

West, who understood his C.O., said soothingly : " More like a week, I'm afraid, sir. Apart from the aileron you've got four bullets that I can see through the petrol tank. You're lucky it's self-sealing, but it still stinks of petrol. Shells've also smashed your turn and bank, rev. counter and undercart quadrant. There are probably other things too."

Bader's anger was cut short. Cork was taxi-ing in and

got out painfully, eyes screwed up and face bleeding. Shreds were hanging all over his Hurricane and the cockpit was a mess where 109 shells had smashed it. Glass splinters from shattered instruments, reflector sight and windscreen had hit him in the face and eyes. He said he was fine but Bader sent him away in the ambulance.

One by one the pilots reported. Turner had got another and had also seen Bader's first 110 burst into flames and crash. McKnight had also got two ; Ball, one ; Tamblyn, one—and others. Jubilantly they added the score. Eleven confirmed. But the other two squadrons had been so far behind that they had missed the fight.

Young Crowley-Milling and Pilot Officer Benzie were not back.

Then a phone call from Crowley-Milling, who had been shot up and cut his face crash-landing in Essex. No word from Benzie. He was dead.

In the morning, a little grimmer, 242 flew again to Duxford, but no call came from 11 Group, though the bombers again were storming London. He could visualise those single 11 Group squadrons climbing up under the German packs, vulnerable to the hovering 109's while they tried to get at the bombers. Often they were picked off like pigeons.

After lunch Leigh-Mallory flew in, and Bader said :

" It didn't come off yesterday, sir. If we'd been higher we could really have got among them and the Spitfires could have covered us from the 109's." Angry that the squadrons were kept so long on the ground, he added : " R.D.F.[1] get these plots of bombers building up over France. If only we could get off earlier we could be on top and ready for them. Why can't we do that, sir ? "

" The Germans might want us to," Leigh-Mallory

[1] Radio Direction Finding—soon to be developed into Radar.

suggested. " If they can decoy our fighters up they can hold back for an hour till the fighters have to go down to refuel again and then send the bombers in."

" It's worth taking that chance, sir."

" So it might be," said Leigh-Mallory; " but it's 11 Group's decision and they feel they should wait till the Germans start moving in."

Next morning to readiness at Duxford again with three squadrons for another day of impatient waiting, and about five o'clock Sector Ops reported that R.D.F. was showing a build-up of enemy aircraft over the Pas de Calais.

Soon Woodhall rang back. " Bombers heading in. Scramble fast as you can ! "

And then in the air: " Hallo, Douglas. Looks like they're heading for London. Will you patrol between North Weald and Hornchurch, angels twenty."

Bader looked at the afternoon sun and thought: I know damn' well they'll swing west and come out of the sun. He forgot North Weald-Hornchurch and climbed his three squadrons south-west over the fringe of London ; ignored the " angels twenty " too, climbing till they were specks at 22,000 feet over the reservoirs at Staines.

And then a few miles in front the sky glinted and around the spot like a film coming into focus the dots appeared ; two great swarms of them cutting across fast in front, heading for London. About the same height. Looked like sixty odd in each bunch. He wheeled to cut them off, still climbing, swinging higher now and between the swarms with the sun behind and calling 19 Squadron urgently to climb higher and cover their tails.

In the corner of his eye a scatter of fighters darted out of the sun and he thought that more friendly fighters had arrived : only a few pilots behind saw that they were 109's and wheeled back to fight them off. Diving now on the first swarm he saw they were mixed Dorniers and 110's. A Dornier was in front leading, and he plunged for it, firing almost point-blank, then diving past and under, pulled up again, but the leading Dornier was falling over on its back, smoke pouring from both engines. Other bombers above! He kept zooming up like a dolphin, squirting at them, seeing flashes as the armour-piercing incendiary bullets hit.

To the side another Dornier was diving, trailing fire and smoke, and a voice shouted in his ears, "F-f-f-f-flamer!" Powell-Sheddon had scored. Black twisting bombs were suddenly falling on Bader as the bombers jettisoned over the fields and turned south-east to flee. He steep-turned out of the way of the bombs, seeing that only about twenty of the bombers still clustered in ragged formation, the rest straggling over the sky, hunted by darting fighters.

Half a mile ahead was a Dornier; he chased it and was soon pulling it back. Five hundred yards now. Two Hurricanes dived in from each side in front of him converging on the Dornier. Daylight robbery! Swiftly the two fighters swept together behind the bomber, and he screamed into his microphone: "Look out. You're going to collide." A moment later they did. The left wing of the Hurricane on the right folded and ripped away, and it spun instantly; the other Hurricane, crabbing crazily on, smashed into the Dornier's tail and the air was full of flying fragments.

A big Heinkel was fleeing about a mile away and well below, and he dived in chase. It seemed to be helpless, making no effort to dodge as he swept nearer—must have been shot up. He held his fire until almost point-blank he jabbed the button and heard only the mocking hiss of compressed air through the breech-blocks. Out of ammunition! He flamed with outraged fury and swung across the Heinkel's nose, but it took no notice.

Back at Duxford two of the pilots, Brimble and Bush, said they saw Bader's first Dornier go down in flames. Bush had also got one. McKnight had collected a couple more . . . and others too, Eric Ball, Powell-Sheddon, Turner, Tamblyn had scored . . . eleven confirmed to 242 Squadron.

But Sclanders and Lonsdale were missing.

The other two squadrons added a further nine enemy destroyed, but two of 310 Squadron had not returned.

Later Lonsdale phoned. He had been shot down, baled out and landed in a tree in the grounds of a girls' school.

Then Gordon Sinclair, of 310 Squadron, phoned from Caterham on the other side of London. He had been in one of the Hurricanes that collided and had managed to bale out.

The pilot of the other Hurricane did not bale out.

But the mathematics were good—twenty enemy destroyed for the loss of four Hurricanes.

Still Bader was not satisfied. He flew to 12 Group H.Q. at Hucknall, and told Leigh-Mallory: "Sir, if we'd only had *more* fighters we could have hacked the Huns down in scores."

"I was going to talk to you about that," Leigh-Mallory said. "If I gave you two more squadrons, could you handle them?"

CHAPTER SEVENTEEN

WING LEADER

FIVE SQUADRONS. Sixty plus fighters! Even Bader was startled. He collected himself:

"Yes, sir. When a fight starts we'd break up anyway. I'd have the Spitfires on top to hold off any 109's, and a mass of Hurricanes below with nothing to worry about on their tails, could crucify a pack of bombers."

Up before dawn next morning for Duxford. And the morning after. Several more patrols to relieve 11 Group but nothing seen. Everyone complained of boredom but that was only the fashionable elaborately casual pose. In the past fortnight 231 pilots had been killed or badly wounded, and 495 Hurricanes and Spitfires destroyed or badly damaged (mostly 11 Group).

Among the survivors fear and tension lay under the surface like taut sinews in a naked body, but always decently covered with understatement. Life was a brutal contrast. Off duty they could joke in a pub and sleep between sheets, to wake in the morning to a new world of hunters and hunted, sitting in deck-chairs on the grass, waiting by the aeroplanes with needles in the stomach. Other men who knew they themselves would still be alive at night brought them sandwiches for lunch and coffee, but any moment the phone might go and they would have to drop the cup: half an hour later they might be trapped in a burning aeroplane crashing from 20,000 feet.

Only Bader had no pose. He swashbuckled around as

though he were about to step into the ring and knock out Joe Louis. His exuberance, the way he utterly ignored the danger, was contagious and infected every other pilot. Morale was extraordinary. He loved the battle and talked and thought tactics, fascinated by them.

About this time he designed the squadron emblem— a figure of Hitler being kicked in the breeches by a flying boot labelled 242. West cut a metal template of it and the ground Crews painted it on the noses of all the Hurricanes.

Bader slept in the mess at Coltishall but used to go and see Thelma every evening. On the 13th September he was having dinner with her at the house in Coltishall when the phone rang for him in the hall. Leigh-Mallory's voice greeted him : " Oh, hallo, Bader. I wanted to be the first to congratulate you. You've just been awarded the D.S.O."

A glow suffused him, and then in the emotion of the moment he could think of nothing to say until at last he managed, " Thank you, sir."

" And another thing," Leigh-Mallory added a few moments later. The next morning 302 Squadron (Hurricanes) and 611 (Spitfires) would also be flying into Duxford. Would Bader be good enough to include them in his formation, which was now to be called the " 12 Group Wing."

Bader managed to convey that he would be delighted to.

Next morning, 14th September, the two extra squadrons flew into Duxford, and twice that day Bader led the armed pack of sixty fighters into the air to patrol North London. They saw no enemy ; the Luftwaffe was coiling for the next leap.

In the cool dawn of 15th September the five squadrons of 12 Group Wing stood in groups about Duxford and and its satellite field, waiting. Broken cloud scattered thickly over the sky offering good cover to attackers, and

R.D.F. began reporting plots of enemy aircraft rising over the fields of Northern France. In clumps the plots crept across the screens towards England, and soon the shield of 11 Group squadrons round London was savaging them over Kent. Then the first stage was over; burning wrecks littered the fields, the remnants of the bombers, some winged and smoking, were streaming back to France and Hurricanes and Spitfires, gun-ports whistling where the patches had been shot off, were coming in to refuel and re-load. At that moment R.F.D. showed another wave of bombers heading for London.

Woodhall scrambled the 12 Group Wing five minutes later.

In the air, the measured voice: " Hallo, Douglas. About forty bandits heading for London. Will you patrol Canterbury-Gravesend."

" O.K., Woodie."

The morning sun still lay in the south-east, and if the bombers were going for London he knew where to look for them. The three Hurricane squadrons climbed steeply in vics line astern with the Spitfires a little to the left, a little above. To the right London lay under the cloud that had thickened. 12,000 feet . . . 16,000 . . . 20,000 . . . they kept climbing high over the cloud. Nearing angels 23 he saw black puffs staining the sky almost straight ahead, and somewhat below and ahead of the flak almost instantly saw the enemy. About five miles away . . . forty odd . . . JU. 88's and Dorniers.

Swinging right, he nosed down to come in diving. He looked for the 109's behind and above and could hardly believe it . . . not a sign. Unescorted bombers.

High out of a veil of cloud near the sun little grey sharks were darting. He called urgently : " Sandy, watch those 109's."

" O.K., chum, I can see them." Sandy Lane, leader of 19 Squadron was already wheeling the Spitfires up into the fighters.

" Break 'em up," yelled Bader and swept, firing, through the front rank of the bombers. He pulled up and veered behind a big Dornier turning away left, fired and fired again. A flash burst behind the Dornier's starboard engine, and flame and black smoke spewed from it. Suddenly he was nearly ramming it and broke off. Aircraft of broken formations darting everywhere in the blurred and flashing confusion. In front—400 yards away—another Dornier seeking cloud cover between the " cu-nims " ; he was catching it rapidly when his eye caught a Spitfire diving steeply above and just ahead. It happened fast. The Spitfire pilot clearly did not see the bomber under the long cowling ; he dived straight into the middle of it and the Dornier in a burst of flame split and wrapped its broken wings round the fighter.

Sweating, Bader looked for others. A Dornier was spinning down to one side, dragging a plume of flame and smoke.

Back at Duxford Eric Ball was missing.

They refuelled, re-loaded, and by 11.45 were on readiness again.

A phone call from Eric Ball. His Hurricane had been shot down in flames but he had baled out and would be back.

Two hours later the Wing was scrambled again to patrol North Weald, and Bader led them through a gap in the clouds. At 16,000 feet, flak bursts ahead, and he saw the bombers ; about forty of them, some 4,000 feet above the Hurricanes. Everything risked again because they were scrambled too late.

A voice screamed : " 109's behind."

Over his shoulder the yellow spinners were diving on them and he yelled as he steep-turned, "Break up!" Around him the sky was full of wheeling Hurricanes and 109's. A yellow spinner was sitting behind his tail, and as he yanked harder back on the stick an aeroplane shot by, feet away. Bader hit its slipstream and the Hurricane shuddered, stalled and spun off the turn. He let it spin a few turns to shake off the 109 and came out of it at 5,000 feet. All clear behind.

Far above a lone Dornier was heading for France, and he climbed and chased it a long way, hanging on his propeller nearly at stalling speed again. Near the coast he was just about in range and fired a three-second burst, but the recoil of the guns slowed the floundering Hurricane till she suddenly stalled and spun off again.

Back at Duxford, Powell-Sheddon was missing.

They found, when they pieced that day's battle together, that the 12 Group Wing had fully justified itself, though in the second battle the rôles had been reversed—the Spitfires had got among the bombers while the Hurricanes tangled with the 109's. But that was merely a quirk of the battle; the main point was that in the two mass fights that day the pilots of the five squadrons of the Wing claimed 52 enemy destroyed and a further eight probables.

242 Squadron's share was twelve. Cork, his face repaired, had got two Dorniers, one on each trip. Young Crowley-Milling, whose cut face was also nearly healed, had flown again for the first time since he was shot down, and avenged himself by chasing a 109 across Kent and sending it smoking into a field. McKnight, Turner, Bader, Stansfield, Tamblyn had all scored. Even Powell-Sheddon, who rang up from somewhere near Epping.

Bader went to Turner and said : " Stan, how d'you feel about taking over B Flight ? "

" Swell, sir," said Turner.

Leigh-Mallory phoned that night :

" Douglas " (using his Christian name for the first time) . . . " What a wonderful show to-day ! "

Bader said : " Thank you, sir, but we had a sticky time on the second trip. They scrambled us too late again and the Germans were a long way above when we spotted them. If we'd only been one squadron we'd probably have been chopped up by the 109's but if they'd let us off ten minutes earlier we could have been just in the right spot to cope.

" It doesn't make sense, sir " (warming to his theme). " As soon as they start building up their formations over Calais we should get into the air and go south. *We* should be the ones to attack them first while 11 Group get off and get height."

" Well, you know I feel the same as you on this point," Leigh-Mallory said.

The chance came on the 18th.

About 4.30 in the afternoon the five squadrons were scrambled. Forty plus bandits were heading for London from the south-east. Bader led the Wing through a layer of cloud at 21,000 feet and levelled off in the clear at 23,000. Not far below, the soft feather-bed stretched unbroken for miles, perfect backdrop for searching eyes. Nothing else in sight. But the invisible world under the cloud ? In a shallow dive he took his fighters down through the thin layer and they cruised under the white ceiling.

Once again the flak-bursts led them. First Bader saw the black puffs away to the south-east and picked up the bombers. About forty in all, were flying about 16,000 feet near Gravesend. More British aeroplanes than enemy! As the fighters circled to close in behind he saw that they were all bombers—JU. 88's and Dorniers. Not a sign of any 109's. The bombers were 4,000 feet below, just where he would have wanted them. No question of coming out of the sun—the clouds hid the sun. He dived, aiming for the JU. 88's in the front rank of the bombers, and the ravenous pack streamed after him.

A Junkers filled his sights and as he fired its port engine gushed smoke and it fell away to the left. Pulling up into the thick of plunging, criss-crossing aeroplanes, he fired at a couple that flashed across his sights and vanished again; then nearly collided with two more bombers. A Hurricane streamed towards him : he yanked the stick over to get out of the way, someone's slipstream and his Hurricane shuddered and flicked into a spin. He got her straight again after losing about 3,000 feet, and saw above that the split-up bombers had turned for home, hounded by the fighters.

Bader summed it up prosaically in his log book: "London patrol. Contact." And alongside it a laconic note : " Wing destroyed 30 plus 6 probables plus 2 damaged. 242 got 11. Personal score : 1 JU. 88, 1 Do. 17."

Goering started to chop and change his tactics more, sometimes sending over squads of 109's in advance of the bombers to draw the fighters up and exhaust their petrol. It was the beginning of the end of the daylight bombing, but no one knew that yet as the aura of ruthless power still clung to the Germans.

Once or twice nearly every day, the wing was scrambled to patrol an arc round London, and Bader had a new grievance—they never ran into the enemy any more. His personal score was eleven confirmed, but that only whetted his zest rather than satiated it. Besides, some others had twenty or more !

The abortive patrols went on till 27th September. About noon that day the wing was scrambled to patrol North London. Woodhall said " Angels fifteen." Bader knew that instruction came from 11 Group and climbed to 23,000 feet.

Woodhall on the air again : " There's a plot of thirty plus south-east of the Estuary."

Bader led his pack over Canterbury. Nothing in sight. He carried on round Dover, headed west for Dungeness and swung back. Woodhall kept talking about bandits cruising about the south-east. Clumps of cloud littered the air below like papers blowing about in a windswept park. Otherwise the sky was empty. Woodhall called again : " All right, Douglas, I think the lunch shift is over. You might as well come back."

" Just a minute, Woodie," Bader said. " I'll do one more swing round."

Turning back from Dungeness, his eye caught glints well below at about 17,000 feet, and soon he could make out an untidy gaggle of about thirty 109's milling round Dover.

CHAPTER EIGHTEEN

HITLER'S FIRST DEFEAT

" O.K., Chaps," he called. " Take this quietly. Don't attack till I tell you." Rather like a huntsman, he began stalking them, turning the wing south over the sea so that they could dive out of the high sun. The 109's were so scattered it would have to be a shambles, every man for himself. Still the Germans weaved in a ragged tangle like unwary rabbits at play. He yelled : " Right. Break up and attack ! " and was diving steeply, turning in behind a 109. At the same speed it seemed to hang motionless in his sights. A two-second squirt and a pencil of white smoke trailed from it—abruptly the smoke gushed into a cloud spewing past its tail and the little fighter rolled slowly on its back, nose dropping until it plummeted vertically.

Another 109 crossed in front, rolled swiftly on its back and dived. Bader peeled off after him, but the 109 was faster and began to pull away. From four hundred yards Bader fired a long-range burst and a jet of smoke spurted from the 109. It seemed to be slowing. Bader fired again and again, seeing flashes of bullet strikes.

Something dark spurted from the 109 and a black shadow seemed to slap him across the face. He felt nothing ; only the eyes sensed it and then saw that his windscreen and hood were stained to black opaqueness by the enemy's oil, that the slipstream was tearing in thin streaks across the glass. Dimly through it he saw the 109

veering aside and turned after it, seeing, amazed, that the
Messerschmitt's propeller was slowing. The 109 was
coming tail-first at him; he yanked the throttle back and
the enemy floated close in front, the perfect shot. He jabbed
the gun-button and heard the psst of compressed air that
hissed through empty breech-blocks. Out of bullets again.

The 109's propeller spun in shaky spasms and then it
stopped dead, one blade held up like a stiff finger. They
were over the sea at 10,000 feet, and the 109, still smoking,
was gliding quietly down into the Channel. That was the
last he saw of it.

The wing got twelve that fight, half of them to 242
Squadron. One Spitfire and two Hurricanes did not come
back.

Leigh-Mallory phoned from Hicknall in what was
becoming a sort of victory tradition and they had a long
discussion about tactics. Bader said that the Hurricanes
flew soggily at 23,000 feet. What about the new Hurricane
II's?

Leigh-Mallory said: "Anything you want, I'll try my
best to get for you."

From that day the tide of battle ebbed. Now the
bombers rarely appeared, but in their place came packs of
109's darting for London and other targets with small
bombs hanging on makeshift bomb-racks under their slim
bellies. They came over fast and very high, dodging
through cloud banks, and as autumn came the cloud
clustered thicker and thicker. The R.A.F. changed its
tactics too. At 25,000 feet the Hurricanes found it harder
than ever to catch the fleet 109's and the burden fell on the
Spitfires, which were scrambled early now so that they were
up there, waiting, when the 109's came.

Goering provided no good " curtain " for the daylight

battles. The Luftwaffe came in like a lion and went out like a lamb. On 12th October Hitler postponed the invasion till the following spring. Some people in England still waited for the next assaults, and the fact that Hitler, the invincible, had suffered his first (and resounding) defeat did not make its full impact until Winston Churchill's phrase " The Battle of Britain " took firmer root with those other famous words : " Never in the field of human conflict has so much been owed by so many to so few." Then the country rejoiced, but Fighter Command had lost 915 aircraft and 733 pilots killed or wounded.

Convoy patrols again ! Life was dull. A few 109's still poked their yellow spinners over Kent, but they were reserved for the Spitfires.

Against the last, petulant stabs of the 109's Bader led his wing on one last flight. Climbing over the Estuary, a lone startled shout came from Willie McKnight, and then a pack of 109's was spitting through them out of the sun. Only McKnight was quick enough to fire ; he caught one as it darted in front and the 109 did not lift its nose like the others but went tumbling down sky like a broken thing that had lost the grace of flight.

As autumn gusts whirled the last yellowed leaves across the aerodrome, the embattled nation realised that not even a madman could invade now. For some time Thelma had been losing her fear for Douglas, and now inside her was an odd feeling that he was invincible.

Then the bombers struck again. At night !

CHAPTER NINETEEN

MORE PROMOTION

OUT OF the black sky they rained bombs on London, the docks, the city, and the huddled houses around. Unable to invade, Hitler tried to destroy the will to resist. The nights glowed with acres of flame but the glow was never high enough to betray the bombers, and apart from anti-aircraft guns the people had almost no defences. Balloons were too low. Some Spitfires and Hurricanes went up, but it was like playing blind man's buff. They had no radar in aeroplanes then. The bombers switched to Bristol, Liverpool, Hull . . . back to London.

The phone rang in the mess one evening and the night controller from Duxford asked urgently : " How many of your chaps can night-fly Hurricanes ? "

" Three," Bader answered. " Myself, Ball and Turner."

" Get 'em into the air as soon as you can," ordered the controller. " The Hun's going for Coventry."

A full moon shone in a cloudless sky as he climbed hard to 18,000 feet over Coventry and was shaken at the sea of flame below.

For an hour he swung grimly round the city, but a full moon was not enough and the bombers flitted unseen in the high darkness. Short of petrol, he turned back and could just see the flarepath 12,000 feet below when the engine coughed and stopped dead.

Trying to force-land a fighter at night " dead-stick " is too dangerous even to be sport. For a moment he was tempted to bale out, but the challenge of it caught him and he decided to try and land it. With the propeller wind-milling, he dropped his nose and glided down in a series of S-turns, keeping his eye on the flarepath. They were lonely moments that picked at the nerves, but he straightened out finally for the last approach, dropped his wheels and did not even have to sideslip off the last few feet. She settled neatly and a lorry towed him in.

Leigh-Mallory rang one day and said : " Douglas, we're having a fighter conference at Air Ministry to thrash out all we've learned from the recent daylight battles. I want you to come with me."

At the Air Ministry building in King Charles Street, Bader followed the bulky figure into a conference room and felt a twinge of alarm when he saw the braided sleeves round the long table. He recognised most of them : at the head the Chief of the Air Staff, Sir Charles Portal, " Stuffy Dowding " looking more craggy than ever, Keith Park, Sholto Douglas, John Slessor, Philip Joubert de la Ferté. And himself, a squadron leader. Leigh-Mallory said to Portal : " I've brought Squadron Leader Bader along, sir." Portal nodded courteously.

Bader sat quietly when the discussion started on the size of fighter formations and the idea of going to attack the enemy at the source when he was building up his formations over the Pas de Calais. Park pointed out that if he sent squadrons over the Pas de Calais the Germans would change their tactics, send up a bogus " build up" (probably of fighters) to draw the British fighters and then send off the real bombers, who would have a clear run while the British fighters were engaged away from the targets they were to defend and short of petrol and ammunition.

Sholto Douglas cut in : " I'd like to hear what Squadron Leader Bader has to say."

The eyes were looking at him and he felt suddenly vulnerable. He pulled himself to his feet.

" We've been learning, sir, exactly what you gentlemen learned in the first war " (that was a crafty start) . . . " Firstly, that the chap who's got the height controls the battle, especially if he comes out of the sun ; secondly, that the chap who fires very close is the chap who knocks them down ; thirdly, it is more economical to put up a hundred aircraft against a hundred than twelve against a hundred.

" I know we can't always put equal numbers against the Germans because their air force is bigger than ours—if necessary we'll fight one against a thousand—but surely we can manage to put sixty aircraft against a couple of hundred instead of only one squadron of twelve."

He went on to develop his theories, and delivered himself of a good, terse homily to the effect that the chap in the air, not the controller, should decide when, where and how to meet the enemy. " In fact," he added, " it might be a good idea to have the sun plotted on the operations board. "[1] Making the most of his chance, he covered every point he could think of, all the things he had discussed with Leigh-Mallory.

A week later, he received a letter marked " Secret." It said that Air Council had decided that wherever there were two squadrons on one aerodrome they were to practise battle flying as a wing and be proficient as soon as possible.

Fighter Command leadership was reshuffled. Dowding went, which upset Bader (and some others) deeply, and Sholto Douglas took over as C.-in-C. Park went to a new post and Leigh-Mallory took command of 11 Group. To Bader's joy he immediately arranged that 242 Squadron

[1] Later adopted.

should go to 11 Group too, posting them to Martlesham, near Felixstowe.

The night skies over England were louder now with the rumbling of bombers dropping hideous loads. The scientists were working to fit radar into aeroplanes, and meantime the R.A.F. was nearly helpless.

242 Squadron still had no part in it. Bader flew convoy patrols with them but felt better the day a phone call came from 11 Group. " I wanted to be the first to congratulate you again," said Leigh-Mallory. " You've just been awarded the D.F.C. I'm afraid it's long overdue."

Thelma sewed the diagonally striped ribbon on his tunic after the D.S.O., and his exuberant exterior was awkward with the effort of hiding his pride when the others saw it. He could—and did—brag about things like squash and golf (often with his tongue in his cheek), but a decoration was different.

Leigh-Mallory sent for him one day and said : " I suppose life seems pretty dull lately."

" Yes, sir."

" What do you think about going over to France and giving them a smarten-up ? "

Bader was glowing again.

The Operation Order labelled " First Offensive Sweep " came to Bader soon after in an envelope marked " Secret." Three Hurricane squadrons would escort six Blenheims to bomb suspected German ammunition dumps in the Forêt de Guisne near the Pas de Calais.

On 19th January Bader, full of hopes for a fight, led 242 Squadron off and over North Weald joined two more Hurricane squadrons led by Wing Commander Victor Beamish.

Over Hornchurch they tagged on to the Blenheims and flew out across the Channel. 242 Squadron was top cover at about 17,000 feet, and Bader felt bold and buccaneering. They nipped over the coast near Calais; France looked peaceful, lying softly under snow. In seconds they were over the Forêt de Guisne, only a couple of miles inland. Seconds later it was over and they were darting out again. No time to look for bomb bursts; the wary eyes roamed the sky looking for 109's but none appeared.

The next days were not so mild. Leigh-Mallory had another idea he called "Rhubarbs"—sending a pair of fighters darting across the Channel whenever layer cloud hung low over the land, to shoot at anything German aground or aloft. If they got into trouble they could climb and hide in the clouds. Some 11 Group squadrons had already tried them, and two days after the sweep Bader got his chance.

They did not get as far as France. Just off the beach between Calais and Dunkirk, Bader spotted two trails of foam on the water, nosed down to look and saw they were German E-boats. Without a second's thought, he dived; the Germans must have thought they were friendly and been shocked when the bullets raked the first boat. At the last moment they started to fire, and Bader had a swift glimpse of two of the crew jumping overboard before he had swept past and was raking the second boat.

For a while the days drifted; they were busy but it was routine. Occasionally when the clouds were thick they tried a few "rhubarbs" but saw nothing. Then they hit a bad patch. It started on 8th February, a cold day with ice cloud, when Laurie Cryderman sheered off from a convoy partrol to intercept a plotted "bandit." They heard him call half an hour later that his engine had cut. He was 600 feet up, far at sea, and never came back.

Only days later Ben Brown, pulling sharply out of a

steep dive low down, spun off a high-speed stall into the ground.

Then Ian Smith, who had taught Douglas "Little Angeline," went out on a convoy patrol and did not come back.

Crowley-Milling caught a JU. 88 over the North Sea, and as he dived to attack his bullet-proof windscreen was smashed into a whitely opaque and splintered shield as a cannon shell hit it; he could not see to aim but went on chasing and firing until the 88 vanished into cloud. Crowley-Milling got back.

Then the steadfast, charming Hugh Tamblyn fought an intruder approaching a convoy. An hour or two later a ship found him floating in his Mae West, but he was dead.

Sergeant Brimble was posted to Malta and killed on the way.

Early in March Leigh-Mallory sent for Bader. "We're working out ideas to carry the attack across to France in the summer," he said. "Fighter sweeps, like that other one you did, but more ambitious. To do it we're building up our 'wing' system and one of the items on that programme is to appoint wing commanders on certain stations to organise and lead the wings there.

"You," he went on, "are to be one of those wing commanders. You'll probably be going to Tangmere."

There are times when words sound like music. In Army terms, wing commander meant a rise from lieutenant to lieutenant-colonel in a year. And Tangmere was in 11 Group—on the South Coast, just across from France.

When L.-M. had disposed of the congratulations, Bader said: "Will I be able to take 242 Squadron with me, sir?"

"Afraid not," Leigh-Mallory regretted. "You'll already have three squadrons there. All Spitfires."

Bader suggested awkwardly that in that case he wasn't sure he wanted to be a wing commander.

Leigh-Mallory said firmly: "You'll do what you're told" . . . and then, because he knew his man: "Look at it this way. If you take 242 you won't be able to help favouring them a bit. I know you and how you regard them."

All he could do then was wait for the posting.

242 Squadron was not pleased. The whole squadron, from the lowest "erk" up, revolved round the C.O. as a tight and exclusive team that had been firmly knit even before the comradeship of the battle. The greatest leaders in the field always have "colour" . . . a certain bravura. Bader certainly had it.

On 18th March the bitter-sweet blow fell. A new man, "Treacle" Treacy, arrived to take over, and Thelma sewed the wing commander braid on Douglas's sleeves. The only man he was able to take with him from 242 was Stokoe, his conscientious and devoted batman.

CHAPTER TWENTY

ON THE ATTACK!

TANGMERE, not far from Southampton, was a pre-war station built for two squadrons. Now three Spitfire squadrons, 145, 610, and 616, and a Beaufighter squadron lived there and the Spitfires were to fly as the wing. He was pleased about 616 because they had been in 12 Group Wing and knew his ways. All the Spitfires were Mark II's, still with eight machine-guns but a little better than the Battle of Britain types.

He arrived on the morning of the 19th, stowed his bags in a room in the station commander's house near the mess, and in half an hour was flying a Spitfire to get the feel again. Two hours later he was leading two of the squadrons over the Channel, having a " snoop " towards the French coast and trying wing formation. The squadrons had not flown as a wing before and in the next two weeks he trained them hard.

Unlike his early days with 242, there was no need to win their confidence. He was famous now, the R.A.F.'s first wing leader, and men and officers jumped to obey his brisk bellows. Most of the pilots (average age about twenty-two) had fought non-stop through the Battle of Britain and he saw that several were showing signs of overstrain. His warm-hearted side became full of love for them, and he felt he wanted to say to them : " Don't you worry, chaps. We'll get you right." He saw Leigh-Mallory and explained that some of the boys should have a rest. Could he have some good replacements and also have Stan Turner promoted to squadron leader to command 145 Squadron?

"By all means," said Leigh-Mallory.

Turner arrived a couple of days later with bad news. Treacy had been leading a 242 formation in a sharp turn when the man behind had collided with him. Bits of the smashed aeroplanes hit a third Hurricane and all three went into the sea, killing Treacy, Edmond and Lang.

As 616 had the least battle experience, Bader attached himself to them and thereafter always flew at their head, leading the wing.

Domineering, dogmatic and breezy, Bader saw everything in blacks and whites, and in this new phase of welding an experimental wing together and evolving new tactics to carry the fight to the enemy he made decisions crisply with a confidence that would have been dangerous in someone else. He startled Tangmere, whose men first regarded him as a curiosity, then were impressed and then, as at 242, became devoted (apart from a few, ruffled by his blunt toughness, who resented him). As the wing knit together he got the itch to fight again, but Leigh-Mallory would not let him cross to the French coast.

Woodhall, newly promoted to Group Captain, arrived at Tangmere to command the station and also to act as controller. Leigh-Mallory wanted his old team together again for the work ahead. To be more easily recognised in the air during wing-flying, Bader had his initials "DB" painted on the side of his Spitfire, which prompted Woodhall to christen him "Dogsbody."

The Luftwaffe's terrifying night raids were easing off a little and the war seemed to be static, though all 11 Group knew it was only a lull. In mid-April Leigh-Mallory called Bader to H.Q. at Uxbridge, and there he found Malan,

Harry Broadhurst, Beamish, Kellett and other leaders. Leigh-Mallory, standing at the head of the table, said quietly:

"Gentlemen, we have stopped licking our wounds. We are now going over to the offensive."

He talked a long time about tactics; the idea, briefly, being to send a few bombers over the Channel surrounded by hordes of fighters, and force the Germans to come up and fight.

On the morning of 17th April a screed came over the Tangmere operations teleprinter headed "Secret. Operations Order. Circus No. 1." There followed details under headings like "Target," "Bomber Force," "Rendezvous," "Escort Wing," "Cover Wing," with heights and speeds and map references.

That afternoon about 100 Spitfires escorted twelve Blenheims to bomb Cherbourg. Bader led his wing of thirty-six and did not see a single enemy. Far away a few puffs of German flak stained the sky, and then they were on the way home again. Leigh-Mallory said later: "We're just poking the bear in his pit, gentlemen. You'll get some reaction in due course."

On the night of 7th May a party developed in the mess with pilots talking shop and skylarking into the night. Bader was surrounded as usual by his pilots, sipping orangeade while they nuzzled cans of beer, and after a while Cocky Dundas said: "Sir, let's have two of the new sections side by side—four aircraft line abreast so everyone can cover everyone else's tail and everyone can get an occasional squirt in."

The wing commander said it sounded fine. Everyone chattered about the new idea, working out, for instance, how to handle it in the air when "jumped" by enemy fighters. They decided that the "form" was for the two on the left at the critical moment to scream round in a full circle to the left and for the pair on the right to do likewise to the right, thus joining up again on the tails (it was hoped) of the foiled enemy.

In the morning Dundas came down to breakfast feeling not so gay as usual, regretting that he had not gone to bed earlier. Bader stumped in and sat at the same table full of rude health. He boomed as he sat down: " That was a good idea of yours last night, Cocky."

Dundas smiled wanly and murmured: " Oh, thank you very much, sir. I'm glad you liked it."

" Damn' good," repeated Bader. " I've been thinking it over. We'll try it to-day."

Dundas thought without enthusiasm that he did not feel like practice flying.

" Just you and me and a couple of others," Bader went on cheerfully. " We'll duck over to France and see if we can get some Huns to jump us."

For a moment it did not sink in, and then Dundas had a moment of lurching horror. He looked to see if Bader were joking. But he wasn't; he was turning to Woodhouse of 610 Squadron down the table and saying: " Paddy, get yourself a number two and come with us."

They took off at 11 a.m., Bader, Dundas (wondering why he hadn't kept his mouth shut the previous night), Woodhouse and a Sergeant Mains, and swept down the Channel at 25,000 feet between Dover and Calais in a slightly curving line abreast, Dundas on the left, Bader fifty yards on his right and slightly in front, a hundred yards to Woodhouse level, and fifty yards again to Mains, slightly behind. Thus they flaunted themselves up and down off Calais for half an hour, seeing nothing. Dundas was thinking with longing in a couple of minutes they would be turning for home again when above, five miles behind, he saw five 109's turning after them. He called urgently: "Hallo Dogsbody. Five 109's five o'clock above."

Bader's voice came delightedly: "Oh, good. I can see 'em, Cocky. I've got 'em." He throttled back a little and the Messerschmitts came up fast. Bader was keeping up a running commentary. . . . "Oh, this is just what we wanted. Wonderful, isn't it?"

Dundas refrained from answering. The 109's were boring in. Bader was going on exultantly: "Keep your eyes on 'em but don't break till I tell you. Let 'em come in. Don't break" . . . He was beside himself with enthusiasm.

The 109's were slanting in for the kill when he snapped "Break now!" and abruptly four Spitfires spun round on their wingtips, Bader and Dundas fanning left, and Woodhouse and Mains right.

In one of the tightest turns Dundas could remember, Bader's tail-wheel bobbed above his windscreen, but his vision kept greying out as the mounting "g" kept loading his lanky, sagging frame, forcing the blood from the brain. He'd heard some theory that Bader could turn sharper than anyone because he'd lost his legs and the blood could not sink that far.

Bader, reefing his machine out of the turn, saw the leading 109 darting just in front, fired in the same moment, saw the flash of bullet strikes and the 109 keel over out of sight, shovelling out black smoke. He heard Dundas, tense and edgy, in his earphones: "Dogsbody, I've been hit." (They had actually turned inside the two rearmost 109's, which had opened fire as the last two Spitfires straightened. Sergeant Mains was also hit.)

With cannon shells in the wing roots and glycol pipes, Dundas was peeling off gushing white smoke. Bader nosed down after him to give cover, but the 109's had vanished. Dundas nursed his aircraft back over the coast to Hawkinge Aerodrome, where it cut suddenly. Desperately he pushed his nose, wheels up, at about 150 m.p.h. on to the grass to try and break the speed, and she bounced and thumped rendingly, just missing a collection of brand-new Spitfires on 91 Squadron's dispersal. Shaken, he climbed out and was met by a furious 91 Squadron C.O. demanding to know what he thought he was doing.

Woodhouse got back to Tangmere all right, and Mains, tail damaged, but unhurt, landed at another field.

Holden flew a Magister two-seater to Hawkinge and took Dundas back to Tangmere, where Bader, seeing he was all right, boomed: " You're a silly clot, Cocky. What the hell did you go and do that for ? Anyway, I'm damn' glad to see you're back all right." Then, suddenly enthusiastic again : " I think I know what the trouble is. Instead of breaking outwards we should have all broken in one circle, all the same way, so we stick together and don't lose sight of the enemy. All it wants is some practice. We'll try again soon."

Bader tried it again with another section the next day, but this time over Tangmere, with a friendly section of 616 Spitfires doing the attacking. Breaking the same way, he found that the "finger four" line abreast was ideal; flexible and good for both defence and attack. Inside a week the " finger four " became the backbone of the wing (and was later copied by other wings and used extensively throughout the war.)

He tried it on Channel snoops and " circuses " to Cherbourg and Le Havre.

In June the Germans startled the world by marching on Russia and it became imperative to force Hitler into diverting more fighters back to France. Leigh-Mallory thought that the Blenheims with a ton of bombs were too light to force the issue, so he pestered Bomber Command till they let him have some four-engined Stirlings which could carry nearly six tons of bombs each. He packed about 200 Spitfires round them and sent them across the coast to an inland target, and with the swarm of darting fighters about them Bader thought it looked like a great beehive. He said so at the Group conference later, and thereafter it was known as the " Beehive."

Leigh-Mallory sent the swarm inland again to blast the rail yards at Lille, an important junction for the Germans.

Leigh-Mallory's tactics began to pay: Goering was pulling fighter squadrons out of Russia. Over France now they were coming up in packs of thirty and forty. The R.A.F. estimated that their fighters were knocking down three Germans to every two Spitfires lost.

On 21st June the Beehive went to St. Omer, and the Tangmere Wing flew ahead to delouse. Several 109's darted overhead, twisting back and forth waiting for a chance to strike at a straggler. Bader watched them intently. The Beehive came and bombed and left, and the Tangmere Wing was following across the coast when out of the sun two 109's dived in a port quarter attack on Bader's section of four. He yelled " Break left ! " wheeling fast.

The Germans must have been raw because they broke left, too, and Bader, turning faster than anyone, saw the belly of a 109 poised on its side fifty yards in front and fired. Bits splintered off the Messerschmitt and it pulled drunkenly up, stalled and spun.

Back at Tangmere, he marked an asterisk in his logbook and sat down to write his first combat report for some time.

Next day he led his wing with the Beehive to Haze-brouck, the day after to Béthune in the morning and to Béthune again in the afternoon.

Next morning to Béthune again at 26,000 feet, and this time he took a new sergeant pilot as his No. 2 to show him the ropes. Crossing the coast, packs of four or six Messerschmitts roamed about like scavengers, darting in now and then, and sheering off when challenged, pecking at the formations and trying to wing the outriders. Fed up with the nibbling, Bader dived 616 on six 109's about 500 feet below, and as they scattered he got a shot at one. Then the sergeant fired a long-range burst. Bader chased and caught it with another burst, seeing bullet strikes but no smoke or visible damage, yet suddenly a parachute blossomed as the pilot jumped and floated into the sea.

After lunch they were off again, this time to St. Omer, where more Germans than ever before were waiting. Eyes warily watched them behind, to the left, and also below, then they were all round, moving dangerously into the sun. Someone yelled a warning as a pack lunged, and Bader sharply broke the wing for independent battle—and in seconds the sky was a milling whirlpool. He caught a trailing 109 at close range and it puffed smoke as it fell into a steep dive. More 109's were diving on him. He got in a short head-on burst at one that flashed past, joined up with Ken Holden's squadron, squirted at one more vagrant enemy and came home, bathed in sweat and exhilarated.

Two more asterisks in the logbook, and a score of two and a half destroyed in a week, plus some damaged. Things were getting better. From then on they averaged a sweep[1] a day, except when the weather was bad.

Bader was still immune from nerves, a rollicking figure in black flying suit and blue and white polka-dot silk scarf, stuffing his pipe into his pocket when he hoisted himself into the cockpit. In the air they assembled over "Diamond"

[1] A " sweep " was nominally a raid without bombers but soon all the mass sorties into France, including the " circuses " (with bombers), were known as sweeps.

(code name for Beachy Head) and set course for France, seeing far below the wash of air-sea rescue launches speeding out from the ports to take station where they might pick up the lucky ones who were shot down alive into "the drink" on the way back. Disconcerting but also comforting.

CHAPTER TWENTY-ONE

INVINCIBLE?

Now THE Messerschmitts were ever more numerous and bolder, every day savaging the flanks. More and more often Bader broke the wings to go for them, and for frantic minutes the sky was full of snarling, twisting, spitting aeroplanes. Several of the wing scored " kills " and three Spitfires did not come back.

The Messerschmitts—quite rightly—never stayed long to mix it with the more manœuvrable Spitfires as they could never hold their own in a round-about tailchase. Despite British propaganda, the 109's were slightly faster and their proper tactics were to dive, shoot and break off. Any Spitfire on its own after a fight was under standing orders to join up with the nearest friendly fighters so there would be at least two in line abreast to watch each other's tail.

Coming back over the Channel one day, Dundas was startled to see Bader, flying alongside, flip back his cockpit top, unclip his oxygen mask, stuff his stub pipe in his mouth, strike a match (apparently holding the stick between his good knee and tin knee), light up and sit there like Pop-Eye puffing wisps of smoke that the slipstream snatched away. Dundas longed to light a cigarette himself, but desire was tempered by realisation that no normal man lit a naked flame in a Spitfire cockpit.

After that he always puffed his pipe in the cockpit on the way back, and pilots flying alongside used to sheer off, half in joke, half in earnest, in case Spitfire D.B. blew up. But it never did, adding to the growing and inspiring myth that Bader was bomb-proof, bullet-proof and fire-proof.

With virtually daily trips now, someone dubbed the wing " The Bader Bus Service. The Prompt and Regular Service. Return Tickets Only." That tickled everyone's fancy and some of the pilots painted it on the side of their cowlings.

On 2nd July they went to Lille, and Bader dived 616 on fifteen 109's. He fired at one from almost dead behind, and as its hood flew off and the pilot jumped, another 109 plunged past and collected a burst. Smoke and oil spurted and he went down vertically. Bader left him and pulled up, obeying the dictum that it is suicide to follow an enemy down. Coming back over the Channel, he dived on another enemy and, as he started firing the 109 rolled on its back like lightning and streaked back into France. Bader was getting fed up with 109's diving out of a fight like that (though he respected the correctness of their tactics), and when he got back to claim one destroyed and one probable, he added as a flippant afterthought : " and the third one I claim as frightened."

He hoped for a bite from Intelligence at Group but they maintained a dignified silence. Instead he got a phone call from Leigh-Mallory, who said : " Douglas, I hear you got another 109 to-day."

"Yes, sir."

" Well," Leigh-Mallory went on in his deceptively pompous voice, " you've got something else too—a bar to your D.S.O."

Coming away from Lille a couple of days later, little schools of Messerschmitts began pecking at them again. Bader fired at three but they half rolled and dived away. Two more dashed in and Bader shot one in the stomach from 100 yards. Explosive bullets must have slugged into the tank behind the cockpit because it blew a fiery jet like a blow-torch and fell out of the sky.

Remembering the three that got away, he claimed one destroyed and " three frightened," and this time got a bite from Group. A puzzled message arrived asking what he meant and he sent a signal back explaining. Group answered stiffly that they were not amused.

He had time to write to a small boy, however. Norman Rowley, aged seven, had had both legs amputated after being run over by a bus in a Yorkshire mining village, and Bader wrote to tell him he would be all right and could be a pilot if he tried hard. (It helped the boy more than anything. He was proud to be Bader's friend.)

In some ways Bader overdid the personal leadership, leaving no one trained to follow him. He could not always lead the wing, and it was obvious what a gap his going would leave. But that did not seem in the realm of reality, and people were recognising now that he had more genius for fighter leadership than anyone else alive.

On 12th July, over Hazebrouck, Bader took 616 down on fifteen 109's, shot at one, and saw a flash on its cockpit as he swept past, then fired head-on at another and saw pieces fly off as it swerved under him. A few seconds later he shot at a third, which spurted black smoke and glycol and wrenched into a violent dive. Then he chased a fourth through a cloud and fired from right behind. An orange, blow-torch flame squirted behind its cockpit and it fell blazing all over. One destroyed and three damaged, but he only put one asterisk in his logbook, no longer bothering to record " damaged."

A couple of days later, coming back with Dundas and Johnson, he streaked after a lone 109 below. Seeing him coming, the 109 dived and then climbed, and Bader, trying to cut him off, pulled up so sharply that he blacked out, hunched in the cockpit like an old man carrying a great weight, seeing nothing till he eased the stick forward and the grey film lifted. Then he still saw nothing—the 109 had vanished.

Back at Tangmere, when he landed Dundas and Johnson came charging over and Dundas said : " By god, sir, that was good shooting."

" What are you talking about ? " Bader grunted.

" Well," Dundas said, " you must have been 400 yards away when the Hun baled out."

" What ! " (incredulously). " I never even fired."

None of them had fired. The patches were still over the gun-ports in the wings. Yet the German *had* baled out.

The wing was re-equipping with Spitfire Vb's instead of the II's. The Vb was faster, could climb higher and had a 20 mm. cannon planted outboard in each wing. Everyone was excited about them except Bader, who developed a sudden, dogmatic aversion, deciding that cannons were no good because they would tempt a pilot to shoot from too far away instead of getting up close. This time, for once, he was wrong, but nothing would budge him ; he was like a choleric colonel barking out obstinately and luridly at anyone who dared oppose machine-guns. At Group Conferences he grunted his vigorous views to Sailor Malan, Leigh-Mallory and even the C.-in-C. Sholto Douglas, but orders still said the wing had to fly Vb's.

As they arrived in ones and twos he gave them first to Turner's top-cover squadron, where their better performance was most needed. Then Holden's team got them, and lastly 616, with whom he led the wing. Stubbornly he himself refused to fly one. Allotting them in this order was ideally correct. A formation leader should fly the slowest aircraft because he sets the pace and people behind must be able to keep up without wasting fuel on constant high power. Not all wing leaders did that, though Bader would have done it the way he did even had he approved of cannon. Finally he got a Va—with machine-guns.

After the war Tom Pike, risen to Air Vice Marshal and Assistant Chief of the Air Staff, said this of Bader at the time : "I think he almost eliminated fear from his pilots. His semi-humorous, bloodthirsty outlook was exactly what is wanted in war and their morale soared. He was a tremendous tonic."

Everyone felt he was invincible, and that this power shielded those who flew with him. Thelma now literally *knew* that the enemy would never get him. Every time he came back from a sweep he swooped low over the Bay House to let her know he was safely back.

Some of the Messerschmitts had shrewdly taken to setting about the Beehive as it came home over the French coast when the fighters were short of petrol. It was suggested that a fresh wing should go out to meet the homing Beehive, and over the Channel on 19th July the Tangmere Wing came down like wolves on an unsuspecting pack of 109's. Bader's first burst sent a 109 spinning down in a sea of flame. His second shot pieces off another, and as the Messerschmitts split up in alarm his bullets flashed on the fuselage of a third. In seconds the fight was over, half a dozen Messerschmitts were going down and the rest hurrying back into France.

On 23rd July, when the weather prevented any sweep, he took Billy Burton on a " rhubarb," and near Dunkirk saw a Spitfire hurtling out of France, chased by a 109. He squirted into the Messerschmitt's belly and it cart-wheeled into the sea with a great splash.

The next weeks were frustrating. Under pressure,

Bader at last tried a Vb, the last in his wing to do so, and only then because the Va was away for a check-up. He grumbled about it mightily because he got into the thick of a lot of fights, but never seemed able to knock anything down now, though Johnson, " Crow," Dundas, and the others kept scoring. He swore one day that his shells from each cannon passed each side of a 109 because he had gone up too close.[1]

He had done more sweeps now than anyone else in Fighter Command and still jealously insisted on leading the wing on every raid, urged by the inner devil, driving himself to the limit and driving others to keep pace.

In seven days he did ten sweeps—enough to knock out the strongest man, still more one who had to get around on two artificial legs.

Peter Macdonald arrived at Tangmere on posting, and was disturbed to note that the skin round Bader's deep-set eyes was dark with fatigue. He and Woodhall began telling him that he must take a rest but Bader refused tersely. At last, at the end of July, Leigh-Mallory said to him :

" You'd better have a spell off operations, Douglas. You can't go on like this indefinitely."

" Not yet, sir," Bader said. " I'm quite fit and I'd rather carry on, sir."

He was so mulish that the A.O.C. at last grudgingly said : " Well, I'll let you go till September. Then you're coming off."

On 8th August Peter Macdonald cornered him in the mess. " I'm going to insist you take a few days off," he said. " I'm taking you and Thelma up to Scotland for a week and you can relax with some golf at St. Andrews."

---

[1] Later he realised that he had been quite wrong in his dogmatic preference for machine guns.

After an argument, Bader said : " I'll think about it," and that evening Macdonald forced the issue by ringing St. Andrews and booking rooms for the three of them from the 11th. That, he thought, would settle it.

Next day everything went wrong from the start.

CHAPTER TWENTY-TWO

DOWNFALL

FIRST THERE was a tangle on take-off and the top-cover squadron went astray. Climbing over the Channel, the others could see no sign of it, and Bader would not break radio silence to call them. Then half-way across, his air-speed indicator broke, the needle sliding back to an inscrutable zero, which meant trouble timing his rendezvous with the Beehive over Lille, and after that a difficult landing at Tangmere, not knowing in the critical approach how near the aeroplane was to a stall. Time to worry about that later: more urgent things loomed. It looked a good day for a fight, patches of layer cloud at about 4,000 feet but a clear vaulting sky above with a high sun to veil the venom of attack. He climbed the squadrons to 28-30,000 feet so that they, not the Germans, would have the height and the sun.

The job that day was to go for German fighters where they found them, and they found them as they crossed the French coast, just south of Le Touquet—dead ahead and about 2,000 feet below, a dozen Messerschmitts were climbing the same way.

Bader said tersely into his mask: "Dogsbody attacking. Plenty for all. Take 'em as they come. Ken, stay up, and cover us," and plunged down at the leading four, Dundas, Johnson and West beside him and the rest hounding behind. The Germans still climbed placidly ahead, and steeply in the dive he knew it was the perfect "bounce." Picking the second to the left, he closed startlingly fast; the 109 seemed to slam slantwise at him and, trying to lift the nose to aim, he knew suddenly he had badly misjudged. Too fast! No time! He was going to ram, and in the last moment brutally jerked the stick and rudder so that the Spitfire careened and flashed past into the depths below.

Angrily he flattened again about 24,000 feet, travelling fast, watching alertly behind and finding he was alone. Better climb up fast again to join the rest: deadly to be alone in this dangerous sky. He was suddenly surprised to see six more Messerschmitts ahead, splayed abreast in three parallel pairs line astern, noses pointing the other way. He knew he should pull up and leave them; repeatedly he'd drummed it into his pilots never to try things on their own. But the temptation! Greed swept discretion aside and he sneaked up behind the middle pair. None of them noticed. From a hundred yards he squirted at the trailing one and a flame flared like a huge match being struck and the aeroplane fell on one wing and dropped on fire all over. The other Germans flew placidly on. They must have been blind.

He aimed at the leader 150 yards in front and gave him a three-second burst. Bits flew off it and then it gushed volumes of white smoke as its nose dropped. The two fighters on the left were turning towards him, and crazily elated as though he had just pulled off a smash-and-grab raid, he wheeled violently right to break off, seeing the two on that side still flying ahead and that he would pass between them. In sheer bravado he held course to do so.

Something hit him. He felt the impact but the mind was numb and could not assess it. No noise but something was holding his aeroplane by the tail, pulling it out of his hands and slewing it round. It lurched suddenly and then was pointing straight down. He pulled back on the stick but it fell into his stomach like a broken neck. The aeroplane was diving in a steep spiral and he looked behind to see if anything were following.

First he was surprised, and then terrifyingly shocked to see that the whole of the Spitfire behind the cockpit was missing; fuselage, tail, fin—all gone. Sheared off, he thought vaguely. The second 109 must have run into him and sliced it off with its propeller.

Thoughts crowded in. How stupid to be nice and warm in the closed cockpit and have to start getting out. The floundering mind sought a grip and sharply a gush of panic spurted.

Get out ! Get out !

Won't be able to soon! Must be doing over 400 already.

He tore his helmet and mask off and yanked the little rubber ball over his head—the hood ripped away and screaming noise battered at him. Out came the harness pin and he gripped the cockpit rim to lever himself up, wondering if he could get out without thrust from the helpless legs. He struggled madly to get his head above the windscreen and suddenly felt he was being sucked out as the tearing wind caught him.

Top half out. He was out! No, something had him by the leg holding him. (The rigid foot of the right leg hooked fast in some vise in the cockpit.) Then the nightmare took his exposed body and beat him and screamed and roared in his ears as the broken fighter dragging him by the leg plunged down and spun and battered him and the wind clawed at his flesh and the cringing sightless eyeballs. It went on and on into confusion, timeless, witless and helpless, with a little core of thought deep under the blind head fighting for life in the wilderness. It said he had a hand gripping the D-ring of the parachute and mustn't take it off, must grip it because the wind wouldn't let him get it back again, and he mustn't pull it or the wind would split his parachute because they must be doing 500 miles an hour. On and on . . . till the steel and leather snapped.

He was floating, in peace. The noise and buffeting had stopped. Floating upwards?

In a flash the brain cleared and he knew and pulled the D-ring, hearing a crack as the parachute opened. Then he was actually floating. High above the sky was still blue, and right at his feet lay a veil of cloud. He sank into it. That was the cloud at 4,000 feet. Cutting it fine! In seconds he dropped easily under it and saw the earth, green and dappled, where the sun struck through. Something flapped in his face, and he saw it was his right trouser leg, split along the seam.

The right leg had gone.

How lucky, he thought, to lose one's legs and have detachable ones. Otherwise he would have died a few seconds ago.

Lucky, too, not to be landing on the rigid metal leg like a post that would have split his loins. Odd it should happen like that. How convenient. But only half a leg was left to land on—he did not think of that.

Grass and cornfields were lifting gently to meet him, stooks of corn and fences. A vivid picture, not quite static, moving. Two peasants in blue smocks leaned against a gate looking up and he felt absurdly self-conscious. A woman carrying a pail in each hand stopped in a lane and stared up, frozen like a still. He thought—I must look comic with only one leg.

The earth that was so remote suddenly rose fiercely. Hell! I'm landing on a gate! He fiddled with the shrouds to spill air and slip sideways, and still fumbling, hit, feeling nothing except vaguely some ribs buckle when a knee hit his chest as consciousness snapped.

Three German soldiers in grey uniforms were bending over him, taking off his harness and Mae West. They picked him up and carried him to a car in a lane, feeling nothing, neither pain nor thought, only a dazed quiescence. The car moved off and he saw fields through the windows but did not think of anything. After timeless miles there were houses and the car rumbled over the *pavé*, through the arch of a gateway to a grey stone building. The Germans lifted him out and carried him through a door up some steps and along a corridor . . . he smelt the familiar hospital smell . . . into a bare, aseptic room, and then they were laying him on a padded casualty table. A thinnish man in a white coat and rimless glasses walked up and down—looked at him.

The doctor frowned at the empty trouser leg, pulled the torn cloth aside and stared in amazement, then looked at Bader's face and at the wings and medal ribbons on his tunic. Puzzled he said : " You have lost your leg."

Bader spoke for the first time since the enemy had hit him. " Yes, it came off as I was getting out of my aeroplane."

The doctor looked at the stump again, trying to equate a one-legged man with a fighter pilot. " Ach, so ! " he said obviously. " It is an old injury," and joked mildly. " You seem to have lost both your legs—your real one and your artificial one."

Bader thought : You haven't seen anything yet.

" You have cut your throat," the doctor said. He put his hand up and was surprised to feel a large gash under his chin, sticky with blood.

The doctor peered at it, then stuck his fingers between the teeth and felt around the floor of the mouth.

"I must sew this up," the doctor murmured. He jabbed a syringe near the gash and the area went numb. No one spoke while he stitched.

Bader grunted vaguely.

"Whereabouts are we?"

"This is a hospital," said the doctor. "St. Omer."

"That's funny," Bader said. "My father is buried here somewhere."

The doctor must have thought his mind was wandering. Two grey-uniformed orderlies came and carried him up two flights of stairs into a narrow room and dumped him like a sack of potatoes, though not roughly, on a white hospital bed. They took his clothes and left leg off, wrapped him in a sort of white nightshirt, pulled the bedclothes over him, stood the left leg, still clipped to the broken waistband, against the wall, and left him there.

He lay motionless, aching all over, feeling as though he had been through a mangle, his head singing like a kettle. Every time he stirred a piercing pain stabbed into the ribs under his heart, cutting like a knife.

A nurse came and held his head while she ladled some spoonfuls of soup into his mouth. She went. His mind slowly cleared and a thought came into focus: "I hope the boys saw me bale out and tell Thelma."

Dusk gathered slowly in the room and he dozed fitfully. Some time later he woke in darkness wondering where he was. Then he knew and sank into misery, black, deep and full of awareness.

No one had seen him go down. He had vanished after the first dive and did not answer when they called him. In the air they had been chilled by the absence of the familiar rasping banter. Back at Tangmere there was stunned disbelief when he did not return. They watched the sky and the clock until they knew he could have no petrol left.

Pike said to Woodhall : " You'd better tell his wife," and Woodhall stalled, saying : " No, give him time. He may have landed somewhere else with his R/T u/s. He'll turn up."

But John Hunt, a shy young Intelligence Officer, thought Thelma had been told and drove over to cheer her up.

She was in a deck-chair in the sun, and only when she said : " Hallo, John. Come for tea ? " he realised that she did not know. Somehow, in an agony of embarrassment, he talked of irrelevant things, trying to find an unbrutal way of breaking it, when a car drew up and Woodhall got out and walked straight up to them. Without preamble he said : " I'm afraid I've got some bad news for you, Thelma. Douglas did not come back."

Thelma stood dumbly.

Woodhall went on : " We should get some news soon. I shouldn't worry too much. He's indestructible . . . probably a prisoner."

Too numb to ask what had happened, she stood very pale and said : " Thank you, Woody."

Dawn brought new strength to Bader. In the light he saw many things more clearly : knew where he was and what it meant and accepted it unwistfully. First things first and to hell with the rest. He must get legs and must get word to Thelma.

The door opened and in came two young Luftwaffe pilots.

" Hallo," brightly said the leader. " How are you ? " His English was good.

" All right, thanks."

Bader was monosyllabic but the Germans chatted amiably. Would he like some books? They'd just come over from St. Omer airfield to yarn as one pilot to another. Spitfires were jolly good aeroplanes.

" Yes," Bader said. " So are yours."

After a while the Count said politely : " I understand you have no legs ? "

" That's right."

They asked what it was like flying without legs. An elderly administrative officer came in and listened, looked at the left leg leaning against the wall and observed heavily : " Of course it would never be allowed in Germany."

Later they left and the next visitor was a Luftwaffe engineering officer, who asked more questions about legs. Bader cut him short : " Look, can you radio England and ask them to send me another leg ? "

The German thought it a good idea.

" And while you're about it," Bader followed up, " could you send someone to look at the wreckage of my aeroplane. The other leg might still be in it."

The German promised to do what he could.

A nurse brought in a basin of water, making signs that he was to wash himself. He did so, moving painfully, and when he got to his legs was shocked to find a great dark swelling high on his right stump.

Later, yesterday's doctor came in, looking precise behind the rimless glasses. Bader showed him the swelling, and the doctor looked grave and prodded it. After a while he said hesitantly : " We will have to cut this."

Bader burst out : " By God, you don't," panicky at the thought of an experimental knife. They argued violently about it till the doctor grudgingly agreed to leave it for a while.

A dark, plump girl came in, put a tray on his bed, smiled and went out. He realised he was hungry till he tasted the bowl of potato water soup, two thin slices of black bread smeared with margarine and the cup of tepid ersatz coffee.

Later it was the doctor again with orderlies. " We are going to put you in another room," he said. " With friends."

The orderlies carried him along a corridor into a room with five beds and dumped him on one of them. A fresh-faced young man in another bed said cheerfully in an American accent : " Hallo, sir. Welcome. My name's Bill Hall. Eagle Squadron." He had a cradle over one leg. His kneecap had been shot off. In the next bed was a Pole with a burnt face, and beyond him Willie, a young Londoner who had been shot through the mouth. All Spitfire pilots. They chatted cheerfully till well after dusk.

Bader asked : " Isn't there any way out of here ? "

" Yes," Willie answered bitterly. " Soon as you can stagger they whip you off to Germany."

" If you had clothes," Bader persisted, " how would you get out ? "

" Out the window on a rope," Willie said. " The gates are always open and no guards on them. They put the guards outside the door."

" How would you get a rope ? "

Willie said there were French girls working in the hospital who might smuggle one in.

Bader slipped off to sleep thinking grimly about that, but he slept well and in the morning did not feel so stiff and sore.

The plump girl came in early with more black bread and acorn coffee, and Bill Hall introduced her to Bader as Lucille, a local French girl.

The doctor came in to see his stump but the swelling was visibly less, which was an enormous relief. In his blunt way Bader told the doctor that the food was awful, and the doctor bridled.

Later a tall, smart Luftwaffe officer came in. He wore the red tabs of the Flak, clicked his heels, saluted Bader and said : " Herr Ving Commander, ve haf found your leg." A jackbooted soldier marched through the door and jerked to attention by the bed, holding one arm stiffly out. Hanging from it was the missing right leg, covered in mud, the broken piece of leather belt still hanging from it. Bader, delighted, said, " I say, thanks," then saw that the foot still clad in sock and shoe stuck up almost parallel to the shin.

" It's been smashed."

" Not so badly as your aeroplane," said the officer.

Bader took the leg. He unpeeled the sock and saw that the instep had been stove in.

" I say," he said, turning on the charm. " D'you think your chaps at the aerodrome could repair this for me ? "

The officer pondered. " Perhaps," he said. " Ve vill take it and see." The officer clicked his heels, saluted, swung smartly and disappeared.

Next it was a new girl, fair-haired and with glasses, carrying a tray. She was Hélène, and everyone goggled to see that she carried real tea on the tray and some greyish-white bread. Apparently the shouting match had been worth while.

In the morning the swelling on the stump had deflated, and that was a great relief.

Later, the officer with the red tabs marched in, saluted, and said " Herr Ving Commander, ve haf brought back your leg," the jack-booted stooge made another dramatic entrance behind and came to a halt by the bed, holding out a rigid arm with the leg suspended from it : a transformed leg, cleaned and polished and with the foot pointing firmly where a foot should be. Bader took it and saw they had done an amazing job on it; the body belt was beautifully repaired with a new section of intricately-worked, good quality leather and all the little straps that went with it. The dent in the shin had been hammered out, so that apart from a bare patch of paint it looked normal.

"It is O.K.?" the officer asked anxiously.

Bader, impressed and rather touched, said : "It's really magnificent. It is very good of you to have done this. Will you please thank the men who did it very much indeed."

He strapped both legs on, eased off the bed, and went stumping round the room, a ludicrous figure in nightshirt with the shoe-clad metal legs underneath. Without a stump sock (lost in the parachute descent), the right leg felt strange, and it gave forth loud clanks and thumps as he swung it. The others looked on fascinated. Beaming with pleasure, the Germans finally left. Bader lurched over to the window and looked at the ground three floors and forty feet below. To the left of the grass courtyard he could see the open gates, unguarded.

They became aware of a drone. The Pole and Willie joined him at the window, and they saw the twisting, pale scribble of vapour trails against blue sky : obviously a sweep and some 109's were having a shambles over St. Omer. Tensely they watched, but the battling aircraft were too high to see. Shortly a parachute floated down. A German he hoped.

A Luftwaffe Feldwebel came in and told Willie and the Pole to be ready to leave for Germany after lunch. He would bring their clothes later.

When they had gone Willie, depressed, said : "Once they get you behind the wire you haven't got much chance."

Bader began worrying that it would be his turn next. He *must* stay in France as long as possible.

Lucille came in with soup and bread for lunch. The guard looked morosely in the doorway, and then turned back into the corridor. Bader whispered to the Pole : " Ask her if she can help me get out or put me in touch with friends outside."

In a low voice the Pole started talking to Lucille in fluent French. She darted a look at Douglas and whispered an answer to the Pole. They went on talking in fast, urgent whispers, each with an eye watching the door. Bader listened eagerly but the words were too fast. They heard the guard's boots clump in the corridor, and Lucille, with a quick, nervous smile at Douglas, went out.

The Pole came across and sat on his bed. " She says you're ' *bien connu* ' and she admires you tremendously and will help if she can, but she can't get a rope because the Germans would guess how you got it. She doesn't know whether she can get clothes, but she has a day off next Sunday and will go to a village down the line called Aire, or something. She says there are ' *agents Anglais* ' there."

English agents ? It sounded too good. But she was going to try, and hope welled strongly. Sunday ! This was only Wednesday.

They took Willie and the Pole that afternoon. Now he had to rely on his schoolboy French.

In the morning Lucille came in with the usual bread and acorn coffee. The sentry lounged in the doorway. She put the tray on Bader's bed, leaning over so that her plump body hid him from the sentry. He grinned a cheerful " *Bon jour* " at her as she squeezed his hand and then the grin nearly slipped as he felt her pressing a piece of paper into his palm. He closed his fingers round it and slid the clenched fist under the bedclothes.

CHAPTER TWENTY-THREE

ESCAPE

HALF UNDER the clothes, Bader unfolded the paper and read : " *My son will be waiting outside the hospital gates every night from midnight until 2 a.m. He will be smoking a cigarette. We wish to help a friend of France.*"

It was signed " J. Hiècque."

He tucked the note in the breast pocket of the night-shirt and stuffed a handkerchief on top. It was red hot. Somehow he must get rid of it. He knew that the person who bravely signed a name to it was liable to death. Lucille, too.

Now how to get out of the hospital ? And he *must* get his clothes back ! Couldn't walk round the town in a white nightshirt. Pretend he was walking in his sleep ! With tin legs sticking out under his nightshirt ! Silly thoughts chased their tails in his head. *Must* get clothes and *must* destroy the note.

He had his pipe and matches.

Reaching out, he picked up his tin legs from the wall, strapped them on and walked out of the door. The sentry stood in his way. He pointed to the lavatory and the sentry nodded.

Inside the lavatory he closed the door, struck a match and burnt the note, then dropped the ashes into the pan and flushed it.

Walking back up the corridor, the sentry gaped at him and he knew angrily how ridiculous he looked in the nightshirt with the legs underneath. It was then that the idea struck him.

When the doctor came in to inspect the stump, Bader said, " Look, I've got my legs back now but I can't walk around in them with this nightshirt on. It's terribly embarrassing. I must have some clothes to wear."

The doctor looked thoughtful and then smiled. " Oh, well, I suppose it is all right in your case."

Half an hour later a German nurse came in with his clothes.

How to get out of hospital! He lay there fiercely thinking about it. No good trying to walk down the corridors and stairs. The guards were on at midnight and all night. He walked over to the window.

He was still there when the fighter pilot with the Knight's Cross came in with his comrade. " Ha," he said, " it is good to see you on your legs again. Look, we haf brought you two bottles of champagne. Will you come and drink them with us ? "

They took him down a flight of stairs to the doctor's room, but the doctor was not there, just the three of them. The first cork popped. It was the first time he had drunk champagne since his second wedding to Thelma.

The Count had obviously shot down some British aircraft but was too polite to mention that.

" Soon you may haf three legs," the Count said. " With the permission of Reichsmarshal Goering, the Luftwaffe has radioed England. They offer to give a British aeroplane unrestricted passage to fly your leg. We have given them a height and a course and a time to drop it over St. Omer."

Bader gave a chuckle. " I bet they drop it with bombs," he said.

The Count grinned amiably and raised his glass. " We will be ready," he promised.

There was another thing he said. The Oberstleutnant Galland, who commanded at their airfield, Wissant, near St. Omer, sent his compliments to Oberstleutnant Bader and would like him to come and have tea with them.

Bader was intrigued. It would be churlish to refuse, and in any case he would love to meet Galland (probably they had already met in the air). It brought a breath of the chivalry lost from modern war. And it was a chance to spy out the country, to see the other side, life on an enemy fighter station, to weigh it up and compare it. Might get back home with a 109 !

" I'd be delighted to come," he said.

The car came bearing the bald little engineering officer, who sat by him all the fifteen miles to Wissant. They drew up in front of a farmhouse. German officers stood outside—it was the officers' mess. As Bader got out a man about his own age stepped forward. He had burn marks round the eyes and a lot of medals on his tunic. The Knight's Cross with Oak Leaves and Swords—almost Germany's highest decoration—hung round his neck. He put out his hand and said " Galland."

Bader put out his own hand. " Oh, how d'you do. My name is Douglas Bader." Galland did not speak English, and the engineering officer interpreted. A lot of others stepped forward in turn, clicking their heels as they were introduced. Galland led him off down a garden path.

He led the way into a long, low arbour, and Bader was surprised to see it filled with an elaborate railway on a big raised platform. Galland pressed a button and little trains whirred past little stations, rattling over points, past signals, through tunnels and model cuttings. Eyes sparkling, Galland turned to Bader, looking like a small boy having fun. The interpreter said: "This is the Herr Oberstleutnant's favourite place when he is not flying."

After playing a little while with that, Galland led him and the others several hundred yards along paths, through a copse of trees to the low, three-sided blast walls of an aircraft pen. In it stood an Me 109.

Bader looked at it fascinated, and Galland made a gesture for him to climb in. He surprised them by the way he hauled himself on to the wing-root, grabbed his right leg and swung it into the cockpit and climbed in unaided. As he cast a professional eye over the cockpit lay-out Galland leaned in and pointed things out. Mad thoughts about slamming the throttle on for a reckless take-off surged through Bader's mind.[1]

He turned to the interpreter. "Would you ask the Herr Oberstleutnant if I can take off and try a little trip in this thing?"

Galland chuckled and answered. The interpreter grinned at Bader. "He says that if you do he'll be taking off right after you."

They had tea in the farmhouse mess. It could have been an R.A.F. mess except that all the other uniforms were wrong. Everyone smiled, exuding goodwill, but it was a little strained and formal and the talk was stilted. No one tried to pump him for information. The interpreter told him that the day he was shot down the Luftwaffe had got twenty-six Spitfires for no loss, which was such obvious nonsense that it put Bader in a cheerful mood, because it confirmed R.A.F. views on extravagant German claims.

[1] After the war Galland sent Bader a snapshot of the scene, and only then did he discover that a German officer beside the cockpit had been pointing a heavy pistol at him all the time he sat there.

He himself had got two that day, and possibly three, counting the mysterious man who had hit him.[1]

Galland gave him a tin of English tobacco, and when he took him out to the car said: " It has been good to meet you. I'm afraid you will find it different in prison camp, but if there is ever anything I can do, please let me know."

He smiled warmly, shook hands, clicked his heels and bowed. At a discreet distance behind, everyone else clicked heels and bowed. Bader got into the car and they drove back to the hospital.

A comatose form lay in the bed by the window and the room stank disagreeably of ether. Bader looked across. " Who's that ? "

" New boy came in while you were out," Hall said. " Sergeant pilot. Shot down yesterday. They've just taken his arm off. He's still under the dope."

The door opened and a German soldier wearing a coal-scuttle helmet came in and said in atrocious English: " Herr Ving Commander, to-morrow morning at eight o'clock you vill pleased to be ready because you go to Chermany."

The words seemed to hit Bader right in the stomach.

Hall murmured : " Tough luck, sir. Looks like you've had it."

Bader roused and said crisply : " Well, I've got to get out to-night, that's all."

He lurched over to the window and pushed it open. It seemed a long way down. He turned back and scowled round the room, austere with its board floor and five prim beds.

Sheets ! Knotted sheets !

Each bed had an undersheet and a double, bag-type

[1] Much later Bader found that his wing had got eight that day for two lost.

sheet stuffed in the continental style. He stumbled over to his bed and ripped the sheets from under the blanket. Need more than that! He clumped to the two empty beds and stripped them the same way. With a sudden idea he began ripping the bag sheets along the seams to get two out of each one. The tearing seemed to scream a warning to the Germans.

" Make a noise," he hissed to Hall, and Hall started on a monologue in a loud American voice. Both were acutely conscious of the guard just outside the door.

" Know anything about knots ? " Bader whispered to Hall.

" Not a sausage."

He started knotting the corners together in an unskilled double " granny " with three hitches, jerking tightly to make them fast and hoping they would stay so when the test came.

The knots took up a lot of length, and when he had finished the " rope " was clearly not long enough.

" Here, take mine," Hall said.

Gently he eased the sheet from under Hall and took off the top one. When he had added them the rope still did not look long enough.

Bader went over to the bed of the sergeant pilot, who was breathing stertorously under the ether. Gently working the sheet from under him, he said : " This is frightful, but I've just got to."

" He won't mind," reassured Hall. " I'll tell him when he wakes up."

Soon he had fifteen sheets knotted together, littered around the room, and prayed that no one would come in. He pushed the sergeant pilot's bed to the window, knotted one end of the rope round the leg and stuffed the rest under the bed. Then he straightened the white blankets on all the beds and climbed back into his own, sweating, heart thumping, praying that darkness would come before the guard.

Time dragged while dusk slowly gathered in the room. It was not quite dark when the door handle rattled, the door opened and a German soldier stuck his head in and looked round. Bader could not breathe. The guard muttered " *Gut Nacht,*" and the door closed behind him.

Three hours to go. As long as no nurse came to see the sergeant pilot!

That evening Thelma, who had eaten nothing for three days, braced herself and asked Stan Turner: " Well, what do you really think ? "

Turner said with simple directness : " You'll have to face it. We should have heard something by this. I guess he's had it."

In London the Luftwaffe's radio message had arrived saying that a spare leg could be flown across in a Lysander communications aircraft. Spitfires could escort it part of the way and then Messerschmitts would take over. The Lysander could land at St. Omer, hand over the leg and then it could take off again.

From Leigh-Mallory and Sholto Douglas the reaction was prompt, definite and identical. No free passage or German escort (with its lump of propaganda plum cake for Goebbels). They would send the spare leg in a Blenheim on a normal bombing raid.

Dundas, Johnny Johnson and Crowley-Milling had gone across to the Bay House to do what they could for Thelma. She sat quietly, a sphinx-like stoic, and only roused when the phone rang. It was Woodhall for her. The others could only hear her saying : " Yes . . . yes . . . yes, Woody." She said " Thank you very much,

Woody," hung up and came back to the room. In the silence she sat down and lit a cigarette, trembling a little. Then she blew out smoke and said quietly : " D.B.'s a prisoner." Shouts of jubilation filled the room but she hardly heard.

Weary æons of time seemed to have passed before a clock somewhere in the darkness of St. Omer chimed midnight. The night was breathlessly still. He eased on to the edge of the bed, vainly trying to stop the creaks, and strapped his legs on. Then his clothes. Praying that the guard was asleep in his chair, he took a step towards the window ; the boards creaked and the right leg squeaked and thumped with a terrifying noise. Hall started coughing to cover it up as, unable to tiptoe, he stumbled blindly across the floor. At the window he quietly pushed it open and leaned out, but the night was coal black and he could not see the ground. Picking up the sheet rope, he lowered it out, hoping desperately that it was long enough.

Holding the rope, Bader leaned his chest on the window-still and tried to winkle his legs out sideways. They seemed fantastically clumsy. Uncontrollable. Sweating, he took a hand off the rope to grab his right shin and bend the knee. Then somehow he was through, legs dangling, hands clutching the rope on the sill. The terrible pain pierced his ribs again, making him gasp.

Hall whispered : " Good luck ! " It sounded like a pistol shot.

He hissed : " Shut up." And then, " Thanks." Then he started easing himself down.

It was simple. The legs rasping against the wall were useless, but the arms that had developed such muscles since the long-ago crash at Reading took his weight easily. He lowered himself, hand under hand, under sure control.

Holding the sheets was no trouble and the knots were holding—so far. In a few seconds he came to a window and knew it was the room where he had drunk champagne with the Luftwaffe. He was horrified to feel that it was open, but inside it was dark and he eased his rump on to the ledge for a breather, hoping the doctor was not sleeping inside. Sitting there, breathing quietly, he looked down but still could not see the ground or whether the rope reached it.

Very gently his feet touched the flagstones and he was standing, dimly seeing that yards of sheet seemed to be lying on the ground.

" Piece of cake," he thought, and moved a couple of yards on to the grass, cursing the noise from his legs. Warily he steered across the grass towards where the gates should be, hoping the mysterious Frenchman would be there.

Something loomed darker even than the night. The gates ! Then a shock—they were closed. He got his fingers in the crack between and one gate opened easily a foot. He squeezed through on to the cobbled *pavé* of the road and instantly, immediately opposite, saw the glowing end of a cigarette. He stumped across the road and the cigarette moved, converging on him. It came to his side with a dark shadow behind it that whispered " Dooglass!" in a strong French accent.

" *Oui*," he said, and the shape took his right arm and they moved off along the *pavé*. The town was like a tomb in which his legs were making an unholy clatter, echoing into the darkness. He could not see, but the silent shape seemed to know by instinct. A pressure on the arm and they turned right and stumbled on.

The Frenchman began muttering to him : " *C'est bon. C'est magnifique. Ah, les sales Boches.*"

Bader thought how funny it was, walking through the curfew in enemy-occupied St. Omer arm-in-arm with a stranger he would not even recognise by day. He began to giggle. The Frenchman said " Ssh! Ssh! " but that only made him giggle more. The Frenchman started to giggle and then it was so grotesque, the two of them giggling and clattering down the street, that it grew into loud laughter mingled with the terror inside him that the Germans would hear. Slowly the pent-up emotion washed away and the laughter subsided.

They walked on—and on. Five minutes, ten—twenty. His right stump without the stump-sock began to chafe. Thirty minutes . . . it was sore and starting to hurt. He was limping badly and the Frenchman made soothing noises like " Not far now " in French. Forty minutes must have passed. The steel leg had rubbed the skin off his groin and every step was searing agony. Stumbling and exhausted, he had both arms hanging on to the Frenchman's shoulders. At last the man took his arms round his neck, picked him up, dangling on his back, and staggered along. In a hundred yards or so he stopped and put him down.

He led the way and Bader stumbled after him up a garden path. A doorway showed ahead, and then he was in a little, low-ceilinged room with flowered wallpaper, and a tin oil-lamp on the table. An old man and a woman in a black shawl got up from the chairs and the woman put her arms round him and kissed him. She was over sixty, Madame Hiècque, plump and with a lined, patient face. Her husband, spare and stooping, brushed his cheeks with a wisp of grey moustache. Fleetingly he saw his guide, remembering mostly the lamplight sheen on the glossy peak of a cap drawn low over the face and the glint of smiling teeth. The young man shook his hand and was off out of the door.

The old woman said gently : " *Vous êtes fatigué ?* "

Holding on to the table, he said " *Oui* " and she led him with a candle up some cottage stairs into a room with a huge double bed. He flopped on it. She put the candle on the table, smiled and went out. He unstrapped his legs with enormous relief, stripped to his underclothes and slid under the bedclothes into a gloriously soft feather bed.

A hand on his shoulder woke him about 7 a.m. The old man was looking down, smiling. He left a razor, hot water and towel. Bader freshened up and examined his stump, which was raw and bloodstained, terribly sore. No help for it. Just have to bear the pain. He strapped his legs on and went wincingly downstairs. Madame had coffee and bread and jam waiting, and while he ate she planted an old straw hat squarely on her head and went out.

Madame came back in great glee. " *Les Boches,*" it seemed, " *sont très stupides.*" He gathered she had walked to the hospital and stood watching mobs of Germans running around searching the area. Great Joke ! In halting French he tried to make her understand that his presence was very dangerous to them. If they found him he, himself, would only be put in cells and then sent to prison camp, but the Hiècques were liable to be shot. He should leave them and hide."

Madame said : " *Non, non, non, non* . . ." The Germans would never find him here. That evening her son-in-law, who spoke English, would come and they would discuss things and get him to the Underground. She examined his right stump and produced a pair of long woollen underpants. Cutting one of the legs off, she sewed up the end and there was a perfectly good stump-sock.

At noon the familiar drone came overhead and they took him out into the shelter of the walled back garden.

Yearningly he watched the tangled con-trails and saw tiny glints as twisting aircraft caught the sun.

At 15,000 feet, just south of St. Omer, the Tangmere wing jockeyed round the Blenheim. Crowley-Milling, close escort, saw the bomb bays open and the long thin box with the spare leg drop out. It looked like a little coffin. A parachute blossomed above it and it floated down, swaying gently.

The quiet, loyal and gallant Stokoe had asked to be dropped by parachute with it to look after the wing commander in prison, but permission had been refused. He had to content himself in helping Thelma stuff the leg with stump socks, powder, tobacco and chocolate.

Madame gave Bader cold pork for lunch and went out again to the scene of the crime. She came back hugging herself with delight. Convinced that Bader could not walk far, the Germans had cordoned off an area round the hospital and were running about like ants, searching every house. But nowhere in this area.

He felt like twiddling his thumbs as the afternoon dragged. Madame went out again to see the fun. About half-past five there came a terrifying banging on the front door and a chill swept through him. The old man jumped as though he had been shot, peered furtively through the curtain, turned and whispered " Les Boches ! "

He grabbed Bader's arm and led him towards the back door. Only at the last moment Douglas thought to grab his battledress jacket. Together they stumbled into the garden, moving as fast as the legs would let him. Three yards from the back door, against a wall, stood a rough shed, galvanised iron nailed on posts, covering some baskets, garden tools and straw. The old man pulled the baskets and straw away, laid him on his stomach, cheek pillowed on his hands, against the corner of the wall and piled the straw and baskets on top.

There was not long to wait. Within a minute he heard voices and then tramping feet by the back door. A vague kind of twilight filtered through the straw but he could not see anything. The boots clumped along the paved path to the shed. He heard baskets being kicked about. The straw over him started moving with a loud rustle.

Miraculously the footsteps retreated, diminishing down the garden path. Elation filled him.

The boots were coming back up the path. Suddenly they clumped again into the shed, then stopped and rasped about a yard from his head. From his heart outwards ice seemed to freeze his nerves.

The baskets were being thrown around, the boots rasped on the paving, and then there was a metallic clang that mystified him. There was a movement in the hay just above and another clang. His eyes turned sideways, saw a bayonet flash down an inch from his nose and stab through the wrist of his battledress jacket to hit the stone floor. He knew what the clang was and guessed that the next stroke would go into his neck.

CHAPTER TWENTY-FOUR

RECAPTURE

IT WAS a lightning decision. He jerked up on his hands, heaving out of the hay like a monster rising from the sea, straw cascading off his back. A young German soldier, bayonet poised for the next jab, leapt back in shock and stared pop-eyed at him, holding rifle and bayonet on guard. He started yelling hoarsely in German. Boots pounded and three German soldiers clattered under the iron roof, all armed. They stood round him in a semi-circle, bayonet tips poised about four feet from him. Slowly he raised his hands.

A little Stabsfeldwebel (staff sergeant) with a dark, thin moustache ran up and covered him with a pistol as he stood there feeling like King Lear, or perhaps an escaped lunatic at bay, with straw in his hair and all over his battledress.

Looking pleased and quite friendly, the Stabsfeldwebel said in perfect, unaccented English : " Ah, Wing Commander, so we have caught you again."

" Yes," said Bader. " Would you mind asking these soldiers to put their rifles down."

The Stabsfeldwebel rattled off some German, and the soldiers lowered the rifles.

Still with his hands up, Bader said : " You speak English very well."

" Thank you, Wing Commander," replied the German. " I lived at Streatham[1] for eleven years."

---

[1] London suburb.

"Did you really," Bader said. "I used to live near Croydon myself."

"Ah, I know Croydon well," the German answered. "Did you ever go to the Davis Cinema ? "

"Yes. And I used to go to the Locarno at Streatham."

"Did you ? " said the German. "Many Saturday evenings I have danced there."

Bader never forgot a word of that dialogue. The German courteously invited him to follow, and he stumped out of the shed into the back door again feeling that the world might well be rid of politicians and that this was a perfect example of the fact that ordinary people never caused wars. He was thinking it made Hitler and Mussolini look " pretty stupid " when he saw the old man and woman standing in the room. They looked pale and he stiffly walked past, showing no sign of recognition.

At the front door he nodded his head back and said to the Stabsfeldwebel : " Those people did not know I was in their garden. I came in last night through that gate in the wall."

Quite pleasantly the German replied : " Yes, I understand that."

By the kerb stood the Germans' car, and as they led him to it the rear door opened and a blonde girl with glasses got out. Rather surprised, he recognised Hélène, from the hospital and said automatically : " Hallo, Hélène," but she walked past him with her eyes down.

They drove him to Headquarters in St. Omer, where a German officer questioned him and got no answers. Then into a room where he was surprised and delighted to see the box containing his spare right leg. They explained, smiling, that it had been dropped that afternoon, and took his photograph standing by it. Then to his annoyance, they refused to give it to him and prodded him instead into an upstairs room. There, for the first time, they really infuriated him ; as he sat on a cot an officer and a soldier stood over him with a pistol and a bayonet, and made him take his trousers down and unstrap his legs : then they took the legs away.

He snarled at them, but the officer said stiffly it was orders from above. Two guards stayed and the rest went out, leaving him on the bed helpless, humiliated and seething. All night two men in full battle order, coal-scuttle helmets and loaded rifles stood over him. It was hot and he asked for the windows to be opened, but the officer came back and refused, saying that " orders from above " forbade that too.

He lay awake all night as the guards coughed and muttered ceaselessly. It was then he realised that Hélène had betrayed him and that the Germans must know about Madame and the old man, and he grew sick with worrying about what the Germans would do to them and to Lucille.

In Fighter Command Headquarters in England next morning the telephone rang in the office of Sholto Douglas. He picked it up and recognised the voice of Winston Churchill saying : " Douglas ! "

" Yes, sir."

" I see from the newspapers you've been fraternising with the enemy, dropping a leg to a captured pilot."

" Well, sir," Sholto Douglas said, " you may call it fraternising, but we managed to shoot down eleven of the enemy."

There was a grunt, and then a click as the phone was hung up.

In St. Omer two guards were carrying Bader downstairs

to an ambulance. Another carried his legs wrapped in a blanket. He gathered as the ambulance jolted along that they were going to Brussels for a train to Germany. It was the most depressing journey he had ever known. He worried about the Hiècques and Lucille and wondered why the Germans looked so square-headed and stupid.

At last Brussels. An officer strutted in front, the two guards carried him and a third brought up the rear with the legs. People turned and stared as they bore him across a square into the railway station.

Thank God the carriage seats were soft. Sourly he watched the officer put his legs up on the rack. The train jolted off and clicketty-clicked through the rain. They passed Liège and then were in Germany.

They came to Frankfurt at midnight and carried Bader to a car, which drove for half an hour to Dulag Luft, the reception and interrogation centre for all Air Force prisoners. Two Luftwaffe men carried him into a stone building, down a corridor and dumped him on a wooden bunk in a little cell.

Tired, he slept well. About eight o'clock in the morning a dapper little man in a grey civilian suit came in, saying brightly : " Good morning." Sonderfuehrer Eberhardt spoke perfect English and was too friendly. He handed Bader a form to fill in, the usual fake form with the red cross at the top that the Germans always used. Bader looked down the headings :

" What base did you fly from ?

" No. of squadron ?

" What type of aeroplane ? " and so on.

He scrawled his name, rank and number on it and handed it back.

" If you will fill in the rest," Eberhardt suggested

winningly, " it will help the Red Cross inform your relatives and forward your letters."

" That's all you're getting," Bader said. " I'm not half-witted. Now if you don't mind, I'd like a bath, a shave and my legs."

Eberhardt went out, saying he would call the Kommandant.

A tall man of about forty-five came in and said : " Oh, good morning, Wing Commander. I am the Kommandant. My name is Rumpel. For you the war is over but we'll make you as comfortable as we can. I was a fighter pilot myself in the last war."

Bader answered shortly : " We're enemies and that can't be overlooked."

" Well, we'll try anyhow," Rumpel said. " We're amused at your call sign. It's Dogsbody, isn't it ? "

" If you know, why ask me ? "

Rumpel probed on, asking questions about aircraft. " We know you're having a lot of trouble with the Rolls Royce Vulture engine."

" If you know," Bader repeated, " why ask me ? "

" We didn't want to fight this war," Rumpel went on, " but the Poles were determined to have Berlin."

" Eighty million Germans scared of thirty million Poles," Bader growled.

" Why did you attack Russia then ? " he demanded.

" We had to have the oil. What makes us sorry . . . it seems such a shame . . . but we Germans and British never seem to fight on the same side. . . . We know you call us Jerries, but . . ."

" No we don't," Bader snapped. " We call you Huns ! "

The charm fled from Rumpel and he stalked out.

Bader yelled after him : " Send me my legs and some tea, damn you."

He was surprised a few minutes later when a Luftwaffe orderly came in carrying his legs (including the new one), some soap and a towel, and took him along to the bathroom. When he got back he found a tray of English tea with milk and sugar, and some bread and butter and jam.

Usually one did a week or so "solitary" in a cell being softened up for questioning before going to the barbed-wire transit cage to await "purging" to a permanent prison camp. Rumpel must have decided Bader was an improbable prospect because an hour after breakfast they took him out of the cell and thrust him into the cage.

The cage was not inspiring : three drab wooden barrack huts on a patch of trodden earth eighty yards square, fenced by double thickets of barbed wire eight feet high and buttressed at each corner by · stilt-legged sentry boxes leaning over the wire with watchful eyes, searchlights and machine-guns. The sight of the gates closing him in was mellowed by the welcome from a few score grounded exiles of his own kind who clustered round, making him feel, if not at home, at least among "chums." From the Red Cross store they gave him a toothbrush, razor and some aircraftman's clothes. Then quite a good meal—the cage had plenty of Red Cross parcels.

A Fleet Air Arm lieutenant called David Lubbock took him to his room, a wooden box with a dusty floor and double-decker bunks round the walls, each with paper palliasse stuffed with wood shavings and two grey blankets. There he found Pete Gardner, a young fighter pilot with eighteen victories, and other kindred spirits, and they gossiped for some time. He felt much better and asked if they knew Harry Day, who was a prisoner somewhere.

"Do we not," said Gardner. "He was here till a few days ago, but he escaped through a tunnel with seventeen others."

Apparently they had all been caught and sent to a permanent camp somewhere else.

At the mention of escape, Bader was on fire, wanting to know all about it. Quite a short tunnel, Lubbock said, because the huts were near the wire. They burrowed from under a bed, and the night they went everyone else kicked up a racket to cover the noise.

"If they could do it," Bader demanded, "why can't we?"

A day or so later they started carving a hole in the floor under a bunk in an end room of the middle hut, and soon they were burrowing into the dark earth under the hut. Bader was no good for the digging; he acted as stooge, watching for Germans outside the window while the others gouged out the dirt.

Day by day, foot by foot, the tunnel lengthened. After a fortnight, when they thought they were nearly under the wire, Eberhardt came one day into the cage and sought Bader.

"Herr Wing Commander," he said, "you must be ready to leave to-morrow morning. You are being taken to Brussels to appear before a court-martial."

Outraged equally by the court-martial and the thought of missing the tunnel, he told the others, but cooled off when one of them, the Irish Paddy Byrne, gave him a bit of paper with a name and a Brussels address on it.

"Wonderful chance to crack off," said the crafty Byrne. "If you can duck the guards and get to these people, they'll hide you and pass you on to the escape chain."

Gratified, Bader looked forward eagerly to Brussels.

This time in the train they let him keep his legs, but a blond young Sonderfuehrer and two helmeted soldiers never left his side.

In Brussels they put him in a car and drove him through

the streets—he hoped, towards a ground-floor room in a lonely house. The car turned through a dirty stone arch and soon they were standing in a cold stone hall.

He said angrily: "This is a civilian gaol. I'm not staying here."

"Oh, but you must, Wing Commander."

"But I damn' well won't."

"Oh, please, please. You *must*, Wing Commander, because it would be very embarrassing to me."

"I won't. I am an officer prisoner of war and you can't put me in a criminal prison. I demand to see the general in charge of this district. Go and get the clot."

Despairingly, the Sonderfuehrer turned and talked to the stolid Army Feldwebel who seemed to be the gaol reception clerk. He turned back to Bader. "The Feldwebel says that perhaps if we could take you along and show you your room you might be willing to stay."

There was not much option really. Sooner or later, they would force him, which would be humiliating, and perhaps they would take his legs too.

Stumping at a leisurely pace, he went with them through the barred gate and along the passage, passing cell doors with peep-holes in them. At one they stopped and pulled the door open. He looked into a tiny white-washed cell so narrow you could touch both walls by putting your arms out. A narrow bed nearly filled one side, and high up was a little barred window.

He snorted: "I'm damned if I'm going in there!"

"Oh, but *please*, Wing Commander," begged the Sonderfuehrer.

"No!"

"But you *must*. I will be shot if you escape."

Bader eyed him amiably. "Will you really?"

"We will give you a servant here."

" What else ? "

" We will leave the door open."

(That didn't mean much—the iron door at the end of the corridor would still be firmly locked.)

" I want a table, too. With a cloth. And tea."

" Yes, Wing Commander. Now will you please go in."

" No. Bring me the servant and table first."

The Feldwebel went off and after a while came back with a little man in a white coat who carried a small table. Good show, a Belgian, Bader thought.

He stalked into the cell and the servant followed and put down the table. They left the door open and re-treated.

Alone at last, he moved quickly and shoved the table under the high window, then grabbed the stool, planted it on the table and climbed up till he was standing precariously on the stool. Hands clutching the bars, he tried to pull himself up the extra few inches to see out : he got his eyes up to the bars but the thick wall stuck out beyond the bars and he could not quite see the ground that he was sure was just below. Using all the strength in his thick hands and wrists, he began shaking the bars violently, trying to loosen them.

A respectful cough sounded behind, and he swung and saw the servant standing looking impassively up.

" *Vous êtes Belge ?* " Bader asked eagerly.

" *Nein,*" said the little man, unwinking. " *Ich bin Deutsch.*"

Deflated, Bader started climbing down. Impassively the servant helped him, removed the stool, put a tray of tea on the table, and glided out on rubber-soled shoes.

About ten in the morning the Sonderfuehrer and guards drove him to a large house and led him into a big room.

This was it ! At one end was a long table and sitting behind it six solemn officers.

Sitting on chairs at the other end he noticed the doctor and some soldiers and nurses from the St. Omer hospital. He grinned at them and said " Hallo " but they only eyed him sourly. A young Luftwaffe officer motioned him to a lonely chair in front of the table, saying : " Will you please sit down ? "

" No, I won't," he answered.

The judges leaned towards each other and muttered among themselves. A hatchet-faced general in the middle spoke to the Luftwaffe officer who acted as interpreter, and the officer turned to Bader : " Will you swear to tell the truth ? "

" No," he answered. " Certainly not."

The officer turned nervously and spoke to the judges, and the bald general's eyebrows shot up.

The officer turned back. " The Herr General wishes to know why you will not tell the truth."

Bader said : " Well, if you're going to ask me questions about the French I will obviously lie."

Another muttered conference. The interpreter seemed to have trouble translating the replies politely. He turned again to Bader. " The Herr General says that the French have already been punished."

(" God," he thought. " What have they done to them ! ")

" What the Herr General wishes to know is whether you think the hospital staff were careless when you escaped ? "

It suddenly dawned on Bader that it was not he who was being court-martialled. He said : " Look, who is being court-martialled here ? "

The interpreter looked surprised. " Why, the hospital staff, of course."

After that it was easy. He turned on the charm and explained that it was not reasonable to punish the hospital chaps because they couldn't guess he was going to climb out of the window. They had been very correct, posted a guard at his door and taken all proper precautions.

When he had finished and the Sonderfuehrer took him out, the hospital staff beamed at him. Thereafter the guards never left his side and there was no chance of bolting.

Back at Dulag, the first thing he asked was : " How's the tunnel getting on ? "

Lubbock said it was plodding along nicely.

Hands in pockets, Bader was idly leaning in a doorway three days later when a Luftwaffe captain called Muller passed. Bader kept his hands in his pockets and his pipe in his mouth. Muller stopped, turned and said : " Ving Commander Bader, you should salute me."

" Why ? "

" All prisoners of war should salute German officers."

Bader said shortly : " The Geneva Convention says I have to salute enemy officers of equal or senior rank. You're only a captain."

Half an hour later an orderly came in and told him to be ready to leave Dulag Luft.

CHAPTER TWENTY-FIVE

PRISON CAMP

FOR TWO days he sat glowering on the hard boards of a third-class train that travelled to Lübeck. Off-loading him there into a farm wagon they trundled him across bleak flats to the lonely barbed-wire compound of Oflag VIB, where they turned him loose among some 400 half-starved British officers behind the wire.

There the real misery started. Lübeck camp received no Red Cross parcels and was ruled by a gaunt, cropped Kommandant who had achieved fame by saying that the Geneva Convention had been drawn up by a lot of old women and he had no intention of observing it.

A few of the inmates were R.A.F. (most were Army), but he knew none of them. The huts were much the same as the ramshackle wooden affairs at Dulag Luft and there seemed nothing to do except talk and think about when the next meal was coming. An entire day's food consisted of three slices of black bread with a scrape of margarine, a couple of potatoes and some soup. Now and then there was *Blutwurst* (blood sausage).

Two days after Bader arrived there Lubbock and Pete Gardner walked dolorously in.

" What happened to the tunnel ? " Bader demanded.

They looked disgusted and said that just after he had left, a posse of guards had trooped into the cage, gone straight to the trap-door under the bed and wrecked everything.

In the next dreary month Bader adjusted to the new life. As years before he had accepted the loss of his legs so he accepted now the loss of freedom, heartened by the thought this time that there was hope of a cure—escape. He talked about it a lot with men who had been a year or more behind the wire, absorbing what lore they had gathered, and learning that getting out was only half the battle. The other half lay in getting beyond the reach of the Germans, and that was the harder half.

Early in October the Germans bundled the whole camp into cattle trucks for transport to a new cage at Warburg, near Cassel, where they were concentrating all British officer prisoners. It lifted the tedium and gave hope of better conditions. Also, there were ways of bolting from locked cattle-trucks. During the night some of the Air Force officers sawed a hole in the floor of a truck with a jagged knife and during a brief halt several dropped out of it and ran into the darkness.

Warburg was a huge cage a quarter of a mile square holding 3,000 men in thirty of the same huts in the same dirt and squalor. But Warburg had Red Cross parcels, enough to give each man a good meal a day as well as the German food.

But confinement was a growing ordeal. Others could let off steam tunnelling for escape, by playing rugger, or by walking round the beaten circuit. Not Bader. The stumps had not taken kindly to captivity, having shrunken a little with hunger. They chafed more easily and there was little powder and no Elastoplast.

At last a letter from Thelma. She did not say much about the wing, of course, except that he was still badly missed, but she had had a letter from Woodhall which said : " I am delighted to be able to tell you that Douglas has been awarded a Bar to his D.F.C."

Warburg had an escape committee headed by a tank major and Bader talked earnestly with them for hours. Unlike others he had little chance of walking out of the gates in disguise; his lurching roll was too familiar.

One outlet still remained—"Goon-baiting."[1] With exuberance he tersely provoked all Germans except "Gremlin George," the Lageroffizier,[2] who had been a prisoner in the last war and was sympathetic because he understood.

His chief butt was Hauptmann Harger, a large, red-faced man with whom he had violent brushes which culminated in a day when Bader refused to stand out in the snow for half an hour on *appell*.[3] Harger found him in his room and ordered him out and in a shouting match Bader refused to budge, saying: "My feet would get cold in the snow. If you want to count me, come to my room and do it."

Harger shouted: "You . . . vill . . . go . . . on . . . *appell*," drew his pistol and levelled it.

The antennæ warned that the time had come and Bader suddenly turned on the glowing good-will and beamed. "Well, of *course* I'll go on *appell* if you really want me to." He picked up a stool and stumped off to plant it on the snow and sit among his squad, leaving Harger seething.

Bader had found a new game, and on more than one occasion after that he goaded his captors into drawing their pistols and then disarmed them by pricking the strained bladder of their ire with maddening charm.

Around Christmas time Lubbock and Gardner came to him, and said: "Look, we've got an idea for escape. Would you like to come with us?"

[1] To prisoners, Germans were always "Goons." It was a satisfying name.
[2] Officer in charge of the compound.
[3] Roll call by count.

Bader said : " I'm in."

Lubbock explained the plot. Just outside the barbed-wire gate was a clothing store hut where prisoners were taken under guard to draw kit. Gardner, a born lock-breaker, had discovered how to open a spare room in the hut and the idea was for the three of them, together with a Commando captain, Keith Smith, to go on a clothing parade, lock themselves in the empty room till darkness, then climb out of the window, walk up a lighted road past some German huts and then melt into the shadows beyond. Just down the road was Doessel railway station where they could catch a train down into occupied France and contact the Underground. The escape committee had promised them several hundred smuggled marks, maps, a compass and forged passes.

Everyone said they were mad to try in winter but on 9th January, when thin snow carpeted the frosty ground, they marched through the gate with a clothing parade to the hut. Someone started a loud-voiced diversion and under its cover Gardener picked the lock and the four crowded into the room.

Darkness fell early and the wait was long and cold. About eight o'clock they heard a clatter of tins by the wire, caused by an unruly flight lieutenant, Peter Tunstall, giving the signal and creating another diversion. All the searchlights obligingly turned towards the noise and Gardner quietly opened the spare room window. Smith, a baldish six-footer, slipped out first and walked up the lighted path, followed by Lubbock and Bader and then Gardner.

Smith reached the shadows but the others were about fifteen yards short when a German soldier ran out of one of the huts right in front of them. He looked with shocked surprise at the three walking in British greatcoats and started bellowing for help. Germans came pouring out of huts for yards around and the three were seized by a jabbering crowd. Smith had vanished.

They started hustling the three over to the guardroom and one of the Germans, not realising Bader had artificial legs, thumped him on the toe with a rifle butt.

In the guardroom the Hauptmann security officer, a Party member, demanded to know how they had escaped, and Bader said flippantly that they had walked through the wire.

" Did you ? " replied the Hauptmann, unamused. " Well, now you can try walking through the bars because you are going into the cells."

He went away to make arrangements and came back slightly flushed. Apparently the cells were already full and there was a waiting list. They would have to go back to the compound and await their turn.

Smith was back in five days, having nearly frozen to death in a cattle truck.

It was about a month before the three were taken across to the wooden cooler[1] for their ten days' solitary. The cells were about as wide as one's outstretched arms, but there were books and Red Cross food and prisoners of the rank of major and above were allowed to smoke. About the seventh night, after the guard had locked up and gone, Bader was lying on his bunk reading when the door opened. He looked up and was startled to see the face of Gardner.

" Hallo," Gardner grinned, holding up a piece of wire, " I've found out how to open these doors."

Delighted, Bader got up and joined him in the corridor, and they unlocked Lubbock's cell. The three of them cautiously explored the place, but no Germans were about and only a couple of flimsy doors lay between them and

[1] Cell block.

freedom. Bader suggested they make a break for it then and there, but wiser voices prevailed. Snow still lay on the ground, and they had no food, maps, compass or money.

" I know," said Bader, " let's finish our time here and wait for the good weather. Then we can all kick that rat Harger in the tail and get sent back. We can smuggle some food and maps in and then make the break."

Brilliant, they all thought. The " Goons " would never expect an escape from the cooler.

Three days later they were released and immediately registered the scheme with the escape committee. The date was set for May.

They were getting ready for it when a rumour buzzed round that some Air Force officers were being moved to a new camp, Stalag Luft III, at Sagan, between Berlin and Breslau. That evening Germans confirmed it and they were shepherding an enraged Bader and fifty others on to the train.

Stalag Luft III was a little cage of six huts for officers and another one next door for N.C.O.s, all on barren Silesian sand, hedged from the world by spindly pine trees. As they walked in, a lean figure walked up to Douglas with outstretched hand and the wry, twisted smile he so well remembered.

" Hallo, Douglas," said Harry Day. " I thought you'd catch up some day."

Behind him appeared Bob Tuck, still debonair in silk scarf.

Being among old chums helped soothe him a little. The Warburg contingent took over one of the huts and Day and the compound " Big X,"[1] Jimmy Buckley, came over to talk escape.

[1] Escape Committees were becoming known as the " X Organisation " and the leaders were known as " Big X." It was for security, not for drama.

Almost before people in the hut had unpacked they had started tunnelling under a stove in the room opposite Bader. Other tunnels were already under way in the compound, but it was slow work because six inches under the grey topsoil lay bright yellow sand which came up in bucket-loads and was a devil to hide from German eyes. Also, Stabsfeldwebel Glemnitz, the leathery-faced chief German ferret,[1] was a shrewd man who had microphones buried round the wire so that tunnels had to be about thirty feet deep.

There was nothing Bader could do in the tunnels; he could only " stooge " outside as a sentry, feeling rather futile. Then Glemnitz found two of the tunnels, including the one in Bader's hut.

Inevitably it inflamed his " Goon-baiting," and his scores of admirers followed his example.

Camp opinion divided; there were the turbulent rebels devoted to Bader who believed in riling the Germans at every chance and others, the wise cool heads, who wanted a judicial amount of Goon-baiting mixed with enough co-operation to ensure peace for escape work.

Now and then a German got him chatting in his room and on those occasions Bader was perfectly charming. But his pride was touchy. One day he was talking quite pleasantly with his arms folded to the Kommandant, Oberst Von Lindeiner, when the mild Lageroffizier, Hauptmann Pieber, came up, and said: " Wing Commander, you should stand at attention when you speak to the Kommandant."

Bader turned and snapped: " When I want you to teach me manners, I'll ask you. Until then, shut up ! "

Von Lindeiner was an erect, elderly soldier of the old

---

[1] Ferrets were the blue-overalled German security guards who ceaselessly snooped round the compounds with torches and probes (for locating tunnels).

school, but, as the baiting campaign worsened, inevitably the reprisals started and the compound lost privileges such as staying outside the huts after dusk, keeping Red Cross tins and others.

Something had to happen.

Pieber came in one day with Glemnitz and found him by the wire.

" Herr Wing Commander, you are leaving the camp. You must be ready to go in the morning."

" Where am I going ? " Bader demanded.

Pieber was vague. " We are taking you somewhere you will be more comfortable."

Bader grunted. " Well, I'd rather live in a pigsty with my friends than in a palace alone. I'm not going."

" The Kommandant says you must go."

" You take me to the Kommandant."

" He will see you on the way out to-morrow."

" No, he damn' well won't. Not unless he drags me out."

Glemnitz angrily snapped an order and a guard cocked his rifle and aimed at Bader's chest. Abruptly the atmosphere was electric as the word to fire trembled on the German's lips and Bader knew he had gone too far. This time he would not give way but glared, defiant and stubborn. The seconds dragged and then Pieber snapped the tension, telling the guard to lower his rifle. He added : " We will see about this. You will go."

That evening the camp buzzed with crisis. Bader said he was not going and would jump into the compound firepool, throw his legs out and defy the Germans to get him. Somehow the Germans heard and knew they would be ridiculed floundering about in a pool after a legless man. What could they do ? Von Lindeiner was too humane to shoot him in cold blood. In any case, that would lose the

Germans far more than dignity throughout the world. They were nonplussed by a man who should have been in a wheel-chair, but even as a disarmed prisoner was an unmanageable enemy.

Towards evening, a company of guards in battle-order marched out of the Kommandantur[1] towards the barbed wire, fifty-seven, with rifles and fixed bayonets. Striding with them was Von Lindeiner, accompanied by nearly all his officers. Prisoners came running up to mass behind the wire. The Germans crashed to a halt outside. Bader stayed in his room. The new S.B.O., Group Captain Massey, went to the gate and talked to the Kommandant while an ominous hush hung over the place.

[1] German administrative compound.

CHAPTER TWENTY-SIX

OUT AGAIN—IN AGAIN

MASSEY WENT back to Bader. "There's one thing we might consider," he said. "It only needs a spark to start an incident and someone may be shot."

After that there was only one thing to do. The watchers by the wire saw the legless man come out of his room and stump down the dusty path between the huts. In silence he went up to the gate, passed through and looked around like a man about to call a taxi, then strolled slowly along the ranks of the German squad.

Bader grinned at the squad and passed on. Von Lindeiner made an impatient gesture and followed with his officers. The tension burst like a bubble and suddenly there was something ludicrous about the sixty armed men who had come to quell a lone and legless man.

They put Bader in a train and Glemnitz climbed into the compartment as escort. The prisoner turned on his charm and soon the two were chatting amiably.

In an hour or so the train stopped at a little halt. Glemnitz motioned him out and they walked a mile along a dusty road to an enormous area of barbed-wire cages. It was Stalag VIIIB—Lamsdorf—where over 20,000 soldiers were imprisoned. Bader was put in a room in Sick Quarters, a hut in a separate cage near the main gate, with another new arrival, John Palmer, a rear-gunner flight lieutenant who needed special treatment for a damaged foot.

Through a window a day or so later they watched a party of soldier prisoners march down the road from the big compound and out of the main gate. Bader turned to Duncan, one of the R.A.M.C. doctors, and asked where they were going.

"Oh, only a working party," Duncan said. "Off to some town a few miles away."

"Mightn't be too hard to escape from one of those."

"Hard?" said Duncan. "It's a piece of cake."

"Could *we* get on to one of those parties?"

"Not legally," Duncan said. "But I know of someone who might help."

That afternoon he presented three sergeants of the Lamsdorf "X Committee," and they started talking escape. First, Bader wanted to know, could he and Palmer get out on a working party?

The leader, eyeing him, said: "You'll excuse me saying so, sir, but you might look a bit obvious going out. Still, I think we could fix something."

A blinding thought struck Bader like a revelation. Leaning forward, eyes alight, he asked: "Sergeant, do these working parties ever go out to aerodromes?"

In his mind was a vision of the map with Sweden only 350 miles away. Stealing an aeroplane was the God-sent answer. Let the Germans take him to one. And then . . . No days of stumbling among the enemy, hopelessly conspicuous, waiting for the end. No trains with police checks or weary miles to walk. No food or langague problems. Just sneak in and take off and—oh, the sweet triumph of landing on friendly ground with a piece of expensive loot and asking the Ambassador for a ticket home!

"Sometimes, sir," said the sergeant. "I see what you mean. Just leave it to us, sir."

Three weeks passed. The hospital was comfortable enough but boring. From the window Bader and Palmer saw many working parties straggle out of the big cage bound for the outside world. But before the main gate opened they were all stripped and searched in a hut next to the hospital. That was the catch. With his legs he would never pass a search stripped. Moodily he used to watch other prisoners sweeping the road right up to the main gates, and an idea began to dawn. He told the sergeant " Big X," who grinned approvingly.

The sergeant arrived one night with two tough-looking sergeant pilots—an Australian, Keith Chisholm, and an Englishman, Hickman.

" Now, look, sir," the army sergeant said, " there's a light working party going out to an aerodrome near Gleiwitz, up on the German-Polish border. Just the sort of thing you want, simple stuff like cutting grass and so on. If you and Mr. Palmer would like to join . . ."

Bader and Palmer said that they would.

The sergeant indicated the two sergeant-pilots. " These two chaps are going and a Palestinian who is a Polish-Jew and speaks fluent Polish. They're all going to escape into Poland and they've all got false identities. We'll fix you up with the same."

Two days later he smuggled brooms and army battle-dress to them and that night Palmer shaved his moustache off.

The morning was warm and they lounged on the front step of the hut, trying to look casual. The working party marched out of the big cage and the escort nudged them into the next door hut to be searched. Bader and Palmer grabbed their brooms, sauntered into the road and started sweeping. One by one the working party emerged from the hut and gathered in a loose knot by the verge. Bader and Palmer swept their way into them. The last man out of the hut dropped his kit which scattered over the ground. The guards looked and laughed. Bader and Palmer handed their brooms to two of the working party who swept nonchalantly on through the others, back towards the big cage. The guards yelled "Komm! Komm!" and the party marched up to the main gate. The escort showed passes, an Unteroffizier counted heads, swung open the gates and they walked through, breaking down the pace to a casual amble and clustering round the limping Private Fenton, alias Wing Commander Bader.

Into a train then at the little wayside halt, and as they rattled and swayed across the country for three hours he hugged the thought that the Germans were taking him to an aeroplane.

On a blazing August afternoon they came to the industrial town of Gleiwitz and started the two-mile uphill walk to the airfield. Within two minutes he was sweating freely and that started his leg chafing. A lanky New Zealand private called Lofty got alongside and helped him along.

The leg was hurting him like that dreadful night in St. Omer and Lofty, pouring with sweat himself, was almost lifting and carrying him. Even so Bader was nearly finished when they came to two huts in a tiny barbed-wire cage isolated on the fringe of what looked like a military camp. No signs of an airfield anywhere. Other prisoners came out to greet them as he staggered through the gate, and sagging with fatigue he asked one of them: "Where's the aerodrome?"

The soldier nodded his head across a rise in the ground. "'Bout a mile over there, mate."

In disappointment, pain and exhaustion he found a room with Palmer, Chisholm, and the other two.

An hour later, reviving fast, he said to Palmer : " We'll go with the other three when they nip off into Poland. If we can find some partisans we might get a wireless message back to England and maybe they'll send an aircraft over one night to pick us up."

A British sergeant had been in the cage some time as camp leader and he came into Bader's room. " We won't let the others know who you are, sir," he said. " It's safer that way. But it won't be so easy to hide it from the Germans. It's hard manual labour here, moving bricks, digging foundations, filling trucks and things like that."

Bader knew his limitations well enough. The work would be physically impossible.

" I know," said the sergeant, with joyful inspiration ; " you can be lavatory man."

Bader stared at him.

" One chap's allowed to stay behind to clean the latrines and huts," the sergeant explained. " You can be him. We'll say you've been shot in the knee and can't walk properly."

Bader started laughing. How the mighty are fallen. " All right," he said.

Chisholm had been walking round spying out the land and came back to report. The wire was only a single fence instead of a double and just outside it at the back of the cage was a field of high corn. There was a wash-house window only a few feet from the wire and it would be easy at night to crawl out of the window and snake through the wire into the corn—except that two guards kept patrolling the cage.

During breakfast next morning the Palestinian went out and started talking to one of the guards through the wire. He came back very excited. " He is a Pole, that guard," he said. " Several of the guard company are Poles, forced into uniform by the Germans. He says they will help us. A Polish guard at night will keep the German guard talking on the other side of the compound while we get out."

Bader said: " To-night ! "

" No. Not to-night. Two Poles are on guard and it would look suspicious."

" To-morrow ? "

" No. There are two Germans on. But the night after will be a German and a Pole."

This was Monday. They set the date for Wednesday.

Germans arrived shouting: " Raus ! Raus ! " to muster the day's working party and as Bader watched them march out a grinning Cockney corporal thrust a bucket and mop into his hands. " 'Ere y'are, Mum," he said. " Get cracking."

He quite enjoyed himself sloshing out the latrines, not caring if he got his feet wet. The only thing that bothered him was whether the Germans would follow the trail from Lamsdorf before Wednesday night.

At evening the workers came back and he asked Palmer, " Did you see any aeroplanes ? "

" Didn't even see the aerodrome," Palmer said.

The next day passed quietly enough. Same fears. Same routine. At sunset the Palestinian talked to the Polish guard who was going off duty and learned that the lone Pole who would be " on " with a German the following night would do what they wanted.

Morning dawned, warm and sunny, perfect weather for escaping, but the day dragged interminably. At last about five-thirty the working party came back and the five rested in their room with the familiar zero-hour feeling fluttering in their stomachs.

At six o'clock boots trampled in the wooden corridor

and a German voice shouted: "Efferybody on parade! Efferybody on parade!"

Wondering what it was all about, the prisoners got to their feet and shambled out. Raggedly they assembled on the trodden ground by the gate, where a Feldwebel stood watching and as they settled down he shouted: "Everybody will take their trousers down."

The order seemed to hit Bader in the pit of the stomach. He looked across at the camp leader who looked back and muttered: "Hold tight, sir. I'll order the men to refuse."

"And get yourself shot," Bader said wryly.

He swung round but yards of open space separated him from the possible shelter of the hut. No escape at all. The mind buzzed furiously and he knew he could not stand the indignity. Heaving himself forward he stumped up to the Feldwebel and said: "I think I'm the chap you're looking for."

The Feldwebel stared as though he could not believe it and at that moment a Hauptmann from Lamsdorf and six guards tramped through the gate. The Hauptmann saw Bader, recognised him and his eyes lit up. "Ah, Ving Commander, I am *delighted* to see you again."

He was very friendly, even when he added: "Now perhaps Mr. Palmer vould come forward."

"Good Lord," said Bader. "Has Johnny Palmer escaped too?"

"No more troubles, please, Ving Commander," the Hauptmann said tolerantly. "Otherwise we take you all back to Lamsdorf to check up."

It struck him instantly that that would wreck the escape plans of the other three.[1] A moment's furious

[1] That night the other three escaped as planned and soon made contact with Polish partisans. Later the Germans caught the Palestinian and Hickman and shot them. Chisholm, after two years of extraordinary adventures fighting with the Poles (including a gallant part in the deadly uprising in Warsaw), got back to England and was awarded the Military Medal.

thought. No way out. He turned to the men and called:
" Come on, Johnny."

Palmer shuffled out of the ranks, the guards closed round
and the two were led away.

The trip back to Lamsdorf was glum, though the
Germans were friendly enough right up to the time they
prodded them into the Lamsdorf guardroom and the
Kommandant came in. Or rather, the Kommandant swept
in like a tornado, in a towering anger. He stood in front
of them, the tirade pouring out till little flecks of foam
flew off his lips. It went on and on, and on, and the
interpreter standing beside him had no chance of getting
in a word. Palmer still had a cigarette in his mouth and
as the Kommandant shouted he drew on it, puffed smoke
just past the Kommandant's cheek, turned to Bader, and
said: " D'you know, I haven't the faintest idea what this
fellow's saying."

Bader started to giggle and the Kommandant crimsoned.
His voice rose in explosive fury. At last he stopped to
draw breath, and the interpreter stepped forward and spoke
a stern summary:

" The Kommandant says you have both disgraced the
honour of an officer by dressing yourself up as common
soldiers and that you have caused a great deal of
trouble."

Bader said: " Well, will you tell the Kommandant
that it's my job to cause him trouble."

The interpreter was tactless enough to do so and the
Kommandant turned a rich red and loosed off another
tirade until they thought he was going to have an apoplectic
fit.

Soon they were in familiar surroundings. An officer
pulled open a cell door and Bader said: " Just a minute.

I'm not going in there. These are common soldiers' cells."

The German security officer said politely: "Ve do not usually haf officer prisoners at Lamsdorf und therefore ve do not haf officers' cells."

"I can't help that," Bader said. "If I'm to have a cell I demand an officer's cell."

"Look, Ving Commander," the German said wearily, "ve haf had a lot of troubles with you an vith the Kommandant. He vus going to take your legs, but I haf talked to him and he has cooled down."

"I can't help that either. Anyway, I demand a spring bed, not that damned plank."

"Please go in, Ving Commander, und ve vill deal vith it to-morrow."

"No, I won't. I want a spring bed, I want a table, I want proper food and a proper chair."

The German raised his eyes to the ceiling, muttering: "*Mein Gott!*" He said with resignation: "Vait here, Ving Commander. I go and get, not, I think, for your sake, the Kommandant, but the second in command."

Soon a dapper German major came in and said heartily: "I'm sorry about this, Wing Commander. You can have a spring bed, a chair and a table, proper food and a book to read and I'll send you a servant."

"Good," Bader said. "I'll wait outside the cell till you get them."

Soon they brought spring mattress, table and chair, and he went in and the cell door locked.

Soon there came a knocking on it and he yelled: "Come in." He heard the bolts being withdrawn, the door opened and in the frame, filling it, was the rotund figure of a young man with a round, red face and glasses. He was in British battledress and said in a strong Scots accent: "Guid afternoon, sir. My name is Ross. I've been detailed to look after-r you. I've br-rought you some tea."

In the morning he and Palmer were taken before the Kommandant who sentenced each to ten days' solitary. Bader again tried the gambit about the incorrectness of putting an officer in a soldiers' cell block and the Kommandant stiffly apologised. He did not have the correct cells so they would have to make do as they were.

The days in the cell seemed interminable. The only bright factor was Ross, who was loyal, willing and unselfish, bringing tea and gossip and spreading a respectful but companionable cheerfulness.

On the ninth day the cell door opened and the Kommandant appeared. Bader got up from his bunk and they exchanged polite salutes. The Kommandant said: " I have some good news for you, Wing Commander. To-morrow you go to an *Offizierlager*."[1]

" Oh," Bader was interested. " Whereabouts, Herr Oberst ? "

" The Offizierlager IVC. at Kolditz."

Bader knew that one.

" Oh, you mean the *Straflager* ? "[2]

The Kommandant looked shocked. " *Nein, nein, Herr Oberstleutnant, Der Sonderlager.*"[3]

Bader started to laugh and then the Kommandant started laughing. Both knew well enough that Kolditz Castle, last stop for the naughty boys, was supposed to be escape proof.

Next day he made one last effort to delay things by demanding an officer of equal rank as escort but the Kommandant said curtly that the only such officer available was himself, and he was the one who was *not* going to

[1] Officers' Camp.
[2] Punishment Camp.
[3] Special Camp.

235

Kolditz. It was an elderly Hauptmann who got into the train with him.

The journey was long and dreary. By the time they got to Kolditz it was dark and the station was blacked out. Then, struggling out of the gloom into the road, Bader looked up and got his first glimpse of the future. The fortress towered over the village, seeming to float in floodlight, enchantingly beautiful like a fairy castle. They moved off along a cobbled road which soon rose so steeply that Ross had to put out his hand and pull him along. He was exhausted when they came to the foot of the great wall that reared above, harsh and scarred in the glare of the floodlamps, giving no inch of cover to any would-be escaper. They trod across a drawbridge over a deep moat into the cavern of a stone archway. Heavy doors closed behind. Fortress guards led them across a courtyard, through a tunnel, along a cobbled path, through another gloomy archway into a smaller courtyard hemmed inside towering walls deep in the bowels of the castle, through a door, up stone steps. A German flung a door open and Bader looked into a small stone cell. He thought : " Oh, God. Is this how we live ? Is this the punishment camp ? "

CHAPTER TWENTY-SEVEN

PUNISHMENT CAMP

As a guard motioned him in, a voice behind hailed:
"Douglas! There you are!"

He swung round. Geoffrey Stephenson was grinning
by the steps.

They were shaking hands, grinning and talking. As
a German started to separate them Bader nodded at the
cell. "Is this how we live here?"

"Good God, no," Stephenson said. "You'll be out
with us to-morrow."

He was hustled away and Bader walked docilely into
the cell and the door clanged behind.

In the morning they took him out, photographed,
finger-printed and searched him, and handed him over to
the hovering Stephenson, who took him upstairs into a
large room with a window overlooking the inner courtyard.

"Your home," Stephenson announced. "Hope you
like it."

He shared it with three others, army officers, one of
whom he already knew, George Young, who had been
S.B.O. at Lübeck. The four single bunks had shelves
over them; there were some wicker chairs and even a
dirty brown wallpaper.

Within two days Bader had his first brush with the
Germans, who then held two *appells* a day. He told the
Lageroffizier, Hauptmann Püpcke, that he was damned
if he was going to spend his days lurching up and down

the stairs and was so determined that Püpcke finally said he could appear at the window till he was seen and counted.

" He had a long talk with George Young and a resolute-looking tank captain, Dick Howe, who ran the " X Committee." Howe, a brilliant escape organiser, pointed out that Kolditz was not like an ordinary camp. Every man was an escape fiend and all sorts of schemes were constantly going on.

Plenty of time for thinking ! The days started early with *appell* and a slice of black bread. Then one could sit and look out of a window or smoke and read, or sit, or walk round the little courtyard like an animal in a zoo. With escape hopes frustrated again he returned like an addict to his old sport and the repetitive theme of life at Kolditz was punctuated by Goon-baiting.

Püpcke was not harried much ; though alive, he was still regarded as a good German. The main butts were the security officer, a Hauptmann Eggers, and a little major, the second in command.

For weeks Bader only acknowledged the major's existence by blowing smoke past his cheek when they passed and when the major at last demanded to be saluted Bader pointed out the difference in rank and suggested that if the major liked to wear the Kommandant's uniform into the camp he would salute him.

He was having other trouble with his legs and the Germans escorted him to a village workshop for running repairs. As he wrote to Thelma : " The leg crisis has passed. A little man has riveted a plate over that crack in the knee. You might tell the chaps who made the leg that I dismantled the knee, the brake and the freewheel and greased and reassembled the lot. It is a very well-made job, the freewheel is most ingenious, but I do want another right leg, sweetheart."

But in London the mould of his right thigh had been destroyed by bombing. The firm of J. E. Hanger and Co. (who now supplied his legs) tried all sorts of ingenious methods of making another one (including telegraphed measurements through the Red Cross), but it just could not be done. They were, however, able to get a spare left leg to him through the Red Cross.

Bader began to suffer from the lack of exercise. Even others found it bad enough walking round the uneven cobbles, but to him it was becoming intolerably irksome and bad for the legs. He asked the Germans if they would let him out for walks on parole, and the Germans, to their credit, agreed, even to letting him take another British officer for company.

As companion he chose Peter Dollar, a ruddy-faced lieutenant-colonel with whom he had become friends, and they signed parole chits and were taken to the castle door where they found a German escort of a Feldwebel with a machine-pistol and two soldiers with rifles.

Bader instantly bridled.

" I've given my parole. I'm damned if I'll be insulted by an armed guard."

The Germans answered that *Befehl* was *Befehl*, and Bader snapped : " Well, I refuse to go."

It was an odd scene that followed. The Germans who went to such trouble to lock everyone in Kolditz then insisted that orders said that the Herr Wing Commander was to go for a walk ; therefore the Herr Wing Commander must go for a walk. The Herr Wing Commander said he refused and there was uproar till the tolerant Püpcke arrived and decreed that the escort should leave the machine-pistol and rifles behind. That still left them with pistols in holsters on their belts, but Püpcke explained that they were part of the normal uniform. Would the

Herr Wing Commander mind? No, said the wing commander, he wouldn't mind, and honour and *Befehl* both satisfied, he walked. They went down through the village and sauntered for a couple of soothing hours beside pleasant fields, the escort ambling discreetly behind.

After that he went for walks twice a week, and mellowed slightly towards the Germans, refraining in good-humoured moments from murmuring " *Deutschland kaput!* " as he passed Eggers and the little major.

The invasion was a relaxing influence too, and when the Allies broke out of the German ring in Normandy even the fervent escape activity at Kolditz eased a little.

As Bader's legs had been giving trouble the S.B.O. suggested that he be repatriated, a suggestion which Douglas emphatically refused, declaring that his legs had not been lost in battle and therefore he was no different as a result of captivity. The S.B.O., however, put his name on the list when the repatriation commission arrived, and then when the Germans called prisoners from *appell* to appear before the commission they left out the names of Bader and two very sick men. It was typical of the spirit of Kolditz that all the sick and maimed who were called refused to see the commission until the three dropped names were restored.

Eggers called guards and tried to force them to appear, but the sick men stood fast and an ugly scene developed until the Germans gave way. It was pure principle. Bader himself had no intention of being repatriated, but the other two needed it. When called before the doctors and asked how he felt, he answered: " Absolutely fit."

The puzzled doctors had known plenty of prisoners who exaggerated their ills, but never one who did the reverse. One of them seemed to think that Bader should be repatriated on mental grounds, but he finally convinced them he wanted to stay and stick it out with the others. The other two, however, were passed for repatriation.

One day the Fortresses came. Bader shouted: " *Wo ist die Luftwaffe ?* "[1] and the rest took it up in chorus because there were no German fighters. It was an emotional moment seeing for the first time the Allied Arms reaching out unchallenged across Germany.

But the armies bogged down on the frontiers of a bravely fighting enemy and as the last leaves fell the prisoners guessed miserably that they were in for another winter.

Then the food parcels stopped coming and hunger came back.

[1] " Where is the Luftwaffe ? "

CHAPTER TWENTY-EIGHT

FREEDOM AND VICTORY

ON THE twice-weekly walks Bader and Peter Dollar began trading cigarettes with farmers for wheat, barley and eggs (which Dollar put under his peaked cap) to bring back to the communal food stores.

Little though it was, the food was such a help that Dollar hung a pillow-case round his neck under his great-coat, stuffed it with grain and came back looking suspiciously swollen.

On the long walks from the farms Bader was not able to carry much for a while. He badly wanted to try and carry a pillow-case like Dollar, but impervious as ever to cold he had never worn a greatcoat and the food committee thought it would look suspicious if he suddenly started. It only needed a search at the gate to destroy the whole scheme. Then an ingenious major, Andy Anderson, made him long, thin bags to hang down inside his trousers. Twice a week they went out looking gaunt and came back swollen like Michelin tyre advertisements.

It was the worst winter of all. For Bader it held some of the joy of accomplishment in bringing back food for his friends, but it took a lot out of him. His stumps were getting emaciated, struggling back with the grain bags across the snow and up the slushy, slippery cobbles.

Returning from a food-gathering walk one day, Bader's left foot seemed to disappear as he put it down and he fell forward on his hands. He looked down, surprised, and saw that his leg was broken by the ankle. The whole ankle and foot came away in his hand and he was staggered to see that the metal had corroded right through, apparently from perspiration which had gathered by the bottom of the ankle. There was nothing he could do except drag himself to the side of the road and send a guard back for his spare leg.

The guard came back with the faithful Ross carrying the leg, and unfortunately, a German officer too. As the officer bent down to help him change the leg it suddenly occurred to Bader that as soon as he took his trousers down the officer would see the full wheat bags underneath. He thought furiously, and then shook his head at the German, and said : " *Nein, nein,*" and tried to pretend he was shy. Watched by the startled German, he dragged himself behind some bushes, coyly changed the leg there and the crisis was over.

Spring came at last and with it the Allies pouring across the Rhine. The secret radio followed their progress on the news, and within the old castle grew a tremulous tension of impatience. On 13th April they heard that an American spearhead was only a few miles down the road and that night they went to bed knowing that it was nearly over, and yet unable to grasp it.

Bader was woken early by a roaring noise. He strapped on his legs and through the window saw Thunderbolts shooting up a nearby target. They went after a while, but soon he heard the sound of engines again and thought it was the Thunderbolts returning until someone yelled : " Tanks ! " Men rushed to the windows and two miles across the river, by a wood, saw gun flashes and the crawling black beetles of armour. A fascinating and glorious sight ! They were here !

The S.B.O., Willie Todd, appeared in the doorway and called soberly: "Listen a minute, everybody. The Kommandant has just ordered that we are to evacuate the castle by ten o'clock."

Bader exploded: "We aren't going to move."

"Don't worry," Todd said. "I'm going to tell him that, but I want you to be ready for anything if he brings up his Goons to winkle us out with guns."

They waited tensely while Todd argued with the Kommandant. Apparently an S.S. Division was going to make a stand behind a nearby ridge; the castle would be in the battleground, and the division commander thought that it and the men inside might impede his defence. Todd threatened that an evacuation would not endear the Kommandant to the Allies.

The prisoners were planning to barricade themselves in when the Kommandant sent in a message to say that they could stay at their own risk.

That afternoon shells started screaming over the castle. Bader was watching through the bars when a blinding light flashed in his face with an ear-splitting explosion and he found himself dizzily on his back in the middle of the floor with plaster falling on him and his ears singing like a kettle. In the top corner of the window the stone had crumbled where the shell had exploded.

No one seemed to know what was happening and at dusk the situation was still confused, though the dogged German guards still stood at their posts and the sentries marched up and down.

That night nearly every one was querulous. Some had been in captivity over five years and the last few hours were unnerving.

The castle was nakedly sandwiched in an artillery duel, and all night the shells screamed and whistled over and banged joltingly on each side. At last, towards dawn, it was quieter.

Bader came drowsily up from sleep to hear tramping feet in the courtyard and shouting. In an instant he was fully awake and strapped on his legs while others less impeded ran down ahead. He heard shouts coming up and impatiently, with a fast and eager dot-and-carry motion, clumped down after them. In the courtyard, through milling cheering prisoners, he was staggered to see American soldiers, and nearby a line of stolid German guards stepping up one by one to hand over their rifles.

It was all over. They were free. How confusing and nerveless it was. No one quite seemed to know what to do, or feel.

Three American newspaper correspondents appeared and started firing questions at Bader. He was amazed to see that one of them was a girl, a real live girl, with red hair, in battledress, in the courtyard. After a while they said they were going back to First Army Headquarters at Naunberg in a jeep. Would he like to come?

He stuffed a few oddments and his books into a kitbag and then he was in the jeep driving out across the moat, down the cobbled hill and through the village.

Around dusk they came to Naunberg, and officers in the school-turned-headquarters greeted him warmly, but they were busy coming and going, and for all the warmth he felt an odd man out again. Then a British major, a young liason officer, greeted him and he found a little footing. They dined on army rations and he filled himself gloriously and guiltily. The army bread looked snow-white and tasted sweet, like cake. Feeling better, he asked the major: " Any Spitfires round here ? "

No, the major said, they were all up north with the British forces.

" Can I get to them ? " Bader asked. " I'd like to grab one and get another couple of trips in before this show folds up."

" Good God, man," said the shocked major. " Give it a miss and go home. Haven't you had enough ? "

Two officers took him through the blacked-out streets to sleep in a private house whose German family had retired quietly behind a blank door at the back. Later, he crawled into a feather bed and lay wide awake all night, not disturbed, just thinking, feeling for a grip.

By dawn he had it. Kolditz was a year away and he was in the present, still a trifle insecurely, but looking forward to the future with the old, practical sense that seldom looked back over his shoulder.

They drove him to an airfield where the busy officer clerks said it was forbidden to fly prisoners back yet, so he thumbed a lift with a cheerful young American pilot who said insulting things about bureaucrats.

They landed on an airstrip in the Versailles woods and he found haven in a house where warm-hearted American officers offered him champagne to drink to his liberty, but liberty did not seem to call for champagne and he drank Coca-Cola instead. Though they were kind and tactful he still felt awkward in his battledress, which was shabby. He was sitting talking, when the commanding general tapped his shoulder and said : " Come on, Doug. I've got your wife on the phone."

It caught him off balance. He got to the phone and recognised Thelma's voice saying : " Douglas ! Douglas ! " Then there was so much to say that they could not say it for a while. A little later Thelma said : " When am I going to see you ? "

" A few days, darling. I'm looking for a Spitfire. I want to have a last fling before it packs up."

" Oh, God," Thelma almost wailed. " Haven't you had enough yet ? "

In the morning they drove him to Paris. At R.A.F. Headquarters he started telling them about Lucille de Backer and the Hiècques, but they knew more than he did ; the Germans had sentenced all three to death, but there was a report that the sentence had been commuted to prison in Germany.

Lucille too ! He went out hoping very, very hard that they would all be found safe—their fate was the only cloud on his liberty. He asked about old friends on the squadrons and heard that a dismaying number were dead. But Tubby Mermagen was in France and they got him on the phone. He was at Rheims, an air commodore, and almost the first thing Bader said was : " Can you get me a Spitfire ? "

From the other end came a chuckle. " We thought you'd say that. I have strict orders from the C.-in-C. that I'm to stuff you straight into an aircraft for London."

That afternoon Mermagen flew to Paris and did so.

The humble Anson ambled over the fields that used to be Bader's hunting ground, but he could not recognise anything. They crossed the coast at Littlehampton and out to the left he saw Tangmere, but only dimly through a veil of haze.

At Northolt Aerodrome the R.A.F. gave him sanctuary while the Great Machine sucked him in again, looking down his throat, planting stethoscopes on him, giving him clothes, forms to fill in, questions to answer and fending off the clamouring reporters.

On the third morning, with leave for two months, he drove down to Ascot and Thelma, free at last and for the first time tasting it fully. He pulled into the drive, walked up the flagged path and as Thelma ran out of the front door, two reporters stepped from behind a bush saying cheerfully: "Got you at last." And the moment was spoiled.

Next morning he and Thelma fled to a private hotel in a little Devon village and suddenly he could not face people, think coherently, make any plans, or even read the letters that came pouring in.

One night he *did* enjoy meeting people. Sailor Malan, Bob Tuck, Crowley-Milling, Johnny Johnson and a dozen or so others of the old 1940 team gave him a welcome-home dinner at the Belfry Club in Belgravia, and that night he felt at ease.

He got his old flying log-book back and entered up his last Tangmere flight of nearly four years before, with the laconic comment : " Good flight near Béthune. Shot down one 109 F. and collided with another. P.O.W. Two 109 F.s destroyed."

And underneath : " Total enemy aircraft destroyed— 30."

From Paris he learned with joy that the Hiècques and Lucille had been found alive in Germany and were now in an Allied hospital, recovering. He wrote asking to be informed when they returned to St. Omer. News came that the French had sentenced Hélène, who had betrayed him, to twenty years in prison. Still feeling no hate, he wrote to the French Government suggesting they cut her sentence to five years and then send her back to live in St. Omer.

One day he drove to see Rupert Leigh at the Empire Flying School at Hullavington and Leigh gave him fifteen minutes dual in a Miles Master. Then he climbed into a Spitfire and twirled her round the air for half an hour, knowing with elation in the first minute that the touch was still the same. He landed with some of the old glow back in his eyes and a new confidence, and from that moment began to feel back in the swim again.

Then in the R.A.F. Club he met Air Commodore Dick Atcherley, the former Schneider Trophy pilot, who said : " Douglas, I want a man to run the Fighter Leader School at Tangmere. It's a group captain's job. Would you like it ? "

He answered with feeling : " Yes, please."

Eager for the comfort of harness again, he cancelled the rest of his leave and early in June drove to the well-remembered Tangmere. He should have known better. The place looked the same, but the faces were new ; above all, the atmosphere was new. Now there was none of the urgency of war, only a team of battle-weary men who wanted to shed the medal ribbons and be civilians again. He tried to revive some of the spirit but there was no spark left in the embers, so when he was offered command of the North Weald Fighter Sector he took it.

It brought him control over twelve fighter squadrons spread over six aerodromes, but there was little joy in that either because there was no dynamic purpose any more : he was presiding over their disintegration. The great war machine of the R.A.F. was breaking up. He tried to preserve a hard core, but the best men would not stay because the R.A.F.'s future did not look encouraging. It was dispiriting. At least he had his own Spitfire again, and had his old " D.B." painted on it.

A letter from Paris told him that Lucille and the Hiècques were back in St. Omer and he immediately got into " D.B." and flew over there. When he knocked and the door opened, recognition was mutual, everyone crying and laughing and kissing each other. The Hiècques had not changed as much as he had feared. Madame, a little more wrinkled, was still the same resourceful and compassionate soul, and Monsieur still brushed his cheek with the wisp of moustache. The brave Lucille was thinner and shy, and he could find no way of thanking them properly. The young man who had led him through the dark streets was not there : he had been missing for two years.

In North Weald Sector one of his squadrons had Meteor jets and as a matter of both desire and duty he flew one. Oddly, the Meteor, which was soon to win the world's speed record at over 600 m.p.h.,[1] was the first twin-engined aircraft he had flown ; oddly also he found that without legs it was easier for him to handle than any other aeroplane because there was no torque and therefore no need to prod the rudder much to correct swing on take-off or in the dive. Comforted by this it occurred to him that when the Far East war moved north to invade Japan the climate would not affect his legs. He was scheming a way of getting out to it when the atom bomb fell and the whole shooting match was over.

A tinge of regret itched for a few days but common sense soon dismissed the past. Now it was the future that occupied him, like so many others, but he knew his own problem was different to theirs.

On 1st September he found a letter from Group in his " In " tray. It said there was to be a victory fly-past over London on 15th September to celebrate peace, and the fifth anniversary of the greatest day in the Battle of Britain. Three hundred aircraft were to take part, with twelve survivors of the battle in the van. Group Captain Bader was to organise the fly-past and lead it.

Stuffy Dowding arrived at North Weald early on the

[1] Flown by Thelma's cousin, Teddy Donaldson.

15th and stood talking to the chosen twelve, looking much the same as five years earlier. The others looked a little different. Crowley-Milling, who had been a pilot officer in the battle, wore wing-commander braid and a D.S.O. and D.F.C. on his chest. So did Stan Turner. So also Bob Tuck and nearly all the others. The atmosphere was different too; they spoke more soberly and hardly mentioned the battle. Bader wound a blue polka-dot scarf round his neck, called: " Let's go," picked up his right leg and swung it into " D.B.'s " cockpit.

Cloud was drooping over London and down in the grey streets the city gathered in stillness, some in tears, watching the cavalcade of three hundred sweep thunderously over the rooftops. Bader hardly saw them—Turner on one side, Crowley-Milling on the other, he was too busy picking his course through the haze. Once, over the city, he remembered the battle and for a moment, nostalgically, wanted to fight it again.

Now THE problem of what to do with life began to concern him urgently. The Air Force wanted him back permanently. Though still there was nothing in King's Regulations to cover his case, they offered to wipe out all the wasted years and give him the seniority he would have had if he had never crashed in 1931.

The Shell Company wrote to him and he dined with his old boss, who said : " We've got just the job for you." Douglas could have his own aeroplane and fly round the world on aviation business.

His own aeroplane ! And what a grand job ! A week or two at a time in the tropics would not upset the legs much. They named a salary that was tempting, and said : " Take your time."

He took four months to think about it, and at the end of February decided. Writing out his resignation from the Air Force, he felt how odd it was that he should choose to turn his back on the old heaven to return to the old hell. Though this time a somewhat transformed hell !

The most heart-warming messages came to him—summed up in a sentence from the Chief of Fighter Command, Sir James Robb. " All I can say is that you are leaving behind an example which as the years roll by will become a legend."

When the time came to leave he did not feel so badly about it. The job was done and now he knew he would feel a part of the Air Force for the rest of his life. It was on a

Saturday after breakfast that he drove away from North Weald. There was no need to start work yet; officially, he was still on leave from the R.A.F. for three months.

Most of that time he spent working on his golf. Practising ardently at the Wentworth Golf Club with Archie Compston, within three months he had reduced his handicap from nine to four, which is not likely ever to be approached by a legless man again, and, in fact, is equalled only by about one golfer in a hundred. Dessoutter once told him he would never walk without a stick. He played Dessoutter, and beat him seven and six.

Late in June he and Thelma moved back to their old flat in Kensington and on the first Monday in July Bader went back to the office. This time he had an office of his own and the manager tossed him a letter. " This'll interest you, old boy. We've ordered a Percival Proctor for you. It'll be ready in a couple of weeks."

A few days later he collected the Proctor, a neat little single-engined cabin monoplane. She was a four-seater, silver with a blue flash down the side, and cruised at 130 m.p.h. He was like a small boy with a new toy. As she was registed " G-AHWU " (in alphabetical code " George Able How Willie Uncle ") he christened her " Willie Uncle."

In August he started his first trip, accompanied by Lieutenant-General Jimmy Doolittle, a Shell Company vice-president in U.S.A.

First stop was Oslo, where they had an audience with King Haakon, who was delightfully informal. (" That silly man Quisling came and stayed at the palace here during the war," he said. " A very foolish thing to do. The people disliked it intensely.")

Then to Copenhagen, The Hague and Paris and receptions in every spot. Doolittle beside him in the

Proctor, he flew to Marseilles, Nice and Rome, across the Mediterranean to Tunis, Algiers, Tangier and Casablanca. With only a day or two in each spot and champagne and goodwill flowing all round, the pace began to tell, though Bader never touched the champagne. It was cumulative weariness that caught up with him in Casablanca where he sat next to a French general at a welcome dinner on a very hot night. His head was drooping on his chest as he tried to do his duty, saying : "*Oui mon générale, oui mon générale,*" until he actually fell asleep sitting there. Her jerked upright with a "*Pardon, mon générale, je suis un peu malade,*" and they whisked him off to bed where he slept for eleven hours.

Back to London via Lisbon, Madrid and Paris, then off again in the Proctor for West Africa, "White Man's Grave," where he could test his legs in the tropics.

Sweat from steamy West African heat soon made the stumps uncomfortable but talcum powder kept the heat rashes under control for three weeks until he was on the way back.

In 1947, on Doolittle's invitation, he went on Shell business to the U.S.A. which had 17,000 amputation cases from the war, and visited several veterans' hospitals to help men learn to walk again.

Back in London he took Thelma with him in the Proctor on his next trip, a tour of Scandinavia, and at Tylosand he entered for the Swedish golf championship and delighted everyone by winning his first round match, then was beaten in the second.

Next journey was down to West Africa again and this time he flew on to Pretoria to meet Field Marshal Smuts, and for a gay reunion with Sailor Malan in Johannesburg, where he also caught malaria and lost two stone in weight in five days. That bout emaciated the stumps so that it was days before he could walk properly again. Later came a trip to the Middle East, Tripoli, Benghazi, Tobruk, Cairo, Cyprus and Athens.

In 1948 he took Thelma with him in the Proctor out to the Far East, and on the way out an Athens newspaper ran his photograph with limbless Greek veterans, referring to him as the " famous cripple." Cripple ! Servicing his own aircraft in all weathers he flew by way of Turkey, Damascus, Baghdad, Basra, Bahrein, Sharjah, Baluchistan, Karachi, Delhi, Allahabad, Calcutta, Akyab, Rangoon, Mergui and Penang to Singapore. From there they went by air to Borneo, Celebes, Java, Bali and New Guinea, covering over 20,000 miles. In the two months they were away Douglas sweated off many pounds and Thelma put on a stone, earning the new name of " Chubby."

In 1949 he took to flying twin-engined aircraft and delivered a Percival Prince to Singapore (taking Thelma again). In 1951 the company thought he should have two engines on his long trips so he changed the Proctor for a twin-engined Miles Gemini which he immediately flew to the Congo.

After a time in London he is off again, sometimes flying himself by Gemini sometimes delivering a new aircraft to out-of-the-way places, sometimes by airliner. For a man who might be excused for living in a wheel-chair he is fantastically peripatetic. He has flown forty-seven different types of aircraft now and some fifty or more countries have known memorable contact with his exuberance.

Probably no one has done as much for the limbless as Bader's example, which inspires them in a way no doctor can emulate.

He is still a mixture of modesty and ego. In a swash-buckling way he is given to bragging about his golf scores as blatantly as a fisherman describing the one that got away. People who do not know him well have resented that, but they have never heard him brag about important things. It was not from Bader I learned that he would have played rugby for England, and the research for this book was nearly completed before I discovered by seeing one of his old uniform tunics that as well as two D.S.O.s and two D.F.C.s he also holds the Légion d'Honneur and the Croix de Guerre.

I agree with all those who class him as the best fighter leader and tactician of World War II (and one of the best pilots). Also, I know of no other fighter tactician so outstanding in other wars. But his main triumph is not his air fighting : that was only an episode that focused a world's attention on the greater victory he was achieving in showing humanity new horizons of courage, not in war, not only for the limbless, but in life.

Skymen

LARRY FORRESTER

ACKNOWLEDGMENTS

IN MY research for this book I am chiefly indebted to Mr. Peter Salton of the *Daily Express*, who with his expert knowledge, his excellent contacts and his newspaperman's eye for accuracy, dug up innumerable cuttings, checked dates, facts, figures and technical names and spellings; personally typed out a great deal of the material and, giving up an enormous amount of his spare time, helped me to accumulate a vast hoard of original matter. In a task of this kind, few authors are fortunate enough to have the enthusiastic aid of a highly-trained Fleet Street journalist.

My thanks are also due to Mr. I. C. Nerney of the Air Ministry Historical Section—and not for the first time, by any means. I owe much to the staff of the Imperial War Museum; the United States Library and Information Centre; the Science Museum, Kensington; and the Reading Room of the British Museum.

Bill Strutton, the film-writer, biographer and novelist, contributed many valuable suggestions and helped in particular with the chapter on Sir Alan Cobham. Wing Commander R. R. Stanford Tuck, D.S.O., D.F.C., gave me his permission to use material from *Fly For Your Life*, the biography of him which I wrote in 1956. For this I am also indebted to the original publishers of that work, Frederick Muller Ltd.

Some of the chapters are developed from a series of articles which I wrote for *Everybody's* some years ago under the title "Victory In the Air."

The books, British and foreign, which I have consulted

are too numerous to list here, but I wish to mention a few which not only were particularly helpful, but thoroughly enjoyable : Ralph Murche's *Song of the Sky* ; Ruth Mitchell's *My Brother Bill* ; Adolf Galland's *The First and the Last* ; Richard Hillary's superb classic *The Last Enemy* ; *While Others Sleep*, by James A. Michener and various works by that prince of air-pioneers, Alexander de Seversky. The files of various publications, such as *Flight*, *The Aeroplane* and *Air Facts*, *Time*, *Illustrated* and *Picture Post*, yielded a wealth of precious detail.

L. F.

AUTHOR'S PREFACE

THE SCOPE and purpose of this book require a few words
of explanation. This is not a history—though it does
provide an outline of aviation's development from the
earliest efforts to the present day. It is a book about pilots,
a collection of personal stories giving the backgrounds,
characters and careers of some of the world's most famous
flyers, men—and women—who have made important
contributions to the conquest of the " newest element,"
the sky.

Choosing the subject for each chapter was not easy.
Some illustrious names are missing, for it seemed to me
pointless to try to write more about Group Captain Leonard
Cheshire, V.C., after his own book *Bomber Pilot* and two
excellent biographies by Russell Braddon and Andrew
Boyle; or about Group Captain Douglas Bader, after Paul
Brickhill's splendid *Reach for the Sky* and the successful
film made of it. In recent years other films have been
based on the achievements of Charles Lindberg and Wing
Commander Guy Gibson, V.C., leader of the "Dambusters."

So I have concentrated on those airmen, equally distinguished, whose names and adventures are not so well-known
that their tales are " ancient history." To the younger reader,
indeed, many of these stories should come completely fresh.

The sky is not the territory of one nation—any more than
the high seas are. Its conquest has been an international
affair. True, the sky often has been a bitter battleground,
yet there exists between flying men of all nations a spirit
of mutual respect and brotherhood which even war cannot

7

destroy completely. Therefore I have included stories of pilots who served " on the other side "—for heroism is heroism, whatever the cause it serves, and a gallant enemy, is a gallant enemy, even if his politics disgust you.

A good many of the stories, of course, have nothing to do with war. But the peace-time sky has a wealth of snares and treacheries of its own. Fighting through a raging electrical storm over jagged mountains, uninhabited jungle, or a freezing waste of ocean, with your radio jammed by static and your petrol getting low, or with ice beginning to form on your wings and your engine losing revolutions as the propeller blades get frosted—this is just as tough a battle as any involving flak and fighter formations, and it calls for just as much skill and cool-headed courage.

Larry Forrester.

CONTENTS

	PAGE
WOOD, WIRE, AND CHEESECLOTH	11
STRONG MEN AND STOUT SHIPS	21
KNIGHT OF THE SILVER CUPS	33
STARS OF NO-MAN'S-SKY	45
THE WORST WEATHER IN THE WORLD	58
LAST HOP TO HOWLAND	71
THE TRAIL ENDS AT WALKPI	89
ONE SEPTEMBER DAY	102
DUEL IN THE MIDNIGHT SUN	111
HEAD IN THE CLOUDS	122
THE AMAZON HAS WINGS	130
CANNON IN THE SKY	146
WINGS OF MERCY	160
SKYMEN FROM DOWN-UNDER	170

WOOD, WIRE AND CHEESECLOTH

THE HURRICANE sliced in from the leaden Atlantic and struck North Carolina's Outer Banks at a desolate place known as Kitty Hawk. The little camp amid the barren dunes was ripped apart.

When the fury had passed, Wilbur and Orville Wright came out of the wreckage of their lean-to storehouse and silently, wearily, began to pick up the pieces. Their " flying machine "—a clumsy, kite-like construction of wood and cheesecloth, forty feet across the wings, with an automobile engine, naked and seemingly precariously balanced in the middle of it—was seriously damaged, and it would take weeks to repair it.

But the Wright Brothers, bicycle mechanics from Dayton, Ohio, were well-used to cruel setbacks like this. For four years now they had come to camp on this remote expanse of sand and experiment with their machine, and they had yet to get it an inch off the ground. This wasn't the first time a howling " twister " had ripped along the dunes, scattering their light and laboriously fashioned equipment, dashing sections of it to fragments, carrying others far out to sea. And each time they made their repairs, and got back to their experiments, they were faced with fresh disappointments ; one idea after another had to be scrapped, their theories modified, more money spent. . . .

At the week-ends trippers came out to stare at the " cranks " and make cumbrous jokes about the machine

—for hadn't Simon Newcomb, the famous American physicist, stated that it was definitely impossible to fly a heavier-than-air device? To the average person, in 1903, the idea of taking to the air in a machine which had no gas-balloon attached was no less ridiculous than the idea of a man going for a walk under the ocean without any sort of diving gear. But the two slim, dark, serious-faced young men kept their heads down over their work and ignored the braying laughter; when they lifted their tired eyes, it was to squint apprehensively at a sky once more darkening and filling with the whip and whine of a nor'-easter.

Looking back now, over more than half a century, it is hard to see where these quiet, unknown and apparently unqualified Americans, so alone, and so at odds with the views of their country's most distinguished scientists and engineers, found the strength to keep going in the face of such cruel and constant discouragement. Certainly history offered them little inspiration—from the dawn of time, the story of Man's efforts to claw his way up from the surface of the planet was little more than a mixture of fable and fiasco.

In Greek mythology, Daedalus and his son Icarus had fashioned wings of feathers, but their flight over the Mediterranean ended in tragedy when the sun's heat melted the bee's wax with which the wings were attached to their bodies. . . . Arab tales of " magic carpets " were as old and numerous as the desert's grains of sand. . . .

The incredibly versatile mind of Italy's Renaissance genius Leonardo da Vinci had conceived a design for a flying machine which was aerodynamically sound, but his age could provide neither the proper materials to build it, nor the source of power to drive it, and so it remained a useless, forgotten scrap of paper. . . .

Over the centuries in every land, various maniacs, "magicians" and misguided inventors had been hurling themselves to destruction from towers and clifftops, wildly flapping wings of feathers, sail-cloth or wood. More than once, church and state had declared such attempts sacrilegious—Man was not meant to draw nearer Heaven, except in spirit. . . . Hundreds of years of failure and official condemnation resulted in "bird-men" and builders of "sky ships" becoming as discredited as the horde of alchemists who, wandering from court to court, long-bearded and mystical, since pre-Christian times had been claiming the ability to transmute base metals into purest gold by a process known as "the secret of the Philosopher's Stone"—but never once proved it. . . .

And yet there were *some* stories worthy of serious study. There was conclusive evidence that as early as 1852 a wealthy and somewhat eccentric Englishman, Sir George Cayley, had constructed at his Yorkshire home, Brompton Hall, a crude sort of man-carrying glider which had made at least one successful flight. But Cayley, being corpulent, elderly and perhaps a little uncertain, was said to have refused to test the contrivance himself, and a reluctant, terrified coachman was forced to take the controls. (If the story is true, then this humble serving man, of whom we know almost nothing—not even his name!—was the world's first true air pilot. Directly after landing, pallid and perspiring, he gave notice, explaining in broad Yorkshire: "Ah coom t'drive coach, not t'fly like blessed bird.") At any rate, for one reason or another, Cayley's activities brought him such derision and enmity from his neighbours that he abandoned his experiments, leaving no worthwhile testimonial record. Only letters and diaries kept by his sister and other members of the family survived to prove beyond doubt that the amateur scientist had in fact overcome the basic problems of heavier-than-air flight.

At the end of the nineteenth century, a German engineer whose hobby was ornithology (the study of birds), had made flights of up to twenty seconds in home-made gliders. His name was Otto Lilienthal. On 9th August, 1896, he crashed and died, but he left valuable records of his work and a number of brilliantly written scientific papers.

Despite the countless follies and catastrophes of past ages, and the pitifully few genuine advances, the Wright Brothers remained infected by a fiery faith in the impossible, and Lilienthal was their hero. They were convinced that now they had something that none of their predecessors had possessed, a source of power compact and light enough to drive their machine through the air—the internal combustion engine. This comparatively recent invention, so successfully demonstrated in the rapidly developing "horseless carriage," or motor-car, seemed to them the key to the main problem which had defeated all the previous, serious air-pioneers. And they knew that other men, in France and other countries, thought the same and were working on experiments similar to their own.

Perhaps, too, they drew comfort from the knowledge that the only previous human invasion of the sky had resulted from the discovery of two brothers. On 5th June, 1783, Joseph and Jacques Montgolfier, of Annonay, France, had sent the world's first balloon soaring one-and-a-half miles across country in ten minutes. The following September, before the King and Queen of France at Versailles, a Montgolfier balloon rose to 1,500 feet, and stayed aloft for eight minutes, travelling about two miles, with three passengers—a sheep, a cock and a duck. The first officially recognised aerial travellers, suspended in a cage beneath the giant bag—105 feet in circumference—were unharmed by the experience. A month later a courageous court official, Jean François Pilâtre de Rozier, made the first of many successful ascents—and " the great Balloon Age " began, with daring " flights " being made regularly throughout Europe before vast and excited crowds.

But balloons did not truly fly—filled with gas which made them lighter than air, they rose into the upper, thinner atmosphere and then floated, drifted, like wood on water, at the mercy of wind and current. All manner of weird steering and " driving " devices had been tried, including huge oars protruding from the sides, with which the occupant was supposed to row his way across the sky; but it had become very clear that the balloonist could never have more than extremely limited control over his craft.

The Montgolfier Brothers had shown merely that it was possible for Man to enter the sky without harm or discomfort : now the Wright Brothers, a hundred and twenty years later, were resolved to show that the sky could be navigated, ranged at will, in time—conquered.

On 17th December, 1903, at Kill Devil Hill, Kitty Hawk, the flimsy framework of wood, wire and cheesecloth which the inventors called an " aero-plane " was repaired once more. Jerkily, it started forward across the hard-packed sands. It had no wheels. The undercarriage consisted of a low truck which ran on sixty feet of rail laid along the beach. Driven by two propellers, the machine weighed 605 pounds, including the very noisy engine.

Gathering speed, rocking and vibrating, it roared along its rail, Wilbur Wright manipulating the makeshift controls, Orville running along after him, clothes flapping in the slipstream, his face a desperate mixture of eagerness and anxiety. Five islanders, members of the local Lifesaving Service, stood well back by the dunes, watching uneasily —the only people in this part of North Carolina who had responded to an open invitation from the brothers to come and see them " fly."

And as they watched, expecting only disaster, the noise of the machine suddenly changed, became smoother. The launching truck was slowing, falling behind, and there was daylight—empty air—between the machine and the ground. . . .

Rocking a little, rising and dipping gently, only a few feet above the sand, the contraption continued along the beach for more than five hundred feet before it flopped down lightly and slid to a stop on its landing skids. The Wrights, glowing with restrained excitement, measured and noted the distance covered and the time taken, carefully inspected their plane, then brought it back to the starting place and prepared for another attempt.

Four times that day, before the tiny group of marvelling island folk, the Wright Brothers got their craft into the air, and kept it there, moving forward in controlled flight, the last time for as long as 59 seconds, covering 852 feet.

Many years were to pass before the importance of this achievement and the heroic efforts of the brothers gained recognition in their own country. At first, most American scientists and newspaper editors simply refused to believe the accounts of those who had witnessed " aeroplane flights "—even though in 1905 Wilbur Wright, in an improved machine, covered 24 miles in 39 minutes !

What now must be rated as one of the most significant events of the twentieth century, at the time caused hardly a ripple of attention within the United States. But three thousand miles away, in France, the birth of the aeroplane on that lonely, wind-battered stretch of Carolina coast caused great excitement, and no little consternation—for various groups of scientists and engineers, working on a bewildering variety of theories and projects, had hoped to claim the honour for their own country.

Prominent among these pioneers in France was Alberto Santos-Dumont, a wealthy Brazilian. In 1898, he had built and flown a cylindrical balloon with a petrol engine. In 1901, he produced a crude form of airship which won a prize, and engendered hysterical excitement in Paris, by making the first flight from St. Cloud around the Eiffel Tower and back. Two years later, at Neuilly, he constructed the world's first airship station, where he soon built up a vast and varied collection of dirigibles.

Now, inspired by the Wright Brothers' flight, he turned his attention to designing aeroplanes, modelled on their machine. In August of 1906, he got his " No. 14 *bis* " biplane into the air for eight seconds, and in November covered 720 feet in 21 and one-fifth seconds. Immense crowds at Bagatelle acclaimed him as a public hero.

Unlike the Americans, the volatile French—conditioned, perhaps, by the thrills of " the great Balloon Age "—looked upon this new form of flying as first class public entertainment, and made a craze of it. And, unlike the quiet, absorbed Wright Brothers, Santos-Dumont did not hesitate to " play to the gallery "—to encourage ordinary people to take an interest in aeroplanes by every possible stunt and trick of showmanship.

In a matter of a few months, aero clubs were being formed throughout the country. New periodicals appeared, specialising in " aeronautical news and adventure stories." In backyards and barns from one end of France to the other young enthusiasts hammered and sawed and tinkered, creating their contraptions—and with remarkable daring, and a good deal of luck, one by one they got into the air. These backyard builders included many who were to become famous names in aviation—Henri Farman (who later designed and manufactured the famous Farman biplane); master-pilot Delagrange, and the amazing, versatile Jean Louis Blériot.

Blériot was chubby, cheerful, incredibly energetic, with a large " walrus " moustache that seemed to flutter when he laughed or got excited. By 1908, he had workshops at Neuilly and a shed at Issy, and had survived nearly fifty crashes. That was the year that Wilbur Wright, despairing of his own government's attitude and fearing that Europe would steal the lead in aviation development, got the idea of taking the latest Wright machine to France and entering the various flying competitions and displays which by now were regular events there.

Many French enthusiasts resented the American's " intrusion," but Louis Bleriot organised a welcoming committee. And when it was found that Wright's machine had been damaged in the Trans-Atlantic voyage, Louis rushed to offer him the facilities of his Neuilly workshops, and any personal help needed to make the repairs.

Wright's French tour began in July, with a demonstration at Le Mans—now a famous motor-racing track, scene of the annual 24-hour Grand Prix d'Endurance event. He gave what must have been the world's first display of a new art, " aerobatics." Banked almost vertically, he turned repeatedly in a circle of just under 31 yards diameter, close above the upturned faces of a huge and wildly demonstrative crowd, then described perfect figure-eights, suddenly swooped down to the gentlest of landings, with his wings reaching the horizontal at the same instant as he touched the ground.

Blériot ran to congratulate him, declared again and again : " This Wright machine is definitely superior to any of ours."

Soon after this, Louis scrapped several of his planes and, in a frantic burst of work, designed and produced a 28-horsepower aircraft with a light framework, only part of which was covered with fabric. This, his eleventh plane, cruised at 40 m.p.h., and after testing her—with unusual secrecy—he expressed the highest satisfaction.

On 25th July, 1909, in this primitive craft—with his burly body jammed into the tiny cockpit, and his big moustache fluttering in the wind—Jean Louis Blériot crossed the English Channel from Calais to the Dover cliffs. He covered the 25 miles in 37 minutes, despite violent air currents over the water. And he did it " by following my nose "—without a compass.

Not just France, or England, but the entire civilised world at last awoke to the serious potentialities of this new device, the aeroplane. Blériot's feat was infinitely more impressive than anything that had been done before, because it had a great underlying significance that was clear to all nations. For the first time a flying machine had travelled from one country to another, across an expanse of open sea which throughout past ages had been a comforting barrier, a shield. . . .

Thus Louis Blériot, the cheerful backyard tinkerer, became an international hero whose achievement transformed, almost overnight, military and social thinking about national boundaries. From the moment that he thumped down, awkwardly and gratefully, on the clifftops at Dover, the world seemed to shrink, and nations felt closer to, and more aware of, each other.

Louis went on to many more successes. In 1912, he became the first man to " loop the loop," and before his death in 1936, he designed more than 300 types of aircraft, including several successful war machines, and built over 10,000 planes. Few men have made greater single contributions to aviation.

Like the Wright Brothers, he was one of the architects of a new and astounding age. An age of incredibly rapid development in which men of all nations, rising after the pioneer brothers of Kitty Hawk, lifted humanity to an enlargement of life which our forefathers—and perhaps the Wright Brothers themselves—would never have dreamed possible.

STRONG MEN AND STOUT SHIPS

IT WAS 1911. The Kaiser was already strutting across Europe with boasts of his formidable army. Germany's neighbours grew more and more fearful, aware that he was building up the finest fighting machine in the world.

But the Kaiser and his Prussian warlords knew they were still far from supreme—they had an " Achilles' heel." The British navy—whether patrolling distant shores of the Empire, paying courtesy visits to foreign ports, or merely riding at anchor in the summer waters of the Mediterranean —was a constant reminder that whatever power the German army could bring to bear on Europe, any war against Great Britain in the end must be won on the high seas. With this in mind, the Kaiser laid the first keels of what were to become the ships of the Grand Fleet.

Yet while the Kaiser was parading his soldiers and brooding over sea-power, the English seemed to be interested only in keeping open their great trade links from the Port of London. So it was that the Royal Navy—for over a hundred years the traditional rulers of the world's seas —had little time to explore and exploit new methods of attack and defence ; without any serious rival, there appeared to be little need. . . .

There were a few individuals, of course, whose thirst for adventure and natural curiosity forced them, even against the temper of the times, to think of the business of

war. Such a man was Charles Rumney Samson, a dapper
naval lieutenant with a Satanic red beard, a vile temper—
and an uncanny inventive talent. This son of a Manchester
solicitor had become a midshipman in 1899, and served
in the Pomone campaign of 1903. But his story does not
really start until eight years later, when the Royal Navy
was loaned planes and an aerodrome so that a few officers
could be taught to fly.

Volunteers were called for ; in the first rush two hundred
submitted their names. Samson was one of the four
accepted. In October of the same year, he completed his
flying course with distinction, and became the first commanding officer of the Royal Navy station at Eastchurch,
Isle of Sheppey.

That appointment led to many a headache for the
traditionalists of the Admiralty. Not many days had passed
before this sprightly little man was badgering his senior
officers to buy two new-type training planes, and to send
him naval ratings to form the nucleus of a naval flying
school. The Admiralty, long experienced in disciplining
the enthusiastic unorthodoxy of juniors, could not shake
off Samson. Like his Old Testament namesake, the man
burned with faith and possessed a strength that would not
be denied. The Admiralty capitulated by the end of the
year, and Samson jocularly considered the two planes they
sent him as " a Christmas gift from their Lordships."

Within the next month he was back pestering Whitehall
with an even more outrageous request : now he wanted
to convert a ship of the line, the doughty H.M.S. *Africa*,
into a " platform " from which he could fly an aeroplane !

The first answer from his superiors was summed up in
one word—" ridiculous." A certain highly placed naval
man went so far as to say : " Samson, rather than being

like a gentleman of His Majesty's navy, is more suited to be a circus clown! "

Such rebuffs only made Samson bad-tempered and more persistent. There were times in this " battle for a floating platform " when he even hectored and argued with admirals, completely disregarding the fact that at one stroke these men could end his career. They were staggered, stunned by the concentration of effort, the variety of approaches and procedures, the persistence—in turn patronising, threatening, and downright abusive—which this extraordinary man was able to deploy in order to get what he wanted.

Samson's strength won the day: on a cold January morning in 1912 he flew one of his little training planes from Eastchurch to Sheerness. With all the hostile fussiness of an old maid watching a stranger fondle her cat, he supervised the machine's loading aboard *Africa*. Then carefully, with his own naval ratings, he manoeuvred the plane into the best position for a take-off from the warship's short deck.

When all was ready Samson paused, looked round him, surveying the faces of the watching ship's officers and men. In all their eyes he could read the same thought—" this poor idiot, for no apparent reason wants to launch his rickety flying machine, this awkward-looking structure of struts and wires and canvas, from this short and gently pitching deck, and in just a few minutes he is going to be dead or, at best, gravely injured. . . ." Infuriated by their expressions, Samson climbed into his cockpit glowering and muttering, in a foul temper, shouted his last, peremptory orders. The ratings fussed round the machine, the engine fired, and then the plane started to roll forward—slowly, much too slowly it seemed.

Up on the bridge the captain of the *Africa* moved his lips in silent blasphemies, braced himself for the disaster he considered inevitable. He had consented to this madcap experiment only under continued pressure. He had no use for aeroplanes—smelly, undignified, unreliable contraptions, a passing fad—and if this young stunt-man wanted to commit suicide he'd sooner he did so elsewhere, and didn't make a nasty mess on *his* shining decks. . . .

The plane lurched on towards the bows, not gaining much speed, seeming to waddle like some clumsy duck. Then, to everyone's great surprise, quite suddenly it lifted into the air. Samson had got his craft airborne, all right—but now it seemed that it just hung there, a few feet above the boards, engine revving madly, wings waggling slightly, struts and wires blurred in violent vibration. The little engine clanking full blast, the flimsy plane could make no progress—it was all it could do to keep up with the steaming warship ! Then all at once, just for a few seconds the fairly strong headwind fell away : slowly, yet steadily enough, Samson climbed, cleared the *Africa's* forward rigging and drew ahead. The officers and men who had watched him with pitying eyes only a few minutes before now cheered wildly and waved their arms as the tiny plane soared higher, then came round to circle the ship in salute.

Senior naval men who witnessed this flight agreed that Samson had great skill and courage, but they still could not see the point of his demonstration. It was one thing to get an aircraft off from a warship's deck—but to land it again obviously was impossible. Supposing in time of war, somewhere on the wide ocean a pilot took off, flew ahead of the fleet and spotted enemy units—how could he get his information to the commander ? Dropping messages in special containers on a relatively small, fast-moving target was at best a chancy business—and in those days, of course, no wireless communication was possible between an aircraft and land or sea stations. Nor were parachutes invented—what was to become of the pilot if he was out of range of land? Were these proposed " aerial spotters " to be a suicide force? And what about the immense cost in lost machines?

Moreover, Samson's success at the first attempt was no guarantee that planes could take off regularly from dreadnoughts, or that other pilots would prove as capable. And, of course, weather conditions would have to be almost perfect for them even to try. . . .

When he heard of these reactions, Samson exploded into a characteristic rage. Did they take him for a wild, glory-seeking gambler, a mere acrobat, a vain and empty-headed death-defier? Hadn't he submitted comprehensive reports of his researches and theories? Didn't they realise that what was needed, what he was campaigning for, *was a new type of naval vessel, specially designed to carry aircraft, on which planes not only could take-off but also land again?*

For many weeks, on a specially marked-out section of the airfield he had practised take-offs and landings in every sort of weather that was " flyable " by the standards of the time. (It must be remembered that the world's first powered flight, by the Wright Brothers, had been made only about nine years before!) Using special techniques, he had found he could get airborne and set the plane down in a surprisingly short distance, and from these results he calculated the minimum safety length of run needed on board a steaming ship. This was appreciably less than on the land, for the vessel's forward speed was a " bonus " which could be deducted from the normal take-off speed of the aircraft. In other words, if an aircraft on land normally

took off at 50 miles an hour, then from a ship moving at
ten miles an hour it would rise from the deck at an indicated
speed of 40. Of course allowance had to be made for wind
—a ten mile an hour wind blowing from the stern would
cancel out the " bonus." But it was a simple matter for the
ship to turn into wind—and then the wind speed provided
an additional aid, and the length of take-off run was even
shorter.

And everything that applied to the take-off held good for
landing, provided the pilots were specially trained. Perhaps in time, he had suggested, not only the ships but the
planes themselves could be specially designed for this
work.

The very next day, still incensed and determined to prove
he was working on a sound scientific basis, Samson flew
his machine from the deck of H.M.S. *Hibernia*, an even
shorter run. The ship was steaming at ten-and-a-half
knots into a light breeze ; he submitted figures which
showed that on land it would have been impossible to
get airborne in such a short distance. This time several
technically-minded experts at the Admiralty sat up with a
jerk, discussed Samson's report at length, planned a
programme of research and development which, many
years later, was to give the Navy wings. Samson, single-
handed and in the face of stern opposition and no little
scorn, had laid the foundations of the Royal Naval Air
Service.

But typically, as soon as he was satisfied that Admiralty
had taken note of his ideas, and at last apparently intended
to do something about them, he switched his attention to
other problems. By the summer of that year he had submitted valuable reports on the trajectory of aerial bombs,
and suggestions for aiming and fusing. The following

year—1913—he began a project that seemed to his fellow officers, and even his most ardent admirers, infinitely crazier, and more pointless, than the business of flying off from a ship.

He actually started trying to fly at night! In complete darkness, he piloted his plane round and round Eastchurch. And by the sparse light of a few oil flares laid out on the airfield, somehow he even contrived to make very respectable landings.

By now their Lordships of the Admiralty were beginning to recognise that this ill-tempered " circus clown " was leading the world in new aviation techniques. They ordered full investigation of his proposals for night-flying instruments and airfield lighting. He was promoted Commander. And at the Review of the Fleet at Spithead in July 1914 he introduced yet another technique—leading two flights of three planes each in a V-formation. This was the first time that such a formation had been used—except by wild geese!

When war broke out a few months later he was posted to Skegness as commander of a detachment of planes patrolling the East Coast. But later he took his squadron to Ostend, and fought in the defence of Antwerp. Just as things were hotting up there, Admiralty recalled the squadron. " Dare-devil " Samson—as he had come to be known—cursed his luck and prayed for fog so that he could stay in this growingly intense theatre of war.

There was no fog and he and his pilots set out for home. Over Dunkerque, one of the planes got into difficulties, spun down, crash-landed in a field. Samson could see very well that the pilot was unharmed, but he ordered the whole squadron to go to his aid. And once on the ground he managed to find a number of mysterious mechanical defects in other aircraft which would delay them here—keep them all, as he put it, " in business."

Over the next few weeks he continued to make excuses to Admiralty for his delay in leaving France, until Whitehall —perhaps unwilling to battle with Samson as well as the Germans—agreed to keep him at Dunkerque for operations against Zeppelins.

With the Allied Armies in retreat, there were opportunities in plenty for a man of Samson's vigour and ingenuity. And not all were in the air. For instance, with his brother, Felix, he built up a squad of motor cars armed with machine-guns—the first armoured cars in history. And he personally led them in battle against German cavalry units.

In the air he was equally active, attacking Zeppelin hangars and submarine bases at Zeebrugge and Ostend. He drove himself mercilessly, seemed hardly to sleep. Then he was switched with his squadron to the Dardanelles.

His base at Kephalo Point, on the island of Imbros, was particularly vulnerable to Turkish air attack. One night, just before the regular midnight raid on Kephalo, Samson ordered his squadron to load up and be ready to take off when the Turks drew near. The pilots thought that they were merely getting their planes out of the way of disaster, but Samson led them to Chanak, the Turks' aerodrome.

The Turkish ground crews thought the British squadron was their own, returning from the raid on Kephalo, and obligingly lit their landing flares. Down swept Samson, leading his force in a fierce, low-level strafing and bombing run that left the airfield a pitted, smoking ruin. After that, the Turks left the British flyers in peace at nights.

In 1917, after a spell as commander of the seaplane carrier *Ben-My-Chree*, Samson returned to England and was given an important but irksome desk job. After a few months he made such a nuisance of himself that his superiors once more gave in, let him return to active duty. For the remaining months of the war he was busy flying defensive patrols, day and night, up and down the coast from Yarmouth Air Station—all the time improving techniques, submitting reports on various tactical and operational experiments, suggesting new methods and devices and training systems and weapons. . . .

After the war he was transferred to the newly-formed Royal Air Force, given the high rank of Air Commodore and stationed at Uxbridge, a few miles from London. It was there that a heart complaint, developed in the strenuous days of the war, became serious. Samson, the Navy's strong man, had burnt himself out. He died in 1931.

A prophetically far-sighted officer, a brilliant pilot and totally brave, Charles Rumney Samson is remembered as "the man who gave the Navy wings." Of his many contributions to naval aviation, undoubtedly the most important was his dream of a new kind of vessel carrying fighters, "a floating aerodrome." His incredible take-offs from *Africa* and *Hibernia* perhaps did not convince all the Sea Lords that this idea was feasible, but they did set a number of expert minds, in the backrooms of Admiralty and the great ship-building firms, to work on this problem, and after many years this activity produced the forerunner of the modern aircraft carrier—nowadays rated more effective than any battleship.

And Samson lived to see this work in progress. After his successful take-offs, he had planned to attempt landings —but this demanded a somewhat larger deck area, and no suitable ship was available. Then came the war, and he put the idea out of his mind for the duration—and con-

sequently was beaten to it. For in 1917 another naval
pilot, Commander F. H. Dunning, became the first man
to land an aircraft on a ship.

Dunning was very different in character from Samson.
Strong too, but in a slower, subtler way. Gentle of voice
and manners, a methodical and skilful airman, he had
served with quiet distinction through the first three years
of the war. He knew of Samson's theories, was deeply
impressed by the strategic implications. Almost diffi-
dently, in the early summer of 1917 he put forward his
startling proposal: could he have permission to land his
plane, a Sopwith Pup, on the fo'c'sle of H.M.S. *Furious*?

" Impossible—suicidal—a pointless stunt. . . ." These
reactions from Admiralty were strangely similar to those
which had greeted Samson's first request, five years before,
to " borrow " the *Africa*. But now there were a few
progressive minds, impressed by the rapid development
of the aeroplane as a fighting machine, and by its success
in France, and uncomfortably aware that in the near future
capital ships would have to be protected by an " air
umbrella." Various schemes based on Samson's proposals
had been held up for lack of funds ; if it could be proved
that a modern fighter could land safely on a ship's deck,
some of the sceptics might be won over and money made
available.

So the few supporters of the Samson-Dunning school
of thought, seizing their chance, fought hard to get permission for the attempt. And by the end of July, after many
violent verbal battles behind locked doors in Whitehall,
they won.

On 2nd August, 1917, Dunning's little Pup hovered like
an uncertain, grumbling bee over the *Furious*. While he
worked out his approach path, hundreds of anxious eyes

followed him and tension on the ship mounted to such a pitch that some of the officers asked the captain to cancel the bid, and turn out of wind. Sternly the captain refused —he was under orders from Admiralty; his task was to " give this young maniac full facilities to kill himself."

The methodical, experienced Dunning, having carefully surveyed his objective and worked out every action beforehand in his mind, brought the Pup down with its nose high and plenty of power, in a beautifully steady approach, until his wheels were two or three feet above the after edge of the frighteningly short fo'c'sle. Then he closed the throttle, held the stick fully back against his taut diaphragm. The aircraft stalled, dropped like a stone, flopped down in a perfect three-point landing. It stopped with yards to spare.

The sceptics at the Admiralty were shaken. The air-minded few launched an all-out argumentative attack, and at last it was agreed that experiments should continue and that money should be provided for investigating the possibility of designing " a sea-going aerodrome." The future of the Navy's air branch, and the coming of the great aircraft carriers envisaged so long ago by " Dare-devil " Samson, were thus finally assured.

On 7th August—five days later—Dunning made his second attempt to land on *Furious*. This time he was watched by several experts, scientists and Admiralty chiefs.

His approach was perfect, down to the last few feet. But when he cut the throttle and hauled the stick back, he was a shade too high. At first the Pup fell vertically as before, but then one wing began to drop, so that he came down hard on one wheel. The plane bounced, rocked crazily, swung to one side, careered across the deck and over the side, into the sea. And sank at once.

Dunning, strapped in his cockpit, went down with her. In just five days this quiet, methodical, brave airman had written his name in triumph and tragedy on the honours roll of Britain's air pioneers.

But Dunning's death spoilt nothing—the matter had already been settled, he had proved once that it could be done. Like Samson, he had had to use as his " aerodrome " a standard ship of the line, never intended for such exotic service. A few more yards of deck, or a sturdy crash-barrier, would have saved him. By his sacrifice, he had emphasised the needs ; he had shown that a vessel specially designed to despatch and receive aircraft could greatly reduce the very dangers which had destroyed him.

When Samson was told of Dunning's fate, somehow he felt responsible. Deeply moved, he said : " Somebody had to do it, but it was really up to me. Now they *must* see the whole idea is practical . . . now they *must* build us what we need ! "

And throughout the years, up until his death, he kept up a valuable correspondence with the designers of the first aircraft carriers, suggesting modifications and additional safety devices—making sure that the Admiralty kept faith with his old colleague Dunning.

KNIGHT OF THE SILVER CUPS

CAPTAIN OSWALD Boelcke was drawn and aching with tiredness. In the last few weeks he had covered thousands of miles, visiting fighter stations, training fields and air headquarters throughout Germany and France, testing and selecting young pilots for the new, special wing which the Kaiser's experts had ordered him to form. Now, on his way back from the Eastern Front, drooping eyelids and stiffening limbs had forced him to land at this remote bomber base at Kovel.

He got a tremendous welcome in the officers' mess. The pilots of this squadron of two-seater bombers, stuck out here in aviator's " Siberia " in the iron-hard winter of 1915-16, detested their work—raids on the Russians, who had no air protection at all—and thought they saw in Boelcke a chance to escape, to transfer to fighters and go to France where " the real war " was being fought and great personal glory could be won. But he told them bluntly : " I'm sorry, gentlemen, the new wing is as good as complete. I'm not here to find candidates—simply to beg a meal and a bed for the night." And as soon as he had eaten he excused himself, thanked them for their hospitality, and went to the room they had given him.

He took off his tunic, and was sitting on the edge of the bed pulling off his boots when there came a short, sharp knock on the door. He groaned, called wearily : " Come in." A tall, slender, very straight and immaculate young

officer entered, clicked his heels. On the bare floorboards
the scrape and thud of the leather seemed extraordinarily
loud.

" Good evening, sir," said the young man, and his
voice was quick, confident, undoubtedly affected. " I'm
Richthofen. You may remember—we met on a train some
months ago." Vaguely, very vaguely, Boelcke remembered,
and he gave him a tired smile and a nod.

" Yes, of course. How nice to see you again, Richthofen. Were you in the mess ? I'm sorry if I didn't recognise you—the fact is, I'm about all in."

" That's quite all right, sir. I *was* in the mess, but I kept
out of the way—I didn't feel like bothering you there.
With all the others. . . ."

Boelcke sighed, let his head fall forward, peering at the
floorboards between his boots.

" All right," he said, " so you've come to bother me
now—you've waited to get me alone, eh ? Very enterprising, but I'm afraid the answer's still the same. I don't
need any more pilots, and if I did I shouldn't look for them
in a bomber squadron."

" But I have experience on scouts and fighters—in
France, before I came here. I have always known that I'm
not temperamentally suited to bomber operations. If you
would only consider me, sir, look at my record . . ."

" I'm sorry, Richthofen. I've picked my men." Boelcke
yawned, went on with the job of removing his boots. But
his visitor showed no signs of leaving.

" May I ask a question, Captain ? " Boelcke nodded,
without looking up. " What do you consider is the most
important qualification of the fighter pilot ? "

" Marksmanship," Boelcke replied without a moment's
hesitation. " A man may be a wonderful flyer, and full of

courage, but if he can't shoot straight it's a waste of time putting him in a plane."

" I was hoping you'd say that, sir ! " The heels clicked again, like some heavy bolt slamming home. " I have the honour to report that I am a crackshot, sir, with any weapon, from a revolver to a machine-gun. I spend hours shooting, every day. As a matter of fact, I supplied your dinner to-night—wood pigeon. Yesterday it was venison. This squadron never has to buy meat or poultry."

The Captain looked up, chuckled softly ; Richthofen was standing straight as a bayonet, chin jutting high, his lean, aristocratic face flushed with pride. This youngster was vain and cocksure, but if he really kept the mess provided with fresh meat, then he must be a very fine shot indeed.

" Good for you," Boelcke said. " I'll remember that, and if there are any vacancies in the future I certainly will consider you."

" While you're here, sir, will you not look at my official service record ? It's in the commander's office."

" All right, I'll look at your record. In the morning, before I leave."

" Thank you, Captain." A stiff, Prussian bow as he backed to the door. " While you're going through it, I'll see if I can bag you a brace of pheasants to take back with you. Good night, sir."

The first thing Boelcke realised, as he began to read through the young officer's personal record file early next morning, was that Richthofen could never have seen this himself—if he had, he certainly wouldn't have let it get into the hands of anyone he wanted to impress ! Officers' official records were supposed to be confidential, of course

—that is, for the eyes of unit commanders and head-quarters " brass " only—but in time of war paper-work was not taken too seriously, the files were not guarded strictly and most pilots had little difficulty in getting hold of them, finding out how they had been rated and reported by instructors and flight commanders right through their careers. But Richthofen, no doubt confident that his file did him credit, probably hadn't bothered to sneak a look.

It was an intriguing document. He had been in trouble frequently, mostly for insubordination. He was described by former commanders variously—as " headstrong," " over-confident," " disrespectful," but nearly all the contributors agreed, if grudgingly, that he was highly, unfailingly enthusiastic, and had great physical courage and stamina. One or two assessments—which struck Boelcke as perhaps more shrewd and thorough than the rest—clearly suggested that this son of an old and noble family was an incurable romantic, terribly aware of the chivalrous traditions of his class, obsessed by a wild sense of destiny and fired by ambitions which were totally unjustified by his very ordinary capabilities.

Not surprisingly, he had started the war as a dashing, sabre-swinging cavalry officer. Reading between the lines, it wasn't difficult to see that it had taken him some months to face reality—to see that his dreams of galloping glory belonged in another age, that there was little scope for cavalry in the muddy drudgery of 1914 and trench warfare. But once he saw this, obviously he had decided immediately that to seek his radiant destiny he must enter the new list of the twentieth century—the air.

At first his regiment would not release him, but his persistence wore down opposition and in May, 1915, he forsook saddle for cockpit. But training schools for pilots were full; he was made an observer, and served on operations in France.

After a few months he had applied for pilot training, and when this was refused apparently persuaded his own pilot to teach him. But for all his confidence and enthusiasm, according to the reports of this reluctant instructor, Richthofen proved a poor student. His touch on the controls was described as " heavy-handed," his judgment of height and distance was " uncertain " and he had a frightening lack of co-ordination. After many hours of dual instruction, suddenly he seemed to improve—to get the knack of it all. On an October afternoon he took off for his first solo flight. Coming in to land he let his speed get too low, the nose too high. The aircraft went into a spin and crashed. The accident report showed the machine was destroyed, but Richthofen was only bruised and shaken and was fit for normal duties as observer within a few hours.

Boelcke's guess was that after this accident Richthofen's pilot had refused to give him any further instruction, for the file contained no more progress reports by him. But Richthofen must have continued to practise alone, and made a successful solo flight without authority, for only a few weeks later he entered the normal examination for pilots, competing against officers, who had been through the full, official training course. He failed—disastrously. Yet nothing could destroy his simple faith in his destiny; he continued his secret, solitary practice, entered the examination again a few weeks later and scraped through with scant marks to spare. His flying had improved only slightly, but his examiners this time took more interest in theoretical and technical matters and were impressed by his grasp of aero-engineering and maintenance, armaments, signalling procedure and air tactics. Obviously he had been studying very hard.

The file contained a letter written by Richthofen on the day he was informed that he had passed the examination. Doubtless and audacious as a prophet, he requested to be posted to a fighter squadron—though at that time only the most skilful aircraft-handlers were assigned to the fast, light and sensitive single-seater machines. Richthofen was given a sturdy, two-seater observation plane.

After that he had served for some weeks quietly, without distinction, spotting for the artillery and reconnoitring British and French rear lines and supply routes. It was noted that under fire he remained utterly unperturbed, but the standard of his flying was still below average.

Then somehow, persistent as the seasons, he had talked a senior officer into " pulling strings " and getting him transferred to a fighter squadron. At last glory was within his grasp, in a matter of weeks or months he would be an ace ; to celebrate his success in advance, he threw a lavish farewell party for his friends at the observation squadron mess.

He had lasted less than fourteen days on fighters. After wrecking two machines, and very nearly colliding in mid-air with his squadron commander, he was swiftly transferred back to larger, slower planes—this time a bomber squadron stationed on the Eastern Front. At Kovel. And he had remained here, complaining and scheming and not very popular, ever since.

Boelcke was about to replace the file in the commander's cupboard when a loose sheet of paper fell out. He stooped, retrieved it, glanced at the writing. It was a letter written by Richthofen during his time with the observation squadron, and in it he reported " a private experiment " and claimed the destruction of two Allied fighters behind the enemy lines. German observation planes at that stage were usually unarmed, or else equipped with only a single, antiquated and ineffective gun mounted on a scarf-ring round the observer's cockpit. Boelcke could not recall ever having heard of one destroying an enemy fighter. He read on, intrigued but sceptical.

The letter described in some detail, how Richthofen had found a way to rig a Spandau machine-gun on the upper wing of the observation plane, and run a cable from its trigger to his cockpit. Attacked on a long-distance patrol, he said he had shot down two fighters. Though his observer and the crew of an accompanying plane added signed statements that they had witnessed this engagement, it seemed that Richthofen's claim had not been allowed— his superiors simply hadn't believed him. But the signature of one of the witnesses now caught Boelcke's eye—a personal friend, whom he knew to be a man of unquestionable honour. If this were true—if Richthofen had managed to bag two small, fast fighters with a crude contraption like that—then he must be a truly wonderful marksman, one of the best shots in the German forces !

As if to confirm this idea, as the Captain left the commander's office a tall figure came out of the thick woods beyond the airfield's boundary. He walked stiffly, almost a strut ; and he was carrying a sporting gun—and three brace of pheasants.

Watching him approach, Boelcke thought of the task ahead for his new, special wing of fighters, and wondered if this strange, stiff young dandy, vain yet courageous, ludicrously ambitious yet loyal and eager—a sort of Don Quixote of the skies—could possibly fit in after all. He was certainly an unusual and colourful personality, and that was important; one couldn't help admiring his earnestness and persistence; and if he was half as good a shot as his record indicated, and as he himself so readily declared, and as those six pheasants testified——?

Boelcke decided to take a chance. He would take Richthofen back with him. On trial. If he didn't fit in, he'd find himself back on bombers or scouts faster than he could click those polished heels.

The other pilots, hand-picked from the finest units of Germany's air force, literally made rings round Richthofen in the practise dog-fights which were part of the new wing's exacting training programme. Despite his hundreds of hours of experience, he was not by any stretch of the imagination a natural flyer; he was still clumsy, heavy-handed in manœuvres, and his landings were shocking, often downright dangerous.

But no one worked harder, tried harder, studied longer or displayed more coolness under long, severe strain.

To get his " cubs " used to the speed and durability of their new Albatross biplane fighters, Boelcke used to take the whole wing up in a loose formation to about 15,000 feet then suddenly, without warning, slam his stick forward, open his throttle and dive, full out, to 1,000 feet. In this, Richthofen was always a poor last—slow to react to his leader's sudden descent, liable to lose sight of the others on his way down and pull out either too early or dangerously late. And on other exercises he was little better.

But when it came to gunnery he was the star performer. And so vain, so infuriatingly sarcastic about the others, that he encouraged every man on the squadron to work hard and improve his shooting " just for the pleasure of beating him, just once. . . ."

By the beginning of September they were ready. Boelcke explained to them their vital task—kept secret up till now for security reasons. In the past, the German air policy had laid emphasis on defence ; the role of the fighters was to protect artillery and troops from air attack, sometimes to escort their bomber colleagues, and to maintain standing patrols over key positions, supply depots and ammunition dumps. In other words, unlike the British fighters, they did not seek battle—they fought only when called upon.

" Now, after more than two years of war, we are changing our tactics," he said. " We are no longer a purely defensive force—we are going over to the offensive, hitting wherever we can, as hard as we can. And this wing, as a new and specially created unit, will open this offensive."

The pilots cheered—too long had the swashbuckling British enjoyed the advantage of picking the time and place of battle between forces of fighters ! Now the Tommies were due for some surprises—they'd find themselves rousted out at odd hours to meet the challenge of a crack German unit hungry for combat !

The man who cheered loudest was Richthofen ; in this new policy of aggression he saw at last the long-sought opportunity which would bring him fame and glory.

The British formation of scout-bombers flew unhurriedly in a wide circle over their own base. In the distance, glinting in the September sun, they could see the German planes—apparently patrolling their " beat " as usual, high above their army's trenches and heavy batteries. Plenty of time ; Jerry never moved until he was attacked. The British could climb, leisurely survey the situation, then simply fly round the obstacle.

And then, almost before the shocked British pilots

realised it, the Germans were sweeping down across no-man's-land in tight, attacking formation; thirteen sleek and graceful Albatrosses. Too late, frantic hands opened throttles, pulled back on the sticks—there was no time to climb to meet this unexpected assault; for once the Germans were going to have the advantage of altitude.

Boelcke, leading his " cubs," had stationed Richthofen next to his own plane, intending to keep an eye on him if he could. But as they sliced down on the British pack, spreading out in order to pick their victims, the ex-bomber pilot with the " shaky " flying record seemed to draw out ahead of his comrades, plunge in first and fasten on to a large, two-seater Vickers F.E.

At the controls of the F.E. was Flight-Lieutenant L.B.F. Morris; in the observer's seat, Lieutenant T. Rees. Rees had a big Lewis gun mounted on a turntable pivot, and Morris had another fixed to the fuselage, firing forward through the propeller arc and fitted with the new Constantinescu synchronisation device which ensured that the bullets did not hit the spinning blades. Both airmen were " veterans " of the Royal Flying Corps, and Rees had a proud reputation for marksmanship.

Richthofen closed to fifty yards, opened fire with his twin Spandaus. Rees retaliated, and Richthofen was forced to dive out of range. He came back, climbing steeply to above and behind the British plane. Rees opened up again. Some of his bullets were very near; at any moment a stream of them could hit home. Richthofen banked into a cloud, circled and prepared to come in to the attack for the third time—at a lower level. Morris was now flying the F.E. straight and level, no doubt thinking the German had been beaten off for good, and for the moment there was no need to twist and turn evasively.

Boelcke had taught Richthofen and the other " cubs " about a certain " blind spot "—a small approach angle which could be covered neither by an F.E. pilot nor the observer. Richthofen now went for this spot. And Morris flew on, unaware that his super-persistent foe lurked still under his tail.

Throttle wide open, Richthofen rose steeply towards the smooth, red belly of the F.E. Thirty yards from his target his Spandaus rattled out. As he came up and passed to one side of his victim, he noticed that the propeller had stopped. The pilot had been hit. The released controls reared and bucked, the F.E. side-slipped, fell away.

Richthofen followed it down. He saw that the observer was also slumped in his seat. Unguided, the plane crossed no-man's-land, passed over the German lines. Then, as it neared the ground, Morris regained consciousness, straightened out and made a good landing. Richthofen, the unscathed victor, brought his Albatross down in the same field—and, clumsy as ever, almost smashed it!

He ran to the British plane and helped to lift Morris and Rees out ; minutes later they died on the way to a hospital. Sadly he flew back to his airfield. There, the sadness lifted, he smirked and strutted, flushed with victory.

Boelcke's " cubs " had acquitted themselves well ; four other pilots had scored kills in the battle. There was champagne in the mess and to Richthofen and each of the other four a delighted Boelcke presented a silver tankard.

But Richthofen, now completely sure of himself, felt this did not mark the victory—the start of his true, lustrous career—with enough emphasis. So he wrote to a Berlin jeweller and ordered a silver cup, two inches high and inscribed : " 1 Vickers 17.9.16." He announced that he intended to have a cup made for each of his future kills.

By 1918, Richthofen—" The Red Knight of Germany," in a scarlet-painted plane—had shot down eighty machines. But he had only sixty cups: the jeweller in luxury-starved Germany had run out of silver !

Those silver cups perhaps provide us with the most revealing clue to the personality of Captain Baron Manfred von Richthofen. Without doubt he was inordinately vain, and revelled in self-glorification. As the tally of his " kills " mounted, he held aloof from his colleagues and became a tough, silent commander when later he formed his own wing—a sixty-strong " circus " of fighters. He remained a clumsy pilot—and an incredibly brilliant marksman. His courage, his love of flying and his passionate loyalty never diminished, but he lost his old romantic idea of chivalry—the sort of impulse which had led him down to try to help his early victims, Morris and Rees.

He met his death in April, 1918, it is said, while attacking a young pilot whose guns had jammed. He failed to notice another British fighter, getting on to his own tail. It was piloted by a very able Canadian aviator, Captain Roy Brown.

A short burst of machine-gun fire. The Baron's red-painted plane reared, dipped out of control, crash-landed behind the Allied lines.

Richthofen, the crackshot, who always told his pilots " Never shoot for the plane—shoot at the man," was found slumped in his cockpit. Shot through the chest.

STARS OF NO-MAN'S-SKY

TONGUES OF orange and white fire lashed the night sky and the crash of exploding shells rocked several miles of Allied trenches. Along the front line troops huddled together in the mud and wondered if this were just another of the regular probings to test Allied opposition, or the overture to a mass attack on the morrow.

It was 1917. A time of terrible uncertainty ; a time when the tide of war on the Western Front could be changed by one sustained German break-through.

After perhaps an hour, there came a pause in the barrage. At a Royal Flying Corps airfield behind the lines, in the sudden silence a violin was heard playing a slow, wistful melody. It seemed like a tiny voice crying out for peace amid the muddy, smoky destruction.

An enemy flare climbed slowly above no-man's-land and its pale, pulsing light silhouetted the musician, sitting outside a tent. A slim, boyish figure, with his head thoughtfully tilted to catch the mood of his own strange, sweet music. Then the flare died and the German big guns again took up the harsh symphony of war.

Nineteen-year-old Albert Ball closed his eyes, tried not to listen to the guns, continued to play his violin. He hated war.

To many of the other, older pilots it was a mystery that this sensitive lad from a well-to-do home in Nottingham had volunteered to fly. Deeply religious, he had in his eyes the look of the early Christian fanatic. And yet it was a fact that he was proving himself a natural flyer and fearless fighter.

Yes, a strange mixture, Albert Ball. Near his tent out there in France stood his Nieuport—the little one-seater " skin-and-bone " plane which was showing itself such a reliable war machine. And on the other side of the tent, picked out in the mud, was a small garden, fresh with early spring flowers. Both the plane and the garden Ball tended with loving care. Both were part of his life—along with his music.

The Royal Flying Corps had suffered heavy losses in the winter just gone. In four bitter months over the Somme, 867 airmen had died. The average life of a pilot was three weeks when Ball arrived in France to join No. 13 Squadron.

At first he had flown in a two-seater B.E.2 and was engaged on artillery observation. But even in this slow and cumbersome craft he managed to shoot down two Germans. He was transferred to No. 11 Squadron, equipped with the speedier Nieuport.

Among his gay, wild young comrades, Ball was a man apart. He was almost oppressively quiet in the mess ; he never went " out on the spree " with the others. He wrote home regularly, but not about the war ; his letters to his father were full of his little garden, and invariably ended with requests for more seeds and plants.

But with the more experienced pilots he would often spend hours—asking questions, talking technicalities and tactics. He was a passionate admirer of the two superb French aces, René Fonck and Charles Nungesser. (Fonck's total of kills reached 75, Nungesser's 45. Both survived, but in May, 1927, Nungesser was lost on an attempted Atlantic flight.)

As in the mess, Ball preferred to be alone in the air. He never wore goggles or a helmet—" I like to feel the wind in my hair," he explained half-apologetically.

Within weeks of joining the squadron he had conceived and perfected perhaps the most dangerous, but most effective technique yet known in aerial warfare.

It was generally accepted that if an enemy plane got above and behind a pilot then nine times out of ten the pilot could not shake it off. But Ball would go out of his way to allow a German to get on his tail. Then with his uncanny ability to sense the instant when the enemy was about to open fire he would turn away sharply and, in a special, brilliant manœuvre he had worked out, with amazing swiftness come up under the other plane and attack in the " blind spot."

As impressive to his comrades was his steel-nerved method of flying head-on against a German, calling his bluff and forcing him to turn away at the last moment. That left the German plane vulnerable for perhaps a second —enough time for Ball, a crackshot, to send home a deadly burst of bullets. Ball's amazing marksmanship was not entirely a gift—on the ground he drilled with rifle and revolver, hour after hour, keeping his eye true. And almost always he supervised the servicing of his plane's armament.

Such methods quickly gained for the young officer a high reputation, and when he went to 56 Squadron even established aces like Rhys-Davies and Major J. B. McCudden became admirers of this strange, quiet youth. His senior officers, noting his unusual talent as a lone wolf, gave him what amounted to a " roving commission." And nobody plagued him to join in mess parties at nights— he could stay out in the moonlight, alone, with his violin.

During this period he went out on solitary patrol one

day and met two German Albatrosses. He dived to the attack and inflicted damage on one of the planes. But before he could turn his attention to the second machine, he ran out of ammunition. The Albatrosses took this chance to turn tail and flee. Ball followed—keeping up his attack with his revolver!

He continued this strange pursuit until the enemy reached their own airfield, and then he scribbled a note on the little pad strapped to his thigh, swooped low and dropped it on the grass. The note challenged the two Albatrosses to a new battle with him at first light of dawn.

Next morning Ball, his hair streaming in the wind, set off for the rendezvous, alone. He arrived in time to see his two adversaries of the previous day circling slowly, reluctantly. He flew towards the nearer one, intending to use his head-on technique—a shrewd tactic against such nervous foes. He was closing fast when machine-gun bullets hosed all round him.

He pulled up and turned tightly, immediately saw that three other planes had joined the attack, diving from the cover of a cloud patch. He was trapped. Ball was famous even to the enemy, and they were not letting a small thing like chivalry stand in the way of such a prize of war. So it was five-to-one against him!

The Germans had planned their tactics well: every time the British pilot tried to close and pick off one of them, all five kept swerving out of his range. Three worked their way back to cut off his line of retreat, while the other two teased him into chasing them further into German-held territory. Ball, firing at long range, for the second time in less than twenty-four hours ran out of ammunition.

The Germans soon discovered this, and the two planes he had chased turned to face him—to finish him off. They opened fire together, and after two short bursts the British plane fell into a steep, tight spin. As the two attacking Germans followed it down, their three waiting companions waggled their wings to signal victory and flew off with the news—the British ace was about to crash far behind the German lines.

But Ball had not been hit, he was only feigning. Nearing the ground, he eased out of the spin, straightened his plane slightly, just sufficiently to make a landing—an awkward, lurching landing that appeared to be a fluke, or at best the last effort of a dying pilot. It was a brilliant display of aircraft handling—a convincing piece of acting. As the plane stopped, he slumped forward, kept still.

The two Germans, who had followed him down, landed in the same field, leapt from their machines. They were running to examine their prize when Ball's slumped figure suddenly came to life. He opened his throttle. The fighter trundled forward, gathered speed, lifted just over their heads. Before the Germans could get back to their own cockpits and follow, Ball was a diminishing speck—scudding at low level back towards the Allied lines.

Very rarely did Ball—soon made a captain—fly with other pilots, but on 17th May, 1917, he was one of eleven fighter men who set out " to look for trouble." By that time the quiet, flower-loving, violin-playing youth had shot down forty enemy machines and been awarded the Distinguished Service Order (with two bars) and the Military Cross.

A cold day, with a hard brightness. Great puffs of cloud sailed high above the bevy of British machines. From the distance tiny specks expanded suddenly into an armada of Albatrosses. The British patrol opened throttles and tore into the enemy formation.

In the first minute of the battle Ball was seen to climb into a cloud in pursuit of a fleeing German. When the dog-fight broke up, and the British pilots re-formed and turned for home, there was no sign of him. That night the airfield still waited, hoping to hear a drone in the darkness—perhaps he had made a forced landing, or put down at another base. . . . But dawn came, and it was clear that Albert Ball would never return. The exact manner of his death remains a mystery to this day.

He was posthumously awarded the Victoria Cross.

Ball's example—his innovations, his unflagging courage and constant drilling—had fired the imagination of another young pilot—a very different personality.

Edward (Micky) Mannock was the son of a regular soldier, one of a large family. He had been handicapped by poverty, lack of education and bad eyesight. At twelve he had been sent out to work as a greengrocer's boy.

After that there had been various, unpromising jobs before, full of determination to gain some sort of security, he packed up and went to seek his fortune in Turkey. He arrived just in time to find that country at war with Britain! At once he was interned, but after a few months, largely because of his defective eyesight, he was sent home with a batch of exchanged prisoners.

Immediately, he joined a Royal Army Medical Corps unit, and later got a commission in the Royal Engineers. In France he used to lie in the mud-choked trenches, watching Albert Ball and the other heroes of the sky fly out to another day of high-speed action in the wide, clear blue. To him, despite the high casualty rate in pilots, theirs was a life infinitely to be preferred to the sluggish, soggy routine of a " sapper."

By now one of his eyes had returned to normal as a result

of treatment by a gifted Army doctor, but the other was still defective—almost useless, in fact. And, of course, top grading in eyesight was essential for flyers. Even so, Micky Mannock applied for a transfer to the Flying Corps.

At his medical examination he had to read letters on a test card with one eye at a time—the other being covered by the examiner. He began with his good eye, and found no difficulty. Then came an enormous stroke of luck. The doctor was called away for a few moments. And in those moments Mannock stared hard at the card with his good eye, managed to memorise all the letters. The doctor returned, and after the " reading " passed the useless eye as top grade !

In training he showed no great promise, qualified with average gradings and was sent to fighters.

On his first squadron he came under the influence of one of Albert Ball's old comrades, the ace " Mac " McCudden.

McCudden liked the highly-strung, argumentative young man—and indeed felt sorry for him, for Micky had strong likes and dislikes and an unfortunate way of upsetting people, losing friends. Through many feuds and sulks, McCudden stuck by him—perhaps realising that Mannock's tough childhood had left him with a feeling of inferiority and an unreasonable suspicion of the motives of others.

A real test of their friendship came after some operational flights when Mannock—the man who was always talking of his relish for adventure and action—seemed to temper his boldness with perhaps a little too much " reliable judgment." His seniors began to doubt whether he had the fibre of a pilot. In the mess his comrades hinted broadly that the newcomer talked big, but had " cold feet."

McCudden alone did not doubt Mannock ; he took him aside, tried to find out the reason for the youngster's apparent failure to press home his attacks and make what appeared simple " kills." But Mannock sulked, would say nothing.

So McCudden watched him closely on the next patrol and suddenly, in the middle of a dog-fight, discovered Mannock's weakness—he was a shockingly poor marksman ! Back at the airfield he ordered Mannock out for machine-gun practice on the range, and in a matter of minutes found out the secret of Mannock's defective eyesight.

The older pilot was uncertain what to do for the best— if he reported his discovery, Mannock would be permanently grounded ; on the other hand, was it right to let a man go on flying when he was not fully fit, when he could not protect himself properly ? And was it fair to the rest of the squadron ?

In the end he decided to postpone a decision—to wait a little and see whether, with practice, the youngster could improve his shooting. Mannock was ready to work till he dropped, and day after day they spent hours on the range. Slowly, together they evolved a method by which Mannock corrected for his defective eye, making allowance for it in aiming—and to the astonishment of both he became a first class shot !

He worked just as hard to improve his flying, taking off alone between operational flights to practise the difficult and dangerous aerobatic manœuvres introduced by the legendary lone-wolf Ball, and the experienced, patient McCudden. Very soon his doubting messmates noted the change ; in a matter of a few months " Cold Feet " Mannock became " Wild Micky " or "Mad Mannock," and his bag of " kills " mounted steadily.

The sulkiness, the lingering sense of inferiority and

defensive truculence, left him as his confidence grew. At last the ex-greengrocer's boy had found " some sort of security "—it didn't matter to him that to hold on to it he had to place his life in jeopardy every day. He became a cheerful, popular figure in the mess, and displayed immense patience with the less experienced pilots—the same sort of patience that McCudden had shown to him. And he was the instigator and leading figure of countless wild squadron parties.

With no fewer than 73 " kills " to his official credit, he was awarded the Victoria Cross. To thousands in the trenches—on both sides of no-man's-land—he was referred to now simply as " the mad Major." After an air battle, he had a habit of swooping down and skimming along the Allied lines—where he himself had spent many miserable months—waggling his wings and waving to the troops. The soldiers looked forward to his visits, cheered and waved back—it gave them fresh heart to know they had this great flyer on their side, a man who understood their grimmer, dirtier, less personal war here on the ground, and who thought about them enough to drop in now and then.

Occasionally, to provide a diversion for the weary, muddy infantrymen, Mannock would put on a display of aerobatics, rolling and looping and spinning his plane, pulling out scant feet above the parapets. Once or twice, where no-man's-land was particularly narrow, Germans following his crazy progress from the other side would open fire on the stunting plane. Then the Mad Major was apt to roar across and, to the delight of the watching Tommies, " beat up " the enemy positions, diving so low that the Germans were forced to abandon their guns and lie flat on their faces in the mire.

On the night of 26th July, 1918—just four months before

the end of the war—Mannock was holding one of his parties at the airfield's mess. Donald Inglis, a young New Zealander who had joined the squadron only a few days before, was standing on one side, a little shy, feeling a bit out of things. Mannock came up, slapped his shoulder.

" Cheer up, Don ! What's the matter—don't you like it here ? "

" I like it fine, sir," Inglis said with a grin. " But I'll like it better once I've broken my duck and bagged myself a Hun."

" What ?—haven't you got one yet ? Well now, soon put that right ! Come up with me in the morning, I'll show you a good hunting ground. Jerry's been sending a two-seater job over to scout this sector every morning, same time to the minute. Up till now I haven't bothered with him. but he's getting too cocksure, coming in very low —taking advantage of our good nature. He's yours, Don. Come with me at dawn and I'll set him up for you."

A few hours later, while the other pilots were still asleep, the fledgling Inglis and the veteran Mannock took off into a salmon dawn. Over the Allied front line, just as Mannock had predicted, they spotted the German—circling, insolently low. Together they dived on him. Mannock pulled ahead, and a little off to one side, neatly drawing the enemy's fire and forcing him to turn his back on Inglis.

Inglis, in his excitement, came up so fast on the slower scout-plane that he almost collided with its tail. He steadied himself, opened fire. The German staggered under the short-range blast, keeled over, crashed in no-man's-land in a big gout of flame.

Inglis and Mannock circled the wreck, then set course for base and breakfast. They were flying at about two hundred feet, nearer to the German lines than their own.

Below—more as an act of defiance than in real hope—
enemy infantrymen sniped at them with rifles. The Mad
Major did not deign to take the slightest notice.

They were almost out of range of the small-arms fire
when Inglis, glancing over at Mannock, saw flames begin
to lick out of the leader's cowling. He waved, pointed
frantically, then Mannock seemed to straighten in his cockpit, kick his rudder hard, struggle with the controls. Down
went the crippled plane's nose, and now the flames gushed
from it, consuming wings and fuselage even as it fell into
a spin. The blazing wreck turned twice, and smote the
ground as little more than a ball of fire.

Inglis knew Mannock could not have lived in that
inferno—he was probably dead before he hit the churned
mud of the battleground where, many months and more
than seventy victories ago, he had lain and craned his
neck to watch, and to envy, the flashing wings of Ball and
the others. The ex-sapper had had his dream, and now
he followed Ball, and countless other aces, into history.
What the best of Germany's fighter force had failed to
accomplish, an unknown marksman in a clogged trench
on the Western Front had achieved with a single, lucky
shot. And this humble soldier would never know for sure
that it was his bullet which had done it.

Filled with these sad thoughts, the young Inglis flew
away from the pillar of smoke, to take the grim news back
to base.

Ball and Mannock are lustrous names in the history of
military aviation, but no roll call of Allied air heroes in
World War One is complete without mention of a third
holder of the Victoria Cross—the Canadian ex-cavalryman
Billy Bishop. Like "the Mad Major," Ontario-born

William Avery Bishop was fond of swooping low over the trenches and exchanging greetings with the troops—and on one occasion he went one better than that ; he and his fighter plane actually took part in a bayonet charge across no-man's-land !

This famous incident took place on Easter Monday, 1917, in the opening phase of the Battle of Arras. British units had been ordered " over the top," and were advancing slowly across the pocked and boggy ground. Heavy and accurate machine-gun fire from the German lines was taking frightful toll, cutting great swathes in their ranks, gradually bring them to a stop.

Bishop, circling overhead, saw the advance falter and no-man's-land become heaped with dead and wounded. But in one sector a determined formation of attackers had got to within a few hundred yards of their objective.

Slicing down, he roared over the heads of his country-men at about thirty feet, saw that they were being halted and pinned down by the cross-fire from two machine-gun posts. Banking, he turned, dropped still lower, flew towards one of the posts, blasted it with long bursts. Then for minutes on end he flew to and fro, ahead of the advancing Tommies, raking both enemy posts and a section of the German trenches in between. At times, as he hauled the plane round in a steep turn, his wingtips were only inches from the ground.

So accurate was his shooting that the enemy gunners were forced to break off. The British forces started forward again, bayonets high and glinting, moving steadily through the drifting smoke in a solid, purposeful line. Bishop circled overhead, waved encouragingly as they broke into a stumbling charge, smashed through the German front line.

And with the objective gained in this sector of the front, troops on either side rallied and continued their attacks. Thereafter Billy Bishop—who survived the war, to become an Air Marshal of the Royal Canadian Air Force, and an important influence in the development of air power—was also given the honoured title which Mannock had first inspired: " the Mad Major."

THE WORST WEATHER IN THE WORLD

THE COCKPIT was awash. Cobham could no longer see ahead, for the force of the monsoon, hitting his goggles as from a high-pressure hose, completely blinded him. He tore them off and, snugging his head below the cockpit screen to avoid the full blast, squinted down over the side, seeking the vaguest shape of land below.

It was 9th September, 1926. Most of the following week the world was to hold its breath for news of Alan Cobham and his two companions, battling through savage storms in a tiny, single-engined seaplane. They had set out to prove that the worst weather in the world need not preclude a regular air service to Australia and back.

And this slight, urgent little Londoner with the trim moustache was on this occasion making no empty, glory-seeking gesture, but a sober investment of his life in the future of aviation. Now it seemed he was going to lose his great gamble.

Flying low over the sea, scanning a very inadequate map, Cobham had tried to zig-zag the little plane between the monsoon storms. But the moment he crossed the northern tip of Sumatra the full fury of the weather, sweeping unchecked across the Indian Ocean, closed round behind him and buried his plane in a terrible deluge.

In the cabin his two engineers—Ward, whom he had borrowed from the R.A.F. in Basra on the outward trip, and Capel, who had joined the venture in Australia—realised they were in gravest danger now. Obviously they couldn't go on. Ahead it was black as the inside of an ink bottle. Cobham turned the plane about, knowing their only hope was to find a gap in the weather behind. But there was no escape. The monsoon had closed completely around them.

Seasoned airmen and realists, they accepted their great gamble as lost and resigned themselves to death. Then suddenly there loomed ahead a dim shape—an island. Cobham strained his aching eyes to penetrate the swirling rain and saw that the water on the leeward side seemed comparatively calm. He knew this was their last chance.

The seaplane came lurching out of the sodden darkness and flopped on the heaving water. Almost before the cloud of spray settled, Ward and Capel were out on the floats. But when Cobham looked shorewards he saw no beach—only a mass of rocks. He would have to taxi out to sea, come in again, and search for a better spot.

Crossways over the big rollers the plane dipped and lurched. The two engineers, clinging precariously to the floats, were human counterweights that kept the machine more or less upright; the tops were blowing off the waves like snow off mountain peaks, and they breathed more water than air. Luckily the next bay showed a good beach. They struggled towards this haven.

Ward had to cast the sea anchor—a long canvas sleeve—before the engine could be cut. But the sudden drag all but hurled him into the sea and he had to let go. The sea anchor was lost.

Nothing for it now but to taxi in and beach the aircraft. Ward and Capel jumped waist deep into the rushing surf and, fighting every foot, tugged the floats up on the sand.

Then they lashed the plane to the nearest palm tree. Almost at once the storm started to slacken.

A lucky sun-shot, between tatters of cloud, fixed their position. They were right off the beaten sea track, on an uninhabited island about forty miles from the mainland of Siam. Rock and impenetrable jungle came tumbling right down to the sea. The only way out was to fly. And it became clear that they must leave soon, for Cobham noticed with alarm that the tide was coming in, lifting the seaplane and bumping its cardboard-thin floats up and down on the beach. The waterline showed that high tide would reach up to the wall of jungle, and that would be the end of their floats—perhaps of the plane.

Taking off out to sea would mean going downwind, and with those giant rollers running across their path they would never get into the air. So he decided to take off across the wind, riding the long way of the rollers.

It was a terrible business. They bumped and crashed over the water, slowly, slowly gathering speed. Twice, as the floats began to lift, a breaker reared and dealt them a mighty blow, swatting them back into the sea. But on the third try the machine staggered into the air, held its way for an agonising second or so, then, gaining a knot or two of air speed, gradually climbed away.

The visibility worsened steadily again as Cobham headed through the downpour for the main coastline. But they had not gone far when a whistling noise joined the engine note, and a bad vibration shuddered through the craft; the rain had ruined the wooden propeller, and some of the fabric was coming off.

Cobham used all his skill and knowledge to nurse the maimed, failing seaplane along until he judged they were near the coast, then he throttled back and eased the stick forward. He could see only a few yards, but his judgment was perfect. They came down on to a heaving sea not far offshore from the tiny Siamese village of Tanoon. Once safely beached, the engineers busied themselves with repairs.

So ended 9th September, a worse day than most, though it marked neither the beginning nor by any means the end of a series of hair-raising incidents in the most epic survey flight yet attempted in the history of aviation.

What kind of man was this Cobham, who undertook such a flight ? What paths brought him to such high adventure ?

Alan Cobham was reared in the Camberwell district of London. As a boy he was impulsive, highly imaginative. After an uneventful journey in a pony trap, or a quiet day on the river, he could conjure up and invent the most hair-raising exploits which he would retell in convincing detail. Friends and members of the family feared that this vivid talent for " spinning a yarn " would lead him into trouble. But his mother defended him. She saw in those wild tales the outpourings of a mind desperate for excitement, a heart hungry for travel and action. And she could see in her son the beginnings of a fine quality which would balance this " romanticising " ; he had a growing sense of responsibility, shown most clearly in his attitude towards his sister Vera—a girl with a weak heart.

The young Alan was Vera's loyal, self-appointed protector, eager for her happiness, constant in his companionship and always firm and shrewd in guarding her from the thousand petty dangers which lurk for the delicate child. With a quaint, almost fatherly sternness he would upbraid her for running while they were out in the park. And in the evenings those imagined adventures, told in gay boyish tones, let Vera share in a world she could never fully enjoy herself.

Perhaps the most memorable day in Alan's boyhood was when his mother took him to Crystal Palace to see a famous balloonist, Captain Spencer. Passionately the boy begged for a chance to go up in the balloon. Mrs. Cobham refused, told him : " You'll have more sense when you grow up—then you'll know it's better to stay on the ground."

When he left school, his first job was with a wholesale draper in the City of London. But a lad with the restless, adventure-craving heart of Alan Cobham could not take life sitting on an office stool. He tried farming—and gave that up too, because he found an open-air routine as monotonous as that of the City. Routine was the enemy— routine, and having to stay in one place.

One night he was returning home, deep in thoughts of how he might find the right job. He took the wrong bus and arrived in Brixton, on the other side of London. He asked his way from a stranger. They fell into conversation, and suddenly Alan found himself pouring out his troubles.

" They want chaps for the Royal Field Artillery—why not join up ? " the stranger suggested. " The Army has routine, all right—but you'll see a bit of the world, and perhaps some real excitement."

That was in early 1914. Cobham was at the front in France within a month of the outbreak of war. He saw plenty of action in the trenches, and in 1917, when a call went out for volunteers for the Royal Flying Corps, he was among the first to step forward. The R.F.C. training and experience convinced him that his destiny was in the air— always on the move, often in danger, never chained by routine. So after the war he went into civil aviation, and in 1922 was the first Englishman to cross the Channel in a light plane. Two years later he flew to Rangoon and back.

Newspapermen who interviewed him after the Rangoon flight saw him as a cheerful, superbly confident and relaxed young airman who seemed to find his work easy and enjoyable as any sport. But in fact Cobham took each and every task with great, almost grim earnestness—planning each detail, budgeting for the most unlikely eventuality. Just being a pilot wasn't enough—he made himself an expert in every branch of aviation, studying navigation, engineering, aerodynamics, aircraft design, radio communications and metereology. He kept abreast of research and development at home and abroad, studied scientific papers, and made long and frequent journeys to see demonstrations of new equipment.

With his growing knowledge of flying and the aircraft industry, he foresaw the day, not far off, when regular air services would link the continents, carrying urgent mail and perhaps even passengers on fixed schedules to the most distant parts of the globe. Other, older aviation experts scoffed at the idea—aeroplanes, unlike ships, were " fair weather " craft ; it would take many years to produce a machine powerful enough, and with the necessary equipment, endurance and structural strength, to make regular journeys over long distances all the year round, especially in tropical areas where storms of extreme violence developed suddenly.

Cobham, sure that skilled piloting and thorough planning could beat all the dangers, determined to prove it by flying to the other side of the world and back. If it could be done now, in an ordinary, frail plane not specially designed for the job, and without special equipment, then the leaders of Britain's aircraft industry surely would see the urgent need for larger, long-distance machines, and seize the chance to beat other nations in the new field of global air travel. It would be a gamble, but calculated—and with the future of British aviation at stake.

Such was the bold dream which now, in September, 1926, so nearly ended in disaster amid the killing combers off Siam.

In this epic flight to explore and map a new air route to Australia and back, Cobham had deliberately chosen to pit courage and wits, and a plane as vulnerable as a moth by to-day's standards, against the monsoon season at its furious height. And all to establish his conviction that the route could be flown throughout the year.

" My plan," he wrote subsequently, " was to make two jumps per day, keeping up anything from seven hundred to a thousand miles continually between dawn and sunset." He knew that in years to come, with the organisation which would follow his example, there would be better mapping and a system of wireless weather reporting which would enable pilots to miss or fly round the worst of the storms. But for him, the pioneer, skill and resolution were the only defences against the elements.

The odds which had faced Cobham when his aircraft rose from the Medway, at Rochester, on the last day of June that year elude the imaginative grasp of the modern air traveller. His machine—a De Havilland D.H. 50, registered " G-EFBO," powered by a single engine of a mere 383 horsepower—was overloaded by half a ton. It was fitted with seaplane floats, yet beyond a few trial " hops " squeezed in during his last busy week at home, Cobham had no experience of seaplane handling.

He had sketchy maps, no radio, hardly any weather prediction system to warn him of what lay ahead. The 13,000-mile route was dotted with volunteer helpers who, beyond instructions by cable and post, knew next to nothing about the requirements for the landing, mooring-up, servicing and taking-off of a seaplane. Some had never even seen one!

In his early planning, Cobham had allowed himself much too little time to organise the flight, and so had overworked himself to the point of exhaustion before starting. He admitted this later.

" I started off," he said, " on the verge of a nervous breakdown. I relied on the exhilaration of getting into the air and away to pull me round." It didn't. For the first week he flew in a state of collapse. More than once he dozed off at the controls. On his first few overnight stops he dreaded the dawn, when he must drag himself from his resting-place down to the seaplane's mooring.

Cobham's real troubles commenced when he ran into a desert dust storm between Baghdad and Basra. It was impenetrable. He nosed down until the plane was flying only a few feet above the reeds of a marsh, while he strove to make out a horizon by which he could hold the aircraft level.

Suddenly there was a violent explosion. He looked round and saw Elliott, the mechanic engaged for the round-trip, huddled in a corner clutching his side. Above the engine Elliott shouted: " Petrol pipe burst! I've been hit, Chief. Losing pots of blood!"

There was nothing for it but to make for Basra and hospital as fast as they could. The heat was furnace-fierce and Cobham landed perilously on a river littered with shipping. When Elliott had been rushed to hospital, Alan examined the plane and was sorely puzzled to find no damage to the fuel system.

The doctors cleared up the mystery: it wasn't a burst

petrol pipe which had hit Elliott—but a tribesman's bullet. He died the next night in hospital.

At that, Cobham almost lost heart. But cables from home urged him to go on, and the R.A.F. offered to lend him an engineer—a cheerful sergeant named Ward. This airman was to prove a jewel, for though the engine behaved gallantly, the way ahead was strewn with enough mishaps and make-do to keep a whole maintenance crew busy.

When they reached Allahabad, in India, they kept inquisitive native craft from colliding with them only by squirting the occupants with water, and narrowly missed hitting a railway bridge on take-off when the wind changed at the last minute. At Calcutta they had to take special care not to fall in the Hooghly River as they clambered about on the slippery, oil-streaked floats; the undercurrents were so strong that they would never have come up again.

Then came the Burmese rains. Blue-black clouds advanced glowering out of the East to meet them. At times the deluge became a solid wall beyond which they could not see. Cobham kept low, twisting and turning to follow the rocky bays and inlets, close enough to be constantly terrified of crashing. He force-landed once, in a creek near Rangoon, frighteningly close behind a river steamer.

For the last leg of the outward trip, over the dreaded Timor Sea, Cobham laid a protractor upon an Admiralty map and took a bearing. He flew into the teeth of the South-East trade winds, which veered him first to port, then to starboard. He juggled with mental arithmetic and made rule-of-thumb corrections on his compass while flying fifty feet above the water. When the first long spit of land that was Australia rose over the horizon he climbed to have

a look round. There, less than five miles away was his
objective—Herne Bay. After 500 miles of dead-reckoning
navigation in fickle winds, he had almost exactly hit his
destination !

Cobham changed the floats for landing wheels at Darwin
and flew across the continent to Sydney simply by following
car tracks, mule trails and telegraph wires. The plains
below, bathed in sharp, vibrating sunlight, seemed like
one vast aerodrome. At Melbourne the largest crowd he
had ever seen—more than 150,000—swarmed cheering on
to the aerodrome and carried him off in triumph.

Despite all he had been through, Alan Cobham decided
to make the return trip a record bid. With Capel, an
extra engineer recruited in Melbourne to help Ward work
on the plane during their brief stops, he took off and headed
back, plunging almost immediately into foul weather.

The monsoon met him with avenging fury above Sumatra,
and brought him down—first at the unknown island, then
at Tanoon, then again at Victoria Point. And it maintained
its onslaught with unrelenting savagery right into the
heart of India. The diversions and delays cost him four
days.

With all hope of a record now gone, the little weather-
stained plane fought its way slowly up to Calcutta, where
there was more bad news. The storm with which they had
first collided, 1,600 miles to the South, had outstripped
them and was now raging at Allahabad, their next stop
600 miles to the North. And yet they had to go on. For
a tidal bore—a wall of water several feet high—was
reported rolling up the Hooghly River. They knew it
would wreck the machine at its moorings.

So the battle continued. . . . At Delhi the plane broke
loose and drifted downcurrent towards a weir, while

Ward, astride a float, furiously plied a paddle. The paddle broke, and they all dived overboard, swimming and tugging at the floats. Somehow they managed to beach her.

Many other incidents and accidents tried their stamina, efficiency and resourcefulness before they neared the milder skies of Europe. Then all three started to scrub and polish the seaplane into cleanliness for the homecoming.

So at last the little blue-and-silver craft came up the Thames. " G-EFBO " circled Westminster, side-slipped daintily and came in, swaying a little, twenty feet over Westminster Bridge, to land on the river opposite the Houses of Parliament. There it glittered while Cobham walked up the Palace landing stairs in stained and rumpled dungarees—for he had jettisoned his " formals " with other non-essentials to offset the extra over-load of Capel. A vast crowd gave a thunderous welcome to the first man to fly to Australia and back.

Many a young London clerk was late back from lunch that day. No doubt some of them, like Cobham, had thought of revolt from a City stool. In this man in dungarees they saw not only a great aviator, but an individual who had rebelled against routine, sought and found adventure. How many clerks and schoolboys who watched round-eyed the return of Cobham, the trail-blazer, later followed him across the same skies—in peace and in war? And how many others, thrilled by his story, were encouraged to find careers in technical branches of aviation? The full extent of this airman's personal contribution to British air power can never be known in exact terms.

That Australian trip brought him the Britannia Trophy and a knighthood. Cobham, in his superb gamble, had challenged and defied the worst weather in the world;

he had proved that a British plane could outwit nature in her angriest moods; he had shown that flying was no " fair-weather sport," and he had set pilots practising a new art—" blind flying," by the new cockpit instruments.

Sir Alan went on to other ventures—a flying-boat expedition round the continent of Africa; a memorable trip to Capetown, and later air displays with the famous " Cobham's Air Circus." Everything he did served to popularise flying, to excite and inspire youngsters.

His weather-warring wings widened the world for coming generations. The boy with the untameable imagination, who hated routine, became one of the greatest trail-blazers in the history of flying; one of the founders of the proud tradition which many years later sustained and emboldened that small, hard-pressed band of pilots known as The Few in their vital defence of Britain against vastly superior forces.

LAST HOP TO HOWLAND

GEORGE PUTNAM PALMER, the New York publisher, looked into the wide grey eyes of the slender young woman who sat, relaxed and yet grave, facing him across his office desk. " Why do you want this job ? " he asked.

" Because I believe a person must try to do difficult, and especially dangerous things—that's the only way to find out the true extent of one's capabilities. If we stop trying, we stop developing, and we never get to know ourselves properly . . . I also believe that nowadays women must try to do things as men have been trying for hundreds of years."

She said all this evenly, unemotionally, with the clearest kind of sincerity. Putnam knew his problem was solved —the problem of finding an intelligent, level-headed, hardy yet attractive American girl willing to accompany his airmen friends, Lou Gordon and Wilmer Stultz, on their proposed Atlantic flight.

In 1928, crossing the Atlantic by plane was still an immensely hazardous business, a supreme test of man and machine. It had been done only ten times, and never by a woman. Gordon and Stultz had hit on the idea of taking along a girl as passenger, because they wanted an American woman to be the first across, and because they believed that such an achievement by " a mere female " would greatly increase the public's confidence in the future of air travel. They had asked George Putnam to find the right girl, for not only was he a fine judge of character, but a

71

man who well knew the qualities needed for such an adventure, having twice led expeditions into the Arctic.

Now, after countless interviews, the right girl turned out to be Miss Amelia Earhart, teacher and social worker. Putnam had known her for some time, and remembering her strong interest in aviation, her self-confidence and her love of travel, after weeks of fruitless searching had sent her a message asking if she was interested in the idea. For answer, she had come straight to his office, full of restrained excitement.

He studied her now, as she read a summary of the primary flight plan. A long, slack girl with tameless, tawny hair and a quick, eager voice. Not pretty—but her boyish, freckled, very American face, those frank grey eyes, and the sudden, warm way she had of smiling added up to an attractive, completely unaffected personality. Not young, either—yet her boyishness, and her earnestness, made it hard to believe she was thirty. Born in Atchison, Kansas, she had first flown with the young and famous " barnstormer " Frank Hawks, then learned to pilot herself. But flying was expensive; she had been unable to keep it up.

" You do understand the many risks involved? "

She raised her head and gave him a steady, faintly puzzled look.

" Of course. If there were no danger, it wouldn't interest me. To achieve something, there *must* be risks."

Putnam smiled, nodded, lifted his telephone to arrange a meeting with Gordon and Stultz.

And so, a few weeks later, Amelia became the first woman to fly the Atlantic Ocean. Throughout the long, difficult and exhausting flight she remained alert and excited, intensely interested in everything the pilots did, tirelessly watching the instruments and, now and then when she was sure she wouldn't be distracting or fatiguing them, asking questions which showed she had a natural understanding of technicalities and a sound grasp of the principles of flight. And when it was all over she announced : " I'm going to do this again—on my own."

By writing and lecturing about her trip she acquired a little capital. From then on aeroplanes became her sole obsession. George Putnam helped her in every way he could to become a top-class pilot, but tried just as hard to discourage the wild notion of the hazardous solo crossing. Again and again he got her to postpone preparations for the attempt, using any convenient pretext—he would tell her that a new type of machine, or engine, was about to be produced which would give her a much better chance ; or some branch of her flying was weak, she must spend a few more weeks correcting the fault. . . .

Putnam not only admired this extraordinary girl, he had gained a deep affection for her, and was determined not to let her risk her life. But Amelia—fiercely self-reliant, and with a passionate sense of freedom—would not allow even this greatly valued friendship to turn her from the target she had set herself. In flying she had found a new life, a new and more powerful self. She was confident she could beat the Atlantic, single-handed—and after that, perhaps other oceans.

In 1931, with several important cross-country flights behind her, she told Putnam : " I'm ready now. Please don't try to talk me out of it again. I won't hear of any more delay."

" All right, Amelia," he sighed. " But I have one more thing to ask before you go." And he asked her to become his wife.

Amelia did not give him an immediate answer. To her, marriage was now a danger, a threat to the great plans she had made; she wanted time to think. As a wife, would she be able to keep on flying as often as she liked, wherever she liked? Or would the responsibilities of a home gradually turn her into just another captive of the kitchen, dreaming sadly over the dirty dishes? And would it be fair to George, who had his own brilliant career, if she kept on with an occupation that demanded fullest attention, took her far from home, and involved constant tension and dangers?

She knew George Putnam was the only man for her, but she was determined that if they married it would have to be on the basis of a clear understanding; he must never try to stop her flying. Never.

Putnam gave this pledge, for he realised now that nothing could keep her on the ground, and he had come to respect her resolution and superb concentration. On their wedding day, a few hours before the ceremony, she handed him a remarkable letter, reminding him of their pact:

Dear G.P.,

There are some things which should be written before we are married. . . . You must know again my reluctance, my feeling that I shatter thereby chances in work which means so much to me. . . . I may have to keep some place where I can go to be myself now and then, for I cannot guarantee to endure at all times the confinements of even an attractive cage. . . .

It was fortunate that Putnam—the former Arctic explorer—understood the restless spirit in Amelia, the honesty and the passion for independence which had moved her to write such words on her wedding day.

The following year—1932—she flew the Atlantic alone. In a crimson Lockheed monoplane, she won for herself the title " First lady of U.S. Aviation " and set up a new record, thirteen-and-a-half hours. A complicated, rough flight through tricky, swirling winds and thickets of foul weather. Flames and fumes from a broken weld in an exhaust pipe leaked into the cockpit. The altimeter and the petrol gauge failed. Only a tough and workmanlike pilot, and an able navigator, could have battled successfully through the murk and the long, lonely, lurching hours.

Her name and her image flashed around the world. Millions came to know the freckled face with the tomboyish grin, under the short, rumpled hair. In the years that followed she remained headline news, making one important flight after another, the world's most famous and hardest-working air-woman.

In 1935, she made the first solo crossing of the Pacific, from Hawaii to California, in eighteen hours and sixteen minutes. She took deep interest in new types of machines —notably the autogyro, forerunner of the helicopter, which she flew frequently—and wrote and lectured brilliantly on every aspect of flying. And she never tired of encouraging young women who wanted to take to the air, often tutoring them herself, and—it was rumoured—sometimes paying their expenses out of her own pocket.

Those who worked with her in those crowded years, when she seemed to be trying to move events faster than they would in normal circumstances, when her tireless endeavours kept knocking cracks in the barriers to worldwide air travel, wondered at her apparent casualness which, combined with her ever-youthful smile, at times made her appear flippant, careless perhaps. It was almost as if she treated this work as an absorbing game, that she did not fully realise the tremendous chances she was taking—that she never thought of herself being destroyed, as so many others had been, by clutching, cleaving metal or hissing flames.

But the flippancy was only a pose. This perky spirit the newspapers dubbed " everybody's kid sister " knew the dangers, and knew fear too, and was not careless in the smallest respect. Only her husband and a few close friends knew that her light-heartedness was tempered by the greatest thoroughness in her labours, an unfailing scrupulosity in preparing for each new venture and, very occasionally, by a strange streak of melancholy.

She knew she was working all the time now very close to the limits of reliability of her equipment, and of her own stamina and skill, yet unless she was close to the limits the enterprise held no thrill for her, and with each fresh achievement the limits seemed to be extended. She was caught up in a fascinating race. She had to keep on striving, improving—she never forgot that she'd been late starting, and felt she had to make up for the lost years before she took to the air. Despite the constant, inner strain it all agreed with her ; adventure was her nature.

To begin with, after each new success Putnam hoped she would give up flying, of her own free will. But in time he came to realise that the story must run on for many more chapters—neither of them could stop the pages turning now, or close the book. Amelia had chosen to be what she was, and had proved herself outstanding ; it would be a long time before she would be ready to return to being just ordinary. And he had given his promise never to interfere.

Naturally he took great pride in her prowess, but he never ceased to dread losing her. He could never quite master this sort of life, never live it with the nerves alone, with his mind and emotions in cold storage. Each time he found himself sitting through endless hours in some airfield control tower, waiting for news of her, watching the clock's hands creep nearer to the limit of her aircraft's endurance, listening to weather reports and newspapermen weighing her chances, speculating on where and how she could have gone down, and chainsmoking and drinking great mugs of coffee all through the night—each time he went through that, he swore to himself it would be the last time. She'd done enough, promise or no promise he was going to take her home where a wife belonged, and keep her home, and for all the other nights she would be sitting by him, safe in the lamplight. . . .

But always, when at last the brave note of her engine reached his straining ears . . . when her wheels rested once more on solid ground and she clambered out of the machine wearing an old flying jacket with a fur collar, with her hair tousled, her eyes glazed and her features blurred with fatigue . . . when the crowds cheered and the cameras flashed, when she raised a weary arm to wave and that old, quick smile lifted the tired lines of her face—always the relief and the admiration for this extraordinary woman welled up so strong in him as he hurried to greet her that he forgot the vows he'd made in his hours of anxiety.

In 1937, in recognition of her great services to aviation, she was presented with a brand new, twin-engined Lockheed plane, the *Electra*, packed with so many up-to-date devices that the press named it " Earhart's flying laboratory." After thorough trials, having familiarised herself with the operation and capabilities of every piece of equipment on board, she told her husband : " This is the plane I'm going to fly round the world."

This round-the-world flight was a dream Amelia had cherished ever since her first success, the solo crossing of the Atlantic. Over all the busy years since then it had kept her going through difficulties, disappointments and occasional fits of depression. Everything up till now had been merely training, a rehearsal for the real test.

Though she didn't admit it, Amelia must have known that at last her staying power was beginning to go. She was 39—she must face the fact that soon her concentration and her judgment would lose their diamond-precision, she would tire more easily. It was now or never.

Deeply grateful to the wonderful husband who had made her career possible, who had been her wise and generous counsellor through it all, and who had kept his word never to try to curtail her flying, she told him with a wistfulness that was rare in her : " I've a feeling that there's just about one good flight left in my system, and I hope this is it. Anyway darling, after this I'm giving up major long-distance trips—I'll be coming home to be just plain Mrs. George Putnam, the publisher's wife."

She took off from Oakland, California, on a fine summer's day. With her was one of the country's most experienced and distinguished aerial navigators, Fred Noonan, who had pioneered the long and difficult San Francisco-to-Manila route for Pan American Airways, and guided that company's great *China Clipper* aircraft safely through many other important survey flights.

Forecasts on the weather ahead were good, but both these seasoned flyers knew how swiftly conditions could change, and their calculations left a margin for squalls, veering winds, and having to climb over thunder-clouds.

Yet surprisingly, there were no sudden changes, everything went smoothly all the way across the American continent to Florida . . . from Florida to Brazil . . . on the long hop across to Africa, and eastward on across baking deserts, jungles, mountains and sparkling seas to India. The skies smiled, *Electra* functioned perfectly.

It was at Lae, in New Guinea, with the flight almost finished, that they ran into trouble. The sky above the tiny air-strip, carved out of primeval jungle, grew black with storm-clouds, boomed with thunder, blazed with livid scars of lightning. Rain hissed down, in huge drops that stabbed deep into the sandy ground, and kept them prisoners for almost three days.

While she waited, Amelia re-checked her flight plans for the final lap. Her next stop was Howland Island, a fragment of coral rock in the middle of the vast Pacific, 2,556 miles away. It was the longest hop she had ever attempted, and to make room for the extra fuel and oil it required she had arranged to lighten the plane by discarding everything but essential equipment and emergency gear—drinking water, first-aid box, iron rations, a two-man rubber dinghy, flares, lifebelts, a Very pistol and signalling lamps. Even so *Electra* would be laden to capacity, and she knew the take-off from this short strip, with the jungle trees reaching up at one end and a cliff falling sheer to the sea at the other, was going to be the most arduous and perilous of her life.

By the light of an oil lamp, with the tropical deluge drumming overhead, she wrote to her husband : " The whole width of the world has passed under us, except this broad ocean. I shall be glad when we have the hazard of its navigation behind us."

On the morning of 2nd July, 1937, the rain stopped. By 9 a.m. the sky over Lae showed patches of blue. Amelia and Noonan conferred over breakfast. Away to the east great, black nimbus clouds still sailed, with the sunlight crashing between them, but available information on conditions for the area between New Guinea and Howland indicated a general improvement. They agreed to make a try. If they ran into heavy cloud before the half-way mark, they would turn back. Both were anxious to reach home for the Fourth of July—American Independence Day.

At a few minutes before 10 a.m. Amelia, wearing slacks and a plaid shirt, took her place at the controls and began her meticulous cockpit check. Noonan fastened his maps to the chart table and once more checked his chronometers. He'd been having a little trouble with the chronometers ; some sort of radio interference had made it difficult for him to set them with the absolute precision he would have liked. If the chronometers were not correct to a fraction of a second, then the position-fixes he took from the stars would not be accurate.

All calculations in astro-navigation depend on very exact timing of each " star-shot " by Greenwich Mean Time. Normally a very slight chronometer error wouldn't have been serious, for Noonan didn't rely on star observations. He had three other methods of fixing the plane's position ; by dead reckoning, by the *Electra's* radio-direction-finder, and by radio bearings sent out by ships and shore stations briefed to follow their progress. But this long hop to Howland, across a featureless waste of ocean where no aircraft had ever flown and even ships were few, was going to call for the most careful checking and double-checking. The target, two-and-a-half thousand miles distant, was only half-a-mile wide and less than two miles long, and its highest point was only about fifteen feet above sea level. The slightest miscalculation, which might not matter on a routine flight, could bring disaster here. A deviation of just half a degree over such a long trip would carry the plane more than ten miles off course, and if visibility were bad at Howland they might never find the island.

Noonan meant to use star observations as a convenient check on the position-fixes he obtained by the other methods. So he had used the waiting time at Lae to re-set his chronometers as accurately as possible under the conditions there, and now he believed them to be trust-worthy.

Amelia, satisfied with the servicing of the machine, looked at the windsock and decided to take off towards the sea. To use every foot of the strip, she manoeuvred *Electra* close back against the inland boundary of trees, held her on the brakes and opened the throttles. When the engines were revving strongly, and the tail was beginning to kick up, she released the brakes. The plane shot forward in a breakaway start.

But not until the brink of the precipice was within forty yards did the heavy-laden *Electra* lift reluctantly, a few inches at first, wings waggling uncertainly. Then her nose nudged up a little, she rose evenly, gracefully, out over the sea. And headed east. Towards the distant storm-clouds.

George Putnam was waiting in the Coast guard radio room at Fort Funston, California, not far from Oakland. He had arranged for all flight information to be forwarded to him there so that he could follow his wife's progress, move by move. Just two days ago he'd even managed to talk with her—over a radio-telephone link with Lae.

This would be the last of these lonely, nerve-gnawing

vigils. Amelia was coming home. She had left Lae, she should be at Howland early next morning, July 3rd. A weather report came in from Howland: " Flying conditions excellent." He drank some coffee, black as anthracite, tried to read a newspaper.

Riding at anchor off Howland was the Coast guard cutter *Itasca*. Her orders were to help guide *Electra* in by radio and to provide local weather information. Her skipper, Commander W. K. Thompson, had been given a copy of the radio schedule worked out weeks before: " Earhart's call letters are KHAQQ. Earhart to broadcast her position on 3,105 kilocycles at every 15 and 45 minutes past the hour. *Itasca* to broadcast weather and homing signal on 3,105 and 7,500 kilocycles on the hour and half-hour." It seemed a straightforward, foolproof arrangement.

But seven hours after *Electra's* departure from Lae the *Itasca*, faithfully following the schedule, had failed to contact her. Darkness closed over the tiny island and Thompson signalled the operators manning a U.S. Navy radio-direction-finder unit on shore: " Have you heard anything from KHAQQ?" Back came the answer: " Negative. . . ."

Shortly after 1 a.m., Howland time, Thompson radioed to the Californian Coast guard: " Have not heard signals from Earhart but see no cause for concern as plane is still 1,000 miles away." Then, right on schedule, he broadcast weather information, by both Morse key and voice: " Howland flying conditions excellent; winds from East, at 8 to 13 knots; sea smoothing, ceiling unlimited."

Not until a little after 2.45 a.m. was Amelia's voice heard, faint and " frying " in static, in the radio room of the *Itasca*. " Encountering headwinds . . . cloudy and overcast . . ."—and then it faded. Thompson immediately ordered transmission of a long series of " A's " by Morse key—a homing signal on which Noonan should be able to take a bearing with his radio-direction-finding device. And then he flashed word to California : " Heard Earhart plane at 0248."

At 3.15, the time scheduled for Amelia's next call, only static—like a million whips cracking—broke the expectant silence of the radio room. At 3.30 a.m. *Itasca* again transmitted her weather report and homing signal and Thompson added this short message : " What is your position ? *Itasca* has heard your phone. Please go ahead on Morse key. Acknowledge this broadcast next schedule."

Amelia came through promptly at 3.45, but she was still on voice transmitter and she did not acknowledge Thompson's message. Her voice was ragged, muffled, frighteningly distant. Only snatches of her sentences could be made out. " *Itasca* from Earhart . . . overcast . . . strong headwinds . . . Will listen in on 3,105 kilocycles at hour and half-hour. . . ." There could no longer be any doubt that she was having serious radio trouble.

Thereafter the carefully detailed radio schedule seemed to be abandoned. Amelia kept breaking through the curtain of static at odd times, faintly and abruptly, with brief, only partly-understood messages. In the cutter's radio room tension mounted ; Thompson and the listening sailors realised that somewhere out in the darkness to the west a great electrical storm was raging, and through it the two flyers were battling for their lives.

Shortly after 6 a.m. the dawn broke clear and still over Howland, and hopes rose. Once *Electra* emerged from the bad weather to the west she should have no trouble spotting

the island in such fine visibility—unless, of course, she was
badly off course. But at 7.42 the voice which suddenly
broke through was decidely strained and anxious :
" KHAQQ calling *Itasca* ! We must be on you now, but
I cannot see you. Gas is running low—we've only about
thirty minutes left. I've been unable to reach you by
radio. We are flying at 1,000 feet. . . ." Sixteen minutes
more, then came a much stronger signal : " KHAQQ calling *Itasca* ! We're circling, but still cannot see you ! Go
ahead on 7,500 either now or on schedule."

Thompson signalled back desperately—confirming her
message, then transmitting another series of " A's." And
now, for the very first time he got a direct response from
her : " Receiving your signals, *Itasca*, but unable to get a
definite bearing from them. Please take a bearing on us
and answer by voice on 3,105 kilocycles." She began to
transmit a long series of "A's " in Morse, but before the
Itasca's eager radio men could line-up on her and at last
determine her approximate position, there came another
riot of static and the vital signal was drowned out, lost. . . .

Thompson kept trying, and with his officers made a rapid
estimate of the situation in preparation for search and
rescue operations. It was clear that despite the foul weather
between Lae and here—encountered too late for *Electra* to
turn back—Amelia had fought on and accomplished the
necessary distance of 2,556 miles in the 18 hours since
take-off. But somewhere in that black labyrinth of twisting
winds and static-clogged ether, not surprisingly she had
gone off course.

The strength of her last signal, and her statement in the
one before that she had thirty minutes of fuel left, enabled
Thompson to calculate that she must now be within a
hundred miles of Howland. If she passed to the south,

almost certainly she would spot distinctive Baker Island, about 38 miles distant—and that would put her right. So Thompson went to his chart and marked off a square of sea to the north as the primary search area.

At 8.45 Amelia was heard for the last time : "Earhart to *Itasca*. We are in line of position 157-337, repeat 157-337. Will repeat this message now on 6,210 kilocycles. We are running north and south. . . ." But even as she spoke, and the radio-men once more swung the antennae of their radio-direction-finder, desperately probing the air, reaching for her, the signal faded slowly, receding—so that Thompson knew the *Electra* had overshot Howland, and was speeding away from them now, into the wide, empty ocean. The *Itasca* cast off, steamed northward at full speed. And as she went Thomspon transmitted to America this tragic news : " Earhart unreported 0900 hours . . . believe down."

In the Coast guard Station at Fort Funston, George Putnam read this message, looked up at the silent group of officers and reporters and said quietly : " All right, so they're down. But they can't be far from that cutter, and the sea's calm. The *Electra* will stay afloat indefinitely— the empty gas tanks will give her extra buoyancy. All they have to do is sit tight till they're picked up."

His eyes pleaded with them to agree. The reporters nodded, scuffed their feet, avoided his gaze. An officer said comfortingly : " *Itasca* won't be alone for long. We're sending out a seaplane from Honolulu to join in the search, and the battleship *Colorado*, in Pearl Harbour, has been ordered to raise steam."

Putnam forced himself to relax, sat back in his chair and looked out through the big observation window at the smiling summer sky. This, the last wait, looked like being the longest and toughest of all—but everything would turn out right, Amelia was coming home. . . .

All through that day *Itasca* searched the sea north of Howland, without result. The seaplane from Honolulu didn't show up, and early next morning—July 4th—came the explanation; a freak storm of sleet had started ice forming on her wings, forcing the pilot to turn back. But *Colorado* was on her way, and from the Navy's great base at San Diego the very fast aircraft carrier *Lexington* had started out.

The sea and air search for *Electra* became the biggest rescue operation in the history of aviation. The *Lexington's* force of 76 planes painstakingly covered more than 104,000 square miles of water, and catapult aircraft from *Colorado* made low level surveys of every spur of coral rock which broke the surface in that area of the Pacific. But as the days and nights passed, and not so much as a spar was found, a reluctant world was forced to face the desolate truth—that "A.E.," the great-hearted, quick-smiling girl who for five years had been making flying history, at last had been defeated, and was gone.

How this had happened would never be known for certain, but the evidence clearly indicated that she had placed most of her faith in *Electra's* radio-direction-finding equipment to get her into Howland, and when this failed just after the half-way mark—clogged by electrical interference—Fred Noonan found himself with an almost impossible task. The static also prevented him hearing the ships and shore stations which were supposed to give him bearings. Very probably the dense overcast made it impossible for him to get more than an occasional, fleeting glimpse of the stars, and perhaps his chronometers were not as accurate as he believed.

So, of the four navigational systems on which he had planned the flight, all he had left was his dead reckoning track—a method based on pure deduction, in which the position is calculated from the plane's speed and compass course, the estimated force and direction of the wind, and other factors. And he had nothing against which he could check his findings. Add to this the fact that for hours on end, as he bent over his chart table, *Electra* must have been bucking and slewing through storm-roughened air.

Perhaps they missed the little island by only a few miles. But they were flying east, into the glare of a tropical sun newly risen above the rim of the calm, mirror-like sea. Ironically, had it been cloudy at Howland, they might have had a better chance of spotting their destination—they would not have been dazzled by the fierce sunlight, reflecting upwards from the smooth water and spanking off the metal and perspex of the cockpit into their aching eyes. This is a heart-rending thought ; they had battled hundreds of miles through a black night of storms, only to be defeated by a clear morning sky. . . .

Why didn't *Electra* stay afloat long enough for them to take to their rubber dinghy ? The most probable answer is that Amelia failed to set her down correctly on the water. Ditching is always a tricky, dangerous procedure, even for the most experienced pilot. It is something that cannot be practised, because it involves the loss of an aircraft. And when you try it with your tanks dry, when your motors are dead, or dying, you get no second chance if you misjudge your approach, because you have no power to pull you out of the stall or see you through a nasty bounce.

Flying-boat pilots, who always land on water, will tell

you they'd rather have it choppy than smooth, because when it is smooth, and the sun is shining brightly, it is sometimes very difficult to judge your exact height above it. When you are looking down at a flat, shining, absolutely featureless surface, there isn't much difference between twenty feet and two feet.

So it seems reasonable to assume that *Electra* hit the water hard, broke up, and sank at once. Especially when we remember how desperately tired Amelia must have been and that the prevailing wind was *from the east*, so that in turning into it to make her emergency landing she would have had that fierce, low sun glaring full in her face. . . .

Not until 10th July—a week after her disappearance— was George Putnam persuaded to give up his vigil at Fort Funston. Haggard, filled with a lacerating sorrow, he had not spoken more than a few sentences in the last 48 hours. Now, as friends escorted him to the car that would take him to an empty home, he paused a moment, looking out towards the Pacific, and said very softly : " If she's really gone, then this is the way she'd have chosen . . . Only, it was to have been her last flight, you see. She said absolutely the last one."

Later he made public a letter which Amelia had left, to be opened only if she failed to return.

" Please know that I am quite aware of the hazards," it said. " I want to do it—because I want to do it. Women must try to do things as men have tried. When they fail, then failure must be but a challenge to others."

THE TRAIL ENDS AT WALKPI

STAFF SERGEANT Morgan, of the U.S. Army Signal Corps, came into the hut breathing heavily, dragging weary feet. In the eerie, tallow-wick light of the early Arctic day his eyes seemed glazed, his face pale and drawn.

He sat down at his radio key by the window and, very still for a long moment, stared out across the wastes of Northern Alaska, thinking out his message. Then slowly his hand went to the key and he began to transmit.

Sergeant Morgan's call from his lonely post at Point Barrow on that August day in 1935, ran to some thirty words—but in a score of capital cities around the globe it spawned deep, black headlines, and in America it plunged millions into shocked gloom.

" Wiley Post and Will Rogers crashed fifteen miles south of here at five o'clock last night," he reported. " Both killed. Have recovered bodies and placed them in the care of Dr. Griest. Standing by. . . ." This terse, unemotional message confirmed the worst fears of the last twelve hours —that America had lost one of her finest and most flamboyant airmen, and with him his friend and passenger, perhaps the most celebrated humorist and " homely philosopher " of the age.

There was a kind of bitter, ironic pattern to this double tragedy. It was as if fate and the elements had conspired to rob America, at one blow, of her two most far-sighted, active and influential aviation enthusiasts. For though the ex-cowpuncher Rogers had never learned to pilot an aeroplane, he spent most of his enormous income on flying, had covered every main commercial air route in the world and " gone along for the ride " on many important flights with various famous flyers. Next to his friend Post—the one-eyed, part-Red Indian pilot who was the first man to fly solo round the world—he claimed to be " the keenest and busiest aviator on the American continent." Certainly no two men had done more to further the development of United States civil aviation, and to increase public confidence in air travel.

Wiley Post, like his Indian forefathers, loved the open air, and a deep, burning wanderlust would not let him rest. Born at Grand Plains, Texas, in 1900, and raised in Oklahoma, as a youth he had roved from town to town, ranch to ranch, job to job. He farmed, worked as oil-driller, lumber-man and cow-hand ; sometimes, while on the move, he washed dishes, or chopped wood, in return for a meal.

To one of the little Western townships where he paused in his wanderings, there came one day an air circus. Wiley and his workmates went along on pay-night to see " the stunters." As he watched the small, brightly-painted biplanes loop and roll and dive in mock dog-fights, dip daringly to pluck handkerchiefs from the grass with spikes fastened to their wing-tips, and finally zoom upside down scant feet over the heads of the crowd, Wiley felt something essential in him stir and grow. He knew now, with a surging certainty, why he'd never been able to stay in one job for more than a few weeks—he hadn't been cut out for ordinary work, he was meant to be a flyer! He slipped away from his friends, went in search of the air-circus manager.

" Mister, I'd sure like to join your outfit. I'll do anything to start with. . . ."

" Sorry, son. Got nothing suitable right now."

" I told you, anything'll do. Watchman, grease-monkey, ticket-seller. I'll do a week on trial, if you like."

The manager eyed the lean, straight, strong frame and the young, eager face.

" W-e-ll . . . there just *might* be something, come to think of it. You afraid of heights?"

" I don't rightly know—I don't think so . . ."

" Ride a horse, don't you?"

Wiley blinked, gasped, grinned widely.

" All my life, Mister. But I don't see . . ."

" Then you're bound to have a good sense of balance. Let's see your hands, boy." Wiley, in a daze, held out big, calloused palms; on his wrists and forearms the sinews stood out like bell-cord.

" Hmm—yeah, these ought to give you a strong enough grip. Okay, I'll take a chance on you, son. Start tomorrow. Week's trial, then we'll talk about dough."

And so young Post joined the air circus. Not as a watchman, not as a ticket-seller—but as " the Flying Redskin," a death-defying aerial acrobat who walked the wings of the planes high over the gasping crowds, and made several parachute jumps every day!

It was a sudden startling introduction to flying, but he possessed incredibly strong nerves, and the manager had been right about his natural sense of balance. Once he got his breath back, and gained confidence in his ability to do this strange sort of work, Wiley experienced an exhilaration he'd never known before. To be off the ground, to feel the wind slapping his cheeks and tearing at his clothing, the clamour of the engine beating on his ears—at nights he could not sleep for thinking back over these sensations of the day.

Between performances he hung around the parked aircraft, listening to the pilots and mechanics talking—discussing technicalities in the half-secret language of their rite. Mostly they ignored him, but they let him watch and listen as they worked on the engines and airframes, and once one of the airmen let him sit in the cockpit and explained the controls and instruments to him. Wiley was surprised; he had expected it all to be highly complicated, but in fact it seemed perfectly straightforward, common sense. He felt sure that if only they'd give him the chance, in just an hour or two he'd learn to control this fast, nimble steed as completely as any of the spirited mustangs he'd ridden out on the range. . . .

But they didn't give him the chance. After only three weeks, he was paid off. It was then that he discovered he had been only a temporary substitute for the circus's regular wing-walker, who had fallen ill, and now had recovered.

Back to earth, back to trudging the dusty roads—but more unsettled than ever now, more morose and purposeless. Nothing, nobody here on the ground could hold his interest, every fibre of his being yearned to get into the clear blue air again, to become a qualified pilot—but he did not know where or how to begin. A penniless youngster of Indian blood, without proper education or technical qualifications, a rootless wanderer whose occupation at times might, if he were to be brutally honest, be best described by the word " hobo," or " tramp "—what hope

had such a lowly, simple soul of ever being able to afford
the hire of an aircraft, the cost of fuelling it, paying an
instructor, obtaining a licence and all the many other
incidental expenses? Flying was a costly business, a rich
man's sport—he must try to rid himself of this crazy,
impossible dream, or he would be miserable all his
days.

Wiley Post almost certainly would have stayed on the
ground, would never have become a pilot had it not been
for an accident in an oilfield, years later. He lost an eye,
and was paid £400 in compensation.

Friends advised him to be prudent—to bank the money,
or invest it safely. Unemployment was rising in the
country, and a man who was disabled, even slightly, might
find difficulty in getting work. But Wiley knew exactly
what he was going to do—he'd never had so much money
in his life, and probably he never would again. This was
his only chance. He went out and bought an old, somewhat
dowdy Lockheed high-wing monoplane. It was destined
to become one of the most famous aeroplanes in history—
" Winnie Mae."

In a very few hours Wiley was flying smoothly, safely,
nervelessly. But when he applied to the authorities for a
pilot's licence, he was refused—on medical grounds. Only
after days of pleading did they agree to give him a test.
There was no more argument—he quickly proved that his
deficiency in sight did not detract from his great, natural
flying skill.

In 1930 he won the Chicago-Los Angeles Air Derby in
nine hours, nine minutes and four seconds. The following
year he teamed up with the experienced Harold Gatty to
fly around the world. Wiley put his last pennies into the
enterprise—if they could complete the trip in ten days,

they would win £4,000. They made it in the record time of eight days and sixteen hours—and Post, solvent again and suddenly an international figure, at last was able to give up "bread and butter" ground jobs and make flying his full-time profession.

At once he began planning another round-the-world flight, this time alone. With scrupulous care, drawing on the valuable experience of his trip with Gatty, he made his preparations, fitted new equipment and navigational aids, tested and practised, amended and modified. By 1933 he was ready.

So well-planned was his flight that everything went precisely according to schedule—until the 1,800-mile hop from Moscow to Novosibirsk. Over the Ural foothills he smacked into blinding fog and thick cloud, a wall of weather that reached from ground level to well above the ceiling of his aircraft. And as he started to burrow through, hoping to find clear skies on the other side of the range, a pilot's nightmare became reality—several of his instruments, on which in this situation he was completely reliant, unaccountably failed.

Buffeted by powerful down-draughts, no longer sure of his height, speed or heading, unable to see anything beyond the cloud-muffled canopy, muscles cramped and aching from days of hard flying and nights with little sleep, Post fought the bucking controls, tried to maintain height and course using the few basic instruments which still appeared to be operating. His strong arms and hands, and his extraordinary sense of balance, somehow held the plane on something like an even keel.

But the long, lonely battle seemed to last for hours, and his strength slowly ebbed. Suddenly the cloud ahead appeared to grow darker, then a black shape loomed up—

something terrifyingly solid. Wiley hauled on the stick with both hands, kicked on the rudder. The plane rose reluctantly, lurchingly, in a climbing turn, and narrowly grazed the jutting rocks of a hilltop.

Drenched in sweat, nearly exhausted, he realised that his altimeter was out of order—he was much lower than the height it indicated. Fortunately the down-draughts were not so powerful here, and he was able to regain some altitude before resuming course.

On and on through the gloom, with no glimpse of the sun or the earth. His head throbbed, his back and limbs grew stiff and numb. He knew he could not last much longer.

This was the greatest crisis of Post's career. Afterwards he admitted : " I believe if I'd had a parachute, I'd have jumped . . . for it seemed quite impossible to get through." But he did get through—scraping over the shrouded mountain peaks into clearer air, reaching his destination with a few pints of petrol to spare. So fatigued that they had to lift him from the cockpit.

By comparison, the remainder of the trip was easy. He completed his global flight in seven days, eighteen hours and 49½ minutes, breaking the record he had set up with Gatty. Of that, 115 hours and 36½ minutes were actual flying time. His average speed was 127.23 miles an hour.

And he was the first man to have flown round the world alone.

Famous and fêted, he could have rested now ; but the old wanderlust still burned in him, he had to keep on the move. So he went on to many new ventures, including an attempt on the world's altitude record. At Akron in Ohio, the one-eyed " ex-hobo " flew higher than any other human had done, reaching the sub-stratosphere, 7.2 miles up.

Though naturally gifted, Post was no " slap-dash," guessing glory-seeker. He worked hard and long to teach himself technicalities, he sought and respected the opinions of experts and he studied every new idea and development. He always planned and practised meticulously before an important flight, trained diligently as a prize-fighter to get himself in the best possible physical condition. And despite his lack of formal education, in time he became an acknowledged authority on all branches of aviation.

Such then was the man who piloted the plane which crashed near Point Barrow, Alaska, on that day in 1935. His passenger was also from the West, also a national figure—grizzled, sly-grinning Will Rogers, a 56-year-old film actor and " extravagant genius," beloved as a great humorist and as a great human being. There had been a time when Rogers was even considered, quite seriously, as a possible candidate for the Presidency of the United States.

Will had started life as a cowboy, and with his homespun wit had risen to become one of the world's most popular entertainers, earning from radio, films and writing something like £200,000 a year, an enormous income for those days. And a good proportion of that money he spent on flying. In breaks between engagements he would travel by air lines to remote regions, and though he never qualified as a pilot he bought various light machines and hired professionals to fly him between Hollywood, New York and other cities where he was due to appear. Even on short trips he seldom went by train or car—his greatest joy was to get into the air, in any sort of weather, in almost any sort of plane.

Once he was flying to attend an important dinner in Chicago with Henry Ford, the great motor-car magnate, when engine trouble developed and the pilot made a hasty, forced landing in a quiet country area. Rogers broke an arm. They walked to a farmhouse, and a local doctor was called. None too gently, he set the fracture, and Will continued his journey by road.

At the dinner that evening he made one of his most brilliant, wittiest speeches—but never once mentioned his flying mishap. He explained later : " It would have been a reflection on aviation." For when it came to flying, the great humorist was completely earnest ; he believed fervently in the future of air travel, in the potentialities of America's growing aircraft industry, and in the need to build up a strong, modern air force to ensure national security. He was constantly trying to make Americans more airminded—a potent, living advertisement for aviation. And it was natural that this knowledgeable, passionate enthusiast should meet and befriend many of his country's leading airmen, notably " rebel general " Billy Mitchell, and the colourful, energetic Wiley Post.

The cowboy and the redskin had much in common. Both were prairie-bred, of humble origin—and despite success, still essentially simple men. Both had flown twice around the world—Rogers by air line ticket, and by " hitch-hiking " on various military and private aircraft—and they shared a strange, Western wanderlust that in this new, venturesome age found its outlet in the air.

For them the aeroplane had taken the place of the horse, and the world's wide open skies were their range. They had become " partners " long before that summer of 1935, when they set out together to blaze a trail across " the top of the Earth "—a new, northern air route to Russia.

The trip had started in an atmosphere of mystery and conflicting reports which, even now, is difficult to understand. The first the public heard of it was a bald statement from the Soviet Embassy in Washington on 6th July, announcing that permission had been granted for Post and his wife to make a flight across Siberia to Moscow. Newsmen found Post curiously reluctant to supply further details. He confirmed that he had applied to the Kremlin for clearance and airfield facilities " to explore the possibilities of a regular, shorter air route over the Arctic ice," but said his departure date was still uncertain and his general plans for the flight " confidential."

Then, from Hollywood, came the strong and startling rumour that Will Rogers, and not Mrs. Post, would accompany Wiley on the trip. Rogers' studios denied this, and the Posts declined to comment.

On 25th July, while the Posts were preparing to take off for a test flight from a Californian airfield, a chauffeur-driven car swung on to the tarmac. Rogers got out, nonchalantly climbed aboard the plane. His luggage—a magazine, and two packets of chewing gum.

The next day all three were in New Mexico, telling reporters they were " just holiday-making." The newspapermen laughed disbelievingly, settled down to watch and wait ; but for over a week nothing happened to confirm their settled conviction that this was some strange, pointless conspiracy—that at the last moment Rogers would take Mrs. Post's place as Wiley's passenger on the trans-polar trip.

Then on 5th August, the reporters were baffled by Rogers' abrupt departure—returning alone to Hollywood. The same day the Posts flew north to Seattle. It seemed as if, after all, the rumour was wrong—that the press had jumped to wild conclusions.

But at midnight Rogers left his Hollywood home by a back door, drove to the airport and, heavily muffled and using the name of Williams, slipped unnoticed aboard a plane for San Francisco. Next day he appeared in Seattle and, in company with Wiley, finally admitted that he, and not Mrs. Post, would be flying to Alaska. But for some reason—still unknown—he refused to say whether he would go on from there to Russia. A few hours later Mrs. Post was with the reporters on the tarmac, waving farewell as the two men took off for the Arctic.

On their arrival at Fairbanks, Alaska, Rogers received a telegraphed message from a New York paper offering him a substantial sum for " the inside story." He wired back a typical, dry-humoured " explanation " about pioneering for gold and exploring the possibilities of a scheme " for growing spinach along the coast of the Bering Sea." Then the two friends took off—and vanished into the icy mists of the North.

Soon the mist became fog, and Post could not find landmarks to fix his position. The temperature dropped dramatically, and the motor began to lose power. Wiley was about to turn back for Fairbanks when, unexpectedly, they broke into a patch of clear air and spotted a tiny Eskimo village. The ground was flat, so Wiley landed, identified the village as Walkpi and found it on his chart.

While Rogers played with the Eskimo children, distributing chewing gum, Post worked on the faulty engine. After an hour he had it running smoothly, but by then the white, Arctic fog was drifting in over Walkpi. Will and

Wiley talked with the weather-wise headman of the village, learned that if the fog closed in completely it was likely to remain unbroken for days, perhaps weeks. They frowned at their chart and at the dazzling white, steadily thickening fog-banks, decided they had no option but to continue—to get off while it was still possible to see a few yards of ground ahead.

A last wave to the villagers, and they roared across the flats. But they had climbed only about fifty feet when the motor seemed to falter. The wings rocked, the nose dipped suddenly. The plane plunged almost vertically, crashed into the shallows of a small lake. And as the Eskimos rushed towards the wreck, petrol, leaking on to the surface of the water, burst into deep, dull roaring flames. So intense was the heat, no one could approach within twenty yards.

A runner was sent to Sergeant Morgan's little post, fifteen miles away. The sergeant commandeered a fast launch, raced down the coast to Walkpi. All that was left of the fuselage was a charred, smoking skeleton. The starboard wing had been torn off, and the engine lay buried deep in a half-frozen hummock of moss.

There were registration numbers on the wing, and he knew there would be markings stamped on the engine. But it wasn't necessary to examine these. Several yards from the wreck a body lay, thrown clear by the impact. A brief glance was enough to identify one of the best-known faces in the world, a face the sergeant had so often seen, sly-grinning under a wide-brimmed hat, and blown up to many times life-size on a cinema screen—Will Rogers.

With the help of the villagers, Morgan carried Rogers' remains to the launch. Then they cut through the blackened, twisted wreckage and recovered the body of Wiley Post. With his sad cargo the sergeant sailed back to Point Barrow, to radio the tragic news to the outside world.

Two wandering Westerners, having ridden hard and risen high, had come together to the end of the trail.

THE ENEMY bombers approached London from the South-East, flying at about 22,000 feet. As the wailing of the sirens rose to mingle with the malicious drone of the raiders' engines, people looked up and saw ugly clouds of aircraft besmirching the immaculate September sky.

The attack was one of the strongest yet mounted by the Luftwaffe in daylight. It seemed that the enemy had put every bomber they possessed into the air, intending that this day—September 15th, 1940—should give Germany undisputed mastery of the skies.

As usual, to hold the whole force close together, the slowest aircraft had been put in the lead—a bunch of about fifty Heinkel 111's. Behind and a little to the side of these, followed large formations of Dornier 215's. Finally, throttled back to a little above stalling speed in order to keep station, came a solid phalanx of about forty fast and formidably-gunned Junkers 88's.

Between 5,000 and 8,000 feet above the bombers, the escorting fighters fussed—a squadron of Me. 110's and another of Me. 109's. In all there were probably about 200 " bandits " heading for the densely-populated centre of London.

It was a hot, windless day. For weeks on end the weather had been perfect, the kind of old-fashioned English summer people had dreamed about before the war, but hardly ever seen. Now, just when rainclouds or gales would have provided respite for the island's severely outnumbered defenders, day after day Britain awakened to bright sunshine.

The raiders' plan was to drop their bombs all together in a comparatively small area, thus blowing a hole in the hub of the city. They reached the southern outskirts unchallenged and turned for the run on to their target. It seemed now that nothing could stop them.

But far below, the sun glinted on metal. Up out of the indigo haze that lay over the sprawling metropolis climbed a wing of R.A.F. fighters—two squadrons of Spitfires, one of Hurricanes. Thirty-six young men rising into the vast blue battleground to face the Nazi armada.

Stencilled on the fuselage of the leading machine of this all too small force—a Hurricane—were fourteen swastikas : curt epitaphs for German aircraft destroyed by its pilot, the leader of the wing, Squadron Leader Roland " Bob " Stanford Tuck.

At this period of the Battle of Britain the Air Ministry's policy opposed the building of " ace " reputations. The emphasis was on teamwork. Perhaps one of the reasons was that people are inclined to credit an " ace " or hero with god-like luck ; he becomes a mascot of success, and like an ancient god must never die if his worshippers are to be saved from despair.

Only three months before that September day there had been another god-like hero of the air, J. E. " Cobber " Kain, a lean, laughing six-footer from New Zealand. The R.A.F.'s first ace of World War Two, his exploits fired the imagination of the whole western world. No wonder ; once, supported by only one other aircraft, he had attacked seven enemy bombers—and chased them back to Germany.

For that he was awarded the D.F.C. Then there was the time he destroyed two Messerschmitts and was himself shot down. Wounded, and with his plane in flames, he baled out only half-a-mile from the German lines, but got back to his squadron, where the doctors found twenty shrapnel wounds in his leg.

God-like luck it seemed.

In March, 1940, Kain was to return to England for special duties, and to marry a beautiful English actress. He looked round his fellow-officers on the edge of the runway at Blois airfield.

" One more beat-up, lads," he called cheerfully, climbed into his Hurricane and was off—on a wild display of aerobatics, flashing across the airfield mere inches off the grass, the fighter rolling and twisting like a demented fish.

Minutes later the cheers and laughter died on the lips of his watching colleagues. Kain could not get out of a low roll. The plane's wing touched the ground. A rending, splintering crash. Kain—the symbol, the god-like indestructable—lay smashed and lifeless in the midst of the mess.

So after that, no more immortal symbols—the emphasis was on teamwork. But it proved impossible to keep secret the spectacular personal gallantry and outstanding skill of other pilots, men like Douglas Bader, the South African " Sailor " Malan, and Bob Stanford Tuck.

At twenty-four, Tuck was a veteran, a " grey-beard " mentor and father-confessor to the fledgling pilots of nineteen and twenty. He was also, despite official censorship, a national legend. It wasn't that he sought publicity in any way—it just seemed that every time he got off the ground he made the kind of news that pumped fresh confidence into his countrymen, and that newspaper correspondents would break rules to print.

Tuck had joined the R.A.F. in 1935 after a brief spell in the Merchant Navy. Long before the outbreak of war, he was one of the first service pilots to fly the Spitfire. The sensational new monoplane, with its eight machine-guns, its incredible manœuvrability, high ceiling, and tremendous speed, fired the exuberant Tuck with a host of ideas for revising air tactics. Nobody listened to him at the time, but later his schemes were to bring immense profits.

He first saw action in May, 1940, over Dunkerque, as a Flight-Commander with a new Spitfire squadron. His comrades heard him whooping with glee over the radio as he led his section into the middle of a large formation of Me. 109's. The squadron destroyed eleven for the loss of one Spitfire which crash-landed on the beach. Tuck was credited with one " kill." That same afternoon, while on a second patrol over the same area, he shot down two Me. 110's. He followed up that " bag " of three for the first day's combat with a couple of Dornier 17's the next day, and another of the same type on the third morning. Six in three days. " This is the most fascinating occupation in the world," he wrote in a letter to his parents at Walton-on-Thames, Surrey.

A fraction over six feet tall, whip-thin, whip-strong, dark and lithe and elegant as a matador, Tuck seemed to embody all those elusive, incongruous qualities which make a great fighter pilot. He had tremendous energy, he was an excellent marksman and a gay and popular character in the mess. In the air, even in the midst of combat, he was always astonishingly calm and workmanlike ; in a job where the blood was apt to boil, and hatred could blur the vision, he

remained a fastidious, methodical, ice-brained craftsman.

Here then was the man who led the thirty-six fighters up
to the defence of London that September afternoon. This
time he flew a Hurricane, for a few days before he had
taken over leadership of a new squadron, 265. His pilots
had flown three previous patrols that day, without incident.
For many weeks they had been averaging about four-and-
a-half hours' sleep a night, and snatching their meals out
of " hot-boxes " brought to them at the flight dispersal
huts. They were youngsters with haggard faces and wary
eyes.

Now, on the fourth " outing " of the day, everything
was against them. There was no time to gain altitude or
get the sun behind them. If they were to break up the
enemy formation before it reached its target, then they
must attack from beneath. This meant there could be no
surprise, that the German fighters would have the advantages of height and, because they could dive to the attack,
higher speed. Tuck ordered the wing to join up in a loose
formation—a method of attack he had himself introduced,
because he believed tight, "copybook " formations forced
the pilots to concentrate too much on watching their
comrades' wing-tips instead of looking out for the enemy.

After months of argument Tuck, and a number of other
experienced leaders, had managed to get the idea accepted
that fighters should operate not in squadrons (units of as
few as twelve machines) but in wings (three, sometimes
four squadrons flying as a single, fairly widely-deployed
pack). Once in combat the fighters operated in pairs, one
attacking, the other covering his tail. So far as possible
they maintained some sort of general formation so that
they could re-group quickly at an order from the wing

leader. (These tactics had been introduced before the war by the great Italian airman Italo Balbo—and Tuck, an avid student of every development in aviation, had devoured all available reading matter on Balbo's theories and work.)

But this time matters did not work out that way. The planes which had been the last to take-off could not catch up with the leading section, and the formation was dangerously stretched out. Yet Tuck and the other leading machines dared not throttle back to wait for the laggards : if they were to catch the raiders while they were still over the southern fringe of London, they must use everything in their engines, climbing on at full power. . . .

Thus, when the leaders came up under the bombers and Tuck called his pilots into line-abreast, only about seven machines were able to draw level with him for the all-important opening burst. The German fighters, of course, had seen them coming all the way. The 109's peeled off and came screaming down through the closely packed formation of Ju.88's, which were still well out of range of the British fighters.

Tuck kept on, ignoring the plummeting fighters, and got a Junkers lined up in his sights. As the bomber's silhouette grew steadily larger on the ringed glass, a 109 came hurtling down on him, wicked little flames flickering along its wings as it sent a stream of fire close over his canopy. Now he couldn't ignore the danger. He was forced to slam the stick over and break off his attack.

He made a steep turn, climbing away, with his Number Two, Sergeant Ronnie Jarvis, following close behind. All at once and straight ahead he saw the Me. 110's making a slow, wide turn, to face the other British fighters which were now drawing near the tail end of the bomber stream.

He picked one out, closed swiftly and pressed the firing button. The enemy machine shuddered, fell lazily out of position and burst into flames. The rest of the formation began to disintegrate. Tuck swung round after a He.111 which had suddenly turned and was fleeing for home. But down on him, almost vertically and very fast, came a Me 109. Its fire went wide, and it plunged past him before he could reply. But he knew there would be another following—the enemy, like the British, operated in pairs.

Tuck craned his neck and, sure enough, spotted the Number Two following its leader down. But this second Messerschmitt pilot either lost his nerve or became confused, for suddenly he pulled out of his dive and turned in front of the Hurricane, flying into the centre of Tuck's sights as obligingly as a homing pigeon to its loft.

A long burst. The machine rolled on its back and went down. Tuck turned in search of more prey, but the battle was over. The fleeing Germans were jettisoning their bombs at random. Most of them would explode harmlessly in open country. The tiny British force, by sheer resolution and accurate shooting, had turned back an armada.

Back at base Intelligence credited Tuck's squadron with the destruction of five enemy planes, and the ground crew stencilled two more swastikas on their leader's air-craft—bringing his official total at that time up to 16.

The events of that September afternoon serve to illustrate how Tuck's methods during the Battle of Britain, his example, and his cool, almost casual personality contributed to the eventual triumph of " The Few."

Tuck survived. By the end of 1941, when the Battle of Britain was won and Fighter Command was able to go over to the offensive, he was a Wing Commander holding the D.S.O., the D.F.C. and two bars, and officially credited with twenty-nine " kills."

The next year, in January, Tuck was out on a low level offensive patrol over France when a German shell blew most of the engine out of his Spitfire. He spotted a long, flat field on the outskirts of Boulogne and went in to make a crash-landing. Not until he was flattening out, four or five feet off the grass, did he realise that there were guns all round the field. At the far end, straight ahead of him, he could see four 20mm. pieces mounted on the back of a huge lorry. He was landing smack in the middle of the enemy A.A. battery which had shot him down . . . !

The crew of the multiple 20mm. had depressed the sights, and they opened fire on the crippled fighter, now only a few hundred yards away. Nobody shot at Tuck and got away with it. Not even when his plane was dying, and he was only a few inches off the ground. He shoved the nose forward, pressed the firing button—and blew the gun-crew off their lorry.

The Spitfire, slowed by the recoil of its guns, thumped down heavily on the field and Tuck was knocked out for a few seconds. When he came to Germans were running towards him from all directions. Rough hands seized him, twisting his arms, and propelled him across the field to the wreckage of the gun lorry.

He looked down, saw the mangled bodies of the gunners he had killed with his last burst, and waited for retribution. He was quite sure they meant to string him up from the nearest tree. But to his amazement, suddenly his captors were laughing, pointing at the back of the shattered lorry. Tuck saw now that by an astounding fluke one of his cannon shells had gone right up the barrel of a gun, splitting it open, like a half-peeled banana. Such marksmanship evidently appealed to the Teutonic mind. A gunner clapped his back: " Goot shot, Englander ! " Again, it seemed, his marksmanship had saved his life.

Tuck later escaped from a German prison camp into Russia, and turned up in Italy in the spring of 1945. To-day he has his home in Kent. Under the very skies where so many of his hardest battles were fought, he lives quietly, a successful mushroom farmer.

DUEL IN THE MIDNIGHT SUN

THEY WERE flying over dreary wastes of ocean far inside the Arctic circle when a faint elongated blob materialised on the radar screen. According to the Intelligence reports no Allied vessels were anywhere near this area. The "blip" was so large that they thought it must be a destroyer.

Cruickshank said crisply : " Stand by," eased back his throttles and put the nose down. The wide-winged Catalina flying-boat—" Y-Yorker "—went into a shallow, graceful dive, cutting through occasional banks and streamers of clean, white sea fog.

The gunners peered out over their sights, straining their eyes in the dim, tallow-wick light of the Arctic's " perpetual dusk," tentatively swinging and depressing their guns while the navigator-bomb-aimer, Flying Officer J. C. Dickson, called out the decreasing range.

At about 800 feet they emerged from a fog-bank and saw their quarry slightly to starboard about half-a-mile ahead. It wasn't a destroyer. Cruickshank's precise Scots voice came clearly over the inter-comm :

" U-boat ! Right, lads, we're going in. . . ."

It was one of the latest types of enemy submarines, about five times the tonnage of the standard U-boats. The conning tower bristled with heavy machine-guns, and 37mm.

and 20mm. anti-aircraft cannon were mounted on the deck fore and aft.

There had been a time, earlier in the war, when a German submarine automatically crash-dived on sighting an Allied aircraft. But now—in July 1944—most U-boats remained on the surface and fought it out, often with considerable effect. This large, well-armed vessel was a truly formidable enemy and Cruickshank knew he must try to make good use of the element of surprise to get in the first blow.

The Catalina banked steeply to starboard, straightened out and dived on her target. Dickson called: " Good luck, Skipper ! " in the cheerful, almost gleeful, tone that so typified his personality, then hurried forward from his navigation table to take charge of the apparatus which aimed and released the depth charges.

Up in the nose of the plane Flight Sergeant Harbison, the engineer/air-gunner, lined up his sights. It would be his task to try to mow down the Germans as they scrambled to their guns, thus smothering the anti-aircraft fire.

Flight Sergeant John Appleton, the wireless operator/ air gunner, and Sergeant S. I. Fidler—making his first trip in a Catalina—manned the waist, or " galley " guns. They stood amidships, with the big " blister " canopies wide open and the icy wind tearing at their clothing, ready to spray the U-boat's deck as they passed overhead. In a matter of seconds the crew of " Y-Yorker," literally a flying warship, were poised at battle stations.

Their bodies were tense and their lungs heaved jerkily, but this was due more to eagerness and excitement than to fear. For this moment they had waited many months— monotonous months of long, exhausting, utterly uneventful patrols.

The air-sea war that Coastal Command had to fight was always exacting, seldom spectacular. The work was entirely unrelated to the screaming turmoil of fighter sweeps over France, or the fiery fury of bombing raids on Germany. Theirs was a world apart from the rest of the Royal Air Force ; in fact, since 1941, Coastal Command had operated directly under control of the Admiralty. There could be no Allied victory unless the convoys got through to British ports. Coastal Command was there to help them to get through.

Now, in the last hours of 17th July, 1944, Catalina " Y-Yorker " of 210 Squadron seized a hard-earned opportunity and, by the light of the " midnight sun," dived to the kill. From here on much depended on the skill, courage and coolness of the skipper.

Flying Officer—later Flight Lieutenant—John Alexander Cruickshank was a tall, long-jawed and somewhat morose Scot of twenty-four. Before the war he had worked in a bank in his home town, Edinburgh. " Jock " Cruickshank had never been an outstanding officer. Throughout his training—under the jurisdiction of the United States Navy at the air " university " of Pensacola, Florida, where he first flew Catalinas—his instructors had used words like " average," " reliable," " conscientious " in their progress reports. He was, by his own admission, " a plodding Scot —and a bit of a dour one at times."

But the crews who flew with him on operations—at first from Gibraltar, then later with 210 Squadron from Sullom Voe, in the Shetland Islands—soon discovered that this quiet young man with the neat black moustache was a considerate, thorough and highly efficient captain. It was strange that Cruickshank, who preferred the solitude of his quarters to the boisterous atmosphere of the mess, should choose as his closest friend the effervescent, widely popular navigator, " Dicky " Dickson.

" Y-Yorker " levelled out about 100 feet above the water and Harbison opened fire from the nose. But the Germans must have heard the plane's engines some time before ; already they were manning their deck guns, and now they filled the air round the " Cat " with bullets and shells. The advantage of surprise was lost.

In the best " copybook " style, Cruickshank continued his run-in—that most perilous of manœuvres, when the reflexes kick and the instinct clamours for evasive action ; when, against all human nature, the attacking pilot must fight to keep his aircraft straight and steady, though the sky ahead and all around him is erupting death, and exploding shells set the controls bucking crazily in his hands.

The American-built Catalina was an invaluable aircraft in many respects. With her exceptional endurance in the air—well over sixteen hours—she was ideal for long-range patrol work. But her top speed in straight and level flight was only ninety knots (just over 100 m.p.h.) which, combined with her huge wing-span, made her a very good target for hostile gunners, especially when making a low level attack.

Grimly, dourly, Cruickshank held " Y-Yorker " on her course of destruction. And as he bore down on the U-boat, the Germans' fire seemed to become much less accurate. Agonising seconds dragged by while Cruickshank flew on relentlessly ; it is a remarkable fact that up until the instant that the " Cat " sedately passed over the U-boat they seemed to have completely escaped the slightest damage.

Dickson, crouching over his aiming gear close behind the first and second pilots, yelled in dismay. He had pressed the release button, but nothing had happened! The release mechanism was jammed—their depth charges had " hung up ! "

It was then that they began to suffer. A stream of machine-gun bullets ripped into the tail unit and after-hull, and jagged hunks of shrapnel smashed through the port side of the fuselage. " Y-Yorker " yawed and staggered sickeningly as she turned steeply to climb away, her wing-tip only a few feet above the waves.

From the waist position Appleton and Fidler blazed away—first downwards, then directly backwards. But the skipper's evasive action threw them off the target after only a few seconds.

" Check the gear," Cruickshank ordered. " We'll have another go at her ! "

From the start of the second run-in the Germans, filled with new confidence, kept up a fast and well-directed fire. As the " Cat " dived Dickson reported he could find no fault in the release gear—they could only hope it would work next time. . . .

" Right," said Cruickshank. " Make sure nothing's burning. Anybody wounded? What about the guns? " All this methodical " pilot's handbook " talk while they continued to fly in through the full blast of the enemy barrage ! In quick succession the answers came over the inter-comm. Nobody was hurt, there was no fire and all the gunners had reloaded.

But half-way through the second run-in a stream of shells smashed through the aircraft, and directly after this a shell came in through the bottom and exploded. Dickson was blown backwards into the waist. He lay limp and twisted among the empty cartridge cases at the gunners' feet.

Fidler stooped to tend him. At that instant there came a thunderous roar and a section of the after-hull burst into flames. In a few moments the whole inside of the plane was filled with smoke and acrid fumes.

Up front, Harbison screamed with pain as slivers of shrapnel pierced his legs, and the second pilot, Jack Garnett, was thrown clean out of his seat when the windscreen in front of him disintegrated. An icy wind howled through, clearing the smoke, but fanning the flames.

Johnnie Appleton was lurching about, dazed, trying to pick pieces of shrapnel out of his right hand. He had to give up, because blood, streaming from another wound in his head, ran into his eyes.

All this time the skipper somehow kept the ship heading straight for the U-boat. Except when shells struck the aircraft, so that she jarred like a car hitting deep ruts, he held her wonderfully steady.

With about a hundred yards to go he glanced round and realised there was nobody to release the depth charges. But Garnett, bleeding in several places, had clambered back into the second pilot's seat. Grasping the situation, Garnett took over the controls and held the aircraft on course while his captain leaned back and—just in time—pressed the release button.

There was no chance to aim properly, but Cruickshank's judgment was true and this time the release gear worked perfectly. The wounded Harbison, lying prone in the nose gun-compartment, forgot his pain as he watched the depth charges go forward and downward, tumbling awkwardly as dustbins, and enter the water close by the U-boat.

The instant before the vessel passed out of sight beneath the plane he saw the surface of the sea quiver and thick, white columns begin to rise. Finally, the sub's steel deck buckled, cracked open ; there was a searing flash of red flame and a violent explosion inside—probably the torpedoes detonating !

There could be no doubt that the U-boat was destroyed, and that all her crew had perished in the fiery blast. But the victors of the air-sea duel were in a desperate condition.

Appleton, having staunched the flow of blood from his head wounds, took a fire extinguisher and, aided by Fidler, managed to put out the flames aft. In the cockpit Garnett suddenly noticed that Cruickshank's face was leprous white, and a corner of his lip was trapped between clenched teeth.

"You all right, Skipper ? " Garnett asked. There was no answer. Garnett went aft and said to Appleton : "I think the Skipper's been hit."

Appleton told him Dickson was dead, killed instantly by a shell which must have exploded only inches from him. They found the first aid kit and went forward.

Garnett took over the controls and Cruickshank indicated to Appleton a jagged tear in his trouser leg. The Flight Sergeant started to cut away the material, but suddenly the Skipper fainted and slumped forward.

With Fidler's help Appleton got Cruickshank back on to the 'midships bunk—the only one that had not been destroyed by fire. They discovered dozens of deep leg wounds, realised that he must have lost a dangerous amount of blood. Obviously he had been wounded early in the second run-in, but had made no mention of it.

After dressing the leg wounds Appleton noticed dark patches on the front of Cruickshank's shirt. He cut away the material and discovered that the skipper's chest was covered with deep gashes; in at least two places it was clear that shrapnel had pierced the lungs.

And then the Skipper opened his eyes. "What about Dickson?" he asked. Appleton shook his head sadly, and prepared to administer morphia, but Cruickshank stopped him. "I want to stay awake, Johnnie, in case there's more trouble."

With Garnett at the controls and Fidler navigating they started on the five-and-a-half hour flight back to base— 600 miles away. "Y-Yorker" was shuddering and wallowing, threatening to founder under them. The comparatively less experienced second pilot did his best to nurse her along, but soon he began to lose height.

After an hour or so Cruickshank heaved himself up and swung his bandaged legs over the side of the bunk. He wanted to go forward and help Garnett. Only with great difficulty did Appleton persuade him to stay where he was.

Cruickshank lay down again, and now the palsy of shock seized him. The violent trembling stretched and twisted his wounds and he felt himself swallowed in a red fog of pain. Beating pain, crawling pain, pain that consumed like fire. Yet he fought to remain conscious, and again refused morphia.

To lighten the aircraft they jettisoned some of the non-essential gear, and after that Garnett, though sick and dazed from his own wounds, managed to maintain height.

As they flew south-east towards the Shetlands the sky darkened to the colour of fractured iron. They were leaving the area of "perpetual dusk," crossing the Arctic Circle, and it was still black, inhospitable night on the other side.

When the last light faded Appleton came up beside Garnett. The second pilot glanced back at the big holes in the bottom of the hull which they had tried to plug. " It's not going to work, Johnnie," he said. " As soon as we land the water will start coming in fast. We'll have to run her up on to the beach or we'll sink in just about two minutes."

It wanted a little over an hour till dawn when at last the battered plane reached Sullom Voe. Somehow Cruickshank sensed they were over base. He had stopped trembling now, but he was so weak from loss of blood he could not talk above a whisper.

" I'm still giving orders," he croaked. " Help me up to my seat." He knew Garnett had made very few night landings in a Catalina, and this wreck would be difficult to set down even in broad daylight. Fidler and Appleton had to carry him forward.

" Ditch the guns," he said. " And everything else that's movable."

Appleton and Fidler opened a " blister " and tossed out into the inky blackness the machine-guns, ammo and all the detachable equipment that remained. The Skipper caught a glimpse of white-capped waves far below. The water was choppy. He ordered Garnett to circle base; they would wait until it was light before tackling the last obstacle which lay between them and safety.

When it was sufficiently light to see the narrow stretch of water which was their runway, Cruickshank stretched out his hands and took the controls. " We'll do this together, Jack," he told Garnett. " But if I pass out, it'll be up to you."

The crippled " Cat " was liable to stall easily, so they made their approach at a higher speed than usual. They levelled out a few feet above the water and flew on, wings rocking a little, until they were nearly opposite the shore station. Then, bracing themselves, they eased back the throttles and let her settle.

The instant the keel hissed on the water they added power again to hold her before she could settle too deeply. Like a speedboat she sped across the dawn-lit bay in a cloud of spray half-sailing, half-flying. By revving up one engine and throttling back a little on the other they managed to turn her in towards the beach.

Water boiled in at half a dozen places, and soon it was swirling round their ankles. She began to slow, settle deeper. Rescue launches started out from the shore to meet them, sure that they would sink before reaching the beach.

" Full throttle ! " Cruickshank ordered.

The two big, sturdy Pratt and Whitney engines strained to full, roaring power, and the spray whipped up by the propellers came through the broken windscreen, stinging their faces, blinding them, making them splutter and gasp for air.

They could feel now that the nose wanted to go down. That would be the finish. Garnett locked his arms round the wheel yoke and pulled backwards with all the strength he had left.

" Y-Yorker," pitching increasingly and filling rapidly, clawed her way across that stretch of rough sea. On the last 100 yards only her screaming propellers kept her afloat, though they were taking as much water as air. She floundered on to the beach with seconds to spare.

The squadron medical officer gave Cruickshank a blood transfusion as he lay on a stretcher on the slipway. This time he accepted morphia and sank into blissful unconsciousness.

At hospital they found he had no fewer than seventy-two wounds. But after weeks of operations he recovered to go to Holyrood Palace, in his native Edinburgh, and receive from King George VI the nation's highest award for gallantry, the Victoria Cross. At the same investiture Flight Sergeant Garnett received the Distinguished Flying Medal for his part.

After the war, unable to shake off " notoriety," Cruickshank left for Rangoon, to work in a bank there. He has always insisted that he did no more than his duty, and that wider recognition should have been given to the members of his crew—in particular to the skill and gallantry of his navigator and great friend, Flying Officer Dickson, the man who guided them accurately through the fog-banks to their quarry.

Whatever this quiet, modest man has said, his own conduct was outstandingly heroic, a glorious example to his colleagues. Captains of Coastal Command like John Cruickshank, in partnership with the Royal Navy, slowly wore down the enemy and in the end denied him the element in which Britain had ruled supreme throughout five centuries.

HEAD IN THE CLOUDS

SHORTLY BEFORE four p.m. Cunningham climbed into his Beaufighter with his radar-navigator, Rawnsley. It was perhaps one of the worst days ever to mock the avouched merriness of May in England; matted black clouds came lumbering down from the nearby hills and Middle Wallop was blurred by sheeting rain.

John Cunningham's weather, this. Most R.A.F. fighter pilots revelled in clear skies and strong sunlight, but the short, blond, baby-faced Cunningham was a lurker in the shadows, greedy for gloom—a superbly efficient killer in the innermost caverns of the clouds and the darkest recesses of the night. Britain's number one night-fighter ace, in fact.

Many tall stories were told about him. For instance, newspapers reported that he ate pounds of carrots, and stayed in his room between dawn and sunset with the blinds drawn, in order to sharpen his vision. And it was said that as visibility faded his blue eyes began to shine and acquired a greenish hue—" Cat's Eyes Cunningham," they called him, " the man who hates the sunlight."

Exaggeration, propaganda. But it was indisputably true that at 25, at the peak of his strange yet brilliant career, this destroyer of the darkness could rise into the foulest sky, stalk a fast and wary prey and get into position to make his kill without once lifting his gaze from the instrument panel—guided only by Ground Control's radioed messages,

Rawnsley's murmured headings and the faint, pulsating
" blip " of his radar screen. In addition to swiftness of
reflex, sureness of marksmanship, high courage and all the
other usual qualities of a great fighter pilot, Cunningham
possessed a quick, logical, scientist's brain. And always
he was relaxed, cool, imperturbable.

His eyes certainly seemed to be shining now, as he
strapped himself into his seat and peered out through the
streaming windscreen. The clouds were thickening, the
light was fading, definitely fading. Somewhere up there,
tunnelling through the murk, the crack Luftwaffe unit
K.Gr 100 was making its first " blind " bombing run on
Britain. According to the Intelligence warning the
Germans were equipped with a new radio aid for flying in
cloud—though just what this was, and how it worked,
nobody on this side of the Channel knew. But surprises
were expected, so Cunningham—with his very special
talent and experience—was going up ahead of the other
defenders to " investigate."

Carefully he checked his treasure-trove of instruments,
took off, rose swiftly. Within seconds the Beaufighter
was swallowed up in the vast, sodden gloom.

Inside their little perspex capsule, burrowing through
the soupy strato-cumulus, Cunningham and Rawnsley
flew and navigated entirely by their instruments and the
directions radioed by Ground Control. They were vectored
to Swanage, to intercept the leading formations of the
Nazi raiders. But when they arrived there was nothing—
—not a " blip " on the screen, and beyond the canopy only
solid, pitchy blackness. Cunningham circled, relaxed in his
seat, eyes flicking over his instruments ; waiting. Long
nights of vigil had given him immense patience.

Empty minutes, then Control came through : " Bandit

in your area . . . Steer 0-2-5, angels nine." Cunningham swung on to the bearing, climbed to nine thousand feet and very soon picked up a faint " blip " dead ahead. He closed up to just over 1,000 yards, and then suddenly the " blip " began to move very rapidly across the radar screen—the raider had turned about, and now was racing back towards him ! In complete darkness, the two machines were converging head-on, at an aggregate speed of over 500 miles an hour !

Seconds to think. Cunningham kept his Mahatma-calm, his shoulders remained resting, relaxed, against the back of his seat even as the enemy's streams of tracer came lobbing towards them, passing so close that the Beaufighter bucked and shuddered. He did not return the fire—it was not John Cunningham's habit to blaze away wildly, he never pressed the button until he had " everything lined up " and was perfectly sure of hitting the target. Smoothly, unhurriedly, it seemed—he banked the plane and went into a tight, climbing turn.

As they rose out of the claws of the tracer, a slender, barely discernible shadow flitted by underneath. " Heinkel," Rawnsley announced quietly. Cunningham wheeled round after it, but it had vanished, his screen was blank. He circled, called up Ground Control : " Standing by—up to you again. . . ."

While they waited, hovering in the high dark, Cunningham reflected that the Germans' new radio device certainly seemed effective—the Heinkel's captain had been warned that a fighter was coming up behind him, perhaps even informed of the pursuer's height and range. And this business of turning back to meet the attacker, head-on, was a new and bold procedure. All this might call for new tactics, a fresh approach. . . .

Ground Control's plotters were not long in tracking down the Heinkel. It had turned north, towards Shaftesbury. A new course and height to fly—and Cunningham was back in the hunt.

He picked up the raider again only minutes later. And once more it wheeled on the instant to face him. Visibility was better here and for fleeting seconds he saw it clearly, charging at him. He kicked his rudder, slid neatly out of its path. Rushing past at close range the German raked the Beaufighter with its 'midship guns, and was gone.

Cunningham knew then that it was his rare—and doubtful—luck to be up against an ace bombing pilot. It is not often in modern war that two truly great pilots chance to oppose each other in personal battle. Cunningham, so far getting the worst of the duel, decided that his best chance lay in a " winding match "—a complicated, physically exacting and extremely hazardous manœuvre in which two aircraft try to out-turn each other. He checked the Beaufighter, could find no serious damage. If only he could tempt the German into this trap, he was confident he could get round inside him and thus bring his guns to bear on the tail. In the meantime he would save his ammo.

The Heinkel had straightened out and resumed its northerly course, cutting through rearing wads of cloud. Cunningham once more groped for him by radar, closed in from behind. For the third time the German started to wheel tightly, to hunt the hunter.

But the Englishman, ready for him this time, turned too, before the bomber could get round—banking the Beaufighter vertically, pirouetting tightly on his wingtip. So tightly it hurt : centrifugal force, like the hands of an invisible giant, pressed on the heads of pilot and navigator, slamming them down into their seats, turning their limbs to immovable lead, draining the blood supply from eye and brain until the instrument dials became blurred, meaningless splotches. When he judged they were round, heading back the way they had come, Cunningham took off some of the bank ; at once the pressure lifted, everything came back into focus. And now the roles were reversed, they had the Heinkel chasing them.

Cunningham continued to turn, but not too steeply now. Sure enough, the German followed him round. Cunningham advanced his throttles, little by little increased bank and rudder, gradually tightening up again. The Heinkel fell into his trap, tried to stay with him.

As once more the wings neared the vertical position several of the Beaufighter's most important instruments went mad, for the spinning gyroscopes that controlled them toppled at this angle. Beyond the windscreen darkened earth and overcast sky were merged in unbroken dimness —there was no faintest hint of a horizon for Cunningham to use as a reference, and as ten, twenty, thirty seconds strained by Rawnsley, slumped in the rear seat, lost all sense of direction, could not tell which way was up and which was down . . . But so skilled was Cunningham that, with only a few basic instruments still operating, he was able to hold the plane steady in its full-banked, full-powered circling. And somehow he managed to keep raising his head to search the darkness around them with those incredible, gloom-piercing eyes, trying to keep track of the Heinkel.

Forty seconds, fifty, sixty. . . . The crushing weight of the centrifugal force increased until Rawnsley could no longer hold his head up ; his chin went down, pressed against his chest, and the cabin seemed to fill with swirling, red mist. He wondered how his Skipper hoped to distinguish anything—even his instrument panel—under so much " G " stress.

Cunningham was fighting to stop himself " blacking out." His locked neck and jaw muscles ached and quivered under the strain, he was having trouble breathing —when he let the air out of his lungs they wanted to remain deflated, and it was hard labour to get them filled again. And even his remarkable vision was suffering as the blood drained from his cranium ; thick black streaks of " rain " appeared, slashing down across windscreen and instrument panel. But he knew the bigger, less manœuvrable Heinkel could not turn as tightly as this, no matter how good the pilot. And he knew he must hold on or be trapped himself—he was committed now, to take off any of the bank would mean flying right into the enemy's sights !

The engines shrieked, the fighter began to vibrate violently, and all track of time was lost. Afterwards they could not be sure how long they had kept up the punishing " merry-go-round " before, very suddenly, the dark silhouette and glowing exhausts of the Heinkel materialised out of the darkness—very close, almost directly above the Beaufighter's canopy ! The fighter had turned in a smaller circle, come up behind the bomber.

Immediately Cunningham eased back his throttles, took off a little bank. The gruelling " G " pressure lessened. He let the enemy draw ahead a little, drew a deep breath and, cool and methodical as a butler setting a breakfast tray, adjusted his gun-sight and laid it on the Heinkel's tail.

But in that instant, just as his thumb took the first, light pressure on the firing button, the bomber flicked out of its steep turn, twisted away in the opposite direction then plummeted down in an almost sheer dive. Perhaps the

German pilot's physical endurance was at an end, or having lost all trace of the Beaufighter he decided to break off the engagement. Possibly his new radio device warned him that his adversary was once again on his tail and, just in time, he saw the trap he'd been drawn into.

Cunningham put the stick forward, dived after him. But beneath lay clouds thick as wool, with hilltops thrusting up into them. The high ground cluttered the Beaufighter's radar with huge shadows, making a crazy jigsaw of the screen and masking the " blip " of the fugitive bomber.

Rawnsley was snarling in angry disappointment but the " imperturbable Baby-Face " merely shrugged, climbed, set course for base.

Not until late the next day did the news reach Middle Wallop : the Heinkel had not escaped, it had crashed on a hilltop near Cranbourne Chase. In his desperate dive to shake off the Beaufighter the German had struck high ground hidden in the dense cloud. Intelligence had managed to identify the pilot as Hauptmann Langar, celebrated Luftwaffe ace and commander of the K.Gr 100 development unit.

Without firing a shot Cunningham had won his duel. By patience, daring tactics and sheer flying ability, he had vanquished a top pilot from a crack enemy unit. And he had proved that the Luftwaffe's new radio device could be beaten by resolute, resourceful defenders.

This single incident—so typical of Cunningham's war —had a profound effect on the future tactics of the entire R.A.F. night-fighter force.

John Cunningham attained the rank of Group Captain, and an official " bag " of twenty enemy aircraft. Men who flew with him declared that in fact he had destroyed at least another ten, but in the darkness and confusion of night operations it was often difficult, and sometimes impossible, to confirm " kills " and establish which pilots had made them.

From early childhood he had been familiar with, and deeply interested in, aeroplanes, for the family home was close by Croydon airport on the outskirts of London. It was natural that he should become an apprentice at the De Havilland Aeronautical Technical School, and later join the Auxiliary Air Force.

And it was natural that when peace was won, and he left the service, this cool-headed, outstanding airman with the scientific bent should become chief test pilot of Britain's proud new jetliner, the De Havilland Comet, and nurse that mighty plane through experimental stages, setbacks and crises, to record-breaking fame.

THE AMAZON HAS WINGS

THE DEEP, vengeful roar of the Russian artillery rolled through the smoky, rubbled streets of Berlin, a dying city. While Adolf Hitler crouched in his bunker—an elaborate, bomb-proof underground headquarters—less than a mile distant his personal suicide troops, the " Praetorian Guard " of the Third Reich, were making a fanatically brave stand against the powerful Soviet infantry formations pouring in from the outskirts, thrusting for the heart of the crumbling Nazi capital.

In the bunker, the din of the barrage and the street battles could not be heard. Closing his eyes and ears to the true grimness of the situation, Hitler studied his maps and explained to the small group of followers who remained his wild, last-hope plan to counter-attack, save the city and himself from the Allied fury. Then he dictated a curt message for his air commanders. Minutes later a diminutive figure in overalls and flying helmet slipped from the bunker into the thundery haze of the outside world.

Thirty-two-year-old Hanna Reitsch, one of the greatest women flyers of all time, carried from the surrounded bunker the most dramatic—and hopeless—S.O.S. of the war. Hitler had chosen her to pilot the last plane out of Berlin, and contact the Luftwaffe chiefs whom he believed were still operational outside the Soviet ring which encircled him. "Only with aerial help," he had written, "can General Wenck's army relieve the capital."

What the Fuhrer did not know—or refused to accept—was that Wenck's army existed only on paper. Russian ground and air attacks had long since smashed it to pieces. And nearly all of the few, isolated Luftwaffe bases which remained outside the range of the invading Allied armies were under constant bombing and strafing attacks—it was doubtful if any could have got more than two or three planes into the air. Hour upon hour, shell and bombfire marched down the runways, smashed the parked aircraft like bugs, crumpled the hangars and control towers like empty cigarette packets. Most squadrons were without reserves of fuel and ammunition, and with the country's main road and rail arteries cut or blocked there was practically no chance of fresh supplies reaching them. Communications were becoming chaotic and many commanders had lost touch with each other, and with the general picture—everywhere was confusion and the bitter stench of defeat.

But the Fuhrer had said Wenck and the Luftwaffe would save him—and Hanna Reitsch even now believed implicitly every word he uttered. A tragically misplaced patriotism, and a complete capacity for loyalty, long ago had made this five-foot-tall, blonde aviatrix one of the Nazi dictator's most passionate admirers and eager servants. In 1942 he had strengthened her pride and devotion by decorating her with the Iron Cross (First Class)—after that there can be no doubt that Hanna was as passionate a Nazi as any of the others who served the swastika.

There can be no doubt, either, that she served heroically. And in this book we are concerned mainly with heroism in the air—the causes and motives involved are of secondary interest.

Hanna's brilliance and bravery as a pilot had won her many friends in England in 1937 when she arrived to take part in the annual soaring competition held by the British Gliding Association at Great Hucklow, Derbyshire. And her endless efforts to encourage women everywhere to take to the air and make careers for themselves in the growing aircraft industries " on an equal basis with men " got a good deal of publicity. She was then 24, and had been given the rank of Captain by the German Air Ministry in recognition of her work as a test pilot. Famed for her precision flying, she had challenged top German airmen to contests involving complicated patterns, instrument flying and aerobatics— and more often than not been judged the victor. She spent every hour she could in the air, and was familiar with scores of aircraft types.

Hanna believed that British girls, like their German " cousins," had certain " national qualities " which were suited to flying. She was full of praise for Amy Johnson, the English ex-typist who had been the first woman to fly solo from London to Australia in 1930, and in 1931 had set up a record by flying alone from England to India in six days.

Amy was about ten years older than Hanna, and startlingly different in personality. The English girl had a simple love of aeroplanes, a natural flying skill and a hard-won, carefully husbanded store of aviation knowledge. Her only purpose was to go on flying, and meeting all the challenges it offered her, for as long as she could. Quiet-spoken and completely unaffected—genuinely shy, many thought—she was entirely without fierce national pride or fashionable theories, and she saw herself as representative of no particular class or cause.

The British public held Amy in warm affection, and to this other girl pilot from abroad—dubbed, indeed, by some newspapers " Germany's Amy Johnson "—a special welcome was extended. Her coolness and outstanding skill in flying gliders through the tricky winds above the hills of Nottinghamshire and Derbyshire brought unstinted praise from air experts, and many leading British flyers entertained her in their homes.

Hanna was eager to recruit enthusiasts in Britain for her " equal rights for women in the air " campaign, and her idea about " national qualities "—which to some English minds had a strong reek of Nordic racial theories. She grew impatient when—despite her lavish tributes to Amy Johnson—none of her hosts seemed to take her schemes seriously. There is every indication that she returned to Germany convinced that Britain was " lackadaisical, backward, decadent "—everything that the Nazis said it was. And two years later, when war came, Captain Reitsch volunteered for flying duties " in an operational capacity." She even offered to form a special squadron of women pilots " to fight for the Fatherland, on the same terms as the men of the Luftwaffe—without any privileges or restrictions."

Nazi propaganda chief Joseph Goebbels saw in her a valuable property, and used her to symbolise the spirit of German womanhood at war—recruiting girls for ground duties with the Luftwaffe, for munitions factories and other forms of national service. She worked as test pilot for many of the latest fighters and bombers ; flew Generals and high Nazi officials in and out of occupied countries and operational theatres (more than once having to run the gauntlet of enemy flak or fighters), acted as liaison officer flying between forward bases and headquarters, and for a time was Hitler's personal pilot. Often as she whisked him across Germany the dictator would ask her advice on aviation matters.

But her repeated requests to be allowed to form and train an all-woman squadron to fly on bomber or fighter operations were tactfully brushed aside. Hitler is said to have told her : " You are more valuable to me in your present duties."

Meanwhile Amy Johnson was also serving her country. She had no grand schemes about forming girl pilots into combat units, and no photographers or propagandists followed her around—as a ferry pilot with Air Transport Auxiliary she was busy flying new aircraft of all types, from fighters to the biggest bombers, from the factories to the R.A.F. bases where they were so urgently needed. All over the country and abroad she flew, by day or by night, often in foul weather.

On a grey day in 1941 a multi-engined plane she was ferrying over Southern England developed a series of faults. Amy fought coolly, using all her vast experience, but she lost control. Over the Thames Estuary she baled out, and was drowned.

In far-off Russia, where even before the war Communism had introduced a greater equality of the sexes, the story was different. In the tense summer of 1941 Marina Raskova, one of the most experienced Soviet airwomen, was checked out by Red Air Force instructors on every type of operational plane in service. She then called together from all areas of the vast Union, all the girls who held pilots' certificates and taught them to fly fighters and bombers.

First woman to hold the Air Force rank of Colonel, Marina got her government's approval of a scheme to form all-women squadrons for combat duties. She herself later took command of a " mixed " bomber squadron—eighty per cent of the air crews were female. Its record was as good as any in the service.

The girl fighter pilots were commanded by Lieutenant Colonel " Niki " Kezarinova, who held the Order of Lenin and the Red Star. Top ace of this " pursuit regiment " was Captain Lydia Litviak who, during the desperate air battles over besieged Stalingrad, destroyed twelve German machines. Lydia was killed during the Soviet offensive at Orel in 1943.

One of the strangest air operations of any war took place over German artillery fortifications at Krimskaya in June, 1943. It might be called " the battle of the Amazons."

Nine Russian dive-bombers, all crewed by women, were ordered to destroy the Nazi guns. They were escorted to the target by a wing of fighters, also flown by women and commanded by Captain A. Timofeyeva—mother of two children, who had worked before the war as a weaver.

Cloudy conditions forced them to approach the target dangerously low—at about 2,800 feet. As the dive-bombers dipped their noses and started to scream down through a thick curtain of A.A. fire, a pack of Messer-schmitts swooped out of the cloud cover in a perfect " bounce " and tried to fasten on to their tails.

Captain Timofeyeva brought her fighters down after the Germans and the Nazi pilots were astonished to hear on their radios high, unmistakably female voices calling to each other! Perhaps the surprise put them off their stride—at any rate, they failed to catch up with the dive-bombers, or to make them break off their attack.

The Soviet bombs erupted in and all around the German battery—and then the dive-bombers, instead of fleeing across country, keeping very low and slewing from side to side to shake off the Messerschmitts, suddenly formed up and wheeled in a neat, pre-arranged manœuvre to face their attackers. Their turn was right—the faster, less manœuvrable Messerschmitts could not get round in such a small circle, but were lured into trying. The German pilots found themselves caught in a deadly crossfire —between the dive-bombers and the escorting fighters.

In a matter of seconds four of the German planes were shot down. The rest broke formation, turning and climbing and diving—heading off in each and every direction to get out of the crossfire. The Red Amazons, with the sky to themselves, turned in orderly formation for home. Three of the dive-bombers were damaged and one, piloted by Maria Dolyena, had flames trailing from the rear fuselage. But all made it back to base.

Intelligence reports of such encounters with Soviet women pilots were kept secret in Berlin, but the news reached Hanna Reitsch. Again she asked permission to train German women pilots for combat, but again she was refused—it was too late, the Allied invasions, and the round-the-clock bomber offensive were cutting production, and it was a big enough problem to keep present squadrons supplied with replacement aircraft.

So Hanna had to content herself with the various assignments Hitler chose to give her. And the last of them was that dramatic S.O.S. from the Berlin bunker, on that April night in 1945.

An armoured vehicle was waiting to take her to Branden-burger Tor, where her Arado 96 was hidden in a special shelter. Accompanying her was General von Greim—pale, hollow-eyed, wordless.

They clambered into the vehicle and Hanna sat beside the driver,—a young, poker-faced S.S. volunteer; von Greim hunched down in the back, consumed with his private miseries. They started off, lurching crazily over hunks of masonry and piles of debris. In the distance now huge fires were raging, washing the night sky with a fierce crimson. Salvoes of shells screamed down, crashed into buildings all around, showered the vehicle with fragments of stone and shrapnel.

Each time they heard the screaming of falling shells, the driver swerved out into the middle of the littered roadway, so that if a building on either side were hit there would be less chance of the vehicle being completely buried by the falling wreckage. And he avoided the narrower streets.

Hanna began to worry that her secret plane-shelter was already in Russian hands. " Faster ! " she yelled, above the storm of the battle. " Forget about swerving—take the shortest route ! "

They were within a quarter of a mile of the Arado's hiding place when a salvo smashed into the roadway so close behind them that the armoured vehicle was lifted into the air, carried sideways by the blast, and dumped down again with tremendous force. It staggered on for a few yards, rocking wildly, then snarled to a halt. The driver, blood running down his face from where he had struck it against a stanchion, could not get it moving again.

Hanna wheeled, shook von Greim's drooping shoulder, then climbed out. The street was full of hot drifting dust and smoke and the sinister, flickering light from a thousand burning buildings. Ducking round shell-holes, scrambling over the rubble, together they half-ran, half-crawled the rest of the way to the plane-shelter. The Arado was undamaged.

While they worked to prepare for the take-off, crouched figures flitted past the end of the broad avenue outside. Machine-guns rasped, rifles barked and whined, grenades crumped, there were hoarse cries and shrill whistles—they knew they were on the very fringe of the street fighting.

Hanna taxied out, pointed the Arado's nose up the dark, smoky roadway which was to be her runway. For all she knew there might be a yawning crater dead ahead, or a barricade of masonry, but there was no time to check. She glanced at von Greim—deathly pale, staring fixedly ahead with those hollow eyes. Then she advanced the throttle and the little craft started to roll.

Just after the tail came up one wheel struck a big stone. The Arado tilted, swung round, one wingtip scraping the ground. Hanna saw the dark bulk of a shattered building looming ahead and knew she had to take a chance and try to haul the plane off before it had built up a safe margin of speed. Both hands on the stick : the plane was reluctant to rise, but came up mushily, wings juddering and dipping, a hair's breadth above stalling point. Hanna fought it round slowly, with the minimum of bank, away from the shattered building. Then she let the nose down a shade, kept going straight on up the avenue, with the wheels scant inches from the littered surface, and held it there until at last she had built up climbing speed.

As they rose above the rooftops into a dark red sky the full, appalling vista was revealed—a great city burning, breaking up, perishing under their wings. Great columns crashed in plumes of sparks, ancient structures blazed like lanterns, exploding shells flashed in expanding rings, and over all the long, glowing spears of tracer stitched a criss-cross pattern, like a vast golden net.

And then the searchlights hit her. Searing, pounding, blinding light—a Russian battery on the outskirts swung all its beams on to the little Arado, held it in a cone while scores of heavy machine-guns and light A.A. pieces clawed for it.

Hanna threw the plane violently from side to side, climbed, dived, side-slipped. Still the vice of beams gripped her, and the blast of the flak made the controls kick furiously in her hands.

" I'm going down ! " she bawled to von Greim, but he stared blankly, apparently not understanding her. She cut the throttle, slammed the stick forward. The Arado plummeted, almost vertically, back into the smoke over the dying city.

The searchlights tried to follow but Hanna did not pull out until she was skimming over the shattered rooftops. Having shaken them off, she stayed at this height—now and then having to tweak a wing up over a broken factory chimney, or a fractured church spire—until they were clear of the suburbs. It was a superb, courageous example of evasive action, of which any experienced combat pilot could have been proud. And it was done in the most dangerous conditions—at night, with drifting smoke and dust obscuring the windscreen at times, and obstacles materialising suddenly out of the gloom.

Reaching open country she climbed to 20,000 feet and set course for the fifty-minute flight to Rechlin, still in German hands and headquarters of a Luftwaffe group.

She knew the worst was still to come—the sky all

around the city was alive with Russian fighters. Convinced that Hitler and the other Nazi leaders would make a last-minute bid to fly out to Switzerland, Sweden or some other neutral country, the Red Air Force had built a thick, high wall of patrols around the city and the pilots had orders to let no plane pass, whatever its type or markings.

Luckily there were occasional clumps of cloud. She made her way from one to another, twisting her neck to search the sky all around as she skipped across the clear patches. Several times, high above or off to one side, she saw groups of Soviet fighters silhouetted against the stars or the red glow of the burning city, and they failed to spot her. But such luck could not last. . . .

Four of them. Slanting down from behind, coming very fast in loose, line-abreast formation, the leading edges of their wings barbed with wicked little spikes of blue and red flame, flickering fiercely, as they fired long bursts. Hanna stood the Arado on a wingtip, hauled it round, dived hard. The fighters followed, but could not turn as tightly. She pulled up again, into the sanctuary of a cloud and lost them. Only then did she discover that the Arado had been hit. Pieces had been chivvied out of the tail assembly and the rear fuselage, but the little craft still responded perfectly to the controls.

She could see the sweat glistening on von Greim's white, misery-broken face. She realised the man was resigned to death, any minute now—he did not believe they had the slightest chance of getting through to Rechlin. But Hanna, aglow with the fire of the fanatic, had the feeling that she held history in her hands; she really believed the message from the Fuhrer which she carried could save the Father-land even now from the hated Bolsheviks. Emerging from the cloud she settled down to fly as never before, putting her neck into swivel-gear, scanning every corner of the night sky ; with her reflexes poised, yet relaxed, her mind highly charged, yet unflustered—remembering even now to check the compass, altimeter, air speed indicator and all the other instruments with regular, swift, custom-learned flicks of the eyes, and managing to keep track of their progress towards Rechlin.

After about two minutes in the clear, two more fighters sliced down, this time almost dead ahead. As they came, they slid apart—to get on either side of her, so that when they opened up they could bring a crossfire to bear. But the watchful, sharp-sighted Hanna spotted them long before they were in range. And a bare instant before their guns blazed she put the Arado into a steep dive, dropped like a gannet for about 2,000 feet, then levelled out, banked steeply and cartwheeled to the right. This rapid, complex manœuvring shook off one of her attackers, but the other had dropped below and was now climbing under her belly, firing short bursts. His bullets drummed on the underside of the port wing, and a piece of the trailing edge fell off.

Hanna threw the nimble machine into a long, violent series of rolls and stalled turns, vertical dives and climbs, bunts and controlled spins, writhing about the sky like a maddened salmon fighting on the hook. She finished up right down on the deck, streaking across fields and villages so low that the plane's shape seemed to merge with the shadows of hills and valleys and pine thickets. She managed to lose the remaining fighter, but soon machine-guns on the ground opened up, and she was forced to climb again.

Now the Russians knew that a plane had got out of Berlin, and was trying to sneak through their blockade. Hanna reckoned that by now they must have realised she was heading for Rechlin—so all their fighters would be concentrated rapidly in this sector, and all ground defences would be warned. To make their tracking more difficult, she began to weave from side to side.

This time she didn't see them coming, the first she knew about it was when tracer flicked close by the cabin. The angle and density of the tracer told her there were at least two, diving from port in a beam attack. She rolled on her left side, turned in to face them—thereby altering the closing angle, shortening the time she would be in the line of fire, and presenting a smaller target. The first of them flashed by close overhead. The second hurtled towards her, head-on now, but he could not reduce his initial angle of deflection in time to get his fire on to her before he was forced to put his nose down and pass just underneath.

The instant both were behind her, Hanna wheeled again, raced after them at full throttle—gambling that this would be the very last thing they would expect. The gamble came off; the Red pilots, taking it for granted that she would be trying to put as much sky as possible between her and her pursuers, turned about and sped off in that direction. She saw them pass underneath. Seconds later she was plunging into a timely wad of cumulo-stratus.

She stayed in the cloud for two or three minutes, circling, then edged out and, scanning the faint grey-and-black pattern of the land below, managed to get her bearings. Her pulse quickened—she was almost through, another ten minutes would take her to Rechlin! And in that direction the clouds were thicker! She gave von Greim an encouraging grin, but he only nodded vaguely, stared about him with those deep, glazed eyes.

On that last stage of the nightmare flight Hanna spotted several more fighters—once a huge pack of them passed within two thousand yards, without sighting her. There was one more attack by a single Russian but there was a lot more cloud now and she managed to bury herself in it before he could get in a well-aimed burst. Then she was through the gauntlet. She dropped out of the overcast, made her landing approach a little faster than usual to allow for the damage to tail and rudder, touched down with the wheels first and taxied at high speed to the control tower, swerving round bomb craters and wrecked planes. As she cut the engine, von Greim looked as if he could not believe they were safely down. He remained perfectly still, blinking uncertainly; she had to shake him hard before he came to life, undid his straps and climbed out.

To the few haggard, listless senior officers of the Luftwaffe gathered at this base, Hanna formally delivered the Fuhrer's message, and General von Greim mustered enough concentration to issue orders calling every available German aircraft to the defence of Berlin. The General was not very convincing; it was plain he had no faith in his own words.

The Luftwaffe officers listened in silence, then explained politely that the small number of aircraft they could get airborne would be completely ineffective against the Soviet might. They had no replacements or spare parts, fuel and ammunition were almost exhausted. And besides, nearly all of them—like von Greim—saw that defeat was inevitable and were loath to send their surviving pilots, mostly very young recruits, on a suicide mission which could gain nothing.

Not so Hanna—furious at their " disloyalty," she persuaded von Greim to fly off with her to Ploen, near Keil, to see Grand Admiral Karl Doenitz, who was earmarked to become Nazi Supreme Commander if Hitler should be killed or captured. Her idea was that Doenitz, planner of the pitiless U-boat war and notorious " strong man " in past crises, would very quickly crack down on these Luftwaffe " shirkers," rally them—and the country— for a final effort.

Ploen was well out of the way of the Russians, and British and American aircraft in that area showed no interest in the light machine, so the flight was uneventful. So was the interview with Doenitz—he seemed suddenly to have aged ; her words clearly did not impinge on his consciousness. It was plain that he was preoccupied with the problems of food distribution, public health and essential services in the foundering Reich, all of which Hanna considered unimportant compared with the need to save Berlin and the Fuhrer.

Refusing to give up, and still dragging the dazed and depressed von Greim with her, Hanna sought out Field-Marshal Wilhelm Keitel, head of the Supreme Command— of which Hitler himself was the Commander-in-Chief. Keitel, his face deep-scored, his eyes bright-glazed as painted porcelain, listened to her passionate plea, that, even without air support, Wenck's army should move at once to the relief of Berlin. Then the man who, in just a few more days, was to sign an act of military surrender— and who eventually was to be condemned by an Allied tribunal and hanged as a war criminal—said very quietly and flatly : " Wenck's army has been destroyed. It is all over."

It was the tragic end of Hanna's hopeless mission. Her flight out of Berlin had been an epic—perhaps the most difficult and dangerous ever undertaken by a non-military flyer in an unarmed plane. Months later, Allied air experts piecing together the facts were forced to acknowledge her immense skill and heroism. Many expressed deep sadness that this outstanding woman pilot should have squandered her talents and loyalties in such a vicious cause. Some even sought to find excuses for her Nazi activities.

But Hanna Reitsch remained a faithful and defiant Nazi, even after news reached Ploen that Hitler and Eva Braun had died in the Berlin bunker, and that Russia's hammer-and-sickle flag was flying over the ruins of the capital.

On 2nd May, when a new German Government was convened at Ploen, she marched into the office of Heinrich Himmler, head of the Gestapo and now home front commander (who later committed suicide).

" Is it true" she demanded, " that you have contacted the Anglo-Americans with peace proposals ? "

" Of course," he said curtly. " There is nothing else to do now." Members of Himmler's staff and other officials and officers turned nervous glances on Hanna.

The five-foot Amazon stared into the hard eyes of the most feared man in Germany—the systematic killer who had ordered the deaths of countless thousands, from nameless concentration camp victims to powerful officials and top-ranking military officers. Her lips curled in contempt.

" Traitor ! " she shrilled. " You have betrayed your Fuhrer, and your people, in the very darkest hour." Then, blonde head high, she turned and marched from the room— soon to face Allied investigators, and pay the price for her misplaced devotion ; for the wasted years which, but for Adolf Hitler and his base creed, could have brought her fame and friendship throughout the world.

CANNON IN THE SKY

OVER THE quiet English countryside came two great shuddering bangs, in quick succession, like the expanding shock waves of a distant, mighty explosion. Workers in the fields of Surrey felt a soft jolt in the air; flocks of birds rose in whirring fright from the treetops, and in farmsteads, hamlets and townships window-panes rattled in their frames.

Everywhere people paused, peered skyward. A few spotted a small, glinting fighter-plane streaking overhead, but there was no reason to associate it with the mysterious bangs—it was flying serenely, trailing no smoke. And besides, aircraft like this were often seen over this part of England nowadays; any schoolboy could identify those swept-back wings—the new DH 108, experimental jet, also known as the Swallow.

But they were wrong to dismiss the little plane as the possible source of the big " explosion." For beneath the Swallow's streamlined canopy was Squadron Leader John Derry, one of the most brilliant and venturesome of that small band of former war-flyers who, turning from bombs and bullets to blueprints and prototype testing, were piloting Britain to peace-time progress. And Derry had just made history; that deep, shuddering noise rolling over the countryside and echoing in the hills was, in one sense, an explosion—Man's crashing of the Sound Barrier, his bursting through into the Supersonic Age.

The time was 10.30 on a Monday morning in the Autumn of 1948 ; the place, an undefined area of the sky between ancient, royal Windsor and Farnborough, home of the Royal Aircraft Establishment and the showplace of modern aviation. By putting the Swallow into a flat-out power-dive from more than 30,000 feet, Derry had become the first human to fly faster than the speed of sound. And as the machine had caught up with the noise of its own passage through the air, there occurred that awesome phenomenon which was soon to become known as " the sonic boom," like two quick blasts from a mighty cannon, rolling across the sky and the land.

In those instants, going through the barrier, the Swallow had been subjected to savage buffeting. The sound waves cramming the air all around it set up a vibration that threatened to shake it to pieces. But Derry, and the creators of this new flying machine, had been well-prepared for this danger ; other pilots had drawn close to the barrier before, and been battered back. One, Captain Geoffrey De Havilland, distinguished military airman and member of the pioneer family which had founded the great De Havilland Aircraft Company, had lost his life only two years earlier, when his plane broke up in a barrier-piercing bid over the Thames Estuary.

Throughout history, the latent power of sound to produce destructive vibrations had been known. There was a clear enough warning in the Old Testament account of Joshua's trumpet razing the walls of Jericho, another in the story of Enrico Caruso, the superb Italian opera singer, shattering wine glasses with his powerful tenor voice !

Derry and his colleagues were sure that the answer was to smash through the barrier quickly—" like a dog jumping through a paper hoop." On the other side, once the juddering jumble of sound-waves had been left behind, they believed there lay an unknown world of safe, smooth silence ; a world which must be reached and opened up for the great jet craft of the future.

Up till now no plane had been fast enough to break through quickly and cleanly, thereby being subjected only to a short, sharp " bump " of turbulence ; but in the new, powerful, swept-wing Swallow they were confident they had the key which would open the way.

At sea level the speed of sound is approximately 760 m.p.h. But it decreases with altitude and with reduction in the density of the atmosphere, so to indicate this variable factor airmen use the term " Mach Number One." Whatever the height of the plane, whatever the *actual* speed of sound there, it is called " Mach 1."

To get a mental picture of this mysterious thing known as the Sonic Barrier, we first must understand that in front of an aircraft's wings as it proceeds through the air there is a kind of faint, restless stirring. Little waves of suction and pressure are continuously advancing ahead of the plane, probing forward, like long-range scouts—as though to warn the air of what is coming and start it flowing into submissive pattern before the machine itself arrives. Let us call this process " the run-ahead."

Now, the slower the plane is moving, the further the " run-ahead " will extend. Thus, long before the slow plane arrives, the sky is beginning to prepare itself, shaping its molecules and currents to accept the approaching wings. Few pilots can explain *why* the sky does this, but many see the phenomenon as startling proof that Man was meant to fly—" that the sky was designed to accept machines."

In faster aircraft, flying at around 600 m.p.h., the " run-ahead " extends only a little way forward—the plane is very nearly keeping up with its sound. And in an aircraft travelling at Mach 1—the varying speed of actual sound—the run-ahead stops entirely, and the " bow-wave " of air, unable to outspeed the machine, remains attached to wings and fuselage, building up with terrifying rapidity into a storm of shock-waves, buffeting and battering and threatening to break the plane in pieces.

To ride such a storm, even for a few instants, a special sort of wing design is needed ; a wing which not only can withstand the wild vibration of passing through the barrier, but which can also ride the still, " unwarned " sky beyond—ram into an atmosphere which has not been made aware of the machine's approach, and by sheer power and strength and delicacy of shape and balance fly smoothly on through air which has not had time to prepare itself for the plane's passage.

And as wings like these crash through the barrier, people on the ground usually hear not one, but two bangs. The second, of course, is an echo thrown back by the land. (Sometimes, in hilly districts, there are three " explosions," growing progressively fainter. But whatever the number of echoes, the occurrence is generally referred to in the singular, as " the sonic boom.")

For Derry, in his all-out dive, it came at 605.23 m.p.h. He felt a brief, brutal buffeting that had the controls kicking, bucking under his hands and feet, and he had to strain every muscle to hold the plane's nose down and the wings straight. And then—with incredible suddenness—he was through, the Swallow was flying smoothly downward through tranquil air ; he knew he was the first man into unknown territory, and he wondered at the deep, deep quietness, realised in a flash that jets of the future would travel in a soundless, pacific element, where the whine of motors and even the moan and hiss of wings cutting through the sky would be swept behind too fast to reach the ears of the occupants.

Then it was time to close the throttle, to ease back the stick—gently, smoothly!—and back out quickly, cleanly, through the breach he had made in the invisible wall. The turbulence this time was considerably less troublesome. In no time at all he was flying straight and level through the soft September sunlight, scudding across Surrey at about 500 m.p.h. towards Farnborough airfield. The Swallow was behaving normally, his body felt no different—oh, it was hard to believe he had been through the barrier, through to the silent world. . . !

A few hours later the Ministry of Supply released the bald, almost meaningless statement: " In the course of recent high speed development trials on the De Havilland 108 research aircraft, an apparent Mach number in excess of 1 was recorded." The people of Surrey heard this on the radio news, but still didn't connect it with the mysterious " explosion "—until the national Press explained, under huge headlines and blown-up portraits of John Derry, that a vital voyage of discovery had been successfully completed.

Derry's only comment to clamouring reporters was: " I cannot say I felt calm. . . . My tummy was full of butterflies." This was typical of the tall, modest, slow-speaking family man, the pilot who hated publicity. " Don't waste time on me," he would tell newsmen. " Go and talk to the men with the brains—the chaps who designed this kite, and planned the whole operation. . . ."

When war came in 1939, John Derry had been a 17-

year-old boarder at Charterhouse, one of Britian's most
famous public schools. Adventure pulsed in his veins
—his father, a doctor, had been a member of an archaeol-
ogical expedition to Egypt's " Valley of the Kings " at
Luxor. There was no hesitation in his choice—he volunteered for flying duties with the R.A.F. The pilot training
schools were full; he was happy to be accepted as a wireless-
operator/air-gunner. Qualifying with high marks, he
served with Coastal Command, won his commission and
in time was appointed gunnery leader of his Group.

But the thrill of flying enchanted him and after a while
being a mere crew-member—" a passenger "—was not
enough ; he kept on applying for training as a pilot. Not
until 1943 was he accepted and sent to a flying school in
Canada.

He sailed through the course, without difficulty of any
kind—he knew aeroplanes, he loved them, he understood
the whole business of military aviation better than some of
his instructors. Graduating with high ratings, he returned
to Europe in time to serve in post-invasion operations. He
won the D.F.C. " for great courage," and was also awarded
the Bronze Lion of the Netherlands. His commanders
reported that he had the simple but most valuable qualities
—determination, and painstaking skill.

After the war there was no question about what career
he would follow. His heart was in flying still, and the
glowing reports in his log-book won him a post as test
pilot with the Vickers-Armstrong company. In 1947, he
moved to the De Havilland stable. With the DH experimental jets he smashed record after record, culminating in
the Swallow's faster-than-sound flight in 1948.

Many more years might have passed before the sound
barrier was pierced, and the honour might have gone to a

pilot in another country had it not been for the genius and
selfless, lifelong labour of an older airman—Group Captain
Frank Whittle, " father of the jet engine." He was one of
the " men with brains " that Derry so often praised, that
rare combination of aeronautical scientist and active aviator.

As a lad of fifteen, Whittle had applied to enter the R.A.F
as an apprentice. He was turned down. His rejection report
said simply : " Poor physique." And there was no arguing
—Frank was barely five feet tall, and very thin. Bitterly
disappointed and very ashamed, he went to a physical
training establishment, asked to see the chief instructor
and explained his problem. The instructor, wholly
sympathetic, gave the boy a list of body-building exercises
and directions for a weight-increasing diet, the basis of
which was olive oil.

In less than six months Frank's chest had expanded three
inches and he'd gained nearly four in height. Once more
he applied to the R.A.F. And once more he was refused.
The air force doctors said he was still too skinny and
muscularly weak.

Frank came home, went through the whole diet and
exercise procedure again, from the very start. Then he
applied for the third time—in another town, not mentioning his previous, unsuccessful applications. He passed all
the tests, at last was accepted as a boy apprentice and posted
to the R.A.F's Cranwell College.

Accepted for pilot training, the future jet pioneer made
his first solo flight in an Avro 504N biplane, which had a
top speed of 105 m.p.h.

In the midst of all this, at the age of 21, while still a
cadet, he wrote a science thesis in which he discussed a
new, revolutionary type of aircraft which would be propelled " by ejected gases." The existing system of piston en-

gines and propellors was, he believed, decidedly limited; even with improved design and development such aircraft could not be expected to exceed speeds beyond 400 m.p.h.

That thesis was, in fact, the world's first clear exposition on the subject of jet flight. It won Whittle the college's highest award for aeronautical sciences.

So outstanding was his flying ability that on graduating he was made first an instructor, and later a test pilot on seaplanes. He devoted his spare time to designing the first jet engine, and in January, 1930, took out a master patent, submitted his drawings to the Air Ministry. The idea was rejected—"because the practical difficulties are too great."

After unsuccessful attempts to interest commercial firms, early in 1935 he formed a partnership with two other R.A.F. men and registered a company, Power Jets Ltd. Shown further designs, the Air Ministry experts now conceded that the basic principles were sound, but they still believed that the idea lay too far in the future. There appeared to be ample justification for this assessment, for the first engines which the company produced failed completely.

Whittle had put his all into the venture. Only a deep faith in his theory, and the same unflagging determination which years before had got him into the air force, kept him going now in his small workshop at Rugby. Through all the days of 1936 nothing but misfortune seemed to come his way. Friends advised him to give up the whole project, to concentrate on being an airman and leave engineering and invention to the great factories with unlimited funds and huge research staffs. Then in April, 1937, one of the Whittle jet engines ran properly for the first time. Scientists and flying men rushed to see a demonstration and were deeply impressed. There was champagne that night, and Frank kept one of the bottles—with forty signatures on its label.

But still he got no official backing. While the shadows of crisis were deepening in Europe, and in other lands air-minded governments were ordering their aircraft designers to begin experiments with a view to producing jet-propelled fighters, the little workshop at Rugby remained silent. Whittle wrote letters, sought interviews in Whitehall, constantly campaigning for an earnest development programme, pointing out that Britain was losing the chance of leading the world into the Jet Age. Not until early 1939—a few months before the outbreak of war—did he receive an order to build an engine which could be used to power a new, specially designed plane.

The job went ahead in strictest secrecy. Whittle worked with demoniac energy, depriving himself of sleep and proper meals, rushing back and forwards between Whitehall, Rugby and the various factories and experimental airfields where the makers of the airframe were conducting tests.

One of the biggest problems in this period was fuel consumption. The jet engine promised to give fantastic speed and rate of climb, but it burned fuel so quickly that the plane would be able to stay in the air only for a few minutes. There were many bitter setbacks before a means was found to make the engine run more economically and to provide additional fuel storage space in the wings and fuselage.

All through the tense Summer and Autumn of 1940, and the first winter of *blitzkrieg* bombing, while the young pilots of the R.A.F. fought by day and by night to defend a sorely beleaguered Britain, the older pilot, Frank Whittle, fought a different sort of round-the-clock battle, on the ground. And on a fine May morning in 1941, all the years of patience and toil were rewarded when a strange, propellerless machine whined across the Home Counties, sending people running to their air-raid shelters—convinced that this was some Nazi secret weapon, a giant bomb with wings.

He had got the first jet aircraft into the sky. The Whittle power unit drove it at a speed which exceeded his highest hopes : fully 200 m.p.h. faster than the swiftest piston-engined fighter of the day !

An intensive programme of tests and modification followed. Many improvements were made in both engine and airframe design, and the plane's endurance was increased still further. As the Gloster Meteor, it went into production for the R.A.F.

The first Meteors saw action in 1944. Their first great success was against the V.1 robot bombs, which were too fast for Fighter Command's ordinary, piston-engined planes.

A famous American pilot, General " Hap " Arnold, had seen some of the early tests with the experimental Gloster jet, powered by the Whittle-1 jet unit. He expressed amazement when he learned that this engine weighed only 650 pounds and provided more thrust than a comparable Rolls-Royce reciprocating engine weighing 1,650 pounds, and had only one-fifth the number of moving parts. It was easier to build and service, and would run on alcohol, diesel oil or paraffin.

Now, as a result of Arnold's report and the success of the service Meteor, United States manufacturers took up Whittle's invention and invited him to Washington to supervise the launching of an immense development and construction plan. But the years of feverish work and unrelenting strain were taking toll of his slight frame; his health broke, he had to retire for long spells of hospital treatment. One of the most important periods of development in the history of aviation went ahead without him.

In June, 1946, pronounced fit again, he handed over to the British government all his interests in Power Jets Ltd., without asking a penny. By this act, he gave his life's work to the nation. Into the British Treasury, America poured millions of badly needed dollars in royalties on Whittle's patents.

He accepted the exacting and responsible post of planning and creating his country's future, all-jet air force. And the man whom many now regarded as the greatest air inventor since the Wright Brothers was content to live quietly in a small, rented house on an income of about £2,000 a year.

But the authorities had no intention of letting his genius and devotion go unrewarded. One day a courier knocked at the door of his little house, handed over a letter from the Royal Commission on Awards to Inventors. It told him he had been granted the sum of £100,000—the highest award Britain had ever made to an inventor.

And in 1948 came another, different sort of reward for " the father of the jet engine "—the news that 26-year-old John Derry had broken through the sound barrier. It was the realisation of Whittle's most precious dream. The way was now open, a bridgehead had been established in the supersonic stratosphere: soon great jetliners would soar in silence, without even noticeable vibration in their pressurised passenger cabins, into a new age of air travel.

In 1949 and 1950, the people of the Home Counties grew accustomed to the deep, double clap of " the sonic boom," as—almost daily, it seemed—Derry and his colleagues continued to thrust through the barrier with newer, ever-faster jets. Sometimes the shock-waves shattered windows or greenhouses : then there would be claims for damages, angry letters to the newspapers. All just claims got sympathetic consideration—it was a small price to pay for mastery of the supersonic sky. . . .

In France, Jacqueline Auriol, daughter-in-law of the President, soon became the first woman to fly faster than sound. Again and again she cracked the barrier, and won recognition as one of the world's greatest Jet Age test pilots.

In 1954, Jacqueline crashed on the River Seine, near Paris, and was gravely injured. Doctors feared her flying career was finished, but with great courage and tenacity she went through a difficult rehabilitation course and less than two years later was back at the controls.

And on 26th August, 1959, Madame Auriol—mother of two children—flew France's new delta-winged Mirage Mark III interceptor at 1,345 m.p.h.—*twice* the velocity of sound, the fastest speed ever achieved by a woman.

In Britain, from 1950 onwards, strangely-shaped, still-secret jet machines began to dominate each annual Farnborough Air Show. In 1952, the greatest attraction there was the brand-new, super-priority DH 110 fighter, to be piloted by the conqueror of the sound barrier, John Derry.

The vast, neck-craning crowd stirred in excitement, television and film cameras swung on to the slender, grey, twin-boomed craft as Derry climbed on board, took off and—with ridiculous ease—climbed almost vertically. The 110 dwindled to a speck . . . vanished from view. And all in a matter of seconds.

Eight miles up, Derry wheeled, put the nose down—

pointing straight at the tiny patch which was the airfield—
and began his barrier-piercing dive. His intention was to
pull out and sweep over the Farnborough crowd, fairly
low, at a speed considerably greater than Mach 1.

Bang-bang—far below the crowd heard the familiar double-
boom—the impact of the plane going through the barrier,
closely followed by an echo from the ground. And then
came a third bang. . . .

An instant later the DH 110 came hurtling out of the blue
distance, trying to pull out of its dive. Thousands of eyes
widened in horror as they saw pieces tearing away from
the fuselage !

Derry made a gallant bid to get clear of the airfield. The
plane was coming apart in his hands, yet somehow he
managed to pull the nose up, haul her into almost level
flight. The 120,000 spectators huddled close together and
the show's commentator yelled, " Look out, look out ! "
over the dozens of loudspeakers as the jet streaked overhead, breaking up as it went. For a moment it looked as if
the pilot's superhuman effort would succeed, that he would
manage to take his machine and himself to die in open
country beyond the airfield. But the 110 gave a sudden
lurch, went into a roll.

And disintegrated.

Jagged pieces of metal sprayed the spectators. One of
the engines sailed in a great glowing arc and, pitiless as a
flensing knife, ripped a long hole through a section of
the crowd on a hillock. Part of a wing slammed down
on the runway. The shattered tail assembly and the
mangled cockpit section spiralled slowly down after all the
rest.

Eighteen spectators died, many more were injured. The
body of John Derry lay not far from them, on a bank of

grass. It was four years to the day since he had broken through the sound barrier for the first time.

And as the ambulances raced out to collect the injured, the show commentator's voice came again over the loudspeakers. " This is one of the tragic risks of high speed research," he said, " but the work must go on."

Mere minutes later Squadron Leader Neville Duke, another famous British pilot and a close friend of John Derry, took his Hawker Hunter jet up to 40,000 feet and brought it down in a great, glinting dive.

Bang-bang

WINGS OF MERCY

" GEIGER ? OH, thank Heaven—look, there's been an accident on Monte Rosa ! A climber's fallen on the rock face up by the summit—they've found him, but he's in a bad way."

Hermann Geiger half-turned, peered out of his window ; all grim and grey and dangerous out there, with the slow, slanting sleet blurring out the streets of the little Swiss town of Sion.

" I'm sorry," Geiger said. " I can't possibly fly in this weather."

" But you *must* come—the search party say if this man isn't in hospital within a few hours he'll die for sure ! To bring him down by stretcher, in these conditions, would take the best part of a day. . . . Hallo, you still there ? "

" Yes, I'm here." Geiger was thinking, arguing with himself—the sane part of him was saying it was suicide to go near the peaks to-day, but the other part, the part that understood the misery and agony of an injured man lying up there in the thin, bone-chilling air, was insisting that he had no right to abandon this unknown climber without at least giving it a try. . . .

" All right," he said after a few seconds, " I'll have a shot at it. But I don't think there's much hope."

The thick cloud made a leaden roof over the whole Rhône Valley at just five hundred feet, and beneath it the sleet reduced visibility to less than a hundred yards as the single-engined Piper Cub, light and small as a toy, took off and headed unsteadily in the direction of the rearing mass of snow, ice and granite which is Europe's mightiest mountain bastion—the Alps. Once again the veteran pilot of the peaks was " giving it a try."

In his early forties, sturdily built and permanently tanned, Geiger had one of the most unusual and dangerous flying jobs in the world. His chief task was to supply food, fuel, medical kits and blankets to the scores of mountaineering huts and shelters which are scattered throughout the high Alps—resting places and refuges for skiers and climbers. In an hour he could complete a " round " which would take a string of pack-mules and drivers several days.

In addition, in the winter months he frequently flew food, medicine or special equipment to remote villages and lodges cut off by drifts or avalanches. Day by day he kept an eye on particularly heavy drifts building up above the passes, gave warning of areas where avalanches were likely. And when a big climbing party was making an assault on the great-fanged Matterhorn, he would check their progress every few hours and report to friends and relatives anxiously waiting at inns and lodges in the valleys below.

No man knew the peaks—the cruel, barren, ice-glazed " roof of Europe "—and what was going on in them, better than Hermann Geiger. And he had unique, superb skill in getting his little plane down amid the tricky, swirling winds and shifting, sloping surfaces of the summits and shoulders.

More than 5,000 times he had landed in the uppermost Alps, and taken off again, without one mishap !

The Piper Cub, which could be fitted with skids, was ideally suited for this strange job. A larger, heavier machine could not have been managed with such delicate precision, would have been more liable to stall and to sink its under-carriage into soft snow. A helicopter could not operate at such heights, and needed a perfectly level surface on which to touch down, but the Cub had a high ceiling and, handled by the gifted Geiger, with his special technique, could be landed on an upward slope, sometimes quite steep, and perhaps uneven. And if it got bogged down in a soft patch, with a little help it could be lifted out.

He regarded himself as a very careful man. He took risks only when a life was in danger—and then they had to be carefully calculated risks, deliberately accepted because of the stakes. He had a wife and a family, he was far from being rich—and the exuberance and opti-mism of youth were behind him. So his mechanics found him fussy about the fine-tuning of the Cub's engine, and no matter how urgent his mission he always made a thorough, calm, pretake-off check of the machine, inside and out.

He practised instrument-flying whenever he could—even on fine, clear days he regularly would pull a canvas sheet over his windscreen and fly "blind" for minutes on end. And in working out his own, extraordinary technique for landing and taking off on tiny, treacherous mountain shelves, this quiet, methodical pilot broke down the problems into scientific terms, studied and mastered the complicated aerodynamics involved.

It never seemed to occur to him that he was running the strangest, and certainly the most successful air rescue service in the world. He was completely, genuinely astonished one day when the authorities informed him that the list of people he had saved from the mountains had reached a total of over three hundred !

Now as he climbed through the deep mattress of cloud, steering the Cub towards the long narrow valley of Zermatt which led to Monte Rosa, he knew how slender were his chances of getting through this time. But at just over 15,000 feet he broke into clear, dazzling sky. Beneath him there were no peaks, no Switzerland—only a vast, unbroken grey sea, stretching into infinity in every direction. Now he began to think how slender were his chances of ever getting *down* again : submerged in that sea of clouds, reaching to within a few hundred feet of the surface, were jagged summits. But this was one of his calculated risks —he was banking on finding a hole in the overcast, somewhere, through which he could descend—grope his way down—before his petrol gave out. Or, if the worst came to the worst, he could always bale out, and perhaps himself finish up lost and hurt, high on some icy tor. . . .

By studying his watch and compass and speed closely, and computing mentally, he tried to keep a rough check on his position as he began to make big, gradually widening circles. After about twenty minutes of this the cloud sagged downward and he saw a great, looming shadow in it— saw it, and with his special knowledge of this wild region instantly recognised it as the Weisshorn. From here, with his position fixed, he was able to fly across to where he knew Monte Rosa must be.

But Monte Rosa had the blankets over her head. He knew she was there, but he couldn't make out even the faintest outline. And if he tried to spiral down through the murk to find her, almost certainly he would see her too late, too close to avoid an annihilating collision. Patience

—that's what was needed now. He settled the Cub into a slow, gentle circle.

Twenty minutes, thirty, forty—and then all at once a rip appeared in the cloud, a rip that widened into a gaping hole. Geiger headed for it, throttled back, dived through the " chimney."

A wandering wind had torn the clouds away from one side of Monte Rosa's crest. He came steeply down and by a stroke of good fortune almost at once saw the hut, and outside it a guide holding at arm's length an ice axe with a handkerchief attached—an improvised windsock, indicating the flow of air over the short, steep slope, above a sheer rock face. Geiger levelled out, flew to and fro for three or four minutes, studying the surface with utmost care. Then he drew away, describing a large semi-circle, losing height.

Heading back towards the short slope, once on a level with it, he tilted the Cub's nose up, adding power. " Hanging on the prop " he let her drop. The ski-undercarriage touched at a point where the slope was almost 30 degrees. *Swoosh, who-oomph*—the steepness cut the speed rapidly, the Cub came to rest in less than a hundred yards. Geiger's special technique. . . .

Out of the hut the guide and his comrades carried the muffled, rigid, stretcher-strapped burden. Gently the load was put aboard. Then, directed by Geiger, they lifted the Cub's tail, swung her round to face in the opposite direction.

The take-off was as easy—or as difficult, and dangerous— as falling off a cliff. Geiger opened the throttle, let her slide down the slope and drop over the edge of the vertical rock wall. The Cub dived into space, picked up speed. He eased her out of the dive, and to his immense relief found he was under the belly of the cloud, about a hundred feet above the floor of the valley.

That homeward flight was torture—" like crawling through a tunnel on hands and knees, not knowing when the roof might come down and make it impossible to proceed." The valley was narrow, twisting suddenly, unexpectedly. At times he was only forty feet above the cluttered, crevassed ground. The man in the back lay still, silent, but when Geiger glanced over his shoulder the pale lips tried to pull into a smile. . . .

Sleet again. Memory more than sight moved the controls, steered the little plane round the jutting elbows of rock, raised her over the sudden snags. At times she squeezed through narrow gulches, wing-tips grazing granite walls.

The cloud kept pressing down, trying to squash them into the rugged ground. They flew across a scarred glacier so low that Geiger imagined he could feel the ancient, deathly chill, found himself shivering violently in the cockpit.

Sweat ran down his face, quickly froze into a clamping mask. Concentrating desperately, he recalled the geography of each writhing gorge, banked round giant claws of rock, lifted the Cub over reaching reefs. His wrists and ankles and knees ached, his tendons were taut and strained. He knew he couldn't go on like this much longer, flying an obstacle race, trying to think faster than the next bend or barricade or bluff.

And then suddenly the ground dipped, smoothed out—they were flying down the gradually widening Rhône Valley. The lights of Sion probed through the sleet. As the Cub's skids touched the air-strip's level ground an ambulance came racing across the grass to take Geiger's passenger to hospital. For just a moment the pilot, bruised and exhausted, thought he ought to go too, but the best treatment was administered by a member of his ground crew : " Well done, Hermann ! Well done again. . . ."

He drank a mug of coffee and went home to sleep—before the next phone call.

Captain Jack Slade of the Northern Territory Aerial Medical Services circled low over the flood-bound homestead deep in Australia's Outback. Even during the dry season there was no landing strip here. Now, after the big rains, there was only the immense, silent, slow-swirling, brown blanket of water—and the mud. Thick, soft, treacherous . . .

Somehow Slade had to find a landing ground. Down in that lonely homestead a child lay sick. Minutes counted.

Five slow, searching circuits—and then he saw the narrow oblong of grass humping out of the flood waters. An overgrown peanut patch, with trees all around it . . . not much, but the only possible landing place in hundreds of miles. He knew he must risk it.

He went down, put her into a wide, slow turn, and made a close inspection of the surface : rough, but it looked solid enough. He pulled up again, and started a careful, slow approach.

On board with him was Nursing Sister "Billy " Hill. This was her first trip, and she had been miserably sick in the bumpy flying conditions. Now she'd drowsed off to sleep, wan and exhausted. He didn't wake her—not even when he'd touched down and, rolling and lurching along, realised that he had only about four hundred yards left in which to pull up. Plainly, there was no hope. And if he tried to swing round, the plane might overturn, or

" ground loop "—in which case the nurse could be injured and unable to tend her young patient.

Only one thing to do—he'd let her run straight into the trees at the end of the paddock, and hope nothing too drastic happened. So he sat there, watching the barrier rush towards him, trying not to go rigid and " freeze " on the controls. He aimed the plane between two giant trees. Only when the massive trunks—just far enough apart for the fuselage to get through—sliced off the wings, did Sister Hill wake up.

She peered out of the cabin windows and said placidly : " Wot . . . no wings ?"

They waded through the floods to the homestead, and Sister Hill began the fight to save the baby. But it was too late : the child died half-an-hour later.

Not all stories of endeavour and self-sacrifice end in success. When you battle daily against the realities of huge distances, harsh climate and some of the wildest country on earth, you have to expect setbacks, failures—and some disasters.

The pilots and medical staff of Australia's Royal Flying Doctor Service—to which the Northern Territory Aerial Medical Services is a companion organisation—look upon floods, dust storms, the lack of landing strips, the hazards of navigating across whole states to pin-point some tiny building on a featureless landscape, as all in the day's toil. Routine. Such men as Captain Slade, and women like Sister Hill, are carrying on the work of compassion started back in 1928 by the Very Reverend John Flynn. A Presbyterian missionary, Flynn became a legend in his own lifetime for his work in the loneliest inland regions of central and Northern Australia.

About 1911, the young Flynn went out to join the

pioneers who were struggling to force a living from the reluctant Outback. He came to know these courageous and resourceful people well—and he realised the terrible fear that constantly nagged at them. The fear of being struck down by sickness or accident, in areas where the nearest doctor was weeks away. In those days Death always travelled faster than help.

But after World War One, two scientific developments began to re-shape the living patterns of the world— aviation and radio. The young Outback clergyman immediately saw the possibilities for Australia. " Flynn of the Inland " set out to spread, in his own phrase, " a mantle of safety " over the inhospitable deserts. His zeal and vision fired other men. By 1928 his dream had come true, when the first Flying Doctor base was set up at Cloncurry, in North-West Queensland.

By the time Flynn died in 1951, Australia had six bases. Today there are fourteen, covering some 2,000,000 square miles, or two-thirds of the continent.

In 1960, from the twelve mainland bases—there are two in Tasmania—1,612 flights covering 594,653 miles were made; 1,292 patients were transported, and 11,754 medical consultations were given by radio. In addition, the doctors flew thousands of miles on routine visits, and bringing preventive medicine to people in the Outback.

The radio networks have long operated beyond their original, basic purpose—they have become the schools through which lonely children are taught, and the back-yard fences over which news and family gossip are ex-changed to lighten the isolation of the empty spaces.

The doctors and nurses, too, do other jobs outside of medicine. In remote areas, they are sometimes called upon to act as judges, government officials, arbiters—any representative of authority who might be needed. On record is a report from a Flying Doctor which reads:

Flew to Marble Bar, saw twelve patients, performed two operations, held an inquest, conducted a court case, pulled teeth, renewed hotel licence, granted applications for mining leases and permits to employ local labour.

Flew home for tea.

The former Governor General of Australia, the late Viscount Dunrossil, described this unique organisation as : " This wonderful service—a combination of medical, aeronautical and radio skill and enterprise that has leapt over distances to bring a really Australian answer, idealistic but intensely practical, to an Australian problem."

The whole history of flying, in peace and in war, is enriched by dramatic, valiant rescue operations—flights of mercy through furious weather, to bring medical aid or food to isolated communities ; helicopters descending through skies full of searching metal to evacuate wounded in the midst of battle ; seaplanes and flying boats risking disintegration to touch down on high-heaving seas and pick up shipwrecked sailors ; long, desperate searches in blizzard, rainstorm or mist, by day and by night, for missing ships, planes, climbers, explorers, prospectors. . . .

A bulky, busy book could be written on this theme alone—the stories of those twentieth century life-savers who, in keeping with one of mankind's most ancient symbols, have descended, godlike, to bring succour from the heavens. But here I have been able to mention only a few of the many who fly, not to fight, but to save; not in combat, but in compassion.

SKYMEN FROM DOWN-UNDER

The vast, sun-baked crowds out at Brisbane's Eagle Farm Airport were having a day of air thrills—spectacle, speed, stunning sound. They clapped their hands over their ears as the huge, majestic turbo-jet airliner screamed past just above them, then marvelled at the nerveless precision flying of the Meteor fighters as they dived, rolled, flashed over the field in the five-star formation of the Southern Cross—symbolic constellation of the Antipodes.

As the formation passed, and the deep rumble of the jet engines faded, a silence fell. Then someone looked up, and a single, silver-glinting speck moving slowly across the dazzling sky caught his attention. He pointed, laughed, and soon everyone was watching the tiny, old " steam " plane 9,000 feet above them. Suddenly thick white smoke plumed out behind it, and the sea of upturned faces followed it as, in a series of leisurely loops and swooping dives it traced out a single word, vivid white against the blue. A word which raised from the throats of those watching thousands a roar almost as mighty as the jets' thunder of moments before—

" SMITHY "

The sky-writing was apt tribute, on that day in August 1958, to an Australian who some thirty years before had endured untold hours of pain and peril to pioneer air routes all over the world—Sir Charles Kingsford Smith.

And now the machine in which he had battled and groped through so many miles of uncharted, often hostile sky— the three-engined, high-winged Fokker monoplane "Southern Cross "—was being officially installed in a permanent home. She would be preserved for all time in an imposing structure of glass and timber only yards from the spot where she had touched down—on what was then little more than a dusty paddock—after Smithy's epic first crossing of the Pacific Ocean in 1928.

Born in Brisbane, Queensland, in 1897, Kingsford Smith showed an early taste for imaginative and dangerous escapades. When he was just six the family sailed for a visit to Canada, and in mid-ocean he was found hanging from a hawse-hole at the ship's bows, showing another boy how it could be done.

At eighteen he enlisted in the Australian infantry. He served as a dispatch-rider in Egypt, Gallipoli and France. And then he transferred to the Royal Flying Corps, in which he was commissioned in 1917.

The trainee pilot showed an immediate aptitude and was quick to learn. Though there was one little setback. A cryptic entry in his logbook at the end of his basic training read : " First solo—crashed ! "

Coming in after his first lone circuit of the field he had made a perfect three-point touchdown—fifteen feet up in the air. The aircraft was a complete write-off, but even the severe knocks and bruises, and the blow to his career, didn't stop Smithy laughing. Throughout his life, he was ever able to enjoy a joke against himself—and it was said that he never waited for others to tell the tales of his misadventures.

He arrived back in Australia after the war—minus three toes, but plus the Military Cross. He was smouldering with ideas and eagerness. Flying was in his blood now, and he had been quick to realise that Australia, with its horizonless tracts of emptiness separating fast-growing towns and cities, *needed* aviation. Air communications could bring the vast continent to the full realisation of its potential, knitting its widely-dispersed centres into a virile, purposeful pattern. And no more would Australians feel remote, cut off from the rest of the civilised world—for aircraft could span the seas as well as the " Outback."

With C. P. T. Ulm as partner, Kingsford Smith set about the task—planning the routes, persuading people to start air companies. Success was slow and sporadic: money was hard to raise in those post-war days. Generous by nature, but with no business head, he fretted at the delays. Air lines would be formed, they would stumble along a while—and go broke. Another round of fund-raising, of working at any job that came along—anything to raise cash. Then the setting up of a new company: and the whole cycle would be restarted. But the nation wasn't air-minded yet, so customers were few.

" What we need," Smithy said to Ulm one despondent day, " is something to make 'em really sit up and take notice. Just one record-breaking flight, that's all it needs—then the funds and the bookings would start pouring in."

Ulm saw the sense. Every shilling they had left went into the gamble. They went to America to raise the rest, and on 31st May, 1928, the " Southern Cross " took off from Oakland, California, for the first-ever flight over 8,000 miles of Pacific Ocean to Australia. And even as she lumbered fully-laden down the runway, creditors were urgently elbowing through the crowds to have Smithy arrested for debt. . . .

The little Fokker plane—17 feet 8½ inches wingspan,

its three Whirlwind engines each developing 200 horse power—was by no means new. She had already given noble service to Sir Hubert Wilkins during his Arctic explorations, but with her crew of four—Ulm was second pilot; Americans Harry Lyon and James Warner had joined the venture as navigator and wireless operator—she was facing her toughest test, and many believed it would prove too much for " a worn machine."

Hour after hour, day after day, Smithy and his crew droned on, hopping great distances from island to tiny hard-to-find island ; cramped, noise-numbed, buffeted by winds and rains. Eventually, the longest hop of all : over 3,000 miles of trackless sea to Suva. Thirty-three hours it took them, and most of the time they were weaving around, making rapid, often huge diversions to avoid vicious squalls. Harry Lyon's superb navigation stood the test : out of all the ocean, after all those confusing course changes—there was Suva, dead ahead.

Their tired hearts sang—until they sighted Albert Park, the only possible landing space. It was incredibly small, bumpy—and entirely surrounded by tall trees and telegraph lines . . .

Smithy groaned, and braced his stiff, weary body.

Throttle back—steady—ease her in just over—cut ! stall !— drop her in !

No one could have judged it more accurately : even so, there seemed no chance of stopping her rolling in time to avoid the trees at the other end. Smithy made his decision : *quick swerve !—full throttle on the starboard motor— full left rudder !*

She wheeled to the left, the port wingtip grazed the ground, and she finished up spinning in a terrific " ground loop ". When the whorl of dust settled the damage proved

slight—nothing compared to what would have been caused
by running into the trees. It is still talked of as one of the
epic landings of all time. Certainly it was only Kingsford
Smith's skill and coolness that saved " Southern Cross "
that day, and enabled them—when some of the taller
trees had been felled—to get out again and finally arrive,
battered and weary, at Brisbane on 9th June.

The flight resulted in £20,000 being subscribed for
Kingsford Smith and Ulm to finance other pioneering
flights across the world, many of them in the same " worn
machine ".

The record books can tell only the barest facts. The
same year, a first Australia-New Zealand flight; 1929,
Sydney (Australia) to Croydon; 1930, light aircraft
England-Australia solo record; 1931, first official Australia-
England air mail flight; 1931 again, and another Australia-
England trip, this time alone; two years later, the return
trip, in the record time of seven days, four hours, 44
minutes; 1934, the first West-East Pacific flight, this time
in a single-engined Lockheed Altair.

The bare facts. With no hint of the conditions under
which the flights were made. Whatever aircraft he flew—
and mostly it was the faithful old " Southern Cross "
—and whether he was alone, or with Ulm or others, every
one of those entries in the Kingsford Smith log book was
written only after many days and nights of intense concentration, and physical and nervous strain—sitting cramped,
ears and senses beaten, blurred by the never-ending roar
of engines. After agonised hours, with eyes burning from
constant searching for landmarks after sleepless nights :
hours of harrowing anxiety over the uncertainties of
navigating across featureless sea and uncharted land,
every moment watching water and clouds for the slightest

wind changes, constantly calculating petrol and oil consumption, wondering whether he had enough left to get him to that day's refuelling stop : dragging, draining hours of sheer bone-weariness and—on the solo flights—desperate loneliness. His string of triumphs justly earned him a knighthood. But that didn't change the warm, simple character of the man. And he didn't rest on his fame and honours.

Once, over Turkey, he felt himself fainting at the controls. That night when he landed the police jailed him, and kept him there for four days—something was wrong with his papers. They probably saved his life, for the doctors later found he had been suffering from carbon monoxide poisoning from leaking petrol fumes. On returning to his plane he spotted the broken pipe and had it repaired.

Kingsford Smith was a man of tremendous, consuming determination, great stamina and courage. And he was always completely honest about his own weaknesses, errors and doubts. Take a look through his own log of the England-Australia solo flight in 1933. He had taken off on 4th October in a Percival Gull, and was soon writing of himself as " a case of nerves ", " terribly sick ". He had to be careful not to fly too high, in case he passed out at the controls. There is a frank, human ring to many of these entries, scribbled on his knee as he flew :

2nd day.   6.40 a.m. Passing Athens. Still getting these nervous attacks. Guess I'm too old and worn for these capers.

At 36, he felt " too old and worn . . ." An indication of how much these trail-blazing flights took out of the man.

Later : Another recurrence of nervousness . . . nasty feeling I was going to faint. Hope I can get through !

October 7. Landed Gwadar (on the Arabian Sea). Terribly sick at 4.15 p.m. yesterday. Couldn't sleep till 2 a.m. No

food now for 36 hours. Left Gwadar 7.15. Beautiful morning
but failed to appreciate it. Wish I was reliable as this machine
and engine . . . 4 p.m. Rested at Karachi four hours but can't
sleep. This is what is killing me. Got some bromide here and
will take a stiff dose tonight.

October 8. Another night with not much sleep. How long
can I stick it?

Later that day, he realised he was over the halfway mark,
and from there on the entries cheer up. But he had flown
the 6,000 miles from Brindisi in Italy with nine hours sleep
in three nights, and almost no food. Small wonder that
the last entry reads :

Am all in, but today is the last day. Have just to hang on
somehow for 9 hours.

Hang on he did, and the record was his.

The story was always the same, flight after flight. But
the hard flying, and the ever-present financial difficulties
took their toll. In 1935 he planned a new attempt on the
England-Australia record, this time in an Altair aircraft.
His old flying partner Ulm had been lost some 500 miles
north of Hawaii on a trans-Pacific flight the year before,
and he took with him J. T. Pethybridge. Shortly before the
trip Kingsford Smith, with his usual frankness, confessed :
" I don't feel fit enough for the job, but I'm going to see
it through."

He wasn't being melodramatic or foolhardy ; it was
just his old, ceaseless urge to overcome the weakness of
the flesh. Did that worn-out, battered spirit fail, just for
once ? Did his over-taxed body finally collapse ? Or was
it a technical fault in the plane ? We shall never know.
They found the wreckage off the Burma coast . . . but no
trace was ever found of the two occupants. All we do know
is that, some time on the 7th or 8th of November, 1935,

Sir Charles Kingsford Smith, airman supreme and pioneer extraordinary, died at his controls.

15th May, 1943—the atmosphere on the bomber base at Scampton, in the heart of England's flat, bleak Midlands, was tense—and getting tenser. For weeks the squadron, newly-formed from the crack crews of the R.A.F.'s Bomber Command, had been training in their big four-engined Lancasters. Hour after hour, by day and by night, they had been practising low-level flying, roaring over England at less than 100 feet. And they had been drilled in a new bombing technique which entailed flying at 60 feet—precisely—above water, and aiming through a strange, Heath Robinson device of wood and nails instead of an orthodox bomb-sight.

The Lancs had been specially modified. The crews were so highly trained by now that it was said they could navigate at hedgetop level to any given tree in the country, and hit any minor crossroads with their practice bombs. Still the only man in the squadron to know the purpose of all this was the commander. Everyone else knew only that something out of the ordinary was about to happen—soon. The arrival of the new, huge bombs, strangely shaped, only heightened the tension, increased the rumours.

And then one morning: " Attention . . . All pilots, navigators and bomb-aimers of 617 report to the briefing room immediately." The blaring tannoy brought a sudden knot to the stomach, a dryness to the throat. Each of the flyers answering the summons was secretly wondering whether he would be alive after the next forty-eight hours . . .

By lunch-time, they were back in the mess ; they knew now, but were forbidden to tell the other members of their crews. The show was " on "—for to-morrow night.

The others—the gunners, the engineers, the wireless operators—had been waiting anxiously. One of them, Australian Toby Foxlee, eagerly sought out his skipper, Micky Martin.

" Well, what's it all about ? "

" Just more training, Foxy," Martin said as casually as he could. " You'll hear all about it to-morrow."

" Training ? I don't believe it ! "

" It's true, boy."

" Aw, come off it, Skip ! Give us the straight gen."

" I swear it."

Foxlee stared hard, then mouthed an oath. " In that case, I need a drink. You ? "

" Shandy," said Martin. Foxlee swung back, eyes small and bright. He knew Martin liked his beer by the pint— but never did any hard drinking before an op.

" Skipper," said the gunner, " you're a horrible ruddy liar."

And the very next night Wing Commander Guy Gibson, D.S.O., D.F.C., led 617 to the Moehne, Eder and Sorpe dams, deep in Germany. One of the greatest air operations in history : the exploit which earned the squadron its glorious nickname, " The Dam Busters ".

Flying alongside Gibson was Micky Martin, in his faithful Lancaster P-Peter (which he irreverently insisted on calling P-Popsie). Born in Sydney twenty-four years before, Martin—tall, fair and slim, with a generous moustache— had done all his war-time flying with the R.A.F. And he had become addicted to, and expert in, the art of low flying. His thinking was supremely simple : if you flew lower than the rest of the bombers in the stream, usually you avoided the enemy fighters ; lower still, and the heavy anti-aircraft fire would burst well above you ; right down to tree-top level, and you would be gone before the light stuff could draw a bead on you—and your gunners had a high old time picking off searchlights and any other targets offered. There was, of course, the risk of being cleaved by the cable of a barrage balloon, but Martin figured that no one put up balloons along main roads and railways—so he flew up those. . . .

All very fine in theory, but a very different matter when it comes to handling a fully-laden, four-engined bomber through hostile night across enemy territory. That calls for rock nerves, instantaneous reflexes—all the highest skills. And Martin had them in plenty. Which is why Gibson had picked him for 617. They'd met at Buckingham Palace, when Gibson was getting his D.S.O. and Martin the first of his D.F.C.s, and they'd talked about low flying. At once Gibson recognised a bomber captain of outstanding talent. The exactly right combination of daring and caution.

True, on the ground Martin had a wild look in his eyes, and he indulged in horseplay and all sorts of escapades. But in the air he was calm and crisp, took no *needless* risks. Early in his operational career he had made up his mind that he was going to die before the war ended, and die unpleasantly, probably trapped in a blazing Lancaster. Having accepted that, he began to live life to the absolute fullest, and in his off-duty hours quickly gained a reputation for boisterousness. But the moment he climbed into his aircraft, he settled down to earnest, professional work. He did his job to the utmost, completely reconciled to the idea that it would kill him. The object of the grim game was to see how long you could delay the pay-off.

When necessary, Martin was audacious—but in a calculating way. Every risk was measured : he meant to spin out his life as long as he could, and every single bomb tell while he lasted.

Micky Martin survived the great dams raid, and was awarded the D.S.O. Other Australians also came through— the incredibly boyish Dave Shannon (he celebrated his 21st birthday a few days later, and went on to win a bar to his D.S.O., plus a couple of D.F.C.s), and Les Knight. In Martin's own crew there were long-chinned Jack Leggo, the navigator, and Bob Hay, the bomb-aimer, who won bars to their D.F.C.s. Among the total of ten D.F.C.s was Gibson's own bomb-aimer, the chunky Australian " Spam " Spafford. Two C.G.M.s and twelve D.F.M.s completed the decorations won that famous night plus Gibson's own Victoria Cross.

Martin, in fact, to his own surprise, survived every raid he went out on. But death grazed by many times— notably in 617's third attempt on the difficult and heavily defended Antheor Viaduct in Italy, when P-Popsie was badly shot up while he was doing impossible things with her in the face of murderous flak. Coming down to almost zero feet to mark the target with flares for the other planes, it seemed that no aircraft could live through the tight cross-fire from batteries all around the target—some of them actually *firing down* on to the marauder. But the tiny koala bear mascot Martin always stuffed into his battledress just before take-off saw them safely through the inferno. And they left the target brightly outlined by their flares.

Limping away, they listed the damage : first they found the port inner and starboard outer throttles gone, and the pitch controls for the other two engines gone too— so they had just enough power to keep the bomber air-borne. A shell had smashed through the nose and exploded in the ammo. trays under the front turret : in the ensuing blasts and flarings of bullets, hydraulic pipes, control rods and fuse boxes were all hit. Two of the crew were wounded, and so was Martin himself—in the leg. Obviously they were out of the fight—if they took her in again to drop their bombs with the others, she would be slow and unweildy and might impede and endanger their comrades. And certainly they would be hit again : no aircraft could survive any more hurt and stay airborne. So Martin pulled her up and began to battle for altitude.

Not a hope of getting home—that was grimly clear right away. They set course for Corsica, only just occupied by the Allies. But the plane became increasingly sluggish. Someone came back from a further investigation, with news that the entire hydraulic systems were useless.

"You'll probably get your undercarriage and flaps down, by the manual emergency system, but you won't have any brakes to pull up with once we're on the deck," he told Martin.

Then another of the crew brought an even more chilling report : "The fuses have had it, and we've still got the bombs on board." A faulty landing, and they'd end in an annihilating explosion . . .

They were at 2,000 feet now, with little prospect of getting higher. They had on board, fused and live, a 4,000 pound bomb and several 1,000 pounders—and the minimum safety height for dropping a 4,000 pounder was 4,000 feet. Any lower, and you got caught in the blast yourself.

Rain came, and then hail. Water was flooding in through the tail—and then they ran into an ice cloud. The wounded Martin felt the controls grow even more soggy. Every moment now he was fighting to keep his height. The crew managed to cut one of the smaller bombs loose, but as it fell Popsie stalled. The starboard wingtip dropped, and they were on the verge of a spin. Somehow Martin regained control—but now they were down to 1,800 feet . . .

Still, they were 1,000 pounds lighter. Slowly, brilliantly, he coaxed her up again. At 2,500 feet two more of the 1,000 pounders were dropped. But they needed still more height before they could get rid of the big one.

A long, sweating, agonising haul took her to 3,200 feet. And then it was plain that she had reached her limit—she was still in the climbing attitude, but not moving any higher. After a conference it was decided that it would be safer to risk dropping the 4,000 pounder from this height, than to try to land with it still " hung up " in the bomb bay. As it left the aircraft, Popsie jumped weakly. She jumped again like a frightened mule when the shock wave of the explosion reached her, but Martin caught her smartly with rudder and they were straight and level again.

But nothing would shift the two remaining 1,000 pounders.

A little later the airstrip on Corsica radioed that there were better medical facilities at a field in Sardinia, and a new course was set. Martin grinned sardonically when he heard that the best approach was over a range of mountains 8,000 feet high, and set about planning his own, lower route in.

They found the field. It ran *across* a narrow spit of land—the runway started at the beach and stopped abruptly at a cliff edge.

When you still have two fused 1,000 pound bombs on board, a belly-landing is ruled out. Then again, the undercarriage might go down, or it might not; the tyres might be all right, or they might be ripped by shrapnel —in which case the plane stood a good chance of ground-looping, so that they could easily collapse on to the bombs. And there was no question of going round again. Everything had to be right first time, for there wasn't enough power left in the damaged engines to climb again for a second approach.

Their chances—after the hours of struggle—seemed very small. But no one wanted to bale-out and leave the wounded men. They'd all see it through together.

Martin started his preparations early. Slowly the undercart swung down, and seemed to stick in place. There was just enough pressure to get some flap down. Martin—muscles aching, throbbing from the tussle of keeping the shattered Lancaster in the air, and his wounded leg feeling oddly numb—headed in on a long, low approach from miles back. At the last moment he cut all engines and pulled the nose up to clear the dunes. At about 85 m.p.h. she squashed down on to the runway. The undercart held, Martin began fish-tailing his rudders. The far cliff loomed alarmingly, and he pushed on full port rudder.

The broken bomber swung sickeningly, jolted over the grass verge. She started to slew, tyres skidding just short of a ground-loop—and came to a lumbering halt fifty yards from the precipice . . .

Bob Hay was dead. Whittaker, the engineer, had come within an ace of losing a leg. Martin, who during the whole of this superb feat of flying had been imagining himself seriously wounded, found that in fact his leg had barely been punctured. His main injury was a huge, numbing bruise.

When they got back to England days later, it was to

find they had been posted off operations. Martin argued furiously, but he found himself behind a desk at Group H.Q. Not for long, though—very quickly he had fixed himself another posting, this time to a Mosquito night-fighter unit. And this man who fully expected to die in the air —who at times seemed to be seeking every opportunity to fly into the highest peril—in fact survived the war, finishing up with a D.S.O. and bar, D.F.C. and two bars.

Group Captain Leonard Cheshire, V.C., D.S.O. and two bars, D.F.C., who led 617 after Gibson, once wrote this of Micky Martin : " As an operational pilot I consider he was . . . the greatest that the Air Force ever produced. I have seen him do things that I, for one, would never have looked at." Coming from as great and brave a pilot as Cheshire, that is a remarkable tribute to a remarkable man.

Martin was one of many Australians who served in the R.A.F. Thousands more came to Britain in the R.A.A.F., and the distinctive, dark blue, " digger " uniforms were familiar all over the country. They had first been seen in " the old country " back in July 1939, when seven officers and fourteen airmen arrived to ferry back nine Sunderland flying boats to help in the defence of the Commonwealth against the looming threat of war. But before they had learned to fly them, war was declared—and they stayed to form the nucleus of No. 10 Squadron, R.A.A.F.

They were quickly joined by an ever-growing stream of their countrymen. They operated in every Command. The R.A.A.F.'s first D.F.C. was awarded in July 1940 to Squadron Leader C. W. Pearce, of 10 Squadron, after he had attacked a submarine in the Atlantic.

They won two V.C.s in the air over Europe. The first was awarded to Group Captain Hughie Idwal Edwards, a Western Australian who had joined the R.A.F. before the war. On 4th July, 1941, he led a force of Blenheim bombers on a daylight attack on the port of Bremen, one of the most heavily defended areas of Germany.

The squadron flew the last fifty miles to the target at little more than fifty feet, passing under high-tension cables, and finally weaving through a thick balloon barrage. On through what seemed a solid wall of flak— *every aircraft was hit*. But they pressed home the assault, led all the way by the dark, thickset Australian.

The citation which resulted said that Edwards had displayed " the highest possible standards of gallantry and determination."

A little over a year later, on 28th November, 1942, 26-year-old Pilot Officer Rawdon Hume Middleton, R.A.A.F., of New South Wales, was piloting a Stirling bomber over Turin in Italy. The flight over the 12,000 foot barrier of the Alps had been difficult and exhausting, and above the target the plane was hit by A.A. fire. A large piece was blasted out of the port wing, and another shell burst inside the cockpit, shattering the windscreen. A splinter took away part of Middleton's face, destroying his right eye. It is probable that he had other wounds, in the chest—there was no way of checking. He lost consciousness and the plane dived to 800 feet before the second pilot—wounded in head and legs—regained control. Somehow Middleton fought through the nausea and waves of pain to take over again. And despite the savage, ice-barbed wind screaming in through the shattered wind-screen, he insisted on tackling once again the Alpine crossing.

His one aim was to reach England so that his crew could bale-out ; he must have known that because of his wounds, the severe loss of blood and his fast-diminishing strength, there was little chance of saving himself. He settled down to coax the last ounce of power out of the damaged bomber, the last degree of concentration out of his failing body and clouding mind . . .

Four hours later, they were over the French coast. And again they were hit by flak. Somehow Middleton summoned the strength to take evasive action, and they wriggled out of the claws of the guns, reaching the English coast with exactly five minutes' fuel left.

Middleton flew parallel to the coast for a few miles, looking down with dimming eyes at the quiet shores, and the fields misted in the early daylight. Then quietly, firmly, he said goodbye to his crew, ordered them to jump. He circled, watched them land safely on the shore. Then he headed out to sea, to die alone with his crippled bomber.

In every phase of the flying war, both in Europe and the Pacific, Australian airmen played a vital part, flyers and ground crews alike. The individual tales of gallantry are endless—more than 3,000 R.A.A.F. men were decorated overseas, another 1,000 in the Australian theatre. Every story has the ring of that same high spirit and self-reliance which has been part of the Aussie character since the days of the hardy pioneers and explorers of the Outback.

And that spirit is perhaps best illustrated by a photograph on the files of the Air Ministry. Taken in London just after the shooting had stopped in Europe in 1945, it shows two young R.A.A.F. pilots, leaning against the bonnet of a sports car, grinning at each other. Both had flown on many ops., and each had been taken prisoner.

Turn the picture over, and the caption gives you their names : Flying Officer Peter Kingsford Smith, D.F.C. (one of three of the great Smithy's nephews who served with distinction in the R.A.A.F. during the war), and

Pilot Officer John Anthony Ulm, son of Smithy's navigator and co-pilot back in the trail-blazing days.

New Zealand doesn't claim much of the world map: just two slim, curving islands deep in the Pacific, with a population even now of only 2,400,000. But its people are no back-yard dreamers; isolated they may be in some ways—but insular, no.

Witness the deed of Richard Pearse, of Temuka in South Island, a taciturn farmer who liked working by himself. In a quaint contraption of his own design, he flew a hundred yards, landing on top of a twelve-foot hedge. The date: March 1904—*only three months after the Wright Brothers had made the first powered flight of history.* . . .

If the belief that Pearse took off under his own power is correct, then he was indeed an epic pioneer—for the Wright plane had to be launched by catapult. Certainly the Temuka farmer was the first man in all the British Commonwealth to fly in a heavier-than-air machine.

Witness, too, the devouring eagerness with which the slim and attractive young daughter of a Rotorua dental surgeon followed the newspaper stories of Bert Hinkler's flight in 1928. She had never flown, but Hinkler's adventures, unfolding day by day, fired her ambition. Within a few years, those same newspapers were carrying reports and pictures of the dentist's daughter, and the slender figure in immaculate white overalls and flying helmet became familiar the world over.

Jean Batten was just twenty when she travelled to England, chaperoned by her mother, her mind and heart set on flying back to Australia. Coolly she told reporters that she'd learned to fly " expressly for this trip." The experts tried to talk her out of the project—dangerous even for a fully experienced male pilot. She smiled, politely, thanked them for their concern—and proceeded with her plans.

She took off from Lympne, Kent, on 9th April, 1933. All went well as far as Karachi, when her engine failed. She crash-landed, and her frail aircraft was a complete write-off. Many thought the experience would " knock some sense " into this imprudent, inexperienced lass. But Jean smiled, said she'd start all over again. Back to England, another hard, often discouraging round of money-raising, and then just over a year later she was off again in a battered old Gypsy Moth.

Disaster again. This time at Rome. But Jean borrowed new wings and flew the plane back to start the whole process for the third time. . . .

Years later, talking of this sad train of events, she admitted : " A great deal of my *enthusiasm* for the flight had gone—but I'd doubled my determination."

In May, 1934, she took off once more. At last, complete success—she landed at Darwin 14 days, 22 hours and thirty minutes later, and had the welcoming crowds wondering how she could appear so femininely neat and trim after such an exhausting solitary journey. They weren't the last crowd to ask this question.

With the women's solo U.K.-Australia record in her pocket (four-and-a-half days under Amy Johnson's time), within a year she became the first woman to make the return flight ; and soon after that she set up a record time of two days, thirteen hours and fifteen minutes for the U.K.-Brazil flight, and became the first woman to fly solo across the South Atlantic.

But perhaps the flight that most enslaved public imagination was her crossing of the Tasman Sea in 1936. Over

1,000 miles of open, shark-infested waters. With radio in its infancy, and aircraft still small, slow and far from reliable, it was a formidable undertaking—one that had daunted many men. Jean Batten was resolved not only to be the first woman to fly it alone—she meant also to do it in record time.

She had already set up a world record for the UK-Australia trip, with five days, twenty-one-and-a-half hours—beating Jim Broadbent's time by close on one day. Now she flew down to Sydney to complete the flight home—the first direct U.K.-New Zealand flight ever.

After two days of fêting, she flew down to Richmond, 40 miles west of Sydney, to make her final preparations. The Richmond field had a longer runway and was thus safer for taking-off in a plane heavy with extra fuel. Once again people, including seasoned pilots, tried to talk her out of the venture, but when favourable weather came, she took off at 4.35 in the morning, refusing the offer of a radio set because of the extra weight, but gratefully accepting a packet of ham and lettuce sandwiches, a flask of coffee and two oranges.

Half Australia and all New Zealand held their breath when the news that she was airborne came through—the thoughts of thousands were with her in that tiny throbbing cockpit, an utterly lonely little world of its own, bobbing, lurching on so slowly above that barren, killer sea. A ten-hour flight was her aim : it was just nine-and-a-half hours and one ferocious rainstorm later that she crossed her homeland coast at New Plymouth.

While the news that she had been sighted flashed around the globe, she flew on to Auckland. There she received her greatest welcome—and a fatherly admonition from the Mayor, " for giving the country such an anxious time."

By now Jean Batten—still only 27—was being honoured by cities, and mobbed by the public. Everywhere people marvelled at the immense spirit and professionalism that drove this gently-natured, fragile-looking girl. They loved her too, for her constant femininity—whenever she stepped from her plane, no matter how long and arduous the flight, she always managed to look *chic* in her white overalls. It was common knowledge that as she came into an airfield, just before she began her landing approach she would add a freshening touch of powder and lipstick.

The dentist's daughter caught the headlines year after year until finally she gave up flying. But she was by no means the only New Zealander to claim a proud place for her country in the history of aviation.

When World War Two came, flying had caught the interest and imagination of thousands of young men in the islands. Yet in September 1939, the R.N.Z.A.F. comprised only 37 officers and 302 other ranks. But in the first weeks of hostilities, thousands flooded in to volunteer, so that by July 1944 the total strength was 42,000.

Soon twenty-six New Zealand squadrons were on service, scattered throughout the world. In addition many thousands of New Zealanders were serving with R.A.F. units, on both ground and flying duties.

Men like Flying Officer E. J. (" Cobber ") Kain, the black-haired, blue-eyed, six foot tall fighter star from Wellington—mentioned in an earlier chapter of this book.

And like Sergeant Pilot J. A. Ward, a 22-year-old from Wanganui, who won New Zealand's first Victoria Cross of World War Two. His Wellington bomber of No. 73 (N.Z.) Squadron was badly hit by a night-fighter while returning from a raid on Munster. Fire broke out close to the starboard engine, and was fed by petrol from a split pipe. Something decisive, perhaps drastic, was called for if they were not all to end up in the Zuider Zee thousands of feet below—and Ward knew seconds counted.

Coolly he volunteered to climb out along the wing, to put out the flames.

His skipper had to *order* him to take his parachute out with him as he clambered through the narrow astro-hatch into the howling night, and clawed his way down the three foot drop on to the wing. Clinging on with one hand he hacked footholds in the plane's fabric with the other, inched his way along the screaming, wind-lashed wing, out to the fire.

The gale gripped him like a giant fist of ice. The cold tore through his clothing, numbing the muscles, probing for his bones. It was a battle to breathe. And then, suddenly, the hot, thick fumes from the fire were stabbing into his mouth and eyes, blinding, choking. . . .

But he beat out the flames somehow, then stopped up the leaking pipe with a piece of rag. No more roasting blast—he was freezing again, in an ice-barbed hurricane. How he managed to drag himself back, he could never remember. But he made it to safety, and so did the bomber.

After the award was announced, Ward was alarmed and embarrassed by the publicity, the " hero " image, the cheering crowds which confronted him on the " personal appearances " at war factories and recruiting centres that inevitably were arranged for him. He hated all " fuss and bull ", and tried every time to dodge it.

But Ward didn't have to put up with fame for long. Two months after his V.C. action, he was shot down and killed over Hamburg.

To survive for long in the air war, a man needed a

charmed life—whatever his skill. One who had plenty
of both was a tough New Zealander who had come to
Britain and joined the R.A.F. in 1937, and who finished
the war as a Wing Commander with the D.S.O., O.B.E.,
D.F.C. and bar, D.F.C.(U.S.) and the French Croix de
Guerre with Plume.

Fighter leader Alan Deere was in the thick of it for most
of the war. His face, under the short fair hair, and with
the fine straight nose, was as well-known to the free
world newspaper readers during the Battle of Britain as
were the features of film stars like David Niven and Robert
Donat.

Five times he escaped death by incredible fortune. Once
German bombers arrived over his airfield just as his squadron
was taking off. A bomb landed immediately in front of his
plane, sent it Catherine-wheeling, to end up a crumpled
mass, upside down, with Deere's head scraping the ground.

He survived several other crashes, and was shot down
three times. He had, they said, " the coolest head, and the
hottest reflexes, in Fighter Command." And like his
friend the great Stanford Tuck, he had an immense amount
of luck.

Between September 1939 and May 1944, Deere was
credited with more than twenty victories. He then became
commander of an advanced airfield of the Allied Expedi-
tionary Air Force during the invasion of Europe. And
among the new, young flyers he led to final victory were
many from his own country : those small slim, islands of
New Zealand, still sparsely populated, but—in this age
of flying—no longer remote from the other free nations
of the Earth.

The Man In The Hot Seat

DODDY HAY

To J. and J.
In that order.

Contents

Prologue   11

Part One   The Parachutist

1 Tail-Gunner   15
2 Men in the Making   23
3 Airborne Army   35
4 The World Sky-Diving Championships   42
5 The Private Pupil   56
6 Introduction to Test Flying   60

Part Two   The Inventor

7   James Martin   71
8   Birth of the Ejection Seat   82
9   The Tests that Worked   94
10 In Hot Blood   106

Part Three   Collaboration

11 The First Meeting   121
12 The Scandal of the V-Force   125
13 Escape from a V-Bomber   140
14 The Secret Test   155
15 About Rockets   166
16 The First Rocket Launching   175

17 Disaster at Le Bourget   188
18 The Ultimate Test   198
19 Recovery   211

    Epilogue   218

Diagrams

Three ejection trajectories 179

The zero-zero test 186

Martin-Baker mk. 6HA ejector seat 209

Prologue

On 14th September 1964, in Manching, Germany, a well-known American test pilot, George Bright, was taking a VJ-101 aeroplane out on to the runway for a proving flight. Cameras had been set up, as is customary in an aviation event of importance, to record all visible details of the performance. Bright's take-off run began ordinarily enough, and for exactly eight seconds all went well.

Then, with no vestige of warning, all went quite unbelievably badly. As the aircraft lifted off the runway Bright lost all control of it, and it spiralled over into a vicious left-hand roll; right round it corkscrewed, as the cameras followed its flight, upside down and over again through 320 degrees, its tail yawing wildly into a 17 degrees sideways slide. It was now in a forty degree bank to starboard, with its nose pointing up into the air and its wing-tip only ten feet from the ground, and the pilot, understandably, decided that it was time to say goodbye. He heaved hard on a handle between his knees, and he shot out sideways and upwards in a sheet of flame to land happy and unhurt beneath an open parachute a couple of seconds later.

Only one device in the world could have saved George Bright's life that day, and that was James Martin's Rocket Ejection seat.

Testing that seat, and two of its predecessors, has proved to be the fulfilment of my professional life. Ultimately, I owe the experience—and the honour—to James Martin but in the first instance to Fate. Only now do I see how every twist and turn in my career prepared me for this strange vocation. How Fate led me to James Martin and how we formed a partnership, the inventor and his guinea pig, is the central story of this book.

Part One

The Parachutist

CHAPTER I

Tail-Gunner

1939-1946

Fate certainly made my first professional decision for me, as she did for several million other young men in September 1939.

When war broke out I was a student at Loughborough College, my enthusiasm for sport having led me to enrol for a three year course in Physical Education. As with so many of my contemporaries, however, suddenly my one desire was to leave College and become a pilot in the Royal Air Force. Accordingly, on my eighteenth birthday in the following April, I volunteered and was accepted for training. The R.A.F. training machine had not yet, however, been geared to deal with the vastly increased flow of pupils, and I was sent back to college to await my call-up.

It was during this period of waiting that Fate delivered what appeared to be a mortal blow to my ambitions. Attempting a complex manoeuvre during an exhibition of high-board diving I misjudged my timing and hit the water chest-foremost and spinning fast. Lying stunned on the bottom of the pool I watched with interest and no sense of its significance a dark spiral rising through the water above me; it was only later, in hospital, I learned that I had ruptured my lungs. That, so far as the Royal Air Force was concerned, was the end. I was not only ruled out as aircrew material; I was sent to a Combined Services Medical Board, who classified me as Grade 4, 'Totally unfit for military service.'

Protesting bitterly I went back to my college in Leicestershire, from where, during the next two years, I became an unmitigated nuisance, presenting myself on no less than seven occasions at different medical centres. Always the result was the same. I would sail through the various specialist sections, receiving an encouraging nod at each, only to end up before the senior medical officer with my documents in his hand and a frown on his face.

'Rather wasting our time, aren't you, young man? You've already been classified.'

Nothing, not even my obvious recovery from my injury, would change their minds. The grading was there in writing, supported by the X-ray photographs showing the tell-tale scars on the lungs. Though playing rugby or cricket and taking part in advanced gymnastics every day of my life, I was 'totally unfit for military service.'

I had no choice but to plough reluctantly on with my college education and with a series of student-teacher appointments, the most interesting of which took me to Gordonstoun, a year or two after Prince Philip had left there but while the school was still dominated by the looming, oppressive presence of that celebrated educationist, Dr. Kurt Hahn.

At last, in 1943, when I had graduated from College and had been appointed head of the Physical Education Department at Robert Gordon's College, Aberdeen, I could stand my civilian status no longer, and it was then I had a flash of inspiration. Aberdeen in the north of Scotland is a long way from Leicestershire in the Midlands of England: tearing up my medical card, I presented myself to the local Combined Recruiting Centre, who in turn passed me on to the R.A.F. Recruiting Centre in Edinburgh. My interview there was a purgatory of humiliation and determination to see it through.

To the obviously contemptuous Squadron Leader who enquired why I had only now, at the age of twenty-one, presented myself for military service, I could give only one answer that would explain also why I had not, like other young men of my age, been called up compulsorily.

'I am a qualified teacher in a specialist subject, a reserved occupation.'

The sneer on his face was like a slap in mine.

'Tell me, *Mister* Hay,' with supercilious sibilance, 'which is your real ambition? To wear a pilot's uniform, or to face the enemy?'

There could be only one answer to that one. I asked him the shortest route into operational flying, he told me, and I took it. Heroic. Nine weeks' training served to qualify me as an air-gunner and within three months I was on a squadron in Italy.

For my first job I had landed one of the hottest seats in flying— hotter, some people thought, than the pilot's. My interest in aircrew survival had begun at first-hand.

The responsibilities of a tail-gunner in this matter were, of course, almost absurdly simple; to keep his guns clear and his eyes open, to rotate his turret smoothly and precisely even during the gyrations and gymnastics of violent evasive action, and to smother at all cost the temptation to hosepipe his bullets in a random spray when attacked by enemy fighters—or by friendly fighters, for that matter, as had occasionally been known to happen. It was a trade, in short, of limited scope and opportunity, but not without its compensations; there cannot be all that many men, for example, congenitally incapable of changing a bicycle tyre, who can strip a Browning breech-block right down to the rear-seat-retainer-keeper, blindfold and wearing leather gloves; and none of us, whatever we might say to the contrary, really hated it when some wide-eyed darling whispered breathlessly 'Is it really true you tail-gunners are paid before every flight?' The widespread belief that a rear-gunner's life-expectancy stretched out a mere three lonely weeks ahead of him offered endless opportunities to the unscrupulous and, unscrupulous, we took cheerful and often delightful advantage of them.

It was not, of course, all honey and roses, and sometimes, cooped up in my little glass gazebo with the ammunition-boxes chafing cold against my knees and the acrid stink of cordite and glycol in my nostrils, I wondered if my choice had been a wise one. But that was only surface wondering, the rueful bewilderment of any man, any time, engaged in trying to kill other men before they can kill him. In fact, as far as one can enjoy such an occupation, I

17

rather liked my time in the turret, with all the world's problems visible, on a clear day, within an arc of one hundred and eighty degrees and a range of a few thousand yards. There was mental comfort amounting almost to pride in the increasing familiarity with the routine, in the ease, eventually, with which one could wriggle into the chilly little cabin behind the bulkhead doors and run through the drill for readying the four black machine-guns, the tools of the trade. Then too there was the nature of the job itself; if danger threatened you could get at it, indeed you damn well had to. Flying in the wingman's crew, facing backwards on the outer edge of the formation, you would often be the first to see what was coming, and after the sudden swallowing of instinctive sick there would be something unnaturally close to exultation in sorting out the probabilities, hunching yourself in tight-gutted behind the guns, waiting for the attack, switching on the headset so that your grotesque running commentary would be heard and acted on by all. It wasn't fun, but it was positive, it was something you could handle, and, in all honesty, it could be pretty damned exciting. Until, that is, it was all over; then it was shameful and sickening, and you had to stop yourself thinking about the next time, because you knew you were afraid of the next time, and you felt that the next time you would be afraid.

The waiting, of course, could be worse than the action. Flying 'first light' sorties, you learned to hate the briefing-room, that gaunt and draughty mausoleum with the big maps on the blackboard carefully shrouded in secrecy until the Briefing Officer had made his entrance—'Well, chaps, we've got a good one for you today,'—like opening the special surprise parcel at a Christmas party, and the Intelligence Officer, dark and sleek as a fat black cat, handing out the signed-for survival packs, salvation compressed into a few shallow inches of Perspex, with his inevitable admonition against prising them open to extract the foreign currency intended to help you buy your way to safety should you end up, regrettably, in the wrong country; you could learn to hate him too, for his sheer, safe, lack of understanding of what these packs, intact, really meant to you and your friends.

'You can expect a fair amount of opposition about here,' and the Briefing Officer's pointer would circle over an inch or two of paper concealing, at the latest estimate, one hundred and forty anti-aircraft 'heavies' and a proportionate scattering of mediums and lights, 'but I don't think you'll encounter any fighters until you're about eighty miles short of the primary target. There are several squadrons of Messerschmitts and Focke-Wulf 190's in that area. Now for God's sake, gunners, do be careful not to confuse the 190's with the Thunderbolts based on Cesenatico. I know they're very much alike, but our American cousins can get awfully shirty about mistakes, and they *are* on our side you know, ha ha, despite what you married men may hear in your letters from home.'

Oh for God's sake, buster, spare us the witticisms, especially the ones that touch the nerve of our unadmitted anxieties, and let's get on with it. Into the lorries, bumping down the rutted tracks towards the aerodrome where the bombers, silhouetted against the first light of an Adriatic dawn, stand waiting for the crews to bring them to life, to rummage through them like newly-qualified Customs officers, checking everything orthodox and the odd thing unusual, like the ready-made tourniquet a tail-gunner might hook handy over the ammunition boxes, practical talisman against his own special fear of the shell splinter that would sever the femoral artery, pumping the bright red life out of him in less than a minute as he struggled with increasing faintness and futility to drag himself backwards out of the cramping claustrophobia of the turret, back through the bulkhead—dear God, if those sliding doors should be jammed—to the body of the aircraft where his parachute was stacked, remote from him, on a ledge. No question of ejection seats in those days; the great thing for the air-gunner was to reach his parachute and then, somehow, to get out, and the worst fear of all was of being trapped, helpless, and on fire.

The rising whine of the starter-motors, the staccato crackle and cough erupting into a roar as the engines caught and the propellers began to spin, the gulping lungfuls of the last cigarette, the thumbs-up of the ground crew as you swung out from the dispersal bay to take your place in the queue of aircraft creeping slowly around to the runway; all this, when you were in the mood for melodrama, could induce a sort of phoney euphoria, a touch of the Hell's Angels syndrome, but that would dissolve in your guts during the endless acceleration of the take-off run, when the height of your ambition was a loss of engine-power noticed in good time by a watchful pilot who would cancel the whole deal for the day and steer you safely back to base to grouse at your bad luck. After take-off, though, there were things to be done, brief smiles or insults to be exchanged as you stooped your way through the long fuselage to the turret, and then you were all right again—eager, almost, to get on with it and get it over; let the others look after their own jobs, you could cope confidently with yours.

There were, of course, the very bad times, when the wrong man was missing from the evening's party or when, over Ploesti, a small figure—British, German? God only knows—went plummeting downwards from twelve thousand feet, arms and legs threshing, parachute canopy ablaze, with nothing ahead of him but certain death and the penultimate indignity, no doubt, of fouling himself in his fear.

* * *

Then quite suddenly, in Europe, it was all over, with a gold-braided character from Group, Gregory Peck ahead of his time, striding into morning briefing, pausing to dramatic perfection, and announcing, all clipped obscurity and suppressed emotion, 'Gentlemen, this squadron is now non-operational,' before adding as an afterthought that the Germans had capitulated and that the local town would be out of bounds to all ranks, including officers, for the next forty-eight hours.

Within weeks the squadrons had begun to disperse, and uppermost in everyone's mind was the question, 'Now what?' I was one of the lucky ones. Far away in his Cairo headquarters the first of two old friends, fellow-students of Physical Education at Lough-borough before the war, who were to alter the whole course of my future, picked up the telephone:

'Squadron Leader Brice here, Command Physical Fitness Officer. There's a qualified teacher sitting on his backside on one of our squadrons in Italy; I want him posted to staff duties as Physical Fitness Officer, No. 1 Base Area, Naples. Name of Hay. . . . yes, immediately.'

Within a couple of days I had exchanged my Irving jacket for a track suit, my flying boots for football boots, and had taken the first step, though I did not know it and would not then have considered it, towards a Permanent Commission in the Physical Fitness Branch of the Royal Air Force.

The second of my Service Svengalis I met months later, boisterously at home in an English pub. Jimmy Blyth, a vast, craggy, rumbustious North countryman, would almost certainly, but for the war, have played rugby for England; now, with shouts of unexpected greeting exchanged and the beer flowing fast from the tankards, I listened to how he had drifted into another game, one in which he was to earn even greater distinction than that of a rugger international, distinction not only in his own country but in America, France, and almost every other Allied country that had parachute troops to be trained. In Britain, by some inspired, deep-seeing decision, the parachute training of the airborne forces, the Red Devils, had been handed over, not to the Army but to the Royal Air Force, and, more specifically, to a specialised sub-division of its Physical Fitness branch. The result was one of the most spectacularly successful examples of inter-Service co-operation in the history of warfare; the pattern and technique of instruction was worked out by men imbued not only with a pro-fessional understanding of gymnastics—which is all that para-chuting really entails, advanced gymnastics with emotional overtones—but with a free and easy conception of instructor-pupil relationships utterly foreign to the admirably disciplined but fundamentally formal traditions of the Army. The nervous newcomers—and never trust a man who claims he wasn't scared of his first parachute jump—were coaxed, cajoled, above all encouraged into the adventure by a team of officers and N.C.O.'s who constituted a contradiction in wartime terms, a *corps d'élite* of non-combatants. And of all these parachuting instructors the best-known, best-loved by far was Squadron Leader (later Group Captain) Jimmy Blyth, A.F.C., veteran of a thousand jumps and twice that number of rip-roaring, morale-boosting, dusk-to-dawn parties, a man who had cursed the morning in every parachute school from Ringway, Manchester, to Fort Benning, Georgia.

Now in the warm, swirling smokiness of the saloon bar, the anecdotes came tumbling out of him, stories of excitement, of companionship in adventure, of first-light flying with the dawn sky alive with parachutes in their hundreds, billowing wide as the aircraft thundered overhead. As we walked out, at last, into the night, Jimmy Blyth, Chief Instructor at the R.A.F. Parachute School, slung a massive arm around the shoulders of Doddy Hay, Chief Instructor at the R.A.F. School of Physical Training.

'This is the job for you, man, not flapping your arms around and teaching a lot of pot-bellied perishers to do press-ups.'

This seemed at that moment a more accurate description of how I earned my daily bread than was actually the case, and when the next, and parting, remark was, 'Put in an application, Doddy, for parachute training; we'd be glad to have you at the school.'

I heard myself answering, straight from the heart, 'Jimmy, I might do just that very thing.'

The future was beginning to take shape.

CHAPTER 2

Men in the Making

1946-1951

Following my meeting with Jimmy Blyth, late in 1946, I did in fact apply for a transfer to parachuting duties, but my introduction to the game was to be gradual. In the post-war reconstruction of the Royal Air Force that began during the next few months I was one of five officers in my Branch selected for a Permanent Commission, and my postings were arranged accordingly. First came a tour of duty at the Air Ministry as assistant to Eric Brice, who had set the ball rolling for me in Cairo and who was now a Wing Commander responsible for the technical aspects of physical education within the Service. While this posting prevented me from engaging full-time in parachuting it did, however, allow me to sample the thrill of the activity, for I used my position at court to win myself a place in a short introductory course at the Parachute School at Upper Heyford in Oxfordshire. What followed was unforgettable.

* * *

Sergeant Ben Cass was like Doctor Ben Casey. He was dark, big, powerful without effort, and he inspired confidence; he also commanded obedience, and when he crooked his finger you came running, your superior rank a thing of no importance, only braid on the sleeves of a beginner. On 8th July 1948, at seven o'clock in the morning, Cass crooked that meaty finger, and I came forward to meet my obligations. Not running—there is small room for sprinters in a balloon-cage loaded with five potential parachutists and their instructor, eight hundred swaying feet above the airfield—but I came. Numb with fear. Fear that had been rising, cold and sick, during the two interminable hours since my batman, God forgive him for his cheerful, insufferable efficiency, had roused me from my bed. Fear of failure, fear of what was now only seconds ahead; fear of a self-knowledge that would destroy me.

I have read the official assessment of my first visit to the Parachute School: 'An excellent performer, calm and confident in the air . . . strongly recommended for transfer to parachute instructional duties.'

If they could have opened a trap-door into my head and heart that morning they might have thought again. But at times like this all the trap-doors are securely battened down against intrusion. To admit fear to yourself is to invite panic; to admit it to others as frightened as yourself is to spread it, to foster it and eventually, worst of all, to excuse it, to rinse out the shame of your weakness in a communal bucket of whitewash. That is why, at the Parachute School, a pupil who refuses to jump finds himself off camp and *en route* before his companions on the course have even got back to their billets; a man who has given in to his fear is a dangerous man to have around. It was this fear of refusal, of proving myself to be such a man, that was the root of my mental misery. I did not expect to refuse; my life's whole ambition at that moment was to jump, and certainly the thought of death or injury literally never entered my mind. But to step voluntarily and unnecessarily from the familiar and secure into the dangerous unknown is fundamentally irrational, a negation of one's deepest and most powerful instincts, and no man, I am convinced, can vouch absolutely for his own response to such a situation until he has actually experienced it.

None of this was showing, it seems, as I made my way forward, first of the novice cage-load to take his place in the open door, left hand outside it, left foot jutting inches over the edge, head held high and eyes on the distant horizon, waiting tensely for the compelling bellow of 'GO' that speeds the trooper on his way. It never came; Ben Cass, hand resting on my shoulder, remarked quietly, conversationally, 'I'm sure you don't want me shouting at you, Sir, now do you? That's for the nervous ones. You're all clear; just go when you're ready.'

I looked round incredulously at this monster who had just kicked my emotional crutches out from under, came face to face with a friendly, utterly confident grin, and found, to my astonishment, that I was no longer afraid. I went through that door, as Cass remarked later, 'like a bloody rocket, probably the first parachutist in history to travel across instead of down', and even during those first uncertain seconds, when you fall a hundred and twenty feet before you know your future, I was wildly, exultantly happy, in love with life and with an activity I love to this day.

Ben Cass had done more that morning than inject confidence into a man who needed it badly; he had given me my first real glimpse into the peculiar psychology of instruction in a subject dominated, at least in its early stages, by fear.

Of the thousands of men I later taught to jump, and to go on jumping, there were many with some special need, need for some little act of example or encouragement coming in just the right way and at just the right moment. To pull a man through his problems, to watch him master his private, individual weakness, was perhaps the greatest satisfaction in an immensely satisfying job, an achievement every bit as exciting in its own way as the sheer personal thrill of the jumping, and it was the memory of that very first lesson from Cass that later helped me more than anything else in some of the hardest, most complex problems of my parachuting career.

That career, however, was once again to be postponed, and once again it was Eric Brice on the telephone who announced its postponement, calling me up one morning in my London flat.

'Sorry to interrupt your leave, Doddy, but you're wanted for an interview tomorrow at Cranwell. They've created a new post for a Physical Fitness Officer of the staff of the R.A.F. College, and you're one of six on the short list.'

'But you promised my next job would be parachuting... you promised.'

'To hell with parachuting—you can do that later. Just listen to me. This is the most important job in the Branch; they are bringing the College back to what it was before the war, and they've vetted about a dozen men for every single posting on the staff. They've never had a P.F.O. before, and the man they choose is made for the rest of his Service career; now you get on up there tomorrow, and make damn sure that man is you. No argument—good luck.'

I didn't argue, and I had the luck. Cranwell will never again be quite what it was during these re-formative years of the late 1940's; by 1951, when my three year tour was over, the madness and the magic were already beginning to fade, standards had been established and the fine frenzy that had established them had no longer any place in the order of things. The first Commandant of the post-war College was the legendary, larger-than-life Air Commodore 'Batchy' Atcherley, hero of a thousand improbable anecdotes, almost all of them true, and as his deputy, in the chief executive role of Assistant Commandant, he had one of the bravest, most fiercely zealous officers in the Royal Air Force, Group Captain J. O. W. Oliver, D.S.O., D.F.C. The Group Captain was later to be awarded also the C.B. for his work during those exciting, unforgettable years, during both Atcherley's time and that of his successor Air Commodore George Beamish, one of the greatest forwards in the history of Irish international rugby. This was the hierarchy who ruled the place and determined the policy, and under them they had gathered a team of officers varying in their ranks and functions but indivisible in their dedication to the job of putting that policy into effect in the shortest possible time, by direct and often wildly unorthodox methods.

These were men who had been in the thick of the air-fighting when most of them had been little more than schoolboys. Some, though not all, had themselves been at Cranwell just before the war, and no doubt the authorities would have chosen to staff the new College entirely with graduates of the old, but the most cursory glance at the Roll of Honour in its glass casket is enough to show why that was out of the question. The new generation of flight cadets, in any event, suffered no lack of leadership from their squadron commanders; men like Bob Weighill, rugger captain of England and the Royal Air Force, one of the finest footballers and by far the greatest skipper I ever played under, who had won his D.F.C. over the beaches of France, and Johnny Dyer, small and effervescent, who had won his over the chilly waters of the North Atlantic. To see Johnny, a magnificent companion but a lousy acrobat, hurl himself suicidally over the highest vaulting box in a spine-splintering bid to encourage his cadets to greater efforts in the inter-squadron gymnastic competition was to understand why he had been made a wartime Wing Commander at the age of twenty-one.

Not that the aim of the College was to churn out a stream of gallant hearties. The cadets were there to fly, to accept and later to exercise authority, to work like ants at their academic studies, and to learn to live in an atmosphere of strict and often formal discipline that would fit them for their future role as the spinal cord of the Service. Their foot-drill would have done credit to the Brigade of Guards—the Graduation Parade at Cranwell is one of the most stirring, splendidly-executed examples of military pomp and circumstance to be seen anywhere in Britain—but the discipline was always the discipline of leaders, and as such it was enlightened and embraced a pattern of activities and behaviour extending far beyond the bounds of the barrack square. My own part in all this was made clear by the Assistant Commandant on the very day I arrived.

'Doddy,' said the Group Captain, and seeing my eyebrows arch he went on, 'yes, I shall use your first name—if I felt I couldn't safely do that, you wouldn't be here. You will be on my personal staff, responsible directly and only, within the bounds of normal discipline, to me. Now, where have you put your personal kit?'

'In the Mess, sir.' (Where else, for God's sake? We've got a rum one here, all right.)

'Have it moved right away; you will be one of half a dozen officers with quarters actually in the College. Your whole life from this minute is wrapped up in the Flight Cadets. I want you to know them, know every single thing about how they think, feel, and act, and I want them to know you almost as well. You and Bob Weighill play rugger for the Royal Air Force—I want you to make these young men want to do the same, and I expect you to make the best of them good enough to do it. On all matters of sport you will work closely with Bob; on all other matters of Physical Education you have a completely free hand. Get to know the College, work out what you want, and come and tell me about it—if I agree with you, you'll have it.'

Cranwell is a vast station comprising several quite important units besides the College; in fact it has the status of a Group. In 1948 it was sadly over-crowded and in the Mess many officers, not just the subalterns, were compelled to share rooms. The quarters that 'Doggie' Oliver had assigned to me were a self-contained, well-furnished flat overlooking the College parade-ground, with a drawing-room, a bedroom, a bathroom, and a batman, Carr, who had been on the staff since the nineteen twenties. Grey haired, silent, and discreet, Carr would glide into the bedroom of a morning to bring his 'gentleman' tea, to shake him gently and announce that the bath was drawn, and to enquire, his hand on the curtains, 'A little light entertainment this morning, sir, or are we perhaps in a hurry?'

If time permitted, Carr would fling wide the windows and the young master would sink back on soft pillows to enjoy for a while the martial music of the College band and the crunching cadence of six hundred boots on the gravel as the drill sergeants ground out their throaty demands for perfection. Carr understood the importance of such things, and of many more besides, and he could deliver a gentle reprimand with the deadly respectfulness of a Jeeves.

'We are dining with the Commandant at the Lodge this evening, sir; I have laid out our Mess Kit, sir, and the socks with the *small* holes.'

The dining-in nights were a delight from ages past, from the rapping of the chairs to the rhythm of 'The Lincolnshire Poacher,' as the musicians in the gallery played the officers to their places among the long rows of cadets, to the growing ease and confidence which circulated later with the port. There were the days, too, out on the sweeping acres of the playing-fields, hammering into these eager, talented youngsters all one had learned oneself in the higher, harder strata of sport; one day in particular, unforgettable above all the others, when the Rugger XV, underdogs trained and transformed into a splendid, spirited team, met Sandhurst on their own ground, Sandhurst inspired by those two magnificent young half-backs, Hardy and Shuttleworth, so soon to play for England, and startled them, stunned them, thrashed them gloriously to their first defeat by Cranwell in twenty years. And sitting in the stand that afternoon, striving mightily to preserve the decorum befitting his rank and position, was Cranwell's Commandant who, as Flight Cadet Beamish, had led his team to that earlier victory twenty years before. There were others of us with no such dignity or rank to consider, and it was not only the fifteen boys who had played their hearts out who greeted next morning with a groan.

'Doggie' Oliver had been right; to live in the College in those days was to live for it, and he provided all the backing he had promised. All the outside excitement I needed was my own rugby football, five years all told of slugging it out as scrum-half for the London Scottish, the Air Force, the Combined Services on their tours to France, and for a couple of Counties besides. Especially to be savoured, even when the blood flowed and the boots bit deep, was the intensity of those inter-Service battles against the Navy and Army at Twickenham; these were the two days in each season when all else was forgotten, but for the rest all my interest was in the cadets, with an occasional wistfulness for the missed parachuting that my good fortune was costing me, and quite suddenly even that faint blemish was removed. Over a drink in my quarters one evening the Group Captain remarked almost casually:

'Our vacations are too long; this isn't quite the same as a university, and the cadets, though they need their holidays, should not be allowed to drift away from the Service altogether. We must increase the scope of our vacation activities so that all of them can spend at least part of their summers with their own companions, preferably doing something that will be not only interesting but useful to them in their career. Any ideas?'

I had one, one so shining bright, so utterly right it lent silver to my tongue. By the end of that evening 'Doggie' Oliver, eyes sparkling, was pacing the floor excitedly, scarcely to be restrained from ringing the Air Council there and then to demand their approval of the scheme. And in truth it had everything to commend it.

I led the first College parachute course that summer, I led the second the following year, and later, as a parachute officer, I commanded several more; not one of those cadets who spent a fortnight at the Parachute School, making two descents from a balloon and six from an aircraft, failed to report an immensely increased confidence in the equipment he might so easily one day be called upon to use in sterner circumstances. Sandhurst soon came in on the act, every bit as keenly as our own boys, and from that evening's conversation between Group Captain Oliver and myself stems a story years later that shows what a parachute can sometimes mean to the man who wears it.

* * *

The facts were simple. The pale-faced boy standing before me in my office at the Parachute School was a jibber; seven times he had hurled himself out of a balloon or an aircraft, but on the eighth, the qualifying descent, first his nerves and then he himself had rebelled, and he had refused firmly, physically, and in defiance of the statutory three commands, to jump. There was nothing, nothing at all, I could do to help him, for the rule, quite rightly, is inflexible—no second chances. A man who has refused once would almost certainly, sometime, refuse again, and next time he

30

might endanger, even kill, his comrades; it is a risk that is never taken.

I felt sorry for the youngster, and I admired the courage with which he stood there, rejecting even a chair and a cigarette, refusing either to excuse his failure or to whimper about his future, which seemed to me even then to be appalling. For he was no ordinary soldier, but a senior Sandhurst cadet, and he was the first from either his own Academy or from Cranwell who had thrown in the towel. To sympathise with this boy, so rigidly under control, would have been an impertinence; I wished him luck, and I sent him to the officer who had brought the course up from the Academy with the instruction that he was to be off the camp within one hour.

That Sandhurst officer, Major Denis Beckett, was a friend, and knowing how badly he must feel about the incident I asked him that evening to join me in the Mess for a drink.

'Rough luck, Denis, about the youngster; poor little devil, he must be feeling dreadful. How was he when he left?'

Beckett toyed with his glass and shifted uncomfortably, as if his bar-stool had had fingers.

'Doddy, I don't know quite how to say this . . . but he hasn't left, he is up in his room. On my authority.'

This from Beckett, unfailingly courteous, most punctilious of professional soldiers, was unbelievable. To countermand the Course Commander's orders, to flout the regulations of another Service, and in circumstances in which he and his cadets were guests . . . impossible.

'The next drink, Denis, I think we'd better have in private; your room?'

The boy, it transpired, was approaching the end of his Sandhurst career, and already he had been accepted into the famous regiment in which his father had served with considerable distinction. That regiment was not airborne, and he would never in the future be called upon to jump, but by an unlucky chance the company in which he had been offered his coveted vacancy was

31

officered mainly by men who had served as parachutists in earlier days. It was not from any instinct for the activity but simply to establish his credit, as it were, with his future companions that the youngster had volunteered for the course, and as it happened he had hated every second of it from the start. By sheer guts and determination he had forced himself through those seven descents, shuddering every time he saw the open aircraft door, sick each time with fear even after the parachute had safely opened; and then, with the end of his ordeal in sight, the last jump for which he was waiting in agony was postponed because of bad weather, and his nerve had cracked completely. The courage, once drained, was gone for good; he was finished, and he knew it. So was his bright new longed-for career; for with this on his record he could not possibly be posted to the regiment of his choice, yet still he could not bring himself to the one last simple act that would avert disaster. Now I knew why Denis Beckett had broken the rules, why he ended his story by saying,

'This lad just *must* be helped, though God knows how, and if there is a way to help him it can only come from you—please will you try?'

The first stage was simple; I had never been famous as the most disciplined of officers. We sent for the youngster and told him to get a good night's sleep, for he would be jumping in the morning, and the whole affair would be forgotten. His answer was like a slap in the face.

'It's very good of you, sir, and I do appreciate what you are offering, but I just cannot do it; nothing could make me jump again, nothing.'

We argued, Denis and I, we coaxed and encouraged—dammit, we pleaded with him, but we could not move him one inch, and at last we sent him off to bed. Wearied, sick, and thoroughly depressed, the two of us moodily lowered the level of the bottle on the table between us until quite suddenly I said, 'Denis, I think I've got the answer.'

The cadet looked all right when he reported to me on the airfield next morning, where a couple of hundred soldiers from a normal Army Basic Course were nervously waiting to make their first jump from the captive balloons now bobbing gently at their mooring. I chatted to him of this and that, strolling slowly closer to the little groups making last-minute adjustments to their equipment, and then, when I saw the first stick of jumpers almost ready to go, I let him have it:

'Put on that parachute, laddie—and that is a military order.'

It was also an illegal order, but only I knew that, and I continued before he had time to figure it out for himself.

'You say you can never be a parachutist, and you think that's the end of it. I want to know if you're fit to be an officer at all. You are going up, number one in the first cage, and you can make up your own mind whether you jump out of it or jib—no-one's going to force you or even persuade you. But there will be four private soldiers right behind you, nervous as hell and looking to you to show them how to do it—and if you just stand there, sonny, they will too, and that's five futures you've busted, not one, for not one of them will get the second chance you've got right now.'

The poor fellow looked green, and I hope I have never been hated as I was just then, but I wouldn't let him shift his eyes, until at last he saluted, saying nothing, and turned slowly to the balloon-cage and the little cluster of waiting men. He must have felt like death as the great silver sausage rose slowly and silently to eight hundred feet, but had he but known it he was not alone in that. The futures at stake were not five, but six; if he failed to jump I too would be off the station that day, my parachuting career over and the certainty of court-martial to follow. I watched the cable tighten as the balloon reached altitude, heard the ringing clatter as the iron bar dropped down from the doorway and the voice of the instructor, well briefed in private, split the morning sky with its rasping, please God irresistible, shattering shout of 'GO.' Out he came, that frightened, brave cadet, and behind him, one by heartened one, four future soldiers of the Parachute Regiment. Beckett and I looked at each other, said not one single word, but very quietly, without affectation or embarrassment, met in a handshake that lasted for many seconds.

I still keep in my desk the very charming letter sent me some days later, a valued memento of one of the greatest moments of my life.

CHAPTER 3

Airborne Army

1951-1954

My three years at Cranwell were followed by a two-year tour of duty as an instructor at the Parachute School, now removed from Upper Heyford to Abingdon, also in Oxfordshire. This was a rewarding experience, with the basic purpose of it all highlighted by memorable moments; long days on the Dropping-Zone, ready with the loud-hailers as the troops came tumbling out of the aircraft, increasingly confident in the ability to spot instantly the man in trouble, to identify him by his position amongst thirty or forty others, and to 'talk him down,' guide him into corrective action, and thrill to the satisfaction of seeing him respond, sometimes only after urgent persuasion, and glide smoothly in to a safe landing on the grass. The half-hour in the canteen afterwards, the pupils going over and over their experiences, all talking, few listening, each convinced that he and he alone had explored one of life's new frontiers; then into the lorry for the long ride back to the School, gradually cooling them down, sharing but containing their enthusiasm, conditioning them into calmness for the lectures and the hours of corrective training that must follow; deciphering the notes dictated during the drop to the ever-present sergeant, shaping them into a reasoned, comprehensive de-briefing, and watching the surprise, growing into confidence, of men slowly realising that each one of them really was being watched, his individual failings isolated and then analysed so that they could later be eliminated—these were crowded, happy, satisfying days.

There were, of course, more private, more personal, thrills to be enjoyed, some jumps out of several hundred that would never be forgotten. Some great ones, like the first night descent, with

35

the flickering cinematic excitement of the scene inside the air-craft, the dark shadows on the pale faces, the stamping feet of the airborne ushers in the aisle, the swift determined rush into the cold hurly-burly of the slipstream and the strange silent blackness beneath, broken only by the yellow pin-points of the goose-neck flares a thousand feet below. Or later, many months later, strolling home in a group, sober but exhilarated, from the Summer Ball, and seeing an aircraft warming up on the runway for the first dawn drop of the day; excuses to the ladies, promises to be back within the hour for bacon and eggs, a mad scramble aboard, buck-ling parachute over Mess Kit and to hell with helmet and boots; and then, pure bliss, floating down on a still and silent summer morning, miniature medals tinkling softly against the rough coarse canvas of the harness, to the final illicit joy of a perfect, forbidden 'stand-up' landing—exactly five yards from the stony gaze of the Commanding Officer who ought by rights to have been miles away in bed.

There were others less idyllic, like the long cold fall from a Valetta, with the parachute flapping limp and useless, closed in a 'Roman Candle', defying all swift and corrective action, down faster and faster from a thousand feet to less than one hundred until suddenly, for God's own good reasons, the canopy billowed three-quarters open—enough, and only just enough, to turn a do-it-yourself grave-digger's act into a forty miles an hour impact that ought to have shattered legs, spine and pelvis but yet, probably because of an automatically-assumed landing attitude, did not. There was the added relief that day that there had been no screams, no panic; the end would have been a decent one, and survival was unspoiled by shame.

Another bad experience even ended, though not without effort, in dead-pan cross-talk comedy. It was a test jump, an evaluating trial of an enormous, one hundred and twenty pound kit bag, and it was difficult enough simply to maintain balance in the open doorway of the four-engined Hastings; a premature 'go' signal, given while the aircraft was flying fifty knots faster than planned,

36

led to a rough and protracted battering along the fuselage and two swift untidy somersaults that tangled the massive equipment in the rigging lines of the newly-opened 'chute, leaving the occupant upside down, suspended by one leg. The glorious fight for freedom was still going on when we crossed a busy highway, far from the open acres of the dropping zone, and it ended when I lowered my precious bundle and swarmed half-way up the rigging lines in a just-successful bid to avoid crashing into the wall of the Military College of Science. Rising, bruised and bleeding, to return the salute of the anxious but impeccably formal Sergeant Major standing to attention between me and the still spinning sky, I remembered my manners and just managed to murmur, before crumpling reluctantly but without choice into the cool shadow beneath the wall, 'Please convey my compliments to your Adjutant, and my apologies for this unwarranted intrusion.'

Cranwell, like murder, will out.

* * *

After all this, in 1953, came the opportunity, almost too good to be true, of running a small show of my own. An appointment as Liaison Officer to the Airborne Forces, scheduled for one year but in the event to be extended to four, gave me a tiny niche in the British Army in Aldershot, myself and my two sergeants the only specks of blue in a limitless desert of khaki. The officers and men of the Airborne Forces Depot were real soldiers, most of them battle-hardened veterans of Arnhem, Normandy, and the Rhine, and to live with them, on and off duty, was Cranwell all over again, with paratroopers to be trained instead of cadets, and with my new Commanding Officer every bit as charming and unhidebound as 'Doggie' Oliver had been in these earlier halcyon days.

Colonel R. G. Pine-Coffin, D.S.O., M.C., who at times seemed obsessed with the macabre connotations of his name, was tall, unbelievably angular, with a long and rugged face softened by eyes that smiled easily and often; he was one of the gentlest, most

37

humorous men I have known. He was also, as a parachutist, utterly fearless—which posed its problems, for this was peacetime, he was the Commandant, and I was responsible for his safety no less than for that of the men under his command; on the dropping zone, in the aircraft, and on all matters concerning the descent, the R.A.F. Parachute Officer is in sole charge, regardless of rank. But my Colonel's approach to parachuting was, shall we say, not so much unorthodox as bizarre, and his peccadilloes began with his choice of boots.

They were splendid boots, handsome, highly polished boots, boots that would have looked quite magnificent on John Wayne or even, perhaps, on John Wayne's horse—but they were not parachuting boots, and though they graced his ankles they did nothing to support them; they flapped wide where they should have clung closely, they offered freedom and comfort where they should have enforced discipline and protection. And my Colonel's ankles, more than most, needed all the protection they could get. The sight of that lanky, bony, where-the-hell-am-I, utterly disjointed figure falling down the sky like a drunken puppet was awe-inspiring enough, but it was in the last hundred feet of the drop, when the ground starts whizzing up at you, that he really struck terror in the heart. At that stage, as I soon learned, it was best to leave him strictly alone, for shouted instructions served only to accelerate the already swift dismantling of any vague pretence to a parachuting position. Arms, elbows, pelvis, knees, every one of them double-jointed, all jerked in and out like broken pistons in an impossible pattern of preparation as Colonel Geoffrey Pine-Coffin, D.S.O., M.C., came swooping down, gaily and gallantly, on his enemy, the ground. Then, dear God, the impact; as those spiky, Texan high-heeled boots drove in the spearhead of the attack, the rest of his limbs would fan out like Panzers in a swift and fragmented pincer movement too fast for the eye to follow. It was not so much a landing as an invasion. And then, as the dust began to settle, and as I drew my hand reluctantly from my eyes, Geoffrey, all beaming smiles, would come stalking

38

across to ask his invariable first question; 'Well, Doddy, did I remember everything you told me? That felt like a really good one.'

With the Colonel's co-operation I built up a display team to 'show the flag' at Air Shows and festivals, and in the constant efforts to produce something out of the ordinary I gradually acquired increasing control over my parachute and a certain ability to handle my problems in the air. Swallow dives and somersaults and 'slipping' the 'chute till it streamed were all very well, but one day I decided to try something altogether new; I would make my next demonstration descent on a bicycle. Not pushing it—we had been wheeling bikes and perambulators out of balloon-cages all over England—but actually riding it; that had not been done.

Harness straps from the back of the seat to the front of the handle-bars ran over my shoulders and held me securely in the saddle; by removing the coffin-shaped floor panel in the cage and by squatting over it in an uncomfortable, undignified, vertical version of the lethotomy position beloved by gynaecologists if not their patients, I could lower myself to a point where the wheels cleared the aperture by exactly one and a half inches at each end. A quick inward jerk of the feet and down I went, with the rigging lines paying out behind me and the shock quite acceptable as the canopy opened; from here on it was simple clowning, tooting the horn, ringing the bell, doffing my hat with extravagant panache as I pedalled my way in over the heads of the spectators. A hundred feet from the ground I pulled the release toggle and the bike dropped away, secured to me still by a fifteen-foot nylon cord, and dragged along behind me like a tail as I made my landing.

Easy: until the day of the demonstration at Biggin Hill, with a hundred and thirty thousand patriots out there celebrating the anniversary of the Battle of Britain, and the wind rising far above parachuting limits to speeds of thirty-five miles an hour and gusting above that. I was wrong, of course, to go ahead with it,

39

and no-one was more acutely aware of that than myself as I crouched there a thousand feet up, trying desperately to keep my balance as the balloon-cage bucked and reared like a bronco with burrs in its back. I was, in fact, scared to hell, and it was a relief finally to judge my moment and drop away—a relief lasting perhaps one half of one second. As I plummeted through the swaying aperture the steering pillar of the bike swung round, the handle-bars hit the rim of the cage, and I was on my back, falling fast, with the serrated rat-trap pedals whirring madly round just one inch from the streaming rigging lines; if they picked up just one line out of twenty-eight they would wrap the white nylon canopy round me like a shroud. I heaved sideways on those handle-bars like an archer at Agincourt, dragging them laterally away from the lethal lines, and my body was twisted sideways and backwards as the parachute at last slapped open in the wind. I thought for one blinding moment all my guts had gone, but at least I was floating, and I managed some semblance of my act; I even got away with the frighteningly fast landing, for the speed of the wind, now rising forty, carried me over rather than into the ground. I rolled up my parachute; the bicycle was lying undamaged beside me. Some gesture seemed called for, if only to Fate. Hoisting my screaming muscles over the cross-bar I rode off through the dense ring of spectators, and as they parted to let me pass, a woman's voice, shrill and derisive above the applause, put my fine gallantry in true perspective:

'Lost 'is nerve, didn't 'e? Got rid of the bleedin' bike before 'e landed.'

Soon, however, there were more exciting things to think about than stunting. In the Spring of 1954 came the announcement that Sir Raymond Quilter, Bt., managing director of the G.Q. Parachute Company, second in British importance only to Irvin's, was going to raise and finance a team of free-fall parachutists to represent Great Britain in the World Championships to be held in France that August. Competition for a place in the team of five would be open to all British parachutists, Service or

40

civilian. Geoffrey Pine-Coffin heard the news the same day that I did.

'Doddy, you must win a place in this British team, to represent us as well as the Royal Air Force.'

I went to bed late that night, yet still I did not sleep.

CHAPTER 4

The World Sky-Diving
Championships

1954

I was skulking behind an aircraft, worried because I was scared.
What was this new, unsuspected flaw in the moral muscle for
God's sake? For this was no ordinary fear that could be hidden,
at least from others; hence my retreat behind the aircraft—my
palms were sweating, my face, I felt certain, was white: I clutched
the metal cylinder in my pocket, trying not to think about its
presence there, yet unable for one second to forget it, and strove
to be rational, clinical, to eradicate the ailment by exposure.

The situation, on the surface of it, simply did not make sense.
My one ambition for weeks had been to represent my country
in the World Championships; now the gateway to selection was
wide open before me; the trials were starting, and I had been
chosen to take part. So, it was true, had others, among them
thirty-five hand-picked instructors from the Parachute School,
each one of them determined as myself to win his place in the
team of five for France; perhaps I was simply afraid of being
beaten? No, that wasn't it, couldn't be it; I had more experience
of top-echelon sport than the whole damn lot of them put together, and I'd had my share of beatings as well as victories, some
of them beatings that I had known in advance were coming to
me. You don't face up to the Army pack at Twickenham expecting
to come out on top. I'd known butterflies in the belly in those
days, certainly, but I had never been afraid; the tendency to puke
before the kick-off had been less compelling, in fact, on the big
occasions than in the hours before the trial matches.

Trials; now, maybe, I was getting close to the heart of things.
Was it fear of failure, perhaps, fear of rejection, that was tempting

me so sorely to cut and run? Faint stirrings of self-contempt confirmed the unpleasant accuracy of this particular piece of probing, but I knew I hadn't yet reached the root. All right, so I wanted acceptance—who doesn't?—but I'd had it before, in other fields, without bragging, and I'd missed it before without moaning, and no yearning for acceptance, especially for acceptance on merit, could explain away that damned metal cylinder burning hot and shameful in my pocket.

OBLIVON. Confidence in a capsule. Emerald green, pretty to look at, soothing to fondle, like a mandarin's jade; a painless substitute for guts. Advertised in the national dailies, sold without prescription in all the better chemists—give some to the children, they'll clamour to be taken to the dentist. Give some to the girl-friend, she'll put her trust in you. How long had I paced furtively up and down outside that chemists' shop, feinting at the entrance, then dodging hurriedly past, scarlet in the face, like any fifteen year old clutching the hot half dollar that will buy him his first packet of contraceptives? And at last I'd given in, and I'd bought my bright green concessions to cowardice—only for use in emergency, of course, but I had them here right now, clutched in my hand, and if this wasn't an emergency, then what in God's name was? There could be no more evasion, no more refusal to face the truth. I knew now exactly what I was afraid of; I was afraid, shivering, sweating afraid of the parachute jump I was about to make. I was afraid of it in and for itself; this was no qualm about my qualities of leadership; for the very first time I was terrified of what would happen to me when I hurtled through the aircraft door, and I had nothing to help me but my vanishing pride and my Oblivon capsules. Twenty minutes before the ordeal was the time recommended for swallowing them, time to let the courage circulate in your blood; well, I had better make up my mind damn soon, for in twenty minutes I would be aboard that flying tumbril, and ten minutes after that would come my moment of truth when, for the first time in two hundred and fifteen parachute descents, *I would fall free through the doorway with no static-line*

43

attached to the aircraft to jerk my canopy into automatic opening,
only a metal D-ring, cold and remote and useless until I myself
had found it without fumbling and dragged it from its housing,
pulling clear the ripcord that held the parachute tight-packed and
unopened in its canvas envelope. Was there a Dead Letter
Department for unopened parachute envelopes? Now there's a
damn silly witticism for a start. Here I was, hoist well and truly
with my own petard, paying—block that metaphor—at extortion-
ate rates of interest for the prodigality with which I had handed
out, gift-wrapped, to my pupils the precious parcels of confidence
in their equipment; 'Your parachute, laddie, is a statichute, and
it opens automatically—it must open, it always opens. It is not a
ripcord 'chute . . . now there you *do* have something to worry
about.' And the pupils had accepted the logic, indeed the truth of
this, and so had I myself, two hundred and fifteen times, and now,
quite suddenly, the truth and the logic were my enemies, not my
friends. No first-timer was ever more frightened and defenceless
than I was, with my two hundred and fifteen anti-jumps acting in
cumulative unison against me.

The marshalling-officer called us over to the aircraft, and I
carefully placed a few personal belongings in my briefcase, to be
collected, I hoped by myself, after the jump. My watch, my
wallet, my silver cigarette case, and a little metal cylinder, its label
stained almost unreadable by sweat, but its seal intact, held there
inviolate not by courage but by grudging, trembling obedience to
unanswerable common sense. 'You'll never, never know, boy,'
said logic, 'whether you made that jump, or whether they did.'
'Don't give a damn about that,' urged fear, 'after the first one
everything will be all right.' But fear, of course, was lying, for
after the first one nothing, nothing at all, would *ever* have been
all right.

* * *

Those early jumps at Weston-on-the-Green took the form of
eliminating trials, and the group that eventually moved on to the

private airfield at Fair Oaks for advanced training had been whittled down to about a dozen. Of those eliminated some had taken their disappointment philosophically, one or two with barely-concealed relief; a couple, inevitably, in a spirit of sour resentment that was to rankle in them for years, and one in sheer bewilderment who could not grasp why the selectors considered him too obsessed with the sport to be safe. Calling on this lad's home one morning, the chief selector saw him spooning sugar into his coffee cup and heard the rhythmic, quite subconscious chanting that accompanied the action; 'One thousand, two thousand, three thousand . . .', the parachutists' time-honoured method of counting out the seconds on a delayed drop. 'Been going on like this for days,' said the wife of the unfortunate birdman, innocently unaware that she was handing over the scissors that would clip his wings, 'even brushes his teeth to numbers, and honestly doesn't know he's doing it. Sounds real funny, it does.' It didn't sound at all funny to the selectors, visualising the boy subjected to the stresses and strains of international competition, and his name was quietly but irrevocably removed from the roster.

Even amongst those selected for further training the *camaraderie*, though genuine enough, was tempered by the awareness that until five of us finally became team-mates, all of us in the meantime were rivals fighting for places, with the odds almost three to one against success. Only one civilian, Arthur Harrison, had made the grade to this stage of selection, but he had more free-fall experience than any of us, and he was good; it was obvious from the outset that one of the five precious vacancies was already effectively filled, leaving the Air Force contingent to slug it out amongst themselves for the privilege of filling the remaining four. It was fun, of course, but it was also a period of tension and of constant experimenting in matters of technique, and a successful jump, notching up personal points on the scoresheet of shared ambition, would be greeted with only qualified delight by the others. 'Nice work—damn you,' was the attitude

45

of British sportsmanship prevailing at the time, and it was hard to conceal a smile of satisfaction as a friend, misjudging the wind, drifted unhappily out to the far reaches of the airfield.

Our coach and non-playing captain was Major T. W. 'Dumbo' Willans, who had jumped for Britain in the Championships of 1952, failing to win the individual title only by a fantastic slice of ill-luck; the final test on that occasion had been made into water and Dumbo, with an unassailable lead over all other competitors, had only to swim a few short yards to the finishing-buoy to become champion skydiver of the world when an official launch, bent on retrieving his floating parachute, failed to notice that he was still attached to it and dragged him half-drowning across the lake—in the wrong direction. It was typical both of Dumbo Willans and of the sport as it was conducted at that time that he did not fight to the death for a 're-run' of the event—international parachuting in its infancy had all the emphasis upon participation rather than victory that de Coubertin had dreamed of in his concept of the modern Olympic Games. Even by my time, just two years later, politics had entered the arena, and now, in the 1960's, the World Championships are a battle ground of national prestige, with the Iron Curtain stretching high and impenetrable across the dropping zone.

Dumbo was good for us. A place in the foreground, as a competitor, was of course his for the asking, yet he ran himself ragged in his role behind the scenes, getting his satisfaction, one must assume, from the confidence and proficiency growing daily in his pupils. Dumbo Willans understood and cared deeply about the problems of competitors, which was just as well, for we sometimes felt that the team sponsor, Sir Raymond Quilter, most emphatically did not.

I liked Sir Raymond, liked him immensely, and in the years that followed I spent many enjoyable hours in his company, but he was an ebullient hedonist fundamentally incapable of drawing any meaningful distinction between an international championship and a champagne party. He financed the whole shooting-

46

match, he piloted the plane from which we made our jumps, he was a most generous and entertaining host throughout the whole of our sojourn in France, and yet, in the emotionally crucial days leading up to the final team-selection, he was the enemy, though he would not realise it, of every last one of us. Later, during the Championships, I was to be his quasi-official adjutant, liaison man between parachutists and officials, sparking-plug of the several quite splendid shenanigans held in the local hotel during evenings with no early jumps to follow, but in these last few days at Fair Oaks, we clashed, head-on, because neither of us could understand at all the other's point of view.

Each jump any one of us had made, good or bad, pin-point accurate or off into the tundra, had been noted and measured, marked for or against us in the tally of talent, and naturally a pattern of probability had begun to form; quite a few of us, in short, knew that we must, on the reckoning, be 'in with a chance.' But there was no exact yardstick of performance, for style as well as accuracy must be taken into account in competitive parachuting; there are points to be scored long before the sky-diver hits the ground. We were learning all the time, and we knew that high amongst the selectors' considerations must be their opinion as to how quickly each man would continue to develop, how well he would react to the strain—and the stimulus—of public competition against the finest parachutists in the world. We too had our doubts and misgivings, about ourselves and about our companions, but what counted was not our assessment, but that of the selectors, and we felt, as time ran out for us, we had the right to know. Morale and sportsmanship, so strong and natural in the early stages, were becoming daily more hard to maintain; tempers were becoming scratchy, little groups were beginning to huddle whispering in corners. I was as bad as the others, but as the only officer I was the one who could speak; I decided to tackle Quilter.

'Look, in just four days from now five lucky fellows leave for France. You must know by now who they are—or at least who they're not—and you've just *got* to tell us. You want a team over there, not a bunch of bloody prima donnas worn out by their tantrums and anxieties. The guys who are out can take it—they've got no choice—and the others should by now be practising, not competing against each other. We've still got a hell of a lot to learn, but do you seriously expect me, or any one of us, to go up now and try out something new, knowing that if it's a stumer it's going to cost us our place in the team? It's not fair, and worse than that it's not even sensible; if you want a man to perform like an international you've got to give him time to realise he is one. Encourage him, flatter him, soft-soap him—or, if you prefer it the hard way, bully him, challenge him, frighten him—but, for God's sake, *pick* him, show him that you at least have confidence and give him the chance to build some for himself.'

Sir Raymond smiled benignly, tolerant of a tiny, irascible, impotent enemy attacking a fortress already scheduled for surrender. 'Relax, Doddy—the team will be announced this evening, and just to put you out of your misery, you're in.' My apology, thank God, had no time to cross my lips before he continued. 'And incidentally, it isn't just five of you; it's seven. We've decided to allow for emergencies and carry a couple of reserves. We'll decide who actually competes once we get there.' I didn't scream, and I didn't strike him: I gazed open-mouthed at the solid, impenetrable wall of his insensitivity and I started right back at the beginning. As he chortled amiably on about how each one of us would have the time of his life, ten days in sunny St. Yan, all expenses paid, with the girls admiring and the wine flowing free, I tried, my God how I tried, to get the simple message across to him. 'It all sounds great, and it's really most generous of you. But I don't want to go to bloody France, and nor do any of the others—I want to parachute for Great Britain, and if I'm not going to I'd rather, far rather, stay at home and get drunk.'

No plea, however, no argument could budge Sir Raymond in his conviction that a free trip to France was all any young man could ask for, that seven fortunate fellows would find in the extra holiday—'It doesn't even count against your leave-entitlement; I've fixed all that with the Air Ministry'—a handsome reward for all the tensions of training, all the bottled-up ambition and the bouts of despondency when things had seemed to be going badly. That for each one of us, the scales were now finely balanced between the honour—an outmoded word, but there is no other— of competing in our country's colours on the one hand, and a crushing disappointment and sense of personal failure on the other, was quite beyond his comprehension. And so, at the end of July, we set out, all seven of us, with only the one official practice day ahead of us before the championships and with the nervy know- ledge that on our performance in just two descents, one from high altitude, one from low, might depend our personal places in the team; if the aim was to keep us keyed-up to the very last, then the aim was most effectively achieved.

The two reserves, in the event, were both Air Force men, Sergeant Sutton and Sergeant Card, and the attitude they main- tained towards the rest of us throughout the whole of the Cham- pionship left me, at any rate, spell-bound in silent admiration, for it was better, far better, in its ungrudging sportsmanship than anything I could ever have achieved myself. When we hit the ground they were there as if by magic to greet us; when we had a good one, their congratulations were immediate and palpably sincere; at the parties they got as happily hooped as the most successful, exhilarated competitor. As team men they were quite magnificent and it is good to record that one of them, Alf Card, was to represent Great Britain in a later World Championship. As for Danny Sutton, a real regular sergeant of the old school, he achieved his moment of glory on the night before we left St. Yan. Throughout the whole of the meeting he had remained obdurate in his antipathy to 'Froggy cooking, all grease and bloody spices,' and had kept body and soul together on a diet of bread and beans; but on that final evening, after a solid hour of persuasion, he turned to me as the waitresses came tripping in with delicious, steaming platters of *filet mignon*, squared his shoulders in true-blue British determination to face danger bravely: 'You're right, sir, mustn't let the side down. I'll try a French omelette—with eggs.'

The set-up at St. Yan was roughly that of an Olympic Village in miniature, with each national team occupying its own quarters but sharing communal rooms for eating and recreation. All sharing, that is, except the Russians, great crop-headed giants of men and stringy, silent—with one charming exception—women who emerged from their lair only to scan the skies, to jump with admirable, frightening efficiency, and to disappear again immediately in a tight-knit regimented group. Their team manager explained to me, the inference in his words varnished over but not concealed by politeness, 'None of our team speaks any language but our own. They have been chosen purely for their sporting proficiency, and not for any social background or accomplishments, you understand.' I searched the faces of my own team-mates, trying hard to see on Sergeants Hoffman, Moloney, and Woods the tell-tale stamp of Eton and Balliol, but decided to let it pass; the Russian manager would be impervious, I imagined, to either argument or irony, and he was, in any case, a liar. All of us already knew, from brief snatches of conversation out on the safe open acres of the dropping zone, that several of the Soviet parachutists spoke quite passable English and that one, at least, spoke it fluently. From him, some days later, I was to receive information that made my serving officer's blood run cold, but in the meantime my interests centred purely on the Championships.

If the Russians on the whole were silent, herded together at the flick of a finger by the Third Secretary from their Embassy in Paris who had appeared in St. Yan 'simply to smooth out any difficulties in interpretation,' there were others, more gregarious, who were not. The French, led by the dapper little reigning world champion Pierre Lard and by the women's champion, the petite, vivacious, Monique Laroche, were unfailingly helpful, offering advice from their vastly greater experience of sky-diving, a national sport in their country for years past. Then there was the lone American entrant, Fred Mason, a soldier who had thumbed his way from his unit in Germany to attach himself to the British contingent, to borrow our parachutes and our aeroplanes, and to give us in return a drawling description of disaster that was to serve us as a slogan when things went badly. 'Fellas,' said Fred, limping back from a descent in which he had missed the airfield entirely to land in the lethal concrete clutter of a half-built house, 'fellas, don't you ever do what ah just done; ain't no percentage in it, no percentage at all. When Mason hit that masonry, ah bloody near busted mah butt.' Before the championships had ended each one of us, one way or another, had come close to bustin' his butt, and Fred's phrasing seemed somehow to ease both the pain and the self-criticism. It was with real sadness that we learned later of his death in a gliding accident, and yet we could scarcely pretend surprise. Fred Mason was a deep-dyed, damn-the-lot-of-them, let's-get-on-with-it aeronautical adventurer, and his courage pushed persistently at his luck.

Finest of all, though, were the Italians, the gayest, the bravest, the most genuinely sporting sportsmen I have ever known. I wined with them, dined with them, talked far into the night with them, and above all watched them with delight and admiration in the air. Enrico Milani, a weather-beaten little walnut of a man, wedge-shaped, would come plummeting down head-first from five thousand feet, legs spread wide and arms folded calmly across his chest, a flying dart aimed straight and true at the target, before trusting his life to an ancient parachute I would not have used to wrap up my laundry. He was an old hand, a sky-diver who had experienced from high altitude the paralysing terror of the back-down spin, when your legs whip round and round above you, faster and faster, and the noise of the wind goes whuff-whuff-whuff in your ears, and in the sheer enervating nausea of it all you need every ounce of strength, both physical and moral, just to reach across your chest to the ripcord before you resign yourself

51

to death. I listened, enthralled, to his description of the phenomenon, and years later I had cause to be thankful that I did, for
only the knowledge of what I must force myself to do enabled me
during one demonstration descent to save myself, with seconds to
spare, as I dived sick and spinning towards the ground.

Less serious-minded than Milani was the Italian champion,
Giorgio Rinaldi, a burly, olive-skinned extrovert whose account
of how he had come to his title seemed to sum up what parachuting,
to an Italian, is all about, and to serve as a reminder that the nation
whose soldiers in their unhappy thousands had surrendered without spirit in the North African desert was also the nation whose
individual heroes had crewed with incredible courage the first
midget submarines. 'Canorrozzo, the last champion,' said Rinaldi,
beaming, 'he and I used to jump out, same height, see which one
of us could be last to reach for the ripcord. You understan'?
Last down's a cissy. One day my friend get too clever, leave it too
late; miss the handle first grab, don't get no chance for a second—
phfft, I'm the new champion, he's a hole in the ground. Bad luck
on Canorrozzo—real nice fella.'

It was Rinaldi again, a couple of days later, who jerked a
contemptous thumb at the Russians' acoustic chronometer, an
ingenious little airborne alarm-clock, fitted into their helmets, that
rang loud and clear at the precise moment for opening the parachute after a long delayed-drop. In competition such delays, of
twenty or thirty seconds, must be timed exactly, for points are
deducted for every tenth of a second above or below the time
stipulated for the test. 'You want to match instrument against
instrument, you go to an International Trade Fair. Come parachuting, you match man against man. *These* my instruments,'
pointing to his shining eyes, '*these* my stop-watch and altimeter.
I jump out, I watch the ground; when I can pick out my friends
I'm getting close, when the green grass start waving—time to
pull, and how. Points? The hell with points, *ragazzo*; have fun.
You watch, one day I show you a real jump, starting way outside

the airfield border, I'll swim right in to the target. You never seen anything like it.'

He was as good as his word, swooping swiftly down the sky in a breathtaking demonstration, years ahead of its time, of the now widely-practised art of 'tracking,' shifting the body-weight and attitude to steer across as well as downwards at speeds of well over a hundred miles an hour. I watched him unbelieving and in that, as I now know, I was not alone. In 1967, thirteen years later, I saw Giorgio Rinaldi again, or I saw, rather, pictures of him, grey-looking and haggard, front-page on every paper, key-man in the biggest international spy-ring scandal since the war, arrested in Italy as an agent of the Russians, operating in espionage throughout the European countries of the United Nations. Poor Rinaldi, victim of his own exuberance, extravagance, and skill. Spotted and assessed by the other side, flattered and suckered and bought into treachery, ruined and disgraced, punished and imprisoned, and all because in the air he had all the talents and knew no fear. Some day, no doubt, I shall tell my eager grand-children 'Once I knew a spy.' And they will thrill to the thought of it; but I should have told them, in any case, 'Once I knew Rinaldi.'*

I shall tell them, too, about the parachuting, about the thrum-ming of the engine and the whistle of the wind as the aircraft droned steadily across the airfield, five thousand feet above the human race; about the tight-lipped concentration of those last crucial moments on the wing, clutching at the struts, defying the slipstream, judging the exact moment before dropping away, ever faster, into the timeless exhilaration of the long free-fall, when the air is a cushion resilient beneath the body; about the exultant, palpitating thrill of thudding hard into the very heart of the target, snug and high-scoring between the very arms of the cross; about the slow terror of recovering consciousness, tumbling

* On Friday, 15th December 1967, George Rinaldi was sentenced in Turin to 15 years' imprisonment for spying for Russia. Angela Marja, his wife, was sentenced to 11 years.

through the air, to see dimly through blood-soaked eyes the inexorable sweep of the stop-watch and to realise I had been falling senseless, stunned and blinded by broken equipment, for nearly thirteen seconds, with my parachute unopened and the ground rushing murderously up at me. I shall tell them all this, whether they like it or not; I shall doubtless be a thundering bore.

It was on the last night of the Championships, at a banquet in Vichy, that I had real conversation with my Russian. This time, for once, the officials could not interfere; marooned in their dignity at the top table, they were far out of listening range and their charges, the new world champions, were visibly, vocally, happily relaxed. So was I, until one chance, well-intended remark by the Soviet competitor at my elbow jerked me wide-eyed out of my euphoria. I had congratulated him on his and his country's success in winning the Championships yet again, in comparison to our own sixth placing, and modesty, beyond question, was in his mind as he answered: 'You are very kind, but really, it would have been disgraceful if we had not won. Our team has been training together for two years for this one event and we are, after all, the picked representatives, the best performers, out of three hundred thousand parachutists in our country.'

I was no longer an amateur sky-diver, but a professional officer. I asked him, very slowly and distinctly, to repeat himself; he did, and his companions, amused at my incredulity, confirmed what he had said. 'We have no class, no money problems in our recreation and sport; a boy or a girl shows talent, interest, we offer training and facilities at the State's expense. This is our Soviet system, and it is good, don't you agree?'

Sure; bloody marvellous, a benevolent, let's all be equal, let's all be healthy democracy, and our teams—we've just proved it—are the best in the world. But I thought of the *Hitler Jugend*, and I thought, in horror, of this ghostly contingent of more than a quarter of a million potential enemies, trained to drop silently from the skies, and I thought of our own pundits in Whitehall adamant, as they were to remain for years, in their blinkered

conviction that there was no military significance in the development of free-fall parachuting. They have come, at last, to their
senses, and our *corps d'élite*, the Special Air Service, has been for
some years amongst our finest exponents of the art, but in 1954
the ripcord parachute, to authority, was precisely what it had
been throughout the thirty-five years since its introduction into
the Services—a life-saver, and no more than that. With that
conversation in Vichy the World Sky-Diving Championships, for
me, were suddenly a light-hearted thing of the past. I went back
to England, back to the Air Force, back to think about my newly-
acquired experience and to wonder how I could put it to work.

CHAPTER 5   The Private Pupil

1954

Fate, however, once again interrupted my plans, with an episode which at first seemed merely a pleasant distraction, but soon became of fundamental significance to my career and my life. That autumn I trained, for the first and last time in my life, a private pupil in the art of parachuting.

Jennifer Cameron Hall was seventeen, slender and very pretty. She was also the daughter of a friend of mine, Alan Cameron Hall, who had retired after thirty-five years as a Shell executive in Shanghai and three years, with his family, in a Japanese prison camp, to run a most delightful pub in Farnham, midway between my Aldershot headquarters and Frensham Common where we did the bulk of our parachute training. This was the haven to which I would make my way after long days on the dropping zone to relax with friends both Service and civilian in the saloon bar, and it was on one such evening that I first met Jenny, home for the week-end from Romanoff's school for Young Ladies, an academy that had nurtured amongst other English misses one now world-famous in show business, Petula Clark.

It was not at this first meeting, however, but several weeks later, that Jenny made the remark I had long since learned to greet with a silent groan; 'D'you know, I'd love to make a parachute jump.'

Now in my experience the number of people, especially attractive young girls, who would 'love to make a parachute jump' is almost exactly equalled by the number who veer sharply sideways when one suggests a day for doing it, and every instructor in the game has learned to dread the gushing aerial aspirants on the cocktail circuit and to recognise them for the pain in the eardrum that they are.

56

This girl, however, was not gushing. She was speaking to me quietly and privately as a friend of the family, and I found myself convinced without argument that she meant what she said. After speaking with her parents I laid down my conditions for the deal, and harsh conditions they were. Jenny was to train at least four times a week for as long as I considered necessary and at the end of it all, if I said 'No', there were to be no tears, no tantrums, no recriminations, no appeals to my sense of fair play. I was promising nothing but a series of punishing training sessions to establish whether, in my opinion, she had the capacity to parachute competently and with complete safety.

Jenny worked, my goodness, how she worked. Night after night for nearly five weeks she was reduced almost to tears in the training area I had rigged up for her in her father's garage; swinging in a parachute harness to learn her flight drill, jumping from a high ramp to master the art of landing 'all round the clock'—forward-left, back-right, directly backwards, directly forwards, side-right, side-left, always adjusting her body in a split second to absorb in the best possible position the shock of landing, receiving the impact on feet clamped tight together, channelling it up two legs locked together as one, passing it diagonally and diminishing it over her bottom and across her back to vanish over the further shoulder. I took her several times to the full-scale training hangar I had constructed at the Airborne Forces Depot, and watched her reactions closely as she moved like a monkey on the swings and slides and practice towers. She went through the mill bruised, scared, but uncomplaining, and she was good, a naturally talented, plucky performer. I applied to the Ministry of Civil Aviation for special dispensation to allow me to despatch her on her first jump before she had reached what was then the minimum age for parachutists, eighteen (it has since been reduced by one year) and, on the strength of my International and Instructor's Licence, permission was granted.

The private grass airfield at Denham seemed the ideal place for the jump, and for the actual launching of my protégée, I called

57

in the aid of Dumbo Willans, the steadiest, most competent, most comforting coach in the business. I would have liked to despatch Jenny myself, for I was her teacher and mine was the voice she knew and trusted, but my place was on the dropping zone with my electrical loud-hailer, to guide her through the flight and landing routine after she had left the aeroplane; Dumbo, I knew, would see her safely away, having nursed her through the nervy, God-awful moment that carries the parachutist from the cabin of an Auster to a crouched preparatory position on the strut beneath the single high wing.

Never have I seen a more confident beginner. Jenny was all smiles as she clambered aboard the aircraft, and I was the one who suffered the agonies of uncertainty, fear, and responsibility as I walked slowly out to the dropping area accompanied by the airport manager, a burly individual in a Harris tweed sports jacket. I stood beside him, loud-hailer clutched in my hand, as we watched the little aircraft spiral upwards, level off, and start its run-in at fifteen hundred feet. It droned interminably towards us, and as it crossed the airfield boundary I could see the little pale blue dot that was my pupil, my friend's only daughter, clambering out to her precarious perch beneath the wing. I cursed her, cursed her father for giving his permission, cursed above all my own stupidity in having placed myself in this position of unbearable, unthinkable responsibility. Supposing I had missed some vital point in my last-minute instructions? Suppose this girl, a mere youngster, should 'freeze' as had been known to happen to first-time jumpers? Suppose . . . ? I sweated silently and wished myself dead.

'There she goes,' exclaimed the airfield manager, and sure enough the little dot was falling away from the aeroplane, now over the middle of the field. Three seconds, I had told her, three seconds of slow acceleration that would carry her well clear of the aircraft before pulling the ripcord. I heard myself counting out loud;

'One thousand, Two thousand'—what was I worrying about?

She was in a perfect sky-diving position, back arched, head high, arms outstretched in an immaculate swallow-dive. What a pupil; what an instructor.

'Three thousand, Four thousand, Five thousand', and the sickness was rising, cold and stifling, but still she did nothing. She was falling fast now, far below the limits of safety, still in a perfect, graceful, controlled position, but still making no move towards the ripcord. 'Seven thousand, Eight thousand.' Jenny was down to less than six hundred feet, only seconds from death, and my bellow had changed almost to a scream—'Pull, pull, P U L L.'

Suddenly her right arm flashed inwards across her body and the ripcord was plucked, clean as a whistle, from its housing. The canopy blossomed open with a resounding slap, her speed changed suddenly from about a hundred miles an hour to perhaps fifteen, and she steered the parachute in like a veteran, responding instantly and correctly to my almost incoherent instructions. A controlled approach, adjusting the body for a side-left landing, a smooth roll on touch-down, and she was up on her feet and running towards me, grinning like an urchin. The airfield manager said quietly, 'Can I have my arm back now?'; on his wrist, pressed there through the tweed of his jacket and the flannel of his shirt, were five purple bruises, the imprints of my clutching fingers.

Greeting this terrifying brat, uncertain whether to kiss her or spank her, I found the matter resolved for me. Flinging herself into my arms, Jennifer Cameron Hall, the newest, youngest parachutist in England, burbled happily, 'Oh, Doddy, I'm so terribly sorry. I know you said three seconds, but it was so wonderful I just couldn't bring myself to pull the ripcord and end it all. You'd taught me all the drill and I knew I'd be all right—and I am, aren't I? Are you very cross with me?'

There is only one way to take care of a girl like that. For the second time in my life I sought her parents' permission, and for the second time it was granted. Not long afterwards, Jenny and I were married.

Just two tree-lined miles up the road from my Aldershot head-quarters stood Farnborough, at the time of my meeting with Jenny one of the most exciting spots in England. It was not beautiful like the Hampshire and Surrey villages that surround it, nor was there anything especially attractive about the quiet avenues of shabby-genteel houses that characterise the district—but that was to look at only one side of the main highway that runs right through it. On the other side of that road, screened from the public gaze by green palings and by the natural declivity dipping downwards to Laffans Plain, lies the aerodrome, the centre ten or fifteen years ago of the most telling developments in British aviation.

This was no ordinary airfield occupied by a few squadrons of bombers or fighters, no echoing terminal for tourists. At the Aldershot end of the airfield, opposite the busy bars and the comfortable lounges of the Queen's Hotel, stood the long blue-carpeted Mess of the Empire Test Pilots' School, one of the finest flying academies in the world, where men of many nations slaved for months on end over the advanced intricacies of their profession; less than a mile along the road, through the main gates with their uniformed police, streamed workers in their daily thousands, scientists and draughtsmen, fitters and electricians, plumbers and physicists, component cogs in the vast mechanism of the Royal Aircraft Establishment. And behind them, scattered around the concrete runways, were the places where they worked, hangars and laboratories and offices, with here and there some assembly of special significance like the long low buildings of the Institute of Aviation Medicine, the catapult sledge on which men subjected themselves to experiments in the effects of swift acceleration and sudden stops, or the two towering tanks of green-painted iron in which whole aircraft could be shaken in controlled vibration to the point of destruction—a legacy, these last, from the tragic aerial disintegration of the early Comets. Farnborough was not a place about which one could feel impassive; it was from here, in the infancy of flight, that Cody had flown his kites, tethered to a tree-stump that stands there still, it was here, in 1952, that John Derry's jet, exploding on its high-speed run, had spread death amongst the packed thousands enjoying the Air Show, it was here that some of the finest aviators in the world had a base from which to explore the new frontiers of flying.

In the No. 1 Mess, used both by the Services and by civilians of officer status, one met men of many and diverse talents and it was arguable—indeed argued, heatedly and frequently—which group of them contributed most to the purpose of the place as a whole. A Senior Wrangler who in calmer times might have been found amongst the courts and cloisters of Cambridge might be seen here, talking higher mathematics with a rather mousy little mannikin, a filing-clerk in appearance and demeanour, acknowledged by people who understood such things to be one of Europe's leading authorities on rocketry; a slim Squadron Leader, sipping sherry, might be heard to compare its flavour favourably with the bitter liquid to be found in tiny quantities within the shells of certain snails, on which disgusting beverage he had been quenching his thirst for days as part of his research into the survival problems of aircrew brought down in inhospitable territory; a technical representative of Decca, evangelist rather than salesman, would be explaining earnestly in a corner why his Company's navigational aids were the most efficient in the world. And amongst all these worthy men, somehow separated from them however warm the social exchanges, wandered a race apart, an aristocracy not so much of merit as of *mystique*, the test pilots.

To pluralise them, though statistically correct, is in one sense irrelevant, almost misleading. To the general public the test pilot,

61

like the cowboy, is less an individual than a type, a composite and traditional character shaped and conditioned by his vocation and his environment. He may have worries and weaknesses, quarrels with his wife, mortgage repayments overdue, colds in the head, but by the outsider he is seen only in the cockpit, facing a singularly unpleasant and imminent death with the calm conviction that his skill and nerve will see him through and the enviable, admirable philosophy that if it doesn't—ah well, it's all in the game, and what better way could a fellow choose to go? And the strange thing is that in all this melodramatic B-movie claptrap there is the germ of essential truth. The job, inescapably, is a dangerous one—in nine black months at Edwards Air Force Base, one of America's most famous fields, sixty-two test pilots died—and one of its fundamental conditions is that the danger must often be quite deliberately induced, which sets it importantly apart from that, say, of the coal-miner, the deep sea diver, or the spiderman. To live with such a condition of one's employment means to come to terms with it, firmly and permanently, both on and off the job, and the latter is often more difficult than the former; the man whose nerves are steel-steady as he flies an aircraft to the point of real danger may find himself funking the explanation to his wife as to why he does it and continues to do it despite his responsibilities to her and to their children. He may find it harder still, if he cares for her, to justify his decision to himself when there are other jobs for the asking and younger men queueing up to take the risks—but the decision, no matter how much he cares for her, will stand; if it doesn't, he has been in the wrong trade all along, and if she cannot understand that, and accept it, he has married the wrong girl. The strains on both sides can be considerable, and the marriage mortality rate within the trade is a high one.

It is this acceptance of deliberate risk and its attendant problems, I think, that makes the test man run true to type in certain facets of his personality and his way of life. Agreed that a certain sort of man is attracted to the work in the first place, it is none the less true that the job, over the years, tends to foster and to accentuate the essential similarities among the men who carry it out. Take drinking, for example; the days of the bloodshot neurotic who flew on alcohol are long gone, if indeed they ever existed—but amongst the many test pilots I have known there are precious few who did not like their liquor and quite a number who loved it like a brother, sometimes a big brother on whose shoulder they leant heavily for guidance and support. But—with one glorious exception, one of God's own eccentrics whose first action on reaching the cockpit was invariably to draw heavily on his oxygen-tube to dispel the carpenters hammering busily in his brainpan—the drinking was always after, not before; the aim was not to screw courage to the sticking point, but to ease off tension after the effort, unassisted, had been made. Many a test man happy in his work has been genuinely surprised in his realisation later of what it has cost him. And he has put the thought aside because such thoughts are uncomfortable, and unbecoming to his image, in which he himself half believes, and he has gone out and got gloriously drunk in the company of other happy half believers like himself, and he has felt very much better for it and has gone back to the job the next morning convinced that all he needs is a couple of rounds of golf or a good night in bed with a blonde. He is lucky, the test pilot, because he is never, of course, afraid.

He is lucky too because he likes his own breed and is happy in its company. There is no stronger evidence of the essential shared quality of the test pilots than the fact that they are fundamentally fond of each other; among them there are of course close friendships, personal preferences, and occasional enmities, but never, not once in a fair number of years, have I heard one run down the work or the achievements of another, and often I have listened with delight to X's exploits described in tones of awe by Y, whom I have known to be himself a man whose courage could frighten his friends. This *camaraderie* is neither fortuitous nor hard to understand; any human relationship is off to a good start if it includes reciprocal respect, any man is at least worth a hearing if

63

his basic qualities are known to include a high degree of fortitude, and there is one other thing that makes the test pilot happiest in the company of men like himself—with them there is no need to explain, to answer damn-fool questions like 'was it awful?', to keep his temper with the plump young insurance broker who 'fancied test flying m'self at one time, but it must get rather monotonous, surely, with the same old routine day after day?' Communication with outsiders is fraught with dangers of under-statement—'affected bastard, isn't he, all silent service and stiff upper lip?'—and of over-statement—'laying it on a bit thick, wasn't he, after all it's his job isn't it?'—and plain rudeness when control has suddenly snapped—'what on earth did he fly off the handle like that for? I only asked if his navigator would have got away with it if they'd had a bit more altitude—dammit, I wasn't blaming *him*.' The test pilot does not like talking with strangers about his job; at large in the outside world he is in essence a loner, with one important part of his make-up wrapped up securely against intrusion. The wrappings may be morose, flippant, even belligerent, but whatever their nature they have one thing in common: they are protective.

In the Mess at Farnborough things were different; here flying was simply shop, and the pilots talked it as enthusiastically and interminably as any other professional group. Any evening might find the bar full of the famous; not only British pilots like Neville Duke, Peter Twiss, Bill Bedford, the two Rolys, Falk and Bea-mont, but, on occasion, their legendary American counterparts—Chuck Yeager, Scott Crossfield, Bob White, all these and many others flitted in and out of the Farnborough scene, and the whole aerodrome was charged with an excitement and sense of purpose in keeping with the gigantic strides being made almost monthly in the progress of military aviation. Jet-propulsion was well out of its infancy and revelling in the lusty developments, difficulties, and exhilarations of its adolescence; stories and anecdotes were told and re-told with relish. 'Did you ever hear about Chuck Yeager flying chase for Bill Bridgeman? Bill was in the Skyrocket, going supersonic straight into the sun, and he couldn't read his instrument panel. Suddenly Yeager moves in above and ahead of him, using his port wing as a bloody parasol—Bill can read everything easily in the shade, and over the intercom comes Yeager, soft and sweet as molasses; "that better, son?" I reckon Bridgeman could have murdered him, for he hadn't said a word about his problem, but he was mighty grateful all the same. Chuck Yeager ... what a bloody man.' And then there was the one about Roly Falk, chief test pilot of Avro, who could be seen, sleek as any stockbroker, sipping cognac in a corner of the bar. 'Brought the Vulcan over for the Air Show, reckoned he'd kill two birds with one stone by showing what it looks like and what it can do all at once. So on the first day he took that bloody bomber off the runway and straight, I swear it, into a slow roll, as if he'd been flying a Spitfire. Honest to God, the sky seemed full of it, just one huge white wedge turning gently round and round like a bleeding mannequin—the Controller nearly had apoplexy. Roly explained afterwards it seemed the simplest way of showing just how big the Vulcan is, but they wouldn't let him do it again. Pity ... it would have stolen the show.'

Such shop-talk evenings, especially at the weekends, stretched far into the night, and it was on one of them that I found, quite by accident, the sign-post to what I was seeking, some employment of my parachuting experience more purposeful than the circus stuff in which, at the time, I was so frequently engaged. Since coming back to Britain as the only serving officer with practical knowledge of the problems and techniques of the free fall I had been constantly on tap for lectures, dinners, and demonstration drops; drops easy and drops difficult, drops from the windswept wing of a Tiger Moth and from the cabined comfort of a helicopter, the sky-diver's dream come true. 'Back a bit, please, pilot—we've overshot the target. Perfect. Thank you so much—goodbye.' It was all good fun, providing both incentive and opportunity for constant improvement in personal performance, but most of it was contributing nothing more worthwhile and significant than a vicarious thrill to a few thousand spectators. There had been some high points—a conversation with Montgomery, set up by Colonel Pine-Coffin, in which the Field-Marshal had struck straight to the root of my story of Russia's parachutists; 'Very interesting; sounds like a job for our fellows, not you Air Force men.' 'His fellows,' the soldiers of the Special Air Service, are now the best sky-divers in Britain, and it takes no great brain to realise that a small detachment of them suitably armed and strategically deployed could be worth its weight in heavy water in anything short of global warfare. A good belly-laugh at the timorous time-servers of the Air Ministry, whose response to a report outlining the possible utilisation of a small nucleus of trained sky-divers within the Service was to impose an immediate ban on all free-fall parachuting, even by the staff of the Parachute School; now the national Press and the Recruiting Offices are full of quite splendid pictures of the School's demonstration team. But someone in the meantime, before committing himself to the decision that made this possible, must have made quite certain of his knighthood or his O.B.E. It was, no doubt about it, a damned risky business; just one fatality, with the attendant adverse publicity, might have wrecked a chap's whole career. But my personal concern, in any case, was not with strategy but with survival, and it was in the Mess at Farnborough that I discovered what I must do, which path I must travel.

I was telling some of the boys about a recent demonstration drop in which, out of curiosity, I had made my exit from an aircraft held deliberately in a vertical spin, and at once the questions were coming at me, fast, frequent, and to the point.

'What was the g force, and was it hard to get out of your seat?'

'Which is the right moment to jump?'

'On the inside or the outside of the spin?'

'How close did you come to the tailplane, and how long did you wait before pulling the plug?'

'Did the aeroplane follow you down or did you drop right away from it?'

Answering as best I could, embroiled in the intricacies of the discussion, I began to realise that these men, my friends, to whom military parachuting with its statichutes, its slow aircraft in steady flight, its unhurried, premeditated preparations for departure, was a thing apart, took a very different view of the free-fall experience I was acquiring day by day. This was something that could suddenly matter to any one of them, flying as they did in a great range of different aircraft some with ejection seats and many others without; these boys had no wish to parachute, they hated quite naturally the very thought of it—but if they had to do it, they wanted to be able to talk about it afterwards. Some of them subscribed, or pretended to subscribe, to the old maxim, 'What's the use of practising something that has to be perfect first time?' but even they were only too willing to absorb the lessons of another man's experience if the knowledge might save their necks in an emergency they had some reason, by the law of probability, to expect.

Realising this, I realised too that I might, after all, have something more to contribute to flying than a few hours of light entertainment. First, though, I must extend my knowledge of my subject; I decided to go back to school. I continued to parachute whenever possible, and I experimented, self-taught, with Rinaldi's technique of 'tracking'; on other drops I let myself fall limp and unresisting, an improbable Petrouchka, through thousands of feet in an attempt to establish a pattern of probabilities for the first-time, emergency jumper, and to figure out for myself the best, essentially simple advice I could offer him against the occasion. I combed the libraries and read everything on the subject I could lay my hands on, and I started my own one-pupil correspondence college with every really experienced parachutist I could trace; I contacted men in France, in America, in Canada, Italy, and Jugoslavia—even, once and profitably, in Mexico—and not one of them, not one, failed to respond enthusiastically to my quest for knowledge. I had a manual of advanced instruction from the French school and I had a treatise on the training of the Smoke

Jumpers, the men who parachute down into danger in their bid to quell great forest fires; I talked with Dumbo Willans—'never trust the boffins, Doddy; they'd drop you in a hurricane rather than set their precious programme back by twenty-four hours,' and I sat shirt-sleeved in his hotel room with a vice-president of the Pioneer Airchute Company of America as he explained to me what was happening to the airborne industry in the United States.

Even my normal duties as Liaison Officer to the Airborne Forces, could to some extent, I found, be harnessed to the drive towards attainment of my new objective. An important facet of my work, apart from lecturing to the new airborne soldiers and supervising the continuation training of the old hands, was to receive visitors, mostly military but occasionally political, from many of the NATO countries and to show them as much as time would allow of the training and technical developments in British parachuting. With my Colonel's blessing I now began to extend this programme to include conducted visits to various outside establishments; I took many of my visitors to the G.Q. Company to meet Sir Raymond Quilter, who was unfailingly hospitable and informative, and I then arranged one or two special sorties to Denham to find out what was happening in the development of the most exciting of all forms of parachuting—ejection. It was on one of these visits, in 1954, that I had the first of many meetings with the man who was destined to give essential purpose to my life, James Martin.

Part Two

The Inventor

CHAPTER 7

James Martin

1929-1944

A tough, stocky, baby-faced Irishman from Grossgar, County Down, James Martin was and always has been a 'pilots' designer,' an engineer true to the basic principles of his profession but impatient to the point of verbal impurity with ultra-cautious theorists without the courage of their calculations. His earliest patented invention, the first of several hundred, had been registered back in 1911, in the infancy of flight, 'when aeroplanes only had two speeds—too fast and too slow. I dreamed up a little gadget to tell the pilots which of the two sins they were committing,' —and he had been head of his own aircraft company since 1929.

In that grim year Jimmy Martin came to Denham with two employees, a few machine tools, and a burning ambition to build aeroplanes, new, exciting aeroplanes that would bear the stamp of their designer's ideas. It was madness, of course, for a small manufacturer with limited capital; investment both by Government and by industry had been cut to the bone, speculation was for fools, and aviation was a highly speculative business. As if that were not enough, Martin's ideas were in themselves revolutionary. De Havilland, Vickers, all the giants of the industry, drawing on their experience of wartime production, had pinned their hopes on biplanes, and the first monoplane, civil or military, had yet to come into general service; Martin's basic concept was of a lightweight, low-wing monoplane. It was with this in mind that he had come to Denham, and Eric Stevens, who was with him then and is with him still, recalls these early days as he gazes out from the boardroom of a Company that now employs more than twelve hundred skilled men.

'There were just four buildings here, one shed made of wooden slats and breeze-blocks, and three derelict army huts abandoned since the '14-18 war. It was a sad collection, musty and peeling like a deserted movie set. There were no roads, no drainage—we drew our only water from the marsh that surrounded us. But the Guv'-nor, he stood in the middle of it all with Jim Clampitt on one side of him and me on the other, stuck his chin out, and had the damned cheek to call it the Martin Aircraft Works.'

Very soon he had the right to. Working sweat-shop hours for starvation wages, the director and staff of the new company swept out their shabby habitat, oiled and burnished their equipment, and began to build. They built—but of course—upon Martin's dreams and blue-prints, and within three months he had inched his way so far out along a fiscal limb that the new monoplane was all but completed. The fuselage, tail unit, and undercarriage had been constructed, the Gipsy engine ground-tested and installed; all it needed was a pair of wings. At this point the limb snapped, overloaded with production costs, and the aircraft did not survive the fall. Martin did. The aeroplane went to the scrap-heap; Martin once more went to work. With the financial backing of Francis Francis, an air-minded businessman who believed in him, he retained his foothold in the aviation business by his invention, *inter alia*, of a patented Wind Indicator, a vast, tubular, arrow-shaped weathercock, balanced and designed to point the path to safety for pilots approaching the shapeless grass airfields of the time. More sensitive than a wind-sock, more positive than smoke, this swinging steel shaft could be festooned with lights to facilitate a landing even at night, and it was installed at airfields both in Britain and abroad.

* * *

Always, however, the dream was of aeroplanes, and by the early 'thirties Martin was ready once again to challenge the big boys, the established manufacturers. The lessons learned from his earlier, abortive efforts were now applied to a more ambitious

72

project, a tandem two-seater powered by one 160 h.p. Napier engine, and this time he built it, wings and all. Compact, cheap, ahead of its time, the new aircraft won the plaudits of the professional Press for the thoughtful qualities of its design; Martin was running true to form. Typical of this thoughtfulness was a built-in facility for folding back the wings, so reducing the span from thirty-seven feet to a mere thirteen and thereby saving expensive hangar-space, and the provision of an electrical starter to obviate the time-honoured but frustrating and sometimes dangerous chore of prop-swinging. The aircraft, in short, was a pretty one, comfortable and well appointed, but it had yet to prove its worth where it mattered most—in the air. Martin had done his work, made his contribution; the rest was up to his new partner, test pilot, and co-director in what was by now the Martin-Baker Aircraft Company.

Captain Valentine Baker, M.C., A.F.C. was one of the most distinguished as well as most brilliant British aviators of the era between the two world wars. He had been a teacher as well as an exponent of the art of flying, a teacher whose pupils had included not only the Prince of Wales, now Duke of Windsor, and his brother the Duke of Kent, but also Britain's darling of the age, heroine of epic flights and of a best-selling popular song named after her—Amy Johnson. He was a quiet man, modest and unassuming to the point of shyness, but he could fly an aeroplane calmly and precisely until its struts screamed. In April 1933 he took the M.B.1. into the air and put it through its paces, and in this and subsequent test flights he progressed steadily from the straight and level to the aerobatic, proving by the end of the programme that the M.B.1 was technically and aerodynamically sound. It might well have been the forerunner of a stable of light aircraft designed for private ownership, as its designer had intended, but Europe by now was preparing for war, and the time had come for Martin to turn his talents to the production of a machine that would carry armament.

Martin's decision to build a fighter aircraft, a simple and logical

73

enough change of plans under the political circumstances of the time, was the first move in one of the minor mysteries of the war. To a nation rightly proud of the countless victories notched up by the Spitfire and the Hurricane it might come as something of a surprise to learn that the first British eight-gun fighter, and an exceptionally good one, was neither of these legendary aeroplanes, but James Martin's M.B.2. In a framework of tubular steel, designed on the principles confirmed by the success of the M.B.1, he fitted a special Napier Dagger 24-cylinder engine that could produce more than a thousand horse-power on take-off. The speed achieved in level flight was three hundred and fifty miles an hour, and the machine was fully aerobatic and highly manoeuvrable despite the fact that for simplicity it had been fitted with a fixed under-carriage. Even this unwieldy appendage, which could later have been made retractable by means of a modification already available, did not prevent Valentine Baker from staging an aerial demonstration that had the aviation Press hurrying back to their typewriters.

Martin, understandably, was jubilant about the success of his aeroplane and about the glowing praise being showered upon it; he could scarely have foreseen that he was about to enter the roughest, most frustrating, and most tragic period of his professional life. The Air Force pilots, many of them senior officers, who had seen and handled the new aircraft, were enthusiastic over what they felt certain would be a new and potent weapon in their sadly archaic armoury. Few of them still harboured doubts that before very long they would have both cause and occasion to make use of it. It was not only James Martin, therefore, who suffered shock and a sense of angry bewilderment when the news filtered down from above that no order would be placed to put the M.B.2 into production. He pleaded and lobbied, argued and fought, pointing out passionately that only minor modifications, such as are introduced to every new military machine during its development, were needed to provide Britain's air defence with the hitting-power it so palpably required. Useless; the dead hand of officialdom was upon the project, and there was nothing more to be said. He had made too many enemies at court.

It was at this time, perhaps more than any other, that Martin exhibited amongst his other qualities a resilience equalled only by his versatility. Savagely slapped down in his capacity as a designer of aircraft, he bounced immediately and importantly up again as an inventor of their vital components, producing not one but a series of ingenious devices destined to play an extensive if highly specialised part in equipping the aircraft of the Royal Air Force for their wartime operations. Of these inventions one of the earliest was an extraordinary piece of equipment known as the Cartridge Operated Cable Cutter, a system of explosive shears fitted to the wings of bomber aircraft that enabled them to slice their way clean through the steel curtain of the enemy's defensive balloon barrages. Set in the leading edge of the wings, the cutter would first gather up the lethal cable, then press it against an anvil, and finally, with the explosion of the cartridge, sever it as the aircraft flew on unimpeded. More than a quarter of a million of these aeronautical cow-catchers were attached to the warplanes of Bomber Command, to whose aircrews the psychological benefit was almost as immense as the practical. They did not even have to wait long to discover whether the device actually worked effectively, for as early as 1940 it was largely instrumental in clearing the skies for the important and highly-publicised raid on the Dortmund-Ems Canal, the operation in which Squadron Leader Learoyd won one of the first Victoria Crosses awarded to the Royal Air Force. The bomber force, thundering low over the target, found the area swept free from cables by the two Handley-Page Hampdens, fitted with the new device, that had gone in ahead of them, snipping away with their explosive scissors to send the balloons floating harmlessly out of the area.

In fighter aircraft, too, Martin's inventiveness was soon making its importance felt, and two of his major contributions stemmed, one directly and the other indirectly, from the experiences and the outcome of the Battle of Britain. The first, an unconscious

75

foreshadowing of the life's work that still lay far ahead of him, was the design and manufacture of a system that sliced seconds off the time required to abandon a Spitfire in an emergency; a man could get out, all right, but with fuel tanks blazing or altitude running low the moments spent in forcing open the canopy of the cockpit might spell the difference between life and death. Martin's answer was a deceptively simple combination of locking-pins, cables, and a little red rubber ball—jerk the ball, and the hood would fly away, ripped clear of the fuselage by the force of the slipstream. He fitted the modification to a Spitfire loaned to him for experiment—a minor change that could later be accomplished, even under field conditions, in a mere seven man-hours of skilled labour—and he handed the machine over for testing to an officer of the Royal Air Force already famous for his exploits outside the world of flying. Wing Commander D. O. Finlay, D.F.C., A.F.C., had made his mark in the Service as a professional pilot of courage and resource; he was also, as an Olympic hurdler, one of the idols of the British sporting public.

Finlay's assignment on this occasion, however, was purely professional and unknown to his admirers. He took the Spitfire through its trials, and he suffered, not once but repeatedly, the swift transition from the comfort of the enclosed cockpit to the screaming uncertainty of the slipstream whistling high-pitched into his cabin. When he finally jettisoned the hood with the aircraft notching up more than five hundred miles an hour, and suffered no ill-effects in the process, he had proved his point, and Martin's. The modification was made standard for all Spitfires, and the company turned out the new canopies in their thousands. How many lives were saved can only be guessed at, but one of them at least was a matter of public as well as personal concern.

On 9th August 1941, Wing Commander Douglas Bader, D.S.O., D.F.C., one of the bravest men in the history of flight, was shot down in a dogfight with the Germans, twenty-four thousand feet above Le Touquet. A grim enough experience for any man, this incident put Bader through the tortures of the damned as he sat there and struggled, trapped by his artificial legs in the cockpit of an aircraft shrieking out of control towards the earth. Half-in and half-out of the machine, battered and buffeted close to unconsciousness as the speed of the dive built up to more than five hundred miles an hour, he had plunged downwards through twenty thousand feet of sky before, by some minor miracle, the straps of his leg-harness snapped and he was sucked bodily from the aeroplane seconds before it exploded into wreckage on the ground. For those precious seconds, Douglas Bader had James Martin to thank; his Spitfire was one of those already fitted with the new jettison device, and his first action, when disaster struck, had been 'to yank the little rubber ball above my head and watch the roof ripped off my Perspex prison.'

* * *

The other by-product of the Battle of Britain that Martin created was occasioned by the Germans' reaction to their defeat. For when Hitler and Goering, infuriated by the failure of Operation Eagle to obliterate the striking-power of the Royal Air Force, decided to intensify the ferocity and magnitude of the night raids against the civilian population of London, there was an immediate requirement for a heavily armed night-fighter force to meet and to break up the attacks. The aircraft available were both sparse and inadequate, and of these the most promising for the purpose were a number of American-built Douglas Havocs, suitable in all but their fire-power, a pea-shooter complement of four Browning 303 machine-guns. From the Ministry of Aircraft Production Air Chief Marshal Sir Wilfred Freeman came hurriedly to Martin, asking if his company would collaborate with another to produce some answer to the problem; Martin without hesitation declined. He was prepared, however, to 'go it alone' if the Ministry would make available one aircraft for trial installation, and Sir Wilfred reluctantly agreed. What he got in return for his confidence was not so much modification as revolution. Martin re-designed the entire nose-cone of the aircraft, packing into its slender streamlining no less than twelve machine-guns, each with its own ammunition box, another of his patented inventions, nestling alongside, feeding in the belts of bullets through a swan-neck chute. This trebled hitting power made the Havoc a significant weapon in the defence of London, and Lord Beaverbrook, Minister of Aircraft Production at the time, spared a few moments from his daily duty of chivvying the manufacturers into achieving the impossible to write congratulating Martin on the conversion. Some short steps down the ladder of authority, however, officialdom quietly paid out James Martin for his insistence on working out the problem for himself; his design was adopted, and more than eighty Douglas Havocs re-modelled, but the contract for their conversion was handed to another firm.

* * *

Nothing, though, could hold him down for long, and already he was hard at work on the next of his aeroplanes, the M.B.3, designed from the outset to meet the requirements of Air Ministry specification F4/34; this time he was taking no chances. It was a smooth development from his earlier models, a sleek and potent machine with a 2000 h.p. Napier Sabre engine, with metal panels replacing the wood and fabric of its predecessors, a pneumatically operated undercarriage, and a top speed in level flight of four hundred and fifteen miles an hour. The six 20 mm. cannon with which it was fitted made it the most heavily armed fighter in the world. It was highly manoeuvrable and easy to handle, and Martin was watching with pride as Valentine Baker, on 12th September 1942, took it up from the airfield at Wing for the latest of its development tests. He saw it flash along the runway, saw it lift gracefully into its climb, and heard, like the others beside him, the cough and the splutter as its engine cut out before it had cleared the field. He watched in horror as Baker, his friend, fought to keep control, slipped and slithered in the sky as he tried desperately to make a forced landing in a nearby paddock and to save not only himself but the aircraft, the only one of its kind. He heard the crash of failure, and he knew without asking that Valentine Baker was dead.

* * *

This was Martin's first meeting, face to face, with death in the air, and the death, moreover, of a friend and colleague for which, until the cause of the crash was established, he must hold himself at least partly responsible. It had been *his* design that Baker had been trying to prove, *his* aircraft he had been striving to save, and beneath the immediate sense of shock was the infinitely sharper, unthinkable fear that the accident might have happened through some fault or failure in his workmanship or design. Investigation, as it happened, proved conclusively that nothing of the sort was true but that a tragically simple error of adjustment by a mechanic had choked off the stream of fuel to the engine; but the terror had been experienced, the burden of potential guilt had been shouldered, never to be put down. I sometimes thought of this, many years later, and understood why, after a test shot in the ejection seat, my first sight on reaching the ground was always of Martin's black Bentley nosing its way across the airfield, ahead of the spectators, the photographers, the Press; he had to know, first and immediately, that the test man had survived the experiment, and the anxiety seemed to stutter out of him like a plea for reassurance.

If the death of Valentine Baker was a tragic blow to Martin personally, the total destruction of the prototype M.B.3 was a shattering setback to what was still only a small company. There could be no question of re-building it nor even of building a replica, for aircraft construction, then as now, was a frenetic business, and with the loss of time the new aeroplane would have been out of date before it could have been put into production. Martin began work on a new version, similar but with a more powerful engine, but abandoned the project before its completion to leap-frog still further forward with an entirely new aircraft designed to meet the latest Air Ministry specification, F18/39.

79

The new machine, the M.B.5, was a beauty, and once again the pilots loved it.

It was not only the performance of the M.B.5 that so pleased the Air Force men who flew her, but also the layout and construction, so clearly planned with the comfort of the customer in mind. The radiators were slung beneath the belly of the aeroplane, the hubs of the two contra-rotating, three-bladed propellers tucked snugly into a long smooth spinner, and the pilot, from the enclosed tear-drop canopy of his cockpit, had in consequence a magnificently uncluttered view over the nose and the leading edges of the wings. The controls and instruments were easily accessible to hand and eye, the fuel was regulated—a boon, this, to the harassed fighter pilot—by a single lever, and the hood had built in to it a clean, simple, and effective jettison-device. One senior Ministry official, commenting with unguarded jocularity on the luxury of it all, received his immediate come-uppance in Martin's brusque rejoinder: 'You'd like a bit o' comfort if you had to fly one of these things. I bet you've even got a cushion on your office chair, and you'd kick up hell, now wouldn't you, if it was missing one morning?' That the meticulous attention to detail was more than mere fussiness was borne out by official reports recommending that Martin's cockpit design be copied as standard for all fighter aircraft. And yet, despite all this, the M.B.5, potentially the finest piston-engined fighter ever built in Britain, was never put into production, and no explanation acceptable to the men who had flown her was ever put forward by the Ministries concerned.

Perhaps the right one was that put forward years later at the Empire Test Pilots' School at Farnborough by the very young, very calm Flight Lieutenant who had spent his afternoon hurtling through the sky in a supersonic Sabre: 'The M.B.5 may have been a very fine aircraft, but it came too late, and its brilliance must have been dimmed by the promise of jet-propulsion.'

The murmur of agreement among his contemporaries, disturbed only by the friendly lapping of beer in a dozen tankards, was shattered by a Squadron Leader older-looking than his thirty-four years. 'Facile, laddie, but not strictly true. If they'd put it into production when they'd seen what it could do, they could have re-equipped whole squadrons that went on flying piston-propelled to the very end in aeroplanes that couldn't touch it. I believe they would have done, too, if Jimmy Martin had been half as busy in the drawing-room as he was in the drawing-office. But he wouldn't kow-tow, wouldn't conciliate; he was a spiky granule, laddie, in the gall-bladder of the bland. He produced the goods but couldn't find patience to wrap them with pink ribbon.' Perhaps this explanation was equally true of Martin's troubles with authority.

But despite these troubles it was to James Martin that Fighter Command turned in 1944 for help in solving one of their greatest problems.

CHAPTER 8

Birth of the Ejection Seat

1944

The problem was a particularly hellish one because it concerned unnecessary yet unavoidable death. With all the glories of the Battle of Britain proudly behind them, with their mastery of the skies becoming daily more self-evident, the squadrons were suddenly faced with a danger unknown since the Dawn Patrol days of Richthofen, Ball, McCudden and Mannock, the legendary heroes of aerial combat over the trenches of the Western Front. In those days pilots had died slowly and in horror, died as it were, unhurt, simply because their aircraft had been hit and they had no means of escape; they had no parachutes, and they dared not get out. Now the story was much the same if for a slightly different reason. Pilots in 1944 were being killed in crippled aircraft because, although—thanks to Leslie Irvin and James Martin respectively—they had parachutes and canopy jettison devices, *they still could not get out*; the aeroplanes had become too fast for them.

For years, in their Spitfires and Hurricanes, the boys of Fighter Command had known that in an emergency, provided they were conscious and had altitude, they stood at least a sporting chance of survival. The drill in times of real trouble was simply to slide back or jettison the canopy, roll the aircraft over on its back, and put your faith in God and Leslie Irvin; the parachute would see you through. But not any more.

The genius of Frank Whittle was bearing its first fruit, and, without the faintest conception of its future significance, we were entering the air-age of the jets. On 24th July 1943 the Gloster F.9/40 prototype 'plane had been wheeled out of its secret hangar to make its maiden flight over Barford St. John, and within a year its progeny, the Meteors, had been handed over to 616 Squadron, Royal Air Force, who were soon flying them with considerable success against the Germans' latest secret weapon, the V.1. Flying Bomb. Citizens of London would watch spellbound as these newest and fastest of fighters went streaking across the skies of Southern England, sidling up to the unwelcome visitors and nudging them gently but firmly from the national premises with the smooth, unanswerable efficiency of a bouncer in one of the better-class nightclubs. It was marvellous, exciting sport for the pilots, who were full of wonderment and delight at the manoeuvrability, the rate of climb, and above all the sheer speed of their latest machines, and who rejoiced in the name enviously bestowed upon themselves by their piston-propelled brothers-in-arms; they were the first of the 'Firecan Jockeys', and they liked that rather a lot.

Behind all the exuberance, however, beneath the exhilaration of the fastest flying then known to man, there was an uneasy awareness that performance, like patriotism, is not enough. High speed demands a high price, and the price, in this case, might well be one's life. For escape, a matter almost of routine at two hundred miles an hour, becomes a physical impossibility at twice or three times that speed, when the gravitational pull imposed on a pilot by a change in the aircraft's attitude may multiply his effective body-weight many times over. No man, however strong or desperate, could force himself out through the shrieking, snatching blast of the slipstream, and if he could it would be only to meet immediate and gruesome death, battered against the fuselage of his aircraft or sliced into segments by its tailplane.

The problem had been brought tragically to the very door-step of the men most obviously suited to deal with it when, in January 1944, a test pilot of the Royal Aircraft Establishment at Farnborough had been killed in his attempt to abandon a Meteor during an experimental flight, and indeed the RAE had immediately set up a committee to study the question of assisted escape. But committees are time-consuming, and scientists are traditionally

83

reluctant to disclose their findings while there exists the slightest danger of their being proved wrong. Several months had passed without tangible results, and the men with their lives at stake were becoming restive. Fighter Command wanted action.

Action is positive, and satisfying, and sometimes successful, but the trouble in this case was that the Command hierarchy had no blue-print, no precedent, no principle even on which to act. They were paying now for the chill indifference with which they and the authorities above them had greeted, fourteen years before, the efforts of one inspired young airman to provide a solution to the problem that he, even then, had foreseen. Back in 1930, when men still flew in open cockpits, No. 208 Squadron, Fighter Command, had just been equipped with new aircraft, stubby, sturdy little biplanes that were rumoured to reach almost two hundred miles an hour in a power-dive, and to one of the squadron pilots, Flying Officer Dudgeon, this potential spelled danger, the danger of being held down in the cockpit by forces beyond one's control. No dreamer, but a young man of action with an inventive turn of mind, Dudgeon armed himself with a drawing board, a set of draughtsman's instruments, and a box of Meccano, and quietly went to work in the privacy of his room in the Officers' Mess. Within weeks he had come up with a plan for modification of the cockpit; the pilot's seat would be remounted on concentric tubes, each containing a powerful spring wound down by a ratchet and key and held in its compressed position by a strong but simple catch. In an emergency, hey presto—the pilot, releasing the catch, would shoot like a Jack-in-the-box to the lip of the cockpit coaming, from which he could roll easily overboard without fear of entanglement. Poor Dudgeon. His ideas were sound, his blue-prints detailed and accurate to scale; his working model, constructed in Meccano, really worked—and the whole concept was strangled by his superiors at birth.

In other countries the authorities had been less obtuse and, as is now known, both Sweden and Germany were ahead of Great Britain in the invention of facilities for assisted escape. Before the end of the Second World War some of the interceptor 'planes of the Luftwaffe were equipped with rudimentary ejection seats, while as early as 1943 the fighter aircraft of the Swedish Air Force were being fitted with SAAB seats, almost certainly the first effective explosive seats ever produced. But with Britain and Germany at war and Sweden preserving her neutrality, nothing of these developments was known in England at that time or, if anything was known, it was ignored.

And so Fighter Command needed help, and so it was that, as I was flying daily in my hot seat over the hostile skies of Italy, James Martin was setting out to wrestle with the very problem that was foremost in my mind—the problem of survival. The story of the British ejection seat, in which I was to play a small but significant role, had begun.

In the early summer of 1944 Fighter Command sent Wing Commander John Jewell down to see James Martin at Denham and within hours, almost, he had accepted the challenge of the airman's urgent need.

* * *

'We could fire them out,' was Martin's first suggestion, but his measuring-tapes proved him wrong. The plan initially was that his designs should be applicable to existing fighter aircraft, not just to the jets of the future, and a study of the cockpits showed beyond question that a pilot shot out of a Spitfire or a Hurricane would leave his lower legs behind him, severed at the knees by the sloping windscreen.

The only acceptable alternative as a means of propulsion was the one that had occurred to the luckless, ridiculed Dudgeon fourteen years before—compressed springs, and it was on the principle of spring-loading that Martin based his first ejection seat. But this was Dudgeon with a difference; instead of a simple lifting device that would raise Jack to the upper edge of his box, Martin designed a lever to run the length of the upper fuselage from the front of the tail-fin to the rear edge of the cockpit, a swinging

85

arm with a U-shaped hand that would engage in the pilot's parachute harness, pluck him clean out of the cockpit and fling him high over the murderous hurdle of the tailplane. To install a spring of sufficient power was entirely feasible, for its function was only to initiate the movement; once the underside of the lever was exposed to the slipstream the natural forces of aerodynamics would provide the 'flick of the wrist' needed to complete the life-saving throw. Martin drew up his blue-prints, checked and re-checked his tables of forces, built himself a scale model, and hurried up to London.

His appointment was with Sir Wilfred Freeman, the Air Chief Marshal who had authorised him, years before, to design the fire-power modifications on the Douglas Havocs, but when he was ushered in to the Ministry of Aircraft Production on 11th October, he found waiting for him a figure of even greater authority, the Minister himself, Sir Stafford Cripps. If Martin had needed any encouragement this spontaneous show of interest at the top provided it; he unrolled his charts and drawings, produced his miniature model, and sailed straight into an exposition of its virtues. Cripps was clearly impressed, and said so. Sir Wilfred Freeman, sure now of backing from above, turned to Martin and asked how the Ministry of Aircraft Production could help in the development of the new idea. Martin, direct as always, stated his primary requirement: 'I must have an aircraft to work on, a Boulton-Paul Defiant. If I remove the gun-turret behind the pilot's front cockpit it will be simple to install my apparatus.' The demand was logical: unless an aircraft was to be sacrificed with every experiment, only a two-seater machine would fill the bill, and the Defiant, its career as a front-line aeroplane already finished, was the most suitable type available. Freeman nodded immediate agreement and Cripps again wished the project well. It was only four months, almost to the day, since Martin had first turned his mind to the problem of ejection.

The swinging arm, however, never swung, for almost immediately Fighter Command and the Ministry changed their minds about ejection policy and decided that escape equipment should be provided only for new jet aircraft and not for the piston-engined fighters already in service. Nothing could have better suited Martin, already keen to experiment with explosives. He reverted immediately to the idea of an ejection gun and he began, as he says, 'to work very hard.' His subordinates are less succinct. 'I suppose he must have slept,' says one, and even as he says it you can see the shadow of doubt in his eyes, 'but God knows when. He'd shut himself up in his office, but you'd know he wasn't resting—he thought a lot, but he never, never rested. Next minute he'd be chasing us round the factory—do this, do that, do it this way. He'd snatch a pencil from a draughtsman or a drill from an engineer, and he'd do each one's job better than he could do it himself; then he'd be on to the next fellow. You couldn't keep up with him, but by God, he made you want to try.'

By the end of November the first seat was built, and despite the rapidity of the design and construction it contained all the main features, though few of the refinements, of the models subsequently to be installed in the aircraft of more than forty Air Forces throughout the world, including those of the United States. Superficially similar to the conventional cockpit seat of a fighter aircraft, it carried beneath and behind it the power pack, a do-it-yourself explosion kit comprising two telescopic tubes and a gunpowder cartridge. Behind the seat was a vertical guide-rail up which, on firing, it would ride smoothly out of the aircraft on four small and closely-grouped wheels.

To test it out Martin next designed a sloping steel ramp, sixteen feet high, with the guide-rail extending right to the top, and with ratchet-stops inserted at three-inch intervals all the way up so that the rise of the seat could be controlled and, eventually, arrested, this too included all the main features of the training-ramp that is in regular use by many air forces to this day. But to visualise it one need only recall the test-your-strength sideshow of the old-fashioned fairground—'Swing the Hammer and Ring the Bell.' The principle was the same, but the 'hammer,' in this case, was a gun.

The bell rang on 20th January 1945 when the ejection seat, loaded with two hundred pounds of sand-bags, roared upwards for the very first time, and four days later, after innumerable trial shots, the inanimate ballast was replaced by the first and the greatest of the Martin-Baker test parachutists, Benny Lynch. A husky, powerfully-built fitter from the factory floor, with a luxuriant cavalry moustache, Lynch, on 24th January, fired himself up the ramp to a height of four feet eight inches. That altitude seems insignificant, but when you're sitting on a cannon you don't query its range; Lynch's courage, as he was later to prove, was immense, and those early experiments, as was soon discovered, were in fact potential killers.

Twice more Benny Lynch shot up the test-rig without discomfort, but on ride number four, which reached a height of nine feet eleven inches, the guinea-pig, for the first time, began to grunt. The charge of the cartridge had been increased, and the resultant jolt had hurt him severely in the back; his complaints were noted, but athough sympathy was expressed, their significance was missed. But not for long. Word of Martin's experiments had spread, and there were others besides Lynch eager to try out the new equipment. John Jewell, who could reasonably claim to have started the whole business, rushed over from Fighter Command, staking his claim to be one of the first. With him came the Command's Chief Medical Officer, Air Commodore E. A. Lumley, while from the Institute of Aviation Medicine came Wing Commander (later Air Marshal) W. K. Stewart. The contribution of Bill Stewart to aircrew safety, right up to his tragically early death in 1967, in all probability ranks second only to that of James Martin himself, but from those very first experiments a name that deserves its place in the record books is that of a journalist called Andrews from the staff of *Aeroplane* Magazine. For Andrews, who volunteered to make trial shot Number Fourteen, was the first casualty in the development of the ejection seat, and the nature of his injury was to alter—almost to determine—the whole future of that development.

Andrews, when wound down from the top of the rig, complained like Lynch before him of violent pains, and when James Martin telephoned next day to enquire after his well-being he too received a jolt. 'I'd like to speak to Mr. Andrews.' 'Sorry, that's not possible, he's in Weybridge.' 'What the hell is he doing there?' 'He's in hospital—he's broken his back.'

A visit to the hospital confirmed the story; Andrews had suffered compression fractures of several spinal vertebrae, and Martin was suddenly, soberly, aware of the dangers of what he was doing, and of the responsibilities his experiments entailed. He was not alone in that; there was a marked and immediate cooling-off in the official willingness to co-operate. The men actually exposed to risk—Lynch, Stewart, Jewell, and several others—remained eager as ever, and took each new trial in their stride, but in Whitehall, where 'danger' meant a tricky half-hour with the Minister, it was felt prudent not to associate oneself too closely with the bangs, claims, and occasional groans emanating from the experimental hangar at Denham. Not for the first time, and not for the last, Jimmy Martin's methods were proving too hot to handle.

For Martin himself, however, there was no escape; something was sadly amiss and it was the job of the designer to identify the trouble, to analyse it, and somehow or another to eliminate it. There were two starting points for study—the injured man and the machine that had injured him. Like any good detective he decided to follow both tracks simultaneously, and straight away he found himself bogged down in a subject he simply did not understand. Not in relation to the seat—the outcome of his investigations into that problem, though they astonished him, did not baffle him; James Martin has rarely been baffled in matters of engineering and dynamics. Puzzled by the fact that a thrust amounting to less than 4 g, a force in other words that less than quadrupled the subject's bodyweight, could produce such devastating and disastrous results, he decided to take a closer look at what actually happened when the ejection cartridge was ignited. A Kodak high-speed camera, running at 1,000 frames a second, came up with the answer: although the mean force generated by the ejection gun was negligible, the rate at which this force was being piled on amounted to an incredible—and in-tolerable—600 to 800 g per second. Small wonder poor Andrews had a pain in the back.

But why Andrews, and not the others? This was where Martin found himself stranded in unaccustomed ignorance; why, from identical experiments, should one man end up in hospital while another walked away with a smile? He *had* to know before it was too late, before some occupant of the seat ended up not on a stretcher, but on a slab.

The answer must lie in the structure, the strengths and weak-nesses, of the human body, of which Martin knew no more than the average layman; this must be his next field of study. He sought the aid of an orthopaedic surgeon, Miss M. Louden, F.R.C.S., and with characteristic disbelief that an initial startled refusal could possibly be meant seriously and intended to apply to *him*, he talked his way into attendance at a number of spinal operations, which he followed step by step with the rapt concentration of an undergraduate on the eve of examination. He brought home with him for experimental purposes a human spine that stands in his office still, stark and grisly behind glass, a silent reminder of the difference between a successful ejection and a failure. That skeletal totem pole, however, during its early days at Denham, was subjected to all manner of mechanical outrage as Martin, checking each new experiment with Miss Louden or with Bill Stewart and the other doctors at the I.A.M., sought to establish the safest means of applying to the human frame history's most monumental kick in the backside. He worked out that while the body could expect to withstand a force of about 21 g, that loading should not be applied at a rate of more than two to three hundred g per second; he learned that to absorb such a hammering the spine should be held erect, with the vertebrae resting squarely, one upon the other. To achieve these conditions he modified the seat, lowering the position of the occupant's legs in order to straighten out the lumbar spine, and he did much more than that. Knowing now that whilst the force of the upward thrust must be sufficient to carry the pilot safely clear of the tailplane, the initial jolt must be limited by the tolerance of the pilot's body, he devised a system of two-cartridge firing in which the first explosion would merely initiate a smooth movement, leaving the second to apply the extra pressure needed to complete the operation. The exact power of these cartridges would be critical, and asked where he would obtain such finely-balanced explosives Martin stared at his questioner in genuine astonishment. 'Buy them, d'you mean? Never on your life—I'll make my own.' Sure enough he did, setting up in his own back yard a sort of private Brock's Benefit where the cartridges are not only turned out but tested under the severest conditions. Samples of them have been baked in hot ovens and frozen till they were encased in ice, and the chap in charge of it all, when I last spoke to him, had produced one and a half million of them without a single malfunction to sully the score-sheet.

During these weeks of calculation and experiment the whole concept of high-speed escape was moving steadily towards its moment of truth. The original ramp was replaced by another steepling up to a height of sixty-five feet, a terrifying tramway on which the test-men could experience the full thrust of an authentic ejection. Lynch, once again, was the first to go, shooting up on the double-cartridge gun to a height of over twenty-six feet. Stewart, exercising the grim prerogative of the research doctor to experiment first upon himself, was photographed hurtling upwards in a dangerous demonstration of the fact that without head-restraint the subject would almost certainly break his neck; he could be seen massaging himself ruefully if surreptitiously for days to come, but he had proved his point, and another vital lesson had been learned.

*   *   *

The Boulton-Paul Defiant promised by Sir Wilfred Freeman early in October 1944 made its appearance at Denham two months later. Elation, however, turned to dismay on first examination, for the machine—DR944—had already been used by the United States Army Air Force for target-towing, and was in such a state of dilapidation that it had to be completely re-conditioned, a process that set the programme back by many weeks. But by the Spring of 1945 it was in first-class order, its structure strengthened to withstand the shocks of repeated ejections. On 10th May, with the aircraft jacked-up stationary on the airfield, the ejection seat was installed in its rear compartment, loaded with sand bags weighing two hundred pounds, and fired by remote control into a huge landing-net on top of a forty foot tower erected specially for the purpose. Stage One was over.

Stage Two, which was to last for one year, two months and exactly two weeks, began the very next day, 11th May, when Brian Greenstead, then chief test pilot for Rotols, flew the modified Defiant up to Wittering, an R.A.F. airfield in Lincolnshire. Here, before a tense and silent gathering of Air Force officers, scientists, Martin-Baker staff and Ministry officials, Greenstead lifted the aircraft off the runway, circled, and came roaring back across the aerodrome. Counting down the seconds, measuring his run-in with stop-watch accuracy, he brought the Defiant to a point level with the spectators, reached for the one unfamilar lever in the cockpit, and pulled; in a flash of flame and a puff of smoke a black bundle exploded from the rear compartment, somersaulted high above the tailplane, and floated to earth beneath its parachute. The tension disappeared, Martin was pounded on the back, an Air Marshal was seen to dance in his excitement. The ejection seat had proved itself, for the first time, in flight.

One week later, at Beaulieu, it made its next appearance when Greenstead, in a series of six runs, accelerated up to an indicated Air Speed of three hundred miles an hour, and on each occasion the seat, with its inanimate burden, made a successful clearance. This, in terms of performance, was as much as could be achieved,

for the Defiant had reached the limit of its capabilities. A long
path of problems still stretched ahead, for the aeroplanes in which
the seat would be installed for operational use could fly twice that
speed and more, and with human lives at stake, nothing must be
taken for granted. Martin, more acutely aware of this than any
man, applied to the Ministry for the loan of a Meteor Mk 3, and
while he was waiting for its arrival went back to the factory, back
to the drawing-board, back to the incessant research into problems
for which there was no precedent, no pattern, and, as yet, no
answer.

CHAPTER 9

The Tests that Worked

1946-1949

Within a year, however, things were in every sense moving fast. On 12th September 1945 Martin accepted from the Ministry of Aircraft Production a contract covering the design, development, and manufacture of two ejection-units and their installation in a high-performance aircraft. One month later the aircraft, a Meteor Mk 5, was delivered, and by June of the following year it had been modified, its bulkhead replaced, its floor-beams strengthened, the ammunition bay behind the pilot converted into a second cockpit, a stark, functional cabin that would contain the explosive, experimental seat.

On the drawing-boards too, and on the 65 foot test-rig, the techniques of ejection were being first calculated and later proved; and with the steady progress the interest in Martin's work became international. In October 1945 two American naval officers, Commander J. J. Ide and Lieutenant R. B. Barnes, had been hugely impressed by the sight of the Denham test-rig in action, and the United States Navy had placed an order for a similar structure, one hundred and ten feet tall, that would be erected, during the summer of 1946, at the Naval Yard in Philadelphia. At Wright Air Development Center, too, the Americans were forcing forward their own plans for a serviceable escape system and Major Mike Sweeney, an aviation doctor of limitless energy and immense personal courage, was pioneering ejection in his own country with an interested eye on what was happening elsewhere, especially in England. Humanitarian in its motives, the drive to produce the first really effective seat was nonetheless fiercely competitive, with prestige no less than profit as the prize, and in the spring and summer of 1946 the race, beyond question, was on.

By May of that year James Martin felt sure that the solution to the escape problem was in sight, and on 8th June he put his confidence to the test, jacking up the Meteor on Chalgrove airfield and firing a dummy into the receiving net. When the seat and its contents cleared the cockpit and the tailplane with smooth, uncluttered efficiency, Martin promptly hoisted the whole programme into the realm where it belonged—in the air.

The early stages of the project, from 24th June when the Meteor started on its high-speed runs, were a pattern of disaster, with the ejection seat proving itself not a life-saver but a tumbling, uncontrollable death-trap. At speeds of more than four hundred and fifteen miles an hour, far less than the Meteor's peak performance, the winner in the battle of survival was the slipstream all the way; parachutes burst open at the seams, tangled like soiled washing in the structure of the seat, dropped both seat and ballast to destruction on the ground. The delayed-action opening device, designed to postpone the opening of the canopy until the first fury of the air blast was over, simply was not up to its job and the situation, if the project was to prosper, demanded immediate and profound re-thinking.

The transition from failure to success, or at least partial success, took less than a week. The first significant happening after the firing of an ejection seat is the automatic opening of a small parachute, or drogue, that serves first to stabilise the seat and then to drag the main, life-saving canopy from its pack; within days of these initial failures Martin had tried and discarded two methods of opening this drogue, the first by spring-loading and the second by hydraulics, and had invented, built, and introduced a third, in use to this day, in which the drogue is fired from its housing by a gun. His troubles, however, were not yet over. The forces to which this drogue is subjected almost baffle belief; on the earliest experiments in which the gun was used the firing was successful, but the shock of opening snapped clean through the cable to which the drogue was attached, a cable with a tested breaking strain of sixty hundredweight. Faced with this new and crucial difficulty Martin reacted as only a man of his calibre would and could; he immediately designed and manufactured a completely new type of drogue, forerunner of the model that has since functioned effectively in the fastest ejections ever recorded. As the weeks hurried past in a frenzy of endeavour the test record-sheets began to read 'Success. Success. Success,' and the stage was being set for one of the great moments in the history of flight.

For Martin it was a time not only of achievement and excitement but also of agonising appraisal, of sleepless assumption of the ultimate responsibility. Two years of research and development were rushing to their climax and his was the word, the only word, that must soon put a man's life in premeditated hazard. 'I thought long and hard about it, and whenever something went amiss on a dummy test, as it sometimes did almost right up to the end, my heart sank like a stone. I hate live tests, Mr. Hay, far worse than you fellows who actually make them, and I think I hated the very thought of that first one worst of all. I've never taken kindly to the idea of vivisection.' But vivisection it had to be, for human tolerance was still the great unknown factor and would remain so until some man had put his body, as well as the seat, to the test. The day Martin finally chose was 24th July 1946, and on that day Benny Lynch, in an act of ice-cold courage that can rarely have been surpassed, fired himself into the utterly unknown in an experiment that was to alter the future of flying.

At Chalgrove airfield Lynch, this fitter from the factory floor, hoisted his considerable bulk into the rear compartment of the Meteor, with a sheet of armour-plating in front of him, one hundred and sixty gallons of aviation paraffin at his back, and a cannon, cocked and loaded, beneath his seat. He wore mechanics' overalls, a leather flying helmet, that luxuriant, improbable moustache, and a huge grin of quite unreasonable confidence. He confirmed his system of signals with the pilot, Captain Scott, and he huddled down behind the bulkhead to get what little shelter he could from the slipstream as the aircraft spiralled its way up to the dropping-height of eight thousand feet. 'It was a terrible anxiety,' recalled Martin, 'just watching it climb and knowing that the decision had, quite irrevocably, been made.' It was an anxious period, too, for Lynch, who remembers the essence of it in the *cri de coeur* of the test man; 'I've never felt so lonely in my whole damn life.'

It can be lonely all right, as must have been discovered by every experimental flyer from Icarus to the Astronauts, but few, I imagine, would have wanted it any other way. When you are faced with problems mental, emotional, and physical with which no-one can help you anyway, it is best, on the whole, to wrestle with them alone after your own strictly personal fashion; the man who wants or worse still needs an audience should never be in this game at all, and the death or glory glamour boy has no place within a thousand yards of an experimental flight. The test man is a technician fitted for his responsibilities by attitude, aptitude, and experience, and Benny Lynch was, every nerve and muscle of him, a test man. As Scott levelled off at eight thousand feet for the approach run, Lynch's tongue was dry in his mouth, but he was absolutely in control of his fear, more so than several of the men beneath him who later confessed to having missed the actual moment of ejection completely, their eyes shut and their heads averted as the Meteor approached the boundary of the airfield.

Captain Scott, his eyes on the instruments but his thoughts, as he says, with the man in the seat behind him, wound the Meteor up steadily to a speed of 320 miles an hour, and the coloured lights in Lynch's compartment began winking out their messages. The red lamp glowed; five seconds to go. Lynch stabbed with his finger at the return button beneath the green lamp to signify his readiness. He reached for the firing handle as the red light faded and he loosened the wire grip in its housing as he waited tensely for the green; suddenly it was there before him, emerald and compelling, and he dragged his hands down sharply to his chest. 'The punch was powerful, of course, but not painful, and my first real thrill came when I cleared the cockpit and the slipstream threw me over on my back. What with the air blast pushing me at three hundred miles an hour in one direction, and a thrust of 16 g shoving me upwards in another, the whole situation was pretty confusing, and on top of that the noise, in the first few moments, was deafening.'

Martin, standing tight-lipped with the others on the airfield, led the sigh of relief just nine seconds later when the tiny black dot stopped tumbling and the huge white canopy, dragged out by the drogue, blossomed wide like a celestial umbrella above the ejection seat and its occupant. The first part of the experiment, at least, was a success. For Benny Lynch up there at seven thousand feet, however, the business of the day had only started, and the worst in many ways still lay ahead of him. There he was, safe and unhurt after an experience many men might envy but few would undertake; floating down comfortably in the seat he could look over the patchwork beauty of the English countryside with the satisfaction inside him that comes from a dangerous job well done—but he could do so for only a very few minutes. His airborne armchair, proud and serene as any throne, would lose its comforting qualities very suddenly when it hit the ground and so, for the second time since climbing aboard the Meteor, he faced with stoicism the Transatlantic maxim 'When you've gotta go, you've gotta go.'

The big canopy above him was there to support the seat, and it had done its job to perfection. But to land in the seat would mean injury both certain and severe, as another test parachutist was later to discover, and Lynch had now to abandon his temporary haven and put his trust in his second, his personal parachute, and pray that it too would function properly. The ejection seats of today are fully automatic, and the pilot's one essential action is to pull the trigger; but for Benny Lynch in that first descent there followed the reluctant rigmarole of cold-bloodedly unfastening the straps that held him securely in his place, kicking himself forward into space, and forcing himself to wait a full eight seconds before reaching for the ripcord in order to obviate any risk of entanglement with the seat. 'It was harder,' he told me later with gallows humour, 'than leaving your fireside seat on a winter evening to open the door to a visitor you don't even want to see.'

But the Visitor he really had cause to fear was not to call on him that day; the parachute opened safely, and the era of assisted escape began that sunny summer morning in Oxfordshire. It was to be a whole year, however, twelve months of ceaseless research and experiment with dummies in the air and with human beings on the test-rig, before the next decisive step forward was ready to be taken, and again the man who took that step was Lynch.

* * *

His second sortie in the seat was not exactly an anti-climax—no live ejection comes quite into the category of the non-event—but it went smoothly and without untoward incident, and Martin now decided that the burden of testing should be shared. The second man selected for the job was P. J. Page, another Company mechanic who had been a trained parachutist in the airborne forces, and on 12th August, an apt enough date, he shot himself from the Meteor at two hundred miles an hour, successfully and suffering no more damage than stiffness and bruising of the shoulders where the harness had bitten into him during the shock-loading as the parachute opened. But just two days later he was to experience one of the most hellish descents in history.

The purpose of this new test was to establish for the first time the effect of ejection at high speed on both the seat and its occupant, and Page went into it under circumstances that raised a rueful grin on my own countenance when I recalled them some fifteen years later, in my hospital bed. Page knew he was facing a high-speed run, but he did not know how fast it would be, and Martin did not choose to tell him. No doubt he would have done so had Page insisted—in my own case, years later, when Martin asked me to make one test without knowing beforehand its exact nature and purpose, he made it quite clear that it *was* a request and that he would tell me if I really wished him to. But he also gave me his reason for secrecy, and I happily accepted both the reason and the result—the eggs are well-broken if the omelette turns out the finest ever cooked. Had Page known that the speed on his second ejection was to be four hundred miles an hour, precisely twice the speed of his first, it would not, I feel certain, have deterred him from carrying out the test, for a man afraid of such knowledge would never have volunteered for test-duties in the first place; nor, again as in my own case, would fore-knowledge have helped him in the slightest when things went wrong. When forces like ejection cartridges and four hundred miles an hour air-blasts are working against you, you are in real danger. This is something you accept from the start, and you just hope to God you can handle your problems decently and with dignity when they come; there is nothing heroic and high-minded about this— every soldier hopes the same.

Page was in trouble from the word go. Just one-fifth of a second after the firing he hit the screaming tornado of the slipstream, and straight away he started to slide. His feet were torn out of the footrests, both legs swung wide out over one side of the seat; the shock of the canopy opening forced him almost out of his safety-harness, and the heavy chunky metal of the quick-release box cut a deep and ugly groove in his chin. In those few frantic, frightening seconds Page, by one of those raw deals of fate that change our lives, may himself have contributed to the mental and physical agony that was to follow. With the main parachute safely open he was now dangling beneath the ejection seat, its ninety pounds of solid steel cutting cruelly into the small of his back, and his one thought was to manoeuvre into a position where he could unbuckle himself from the harness and fall free. He reached round behind him to check the position of the seat-pack, his personal parachute, and then, in one appalling second, every emotion drained out of him but fear; instead of the solid bulk of the parachute envelope his hand was clutching only a thin bundle of rigging-lines. Twisting round in his terror he searched wide-eyed for the parachute, and almost wished he hadn't as he found it, its nylon folds wrapped inextricably around the cavities and projections of the seat. During his nightmare gyrations in the slip-stream something, very probably his own frantically clutching hand, had dragged the ripcord handle from its housing.

There come times in testing when it is hard to make up your mind, when you know that the wrong decision will almost surely be your last, and Page, six thousand feet above the airfield, was now sorting out his chances. He could unfasten his seat harness and hope to drop clear—but then the parachute might be ripped to shreds, and he was carrying no reserve, for under test conditions there just is not room for one, and a man falling helpless from that height takes a very long time to die. He thought about that course of action several times during the descent, and suffered terrible temptation each time he thought of the metal burden on his back and what it would do to him when he hit the ground. But gradually, firmly, he made up his mind to stay with it and take his chances; he knew he must inevitably be injured, but he could cling to the hope that he would not be killed. He tried desperately to struggle upwards into the seat but could find no way, and at last, before the horrified, helpless gaze of Martin, he came sweeping down and across the airfield to land backwards with a sickening crash on— with luck deserting him to the bitter end—the concrete surface of the runway. His heels hit first, and as he rolled there came the searing agony of his knee-ligaments tearing and a sudden terrible pain that shot through his body as his shoulders and the seat smashed down on the concrete. Worse than all the physical torture, however, was the old enemy, fear, for as he lay broken on the runway, Page found himself totally paralysed, unable even to breathe; his lungs, though full of air, would not function, and he felt himself drowning on dry land. It was the sheer determination not to die that enabled him at last to force out the air that was choking him, and when they lifted him gently from the wreckage of the seat he was soaked in sweat from the effort and the agony.

After a seven mile ride to the hospital the doctors gave their verdict; Page had broken his neck and was the luckiest of men to be alive. To others would go the glory; his future for some long time to come would be a grim succession of sleepless nights and plaster jackets.

Page's sufferings, however, would not be wasted, and to realise this is to understand both the principle of testing and the nature of the men who test. For the actual firing of the seat, and even its subsequent behaviour, had been largely successful, and in experiencing and later reporting what had happened to him in the slipstream, Page had fulfilled his function. Martin's modifications were of the simplest, and a safety-strap placed over the ripcord housing was enough to obviate the risk of another premature development of the personal parachute. Two weeks later, the lesson learned, Benny Lynch went up again in the Chalgrove Meteor and blasted himself out of it painlessly and successfully at a hundred miles an hour faster still to set a new world record for high-speed ejection of 505 m.p.h. Page was quoted as saying from his hospital bed that he was 'satisfied that he had done his stuff by paving the way.' He had reason to be satisfied, for he had played his part in what was by now, unquestionably, a success story.

* * *

Delighted with the results achieved on the Philadelphia test tower, the United States Navy had installed a Martin-Baker seat in a Douglas A 26, from which Lt. Furtek, U.S.N., had made a live test ejection on 1st November 1946. Now, in the summer of 1947, orders were given for the seat to be standardised for installation in all new jet aircraft of the Royal Air Force and the Royal Navy, and a production line was started to equip Meteors, Attackers, Wyverns, Canberras, Seahawks, and Venoms.

The work of the test men went on, both in Britain and in America. For Martin-Baker Benny Lynch continued to prove each major innovation; in the United States Mike Sweeney and the men who followed him did the same. With the U.S. Navy an early convert to the British seat, it is probably fair to say that the most important developments in American escape systems were carried out by the Special Projects Section at Wright Air Development Center. There much of the 'routine' testing during the late 1940's and early 1950's was the responsibility of a pair of dedicated young officers of the U.S. Air Force, Capt. Ed. Sperry and Lt. Henry Nielsen. They were not the first in the field, but they were most certainly among the best, as a couple of incidents will show.

While the Americans were concentrating on the development of a seat that would fire its occupant downwards, so obviating the risk of entanglement with the tailplane, Nielsen made a test ejection at about five hundred miles an hour. It was a painful experience, for on clearing the aircraft he broke an arm and chipped a shoulder blade. He also stated that he had not contributed to his injuries by any careless action of his own. Sperry, believing him and therefore knowing the danger involved, nevertheless went up next morning in the same aeroplane under the same conditions in an attempt to establish the flaw in the escape system.

He did; his injuries were almost identical to Nielsen's, but now he knew what had caused them. On this test each had allowed himself to be fired by remote control by the pilot, and each had chosen in consequence to use the firing handle between his knees as an anchor, something to hold on to at the moment of sudden explosive acceleration. Their arms, extended rigidly downwards in front of their bodies, had as a result presented a flat and unbroken surface to the slipstream, whose blast, more powerful than mere flesh and blood, had promptly flung them upwards and backwards, hammering them viciously against the upper edge of the seat. Nielsen and Sperry were well content. Confidence and courage had done the trick; they knew now that there was nothing wrong with the seat itself, and that nobody subsequently using it in an emergency would be exposed to the risk of the injuries they themselves had suffered under test conditions.

Another trial of Sperry's and Nielsen's nerve and teamwork came when they were experimenting with high-altitude ejection at Eglin Air Force Base in the West of Florida, and once again the pattern was of Nielsen's experiencing a new phenomenon and

Sperry's duplicating the circumstances and coming up with the answer.

Firing himself out of an aircraft at fifty thousand feet, Nielsen within seconds was automatically released from his seat and began the long free fall down towards the green and white ribbon of demarcation between the coast of Florida and the Gulf of Mexico. Soon he began to spin, and as the speed of the flat rotary movement began to build up he attempted the orthodox remedial action of rolling himself up into a ball in order to reduce the area of body-surface being presented to the air. This time, however, he found that try as he would he could not bring his knees up to his chest. He was lying flat on his back, a human centrifuge, with the blood being dragged out of his stomach and chest and forced towards both his head and his feet.

As the speed of the spin continued to increase the pain became almost intolerable until, through no conscious action of his own, Nielsen found himself lying on his side, a position that offered some measure of relief. He was still spinning, however, and the pain in his head and legs decided him against waiting for the action of the barometric device that would open his parachute automatically at a height of 11,000 feet. The function of this device is to allow a parachutist falling from very high altitude and possibly injured, or even unconscious, to drop rapidly to a height at which an oxygen supply is no longer a prerequisite of survival. Nielsen, however, had no such problem, for his oxygen mask was working, and as he plunged downwards towards fifteen thousand feet he decided to go for the emergency ripcord. Luckily for him, although his arms were pinioned to his chest his right hand was squarely on top of the ripcord housing, and by an almost superhuman effort of strength and will he managed to drag the handle free and so put an end to his agony.

Sperry's reaction to his subordinate's report of this singularly unpleasant and dangerous experience was entirely predictable. He pondered coolly and methodically the probable causes of the spinning phenomenon, of which little or nothing was known at the time, and he then went up to duplicate Nielsen's ejection under identical conditions. He had a theory; now he must prove it.

As soon as the seat fell away from him, a few seconds after the ejection, and as he began to plummet down at a speed building up rapidly to almost a hundred and fifty miles an hour, Ed Sperry began to thresh around wildly with his arms and legs, kicking and punching in every direction. He must have looked like a man demented, but this was no madness. His random gymnastics served to break up the air-flow over the surface of his body, and the forces of aerodynamics were cheated of the chance to take control. The knowledge gained that day over the Gulf of Mexico was of potential life-saving value to every high-performance pilot in the world.

Such, then, was the work of the pioneer test men in the early days of the ejection story, Lynch and Page in England, Sperry, Nielsen, and others in the United States. They had brought the seat up to a level of efficiency and performance adequate for the aircraft of their time. Their courage and dedication were immeasurable; their contribution to aircrew survival was immense. Within a few years of Benny Lynch's first live test the ejection seat was beginning to fulfil its true function of saving life.

CHAPTER 10

In Hot Blood

1949-1954

The first man to use a Martin-Baker seat in hot blood—the first of more than two thousand to date—was J. O. Lancaster, a well-known test pilot whose A.W.A. 52 prototype aircraft began to oscillate wildly during a routine proving flight near Coventry on 30th May 1949. At a speed of 320 m.p.h. the aeroplane became completely uncontrollable, and Ossie Lancaster made his explosive entry into the annals of aviation. Apart from the fact that it was the first, and that it was successful, however, little is known about that escape, for the pilot, perhaps understandably, could not remember even the sequence of events leading up to his ejection.

Of the men who were subsequently to use the seat, however, there were many whose recollections of the experience were all too vividly clear, and of these one of the earliest was Ken Blight.

On 11th November 1951—to most of us just one more half-remembered Armistice Day—Flying Officer K. J. Blight was flying his twin-engined Meteor jet against the Communists in Korea. His squadron, No. 77, Royal Australian Air Force, returning from a fighter sweep over Sinangu, was 24,000 feet up in a cloudless sky, twenty miles off Pyongyang, and dangerously deep behind the enemy lines.

The attack had been successful; the squadron, intact, was tucked neatly in formation, and Blight, holding number four position in the first of three flights, was heading happily for home with no premonition of disaster. One more operation was almost over, one more lethal sortie to be recorded laconically in his log-book. Just a few more minutes of routine mastery over his aircraft and he could relax, file his de-briefing report with Intelligence, and savour the delight of a long, cold beer in the Mess.

106

Danger, for that day, was a thing of the past; flying was still the cleanest, most civilised, most *comfortable* way to win a war. Often exciting, always impersonal, a job to be done and, when done, forgotten until the next moment of truth. And the next moment, just then, seemed a long way off.

Until, out of the afternoon sun, another aircraft suddenly broke formation, swooped crazily downwards, and slewed into Blight's Meteor with a rending, grinding, terrifying crash that left him, as he reported later, 'too stunned even to speak to the other pilots in the squadron.' His first coherent thought was that he had been hit by a burst of 37 mm cannonfire from one of the enemy Migs that habitually patrolled the area, but as he waited helplessly for the next fusillade, the coup-de-grâce, he caught a glimpse of the aircraft that had collided with him, saw it plunge downwards in a screaming spiral that could have only one end. As he watched it, dazed and sickened, his own Meteor skidded wildly across the sky and whipped over into that aerial nightmare, a vertical spin; shocked out of his inertia, Blight, as of instinct, began to react.

Fighting fiercely with stick and rudder, winding on full left trim and making maximum use of his 'inside' engine, he somehow succeeded in regaining some measure of control, nosed gingerly around into what he hoped was the general direction of his distant base, and gazed about him to take stock of his circumstances. They were grim. Four feet of his starboard wing had been sheared away, leaving only a grotesque and ragged stump; a hurried glance at the jet pipe temperature gauge showed the reading for the starboard engine racing far beyond the bounds of safety. The altimeter, too, told its tale of trouble, for he was losing height rapidly and ultimate catastrophe, it seemed, could not be many minutes away.

Down below, however, now menacingly close, were the Communists, and Christmas in captivity formed no part of Blight's plans for his personal future. Using all his skill and physical strength to keep the shattered aircraft level he began to experiment with the controls. After one or two anxious, heart-stopping miscalculations he discovered that by applying full power on the starboard engine and none at all on the port, by piling on full left rudder trim, and by holding the control column hard left back into his stomach, he could steer a reasonably accurate course for home. So much, then, for direction; but there still remained the problem of distance.

The altimeter confirmed his fears; he was still losing height at the rate of fifteen hundred feet a minute, and home and hope at that moment seemed equally and dishearteningly remote. Action was imperative, if only to ward off fear and resignation. To lower the dangerous level of the jet pipe temperature, which was threatening at every moment to transform the aircraft into a blazing torch, he tentatively eased off the power of the crippled starboard engine, but at the first hint of a reduction the Meteor went wallowing once more out of control, and he was forced to continue at the same high speed his shallow, dangerous dive towards security.

Throughout all these complex, nervy manoeuvres Blight had been trying desperately but without success to make radio contact with his base and to establish a fix on his actual position. At last, after an age of waiting, came the longed-for crackling in his headphones; just a few more miles, a few more minutes, and he would be over friendly territory. A few more minutes; it seemed little enough to ask, but his strength was running out fast, his muscles aching and trembling in an agony of exhaustion, and Blight was by now forecasting in seconds the time he could hold his aeroplane in level flight. Almost automatically, numb rather than afraid, he went through the preparations leading up to abandonment. He retracted the gunsight, de-pressurised the cockpit and, wondering despondently what lay in store for him, he threw the switch to open the canopy above his head. Yet still he hesitated, eking out the last of his strength in his running battle with the controls; to survive such an aerial collision, to come literally within sight of safety, and yet to end up prisoner, or worse, was unthinkable.

Again the headphones chattered into action: 'Well done, boy, and welcome home. You're with us again.' Exhaustion disappeared, despondency dissolved, and in a wild surge of optimism he began to think of saving not only himself but his aircraft. But it was hopeless, utterly beyond his powers; the slightest deviation set the Meteor rolling, and he found it impossible to cut down his speed to less than a hundred and ninety knots, out of the question for a forced landing in this lop-sided, limping, ultra-inflammable wreck. Accepting the inevitable he leaned forward, pulled the lever to jettison the hood, and watched with a strange air of detachment as the dust swirled up from the cockpit floor and the hood was swept clear and away, down past the port side of the fuselage. He checked his altitude, now down to five thousand feet, tightened his seat harness till it bit into his shoulders, and reached up tentatively to a wire and rubber loop above his head.

As the nose of the Meteor, now out of control, dropped steeply, Blight yanked both hands suddenly, savagely, downwards. A gun crashed out beneath him, and instantly he found himself soaring high above the aircraft, his legs flailing wildly in the slipstream, but his body still firmly attached to the seat. Coldly conscious of his actions now, he looked down at the matrix of straps and buckles in which he was enmeshed. On his chest were two large metal D-rings; a determined tug on the nearest of them released him from his seat harness, and at once he tumbled forward out of the metal bucket and began to somersault, with the empty air driving painfully into his eyes. One blurred glimpse of the earth rushing up at him sent his hand grasping for the second D-ring, the all-important, heaven-be-praised, where-the-hell-is-it miracle of the ripcord. He felt the cold metal in his hand, dragged it fiercely across his chest to the full extent of his right arm, and almost shouted his exultation and relief as the canopy, with a crack like a pistol, billowed out above him. His head was being forced painfully backwards by the rough canvas lift-webs twisted and crisscrossed beneath his chin, but no matter—he was safe, safe from the enemy, safe from the aircraft now diving to destruction far below. He dragged the strangling lift-webs apart, eased his aching neck, and moments later, from four thousand feet, Flying Officer K. J. Blight floated gently into the soft and soggy comfort of a paddy-field, one of the first pilots on active service to have saved his life in a Martin-Baker ejection seat.

After Blight came many more, in peace-time flying and in war, and with the seat in general service the stories were soon pouring into the Martin-Baker headquarters at Denham; stories of gratitude, of lives saved when no escape had seemed possible. From aircraft falling in flames, from aircraft hurtling out of control along the runway, from aircraft deep beneath the surface of the sea, the pilots came shooting out, alive, each one with a tale to tell of having looked death in the eye—and having winked. Each escape, to the man most intimately concerned in it, was a moment of high adventure, and many of them bordered upon the miraculous, but for the purpose of authorship it is necessary to be selective.

*   *   *

One day in 1954 Flying Officer Sam D'Arcy, whom I had known three years earlier as a cadet at the Royal Air Force College, Cranwell, took off from the aerodrome at R.A.F. Fassberg in Germany on a mission he frankly looked forward to, high-level practice bombing in the single seater Venom with which his squadron was then equipped. After a swift and steady climb to seventeen thousand feet he checked his instrument panel, set his course, and rolled the aircraft over into a dive at seventy degrees downwards towards the target area. Lining her up nicely, eyes glued to the bombsight, he pushed the nose of the Venom steadily towards the range, released his first bomb as he swept across it, and started to climb away. This, by God, was the life.

'Then,' as he told me later, 'all hell broke loose. I was just pulling her up at about eight and a half thousand feet, travelling around four hundred and fifty knots, when the stick simply gave out on me and I lost all control. The situation had nothing to offer, absolutely nothing at all.'

This conversation of ours took place years later, during a dinner held at the Dorchester to celebrate the thousandth life saved by the seat, yet there was even then, I swear it, more than a touch of sheer awe in D'Arcy's voice as he went on with the story.

'The aircraft was spinning all over the sky, rolling and twisting like something alive but demented. It was also, within seconds, one roaring sheet of flame, with bits dropping off it right, left, and centre. As for me, I was sitting well forward, my shoulder-straps loose to allow me close to the bombsight, and all I could think about was the ground coming up at me at one hell of a rate of knots. I knew I was going in, of course, and even though you think about it quite coldly, in fact calmly, at the time, it's still not a very nice feeling; actually it's downright unpleasant.' Sam D'Arcy is one of that blessed breed, very clipped, very Cranwell, who can talk like that, dead-pan, and get away with it.

'Suddenly I remembered the ejection seat. Of course, in a power-dive like this I had no time for any of the drill, and the instructors wouldn't have approved at all of my performance. I didn't tighten up my straps, didn't even jettison the hood; I just heaved down on the handle and shot straight through the bloody roof, and as it happened it was just as well. I was streaking through the air face downwards and still, of course, fastened in the seat; I got rid of that rather smartly and immediately pulled the plug. I watched the parachute pay out over my left shoulder, and it opened just in time, but the ground was really very close.'

It was indeed. Next morning, when Sam D'Arcy walked out alone to visit the scene of the accident, he found the cockpit, or what was left of it, of the plane from which he had made his escape.

'It was just a heap of twisted metal and broken controls. Few things were recognisable; it was like a jigsaw puzzle shaken up and thrown into a hole in the ground. And that, I thought, is where I was sitting just twenty seconds before the impact. It was all so unreal—the seat was lying only fifty yards away, almost intact. I walked over and patted it; I felt I had no right to be alive.'

D'Arcy's squadron companions, several of whom were later to

suffer a similar if not quite so close-run adventure, clearly thought the same, and two days after the ejection, the first ever made from a Venom, they dreamed up another little incident to add to the tales with which he will no doubt some day enthral his grand-children. The Mess were having a dining-in that night to wish Godspeed to a departing member, and D'Arcy, sipping a sherry in the ante-room before the meal, found that he had been nominated Mess Vice-President for the occasion. Now this in itself was in no way unusual; 'Mr. Vice', whose principal duties are to propose the Sovereign's health and to remain at table after the President and the most important guests have retired to the ante-room for the first crack at the post-prandial plonk, is always appointed from among the more junior members, and D'Arcy thought no more about it except for some faint surprise that he should have been chosen, under the circumstances, for what is understandably regarded by healthy subalterns as less of an honour than a chore.

But this was to be no ordinary evening. Flying Officer D'Arcy, walking in all innocence into the dining-room, found at the Vice-President's place not a chair but an ejection seat—*the* ejection seat. As he told me later, 'I damn near cried, but the President called out, "Sit in it, Sam," so I sat in it, and we all had a party I shall never, never, forget.'

Now that tribute to Sam D'Arcy by the officers of R.A.F. Fassberg stemmed mainly, of course, from their relief that a most popular member of the Mess was there, against all probability, to appreciate it; but there was more, much more to the matter than that. These men, rejoicing in the survival of a friend, were also celebrating the welcome evidence of a dramatic upsurge in their own life-chances should things, in the future, go wrong for them. It is unlikely, to say the least, that there was one single stain of cowardice amongst the lot of them, but it is no less certain that there was not one man in all that gathering to whom D'Arcy's escape in the ejection seat did not bring the strictly personal comfort of increased faith in a future full, by its very nature, of hazard. As the hero of the incident himself reported later, 'This whole affair has spread enormous confidence amongst the Venom pilots throughout Germany.'

Within months there came the Macfarlane incident, a first-of-its-kind-in-the-world rescue made all the more dramatic and significant because it happened under circumstances in which not even the seat's inventor could have prophesied success and because this one not only saved a flyer but prevented the tragic metamorphosis of a wife and baby daughter into a young widow and an orphan.

* * *

On 13th October 1954, Lieutenant B. D. Macfarlane, R.N., climbed into the cockpit of his Wyvern aboard the aircraft carrier H.M.S. Albion and settled down to his preparations for what is always a somewhat startling experience, a launching by catapult. With the canopy shut tight over his head he checked that his seat harness was securely fastened and his parachute straps all in order; the inflatable dinghy pack was fastened by a lanyard to his Mae West life-jacket; as the engine started up he switched his oxygen supply on to normal flow. After another ten minutes the engine was warmed up, all was ready, and on the given signal his aircraft hurtled forward under the thrust of the catapult.

This is a moment of savage acceleration when even the most experienced of pilots tends to suffer a slight and short-lived blurring of the wits, but even before he had cleared the carrier deck Macfarlane was only too well aware that from this particular sortie one vital factor was missing—engine power. As he shot over the bows of the Albion, he tried desperately to force the throttle wide open, only to find it already in that position and locked there. Travelling at only seventy knots, with the undercarriage still down and the flaps in their take-off position, the aircraft could not fly, and as it dived, with no possible hope of correction, over the prow of the ship and downwards in a thirty degree slant to the sea, Macfarlane faced the first of many horrifying thoughts and experiences that were to follow. His mind was now crystal clear, clear enough to remember that the aircraft he was flying was notorious for its unhelpful characteristics in the event of a 'ditching' and clear enough, even worse, to recall vividly an incident some eighteen months earlier when he had actually seen such an aircraft hit the sea and sink instantly without trace or hope of retrieval. As the waves came up at him he had just time, as he said later, to acknowledge the near-certainty that this was the end. Next came the stunning impact of his collision with the water, and the Wyvern, true to form, dived straight and steadily down.

By the time Macfarlane had unscrambled his responses he was sinking fast and the water all around him was growing darker. The Albion, however, was of course ploughing onwards through the sea, and observers in a helicopter overhead were sickened to see its iron bows shear clean through the fuselage of the stricken aircraft, ending, as it seemed to them, any glimmer of hope that the pilot might by some miracle survive. Macfarlane was, however, very much alive, and with the single thought in his mind to remain so. But he found out at once that although his brain was registering his desire to avoid drowning, it had not yet re-established a satisfactory working partnership with his body. Only one part of him, or so it seemed, would obey orders: his left hand. With this he stretched out, searching through fogged and feeble vision for the yellow-painted knob that would jettison the hood from the cockpit; he was grateful for its intentionally bright colouring, and grateful too for his own earlier good sense in practising, over and over again, the sequence of actions in just such an emergency as this.

At last he found the knob and hit it fiercely, and even as the hood began to move, his left hand, still the only one that would respond to his mind's instructions, reached upwards to the firing handle above his head. He pulled downwards, and hope died within him as the seat failed to fire; but then he remembered a similar experience when carrying out a simulated ejection on the test-rig at his base. All that had been wrong then had been his own failure to pull the handle far enough; this time might be just the same—God knows, it was worth a try. He heaved down with all his strength, and he blacked out as the gun roared beneath him and he was thrust upwards through the massive wall of water in which he was entombed. Recovering consciousness immediately he realised, almost without believing it, that he was clear of the sinking aircraft.

He was not yet, however, clear either of the seat or of desperate danger. Patches of yellow nylon and skeins of snaking white rigging-lines writhed all around him as he tossed and tumbled in the turbulent water; over and over he went like the contents of some gigantic, malignant washing-machine, for as he emerged from the cockpit of the Wyvern the huge mass of the Albion was thundering onwards over his head. By some freak of fate he escaped the ancient horror of a keel-hauling, but he was still floundering beneath the frothing water and he was, of course, drowning. It must have been the sheer instinctive discipline of his flying training that freed him from the strangling straps of his parachute harness, for he has no recollection of any deliberate action to cast them off. But he does remember all too well the strange, eerie euphoria of a man on the brink of death by drowning: 'After a time, when I had choked down a great deal, it was no longer unpleasant; in fact it was just like taking a long drink of fresh water.'

At last, when the ship had passed over him, the tumbling ended, and for the first time Macfarlane really believed that he was going to live. Bitter disillusionment was to follow at once, for he found that instead of rising he was being dragged deeper and deeper into the sea. It was at this moment that he acknowledged the inevitable and resigned himself to his fate.

'I must,' he said, 'have reached an advanced stage of drowning. I was in a dreamy, relaxed state, comfortable but sad; slowly "floating" deeper, and not frightened about it, just sorry. I had given up.'

Suddenly, when he must have been on the very point of death, came one sharp stab of hope, and with it the will to fight on. The tangle of lines and fabric in which he was enmeshed abruptly freed itself unaided, and he realised that only a single force was now dragging him down—the bulky dinghy-pack beneath him, secured by its long white lanyard to the life-jacket on his back. With numb and feeble fingers he inched his left hand down the length of the lanyard until at last it could grasp the release-catch of the dinghy. At first he fumbled badly, but at the third attempt the catch worked, and he was free. He began to rise, very slowly, and for the first time he began to suffer the agonies of his bursting lungs. In his desperate need for air he tried frantically to swim upwards, but his actions had no effect, and it was with death staring him yet again in the eyes that Macfarlane remembered, almost too late, the one life-saver still left to him.

Reaching around the edges of his Mae West he found the instant-inflation valve and pulled it; at once, like a cork from a bottle of Bollinger, he shot upwards to break the surface two hundred yards behind the ship from which he had been catapulted, so recently and yet so long ago. The sun was shining brightly, and within less than two minutes the crew of the helicopter above him, the men who had thought him dead, had hoisted him to safety, to a long leave far away from flying, and soon to a Christmas he had never expected to share with the wife and baby daughter who throughout all the ordeal of that watery hell had been waiting for him, untroubled, at home.

* * *

This has been the story, so far, of the early test men and of the importance of their work to the military men of their era: but these *were* early days within the context of jet-propulsion. Lieutenant Macfarlane was only Number 53 in the Martin-Baker Club—almost, so to speak, a founder member—the aircraft in squadron service were not yet supersonic, and there were still many problems to be anticipated and, ultimately, solved.

For prototype warplanes were forever flying faster and higher, probing deeper into the impossible, and escape from these was becoming increasingly difficult. A military test pilot frequently has to take the calculated risk of flying an experimental aircraft in which the escape facilities cannot match up to the aeroplane's performance, a circumstance totally unacceptable once a 'plane has been brought into squadron service. This is harsh, but it is inevitable, and it is reasonable. The test pilot does not have to worry about enemy action; it is his duty, indeed his *raison d'être*, to ensure that the combat flyer does not have to worry about anything else. The squadron pilot flies in the face of the enemy; the test pilot in the face of Providence.

The test pilots accept this, but that is not to say that they relish it. Their attitude was once perfectly exemplified and defined by the late Major Charles 'Chuck' Yeager, U.S.A.F., first man ever to break the Sound Barrier in level flight and one of the greatest of all test pilots. Touched down on the runway after an experimental flight at almost twice the speed of sound, a flight in which he had suffered a gruesome battering that had all but destroyed him both physically and mentally, Yeager's first remark to the admiring circle of men who rushed to greet him was, 'Don't stand there congratulating me—get me out. If I'd had an ejection seat I wouldn't be sitting in this crate now.'

As it is the function of the test pilots to fly constantly improving aeroplanes, so it is the function of the test parachutists to try out new and improved systems of escape from them. Already in the mid-nineteen fifties it was obvious that not merely minor improvements but new ideas would be called for to meet the requirements of the high-performance aircraft of the foreseeable future. In these new developments, when they came, I was privileged to play a leading part.

Part Three

Collaboration

The First Meeting

1954

When I first met James Martin in 1954 I knew a great deal about him and his achievements, but it had not at that time occurred to me that I might find at Denham the perfect opportunity for employing the various skills that I had acquired piecemeal over the last ten years. I was visiting Denham simply to introduce to Martin a U.S.A.F. Colonel who was eager to meet him.

I found Martin as impressive as his reputation. With the years his figure, still powerful and broad across the shoulders, had thickened into a comfortable rotundity; the jacket and waistcoat, both unbuttoned, were sprinkled with ash from the cigarette hinged permanently like wall-lighting to the very centre of his lower, protuberant lip. The gait, as he slowly circumnavigated the great desk strewn with blue-prints and bits and bobs of aluminium, the paraphernalia of his profession, was almost a shuffle, though in no sense enfeebled; unhurried, rather, deliberate and economical of effort. The face, a tolerant twinkle of blue eyes in a pink, cherubic roundness, was that of an ageing Botticelli boy, an angel who had been around.

Accentuating this air of experience was the ragged, deep-cleft scar running down the balding skull to the broad, unwrinkled forehead, a scar recalling the near-fatal night he had gone out to remonstrate with a roving band of gypsies raising hell in the grounds of his beautiful, six hundred year old home, Southlands Manor. His chiding may have been over-forcefully phrased, for the marauders came at him swinging picket posts and iron bars; Martin himself could not remember exactly what he said to them, and small wonder, for he next saw the light of day more than two weeks later, from a hospital bed. What he did recall was his first remark on recovering consciousness, a rebuke to the doctor bending anxiously over his badly broken leg: 'Never mind that end of me, sonny—come and do something about this terrible headache.'

His headache resulted from a fracture of the skull so severe that medical opinion still puzzles as to how he survived. Yet Martin, only weeks after this awful injury, had dragged himself from his bed, a silver plate glistening grotesquely in his skull, to haul himself painfully over to America, where the United States Navy were eagerly awaiting a demonstration of his ejection seat.

This incredibly tough character, far past the first flush of youth, had returned triumphant from that American trip to face another operation on a leg that looked likely to be permanently lame; he had studied the X-rays of his injuries, talked with the surgeon about the chances of complete recovery, and learned that to mend his fractures would be a complicated task with no certainty of success. 'What you need,' said James Martin, 'is the right tools for the job. Now tell me about it once more and let me see what I can do about that.' He then did an engineering specification job, had the tools made in his own factory at Denham, and handed them over to the surgeon with the cheerful challenge, 'now it's up to you.' The challenge was accepted, and the operation was a complete success.

Knowing all this about James Martin, and a great deal more besides, I was eager, naturally, to hang upon his every word. His greeting was predictably unorthodox. 'Have an apple,' he said, and sure enough the hand extended in greeting contained two bright-polished Cox's Pippins, one for the Colonel and one for myself. There followed a brief but fervent homily on the virtues of vegetarianism, with Martin exhorting us to eat the apples 'pips and all—the very seed of life, God-given,' before sitting down to enjoy with us a steaming bowl of beef broth followed by liberal helpings of chicken and ham. 'It's true what I was telling you about vegetarianism, every word of it,' he explained earnestly, 'but then I'm a little too old to take full advantage of my knowledge, and you're too young to listen to sense.' Conscience thus satisfied, he beamed benignly and chewed happily on another forkful of flesh and fowl.

Any suggestion, however, of amiable eccentricity disappeared when the conversation turned at length to the purpose of our visit. James Martin is not the only tycoon who lives for his business; even in England he is probably not the only Managing Director who knows more about every facet of his Company's functions than the men who work for him, who reaches his office every day an hour before his secretary, and who turns the place over to the night watchmen long after his employees have settled down to television or a night on the town. But he must be one of the very few industrialists whose sole business is the saving of human life under increasingly impossible conditions, and though his descriptions and discussions of this work may be humorous, they are never flippant. At the time of my first visit the seat had already begun to save lives—the score, I think, was between thirty-five and forty—and for an hour or more the American Colonel and I were exposed to the laser beam of dedicated enthusiasm that had made this possible; spinal anatomy, the principles of ejection, the critical measurement of explosives—one subject after another was expounded and illustrated by broad sweeps of the blue pencil on the sheaf of drawing paper that was never far from his hand. Suddenly Martin interrupted himself to look straight at the U.S.A.F. Colonel:

'Now you're a flying man; d'you think you could use one of these things properly?'

'Sure I could—just wish I had the chance.'

'Could you now? Right. Just sit there in your chair and show me how you'd use it.'

Dubiously, caught unawares by this piece of post-prandial pantomime, the Colonel raised his hands tentatively to the imaginary firing-handle above his head and held them there for a moment, looking sheepish. Martin roared with laughter.

'All right, Colonel, forget it. Don't bother. You're dead.'

As a slow flush of anger and embarrassment began creeping

123

up from the Colonel's collar, Martin leaned forward, all charm and conciliation, and placed a hand gently on his guest's shoulder.

'Now now, Colonel, don't let me upset you. I wasn't trying to make a fool of you or embarrass you; I just wanted to show you something clearly, so you'll never forget it. This seat of mine may save you one day, but only if you give it a chance. I won't tell you how to fly an aeroplane or when to abandon it—that's your job, and you know far more about it than I do. But what I will tell you is this: when you do decide to go, go fast. This time you hesitated because you were confused and embarrassed; next time you may hesitate because you're confused and scared, mebbe. Don't—don't ever hesitate, for your life-chance may disappear in half a second or less, and you won't get another. You remember that, Colonel—now have another apple and let me show you around the works.'

We toured the plant that day, led by the Guv'nor through the whining, grinding, deafening beehive of drills and lathes and clanking stacks of seats in embryo; we caught only a swift glimpse of Lynch, en route to a lecture he was giving to some visiting mechanics, but we saw film of him in action, and we talked with Captain Scott, the pilot who had flown him on that first epic test. We were shown the first-hand reports of the earliest emergency ejections, and we read the letters of thanks from the flyers who had made them. Cruising back to Aldershot that evening, sunk deep in the leather upholstery of our staff car, the Colonel turned to me out of a long and thoughtful silence: 'Judas Priest, there certainly is one hell of a man.'

'Colonel,' said I, 'I can only agree with you, and I'll tell you now, sir, just one other thing—one day I'm going to work for him.'

CHAPTER 12

The Scandal of the V-Force
1958

My prophecy was not to be fulfilled for some time, and for the three years following that first meeting with James Martin I remained in my liaison post with the Airborne Forces, enjoying not only my parachuting but another sporting thrill that had unexpectedly come my way. As games to be taken seriously, Rugby, Cricket and Boxing were all now far behind me, and I had imagined that my days of high-speed sport were over. I was ready to turn my mind and my leisure hours to casual games of golf.

But it was not to be. Six months after the sky-diving championships I was invited to compete for a place in the Royal Air Force Winter Sports Team, and the challenge was too tempting to resist. One of my friends at Farnborough, a test pilot, was Flight Lieutenant Colin Mitchell, who at that time held the world speed record on the Cresta Run, and it was for a berth in the four-man Air Force team for the inter-Service Cresta Championships that I was being considered. My total lack of experience on the single-handed skeleton toboggans might be offset, according to the selection committee, by my recent activities in another game calling for qualities of gymnastic awareness, balance, and speedy reaction, sky diving.

I travelled, nervous and uncertain, but excited, to St. Moritz, and after some hair-raising moments during the trials I did, as it happened, make the team, which went on to beat the Army and Navy and so win the Championship. Riding the Cresta is, I think, the most exhilarating sporting sensation I have ever experienced. To whistle down the twisting, icy channel at speeds of up to seventy miles an hour, head and chest well forward of the toboggan, chin only inches from the ice, body-weight shifting constantly and with hair-trigger rapidity to hold the rudderless 'skeleton' under control and within the boundaries of the run as it flashes through the towering corners with the magical names—Battledore, Shuttlecock, Scylla, Charybdis, and the rest—this is a supreme physical and emotional experience that leaves one gasping, glowing, and wondering what else one has ever done that made life seem so wonderfully worthwhile.

So far as work was concerned, I carried on as before, putting the troops through their parachuting paces, touring Britain and other European countries in search of suitable dropping zones for major airborne exercises, and maintaining my social-professional relationship with such firms as Irvin, G. Q. Parachutes, and, of course, Martin-Baker. I came to know James Martin quite well, but my diffident suggestion that I might carry out experimental work for him met with an instant application of the icy douche.

'I would like that very much, Mr. Hay, for Lynch's testing days are honourably over, but I'm afraid it simply isn't possible. For the work I see ahead of me in the next few years I shall need continuity. You are a regular officer, and the Air Ministry, you know, are not unfailingly co-operative where I'm concerned.'

I stored these comments away in my mind, but did not think very much about them, not seriously, until 1957, when my Service superiors, suddenly waking up to the fact that I had spent six unbroken years in the specialised sub-division of Parachute Training, decided that for career reasons I should now be posted to a staff job in general Physical Education. My appointment was to No. 1 Group Headquarters, Bomber Command, and at once my mind was switched back to the work of James Martin because, by a wild coincidence, the very first file to reach my office desk contained the specifications and designs of his proposed escape-system for the aeroplanes being flown by the Bomber Command Squadrons at that time. I had run face-first and horrified into the scandal of the V-Force, a story so sick, cynical, and full of shame that it will always disgrace the memory of the men, both officers and politicians, who must bear the responsibility for it.

When the first of the Delta-wing bombers, the Victors, Vulcans, and Valiants that ever since have constituted the major hitting-power in Britain's national defence had been introduced some years before, there had been one quite incredible and inexcusable omission from their design specifications: though they were to fly at more than five hundred miles an hour, no demand had been made by the authorities for the provision and installation of any system of assisted escape. That, in itself, may, just may, have been nothing more sinister than monumental folly—but for what followed there can be no such charitable explanation.

The first men to complain, forcefully and understandably, were the test pilots putting the new planes through their early paces, and gradually, grudgingly, authority was compelled to admit that a major error had been made and that something must be done to rectify it. What authority then did was to come up after months of reluctant discussions with the almost unbelievable decision to install ejection seats for two, and two only, of the five crewmen who would fly each plane in its operational role. Come most emergencies, in short, the team could be neatly and decisively divided, ratio two-to-three, into the living and the dead; and as if that were not an evil enough concept in itself, they compounded it by giving the life-chance to the wrong men, the pilot and the co-pilot, so cutting clean and irrevocably through the very first principle of Service leadership. There are those who sneer at the old tradition of the captain going down with his ship, and they have a point—but no-one, surely, would question that he should be the last to leave?

This was no mere matter of protocol. No man was accepted into the V-Force unless he had five years of flying ahead of him; and once he was crewed up, he really was crewed up. Five men trained together, flew together, came to know and rely on each other, became godfathers to each other's children, and if one of

127

them had a heavy cold not only he but his whole crew was grounded until it cleared up. And the leader of those five men, by definition and by Air Force Law, was the pilot, with the man in the seat beside him as his deputy. The other three, important in their flying functions but impotent as regards their futures, were tucked away, busy and oblivious at their desks deep dark down in the bowels behind the bulkhead—blind except through their instruments, and in every sense dependent upon paterfamilias up front. These three were the ones authority had decreed should, in an emergency, be ditched, deserted, left to die. The implications were immediately and disturbingly obvious to the men to whom they mattered, the aircrew, and the end-product was a gradual erosion of morale, sub-surface, controlled, but undeniable, in the manpower of the greatest striking-force in British military history. Not cowardice, certainly, yet in a sense more dangerous than that, for this *malaise* was deep-rooted in reason, fully justified, and shared by all. At first sight its symptoms seemed innocuous enough, a mere surface rash of badinage in the Mess—but the quips seemed casual only until you looked into the eyes of the quipper: or of his wife.

'Now Henry, dear,' from a Navigator to a Pilot, 'you really must promise me just one little thing: you won't ever leave me without at least saying goodbye.'

'I'll do just that, Charles, I promise. But don't bother to answer, for I won't be there to hear you.'

The realities of the situation, however, were grim, and if luck seemed loaded against the prisoners in the crew-compartment, the moral agonies were greater, by far, for the pilots. Every V-Force captain lived with the knowledge that any day, at any moment, he might be faced with the most appalling decision of all—to eject from a crippled aircraft, as his orders told him he should, leaving three of his closest friends trapped in the near-certainty of death, or to struggle on for a few more seconds against impossible odds before joining them in the final inferno? The second course was simple, perhaps senseless suicide, yet there is strong evidence to suggest that several pilots chose this action in preference to the sad, soul-searching, perhaps even shameful aftermath of personal survival—the widows to be faced, the children wondering why only their father and not his leader would not be coming home again, ever; the nights of sleepless speculation, of tortured doubts, unanswerable, as to whether a few more seconds even might have given the boys in the back at least some chance of 'conventional' escape.

This situation had been brought tragically and spectacularly to public notice in October 1956 when a Vulcan, returning from an epic and highly-publicised flight, had ended its journey a hideous mass of molten metal strewn along the runway of London Airport. The pilot that night was Squadron Leader 'Podge' Howard, the co-pilot Air Marshal Sir Harry Broadhurst, Commander-in-Chief of Bomber Command; behind them were not three other passengers, but four. As the huge aircraft swept in to land there was a critical misunderstanding between pilot and ground control as to its altitude, and Howard made his first touchdown not on the tarmac but in a sodden cabbage-field whose soft, adhesive surface clutched and tugged at the Vulcan's undercarriage, dragging down the flying speed and throwing the aeroplane completely and irretrievably out of control.

Howard forced the nose up, fighting tooth and nail for the power that would carry them into the climb, but as they crossed the airfield boundary the height was zero, the speed insufficient, and the aircraft no longer responded to the controls; there was no hope, no vestigial chance of saving it. Pilot and co-pilot looked at each other, saw agreement in the gaze, and reached for the firing-handles. They had stuck with the situation, and with their aeroplane, to the last possible second, and almost beyond it, for even with the seats' explosive upthrust their parachutes barely had altitude to open. Broadhurst broke his leg as he hit the ground, and as he did so his four companions died, trapped helpless in the blazing Vulcan.

This incident surely should have been the spur—but no. The

aircrews of Bomber Command continued to fly, and to die, in double jeopardy. James Martin, like many others, was appalled.

'Of course if they'd come to me in the first place I would have told them these young fellows must all have seats, and I'd have shown them how these seats could be installed. But I seem to be the very last man they think of consulting—until, of course, it's too late.'

I had known, of course, for years, about the hazards faced by the crewmen of the V-Force, but it was only now, gazing down on the dusty office file, that I realised, almost unbelieving, that the death of several dozen of Britain's most valuable, most highly trained aircrew had been the result not of inevitable, and therefore acceptable, constructional limitations, but cold-blooded, deliberate policy. For Martin's answer to the problem was there on paper, and Martin's answer was being systematically ignored. This was more than I could stomach. I had been a dependent member of an aircrew myself and knew what it felt like in moments of danger; I had seen enough of James Martin's achievements to realise that no blue-prints he offered could be dismissed as a pipe-dream; I felt that there was, there must be, work to be done, and that I was the man to do it. For the first time I began to believe, with inner conviction, that my future lay in testing, and began also to consider the implications and consequences of resigning my commission in the Royal Air Force. Such action might be disastrous, and might not even be easy to accomplish; a permanent officer could not simply walk out on impulse. I decided, nonetheless, to try.

* * *

Almost anything is within reach if you want it badly enough, believe it will be worth having when you get it, and don't look too closely at the mounting bill. It took time, of course, and some heart-searching, but by six o'clock on the evening of 8th July 1958 my confident prediction to the U.S.A.F. Colonel had become an established fact. At that hour exactly I walked out of the Denham offices with James Martin's earthy endorsement of my ambitions ringing in my ears.

'Well, Mr. Hay, since you seem so determined to get yourself an almighty kick in the arse, and since you're so remarkably well qualified to receive one, I reckon the least I can do is to give it to you. I only hope you'll enjoy it as much as you seem to expect, for I promise you it won't be any nice little love-pat. But I know from your record you've been hammered before, and you don't talk like a fool or act like a would-be hero. I'll be glad to have you test for me, and I'll send your contract along in the morning.'

Sitting in my car it was minutes, or so it seemed, before I could trust myself to press the starter or engage the gears; my hands, I noticed, were hot and trembling. I wanted a cigarette, badly, but I decided to wait. The flame of the lighter might flicker in a dead give-away and *he* might be watching from the window ready, at the first sign of nerves, to rush out and cancel the whole deal. I must be cool, matter-of-fact, as if this sort of thing happened to me every day, at least until I was out of sight of the factory. Reverse gear, for the very first time, was hard to find, and I cursed my stupidity in not having parked the Consul nose-outwards from the wall; it would look just great to stall the engine right under the Guv'nor's window. My God, he'd think, I've picked a real beauty here—can't even handle a car. Panic was rising, and I had to stifle an impulse to slide out of the driving seat and hand over to Jenny, sitting calm but enquiring by my side. Then the humour of the situation struck home and common sense, cool and refreshing, came flooding in on a wave of relief. My fingers were suddenly lean and firm on the wheel, the gears meshed smoothly, and we were gliding through the gateway with a farewell wave to the watchman; everything was once again easy, familiar, and under control.

It was a long time, though, before I allowed myself that cigarette. Not this time because I was nervous, but because I wanted nothing, not even smoke, to cloud my vision of what was happening in and to my life at that very moment. Jenny, sensitive and selfless, said nothing, asked no questions; she must, I suppose, have known the answers. Along the narrow lane we drove in silence, out across the busy Watford highway, then westwards through Rickmansworth and Windsor towards home. Through the lights and over the hump-backed bridge at Bagshot, I swung the car into the courtyard beside the timbered whiteness of The Cricketers, ordered up two brandy and ginger, tall and full of ice, lit the longed-for cigarettes, and spoke for the first time since leaving Jimmy Martin almost an hour before.

I was in. The private discussions, the difficult decisions, the repudiation of sound advice from uncomprehending well-wishers like the fat, bewildered, irascible senior officer serving out the fag-end of his career in the Air Secretariat——

'But Hay, I've just told you; your next promotion must come within a matter of a month or two, probably within weeks. And by that time, as you know, the new pay structure will mean an enormous increase in your income. I simply don't understand your application to resign, of all things, one of the very few permanent commissions in your branch.'

All this seemed suddenly, overwhelmingly worthwhile. Pre-destination is a pompous word and a suspect philosophy, yet looking back to that day and to the events leading up to and beyond it, it is not hard to read into the story some traces of the inevitable; too many doors deliberately, almost wantonly, thrown open to the unknown had led through tortuous corridors to rooms that might have been held ready for me since childhood. Too many risks taken had, against the odds, produced results. Any pattern of life in which the *status quo*, usually a satisfactory one in the eyes of outsiders, is deliberately destroyed not once but repeatedly and for no obvious reason, must surely be based either upon madness or upon some instinctive response to subconscious direction. Madness I would not admit; all I do know is that on that summer evening in 1958, with my Air Force future smoulder-ing in ruins behind me and with God knows what ahead, I was warm, comfortable, happy and secure in the knowledge that I had at last come home. There was no sense in it, of course, if you rule out that instinct for basic purpose; Martin, idealist and saver of life on the grand scale but as realistic as nuts and bolts on day-to-day administration, had offered me not a job, but an opportunity—an aim in life, but not a means of living.

'By birth, ability, and education, Mr. Hay, you're an executive, but as you say yourself, you're not an engineer. Now I have no room for executives who cannot contribute directly to the product, and I won't employ you to sweep the factory floor. I want your services, and I value your experience, but I won't have you kicking your heels around the Company, and you would hate that too, whatever you may think at the moment. When you make your contribution it will be a big one, perhaps the biggest one of all, but that won't come often—the only thing that justifies a live test is the need to try something that has never been done before, not by anyone.

'I calculate—you tell me if I was right. That is a huge responsibility, with a lot of lives depending upon the answer besides your own, and I'll gladly pay you a decent retainer to have you available whenever I need you, and pay you in addition for the actual tests. If you go away from home for more than forty-eight hours I shall want to know where I can contact you, and I'd like you to check with me before you plan any holidays; I'd like to you come up every now and again for a talk with me about what is happening, and I expect you to be fit and ready for a test at any time, on the shortest possible notice. I'll look after you if you get hurt, and your contract will spell out the terms of your insurance cover—tell that to your little girl out there in the car, and tell her she's looking worried about the wrong thing. I've never killed a parachutist yet, not even Lynch, but a few weeks after anybody uses my seat, his wife starts morning sickness.'

I stared, and saw the very start of reciprocal understanding.

'You're on the right lines, Mr. Hay; when you've done your stuff you'll come up here one day and you'll meet, just by chance, one of these fellows who's used the seat. He'll be here, very nicely, to say thanks, and his wife will be here with him, looking very young usually and not very sure of what she should say. And that's not all she'll be looking—she'll be looking pregnant, and she knows just why. Because she knows one night she got her man back when he ought to have been dead, and she gave herself to him in a way she probably hadn't done since her honeymoon. That's the life-chance, Mr. Hay; that's what the ejection seat really means; it gives a man the chance to die twice, and to take advantage of the experience if he's got the sense. And now I'll tell you something else, Mr. Hay—I'll tell you why you've got this job. All your international competitions, all that teaching of soldiers—you think it's credentials, I think it's crap. Now don't start getting up on your dignity—you're a good parachutist, and you have a good record, and that's fine, but what the hell do you think it matters to me?'

'It ought to matter: it's what you're after, surely?'

'Not at all, boy. There are plenty of good parachutists and plenty with good records. Agreed I wouldn't touch you if you didn't have the experience and some proven ability, but it's two other things that you offer and I'm after—I believe you really do want to make a contribution to air safety, I believe you really *care*, and you've got this queer damn disease that makes some men want to explore the unknown. To most people that's the most frightening thing on earth; to a few it's also the most fascinating. I believe you are one of the few; you'll be frightened all right, whatever you think now, but I don't think you'll back out or do something foolish. And that's what I want from you, not fancy bloody swallow-dives. Leave them to the stunt-men, the circus-boys. Your job is experimental flying with aircrew survival as its aim, and you'll start earning your pay when you walk up to a new seat knowing you're going to be the very first man to try it out, to find out whether James Martin is as clever as he thinks he is, or just a doddering old idiot as some of these wise men with lots of letters after their names seem to believe.'

That, then, was the prize that had me simmering with excitement, understandably, and with the satisfaction of achievement, ludicrous. A few hundred a year—'for the period of one year' the contract would read, though in the event it was to run for eight— no job, no pension, no prospects apart from an impending explosion beneath my backside heralding perhaps premature departure from this world in a singularly unenviable demise. Ridiculously happy I stirred on my stool, beamed at the barmaid, and ordered two more celebratory drinks.

'Jenny,' I bubbled, 'I simply can't believe it.'

'Neither can I.' Her tone was dry but her eyes, when I jerked up sharply to meet them, were warm and smiling.

'I must find a job, of course.'

'Teaching?'

'Never.'

It was surprising, the vehemence, the absolute certainty that I would not, at any price, go back to schoolmastering, the profession for which I was trained and qualified. Teaching was the job I did best, and I had enjoyed it thoroughly wherever and whenever I had engaged in it. I had taught in good schools, exciting schools, as a student teacher and as a qualified professional, and it had always gone well. But what I had seen in these schools had made its mark on me.

I had, as I say, enjoyed my brief teaching career, and much of my work in the Air Force had kept me at least tenuously in touch with post-war professional trends. I was thirty-six, young enough yet to pick up the threads and even to step on the sports field in shorts without starting giggles amongst the pupils—I was still, in fact, playing an occasional game of third-rate rugby, looking smooth, stylish, and supremely experienced some fifteen yards behind the scene of action and the threat of violent contact—yet I was a bit long in the tooth for spurning the one sure source of income and advancement for which I was qualified. The reasons for this refusal? I think two. First an almost pathological aversion to turning back—perhaps, because of a sense of adventure; more likely, I suspect, because of an instinctive awareness of talent and opportunity thrown away, of success and self-respect to be captured only in some new field entirely. Admission, early on, of weakness, and the firm intent, at all cost, to repay. And then, secondly, a creepy remembrance of the childish spitefulness and small-minded sniping of ageing schoolmasters growing in on themselves in every staff common-room I had experienced. I came from an academic family—my father was, I think, the greatest and best-loved teacher I ever met—and the profession meant a great deal to me, but I had seen, at first hand, its end-product. I had even seen, at one well-known school not hitherto mentioned, 'Mr. Perrin and Mr. Traill' acted out, under a weak and ineffectual headmaster, almost to the life, and I had shuddered with loathing and with pity at the sight. I had seen naked hatred and unspeakable mental cruelty at a sensitive, impressionable age, and so schoolmastering, irrevocably, was off the agenda. I started to look around.

If the ad. in the *Telegraph* had asked for a man to sell insurance I should have scanned the next column; I know my limitations as well as the next guy, and high among them, professionally that is, stands a built-in block against selling anything except maybe ideas. But the ad. didn't say anything so crude; it called for a character to be trained as a 'Life Underwriter', and it demanded some qualities I thought I could muster up at a pinch, at least for the purpose and duration of an interview.

Johnny van Haeften, my boss-to-be, was dapper and debonair, an Old Etonian and a sometime Colonel of the Brigade of Guards, one of the kindest, most easy-going men I have ever met; the interview went as smooth as cream. Perceiving within seconds that I had been conned completely by the wording of the *Telegraph* advertisement, I none the less kidded myself into subscribing to Johnny's enthusiastic assessment of my selling potential and I took over my desk, my telephone, my rate-book, prospect-book, day-to-day diary, and secretarial services within the week. I made a bull point immediately by memorising in its entirety but amending to its betterment a sales-talk I was supposed to deliver only from a script, for practice, and Johnny's admiration was unbounded, tempered only by the gentlest of chiding at the end of the performance.

'That was really quite magnificent, Doddy; you're the first chap who's ever pulled that one out of the bag, and you're going to sell a lot of Assurance. Just one little point, though. We are the Imperial Life Assurance Company of Canada. Canada Life, whose services you have been promoting throughout this most persuasive little chat, happen to be amongst our biggest rivals: do try, my dear chap, to sort them out quite, quite clearly in your mind before you start turning your talents on the clientele.'

I did. I re-wrote and memorised all the statutory sales-pitches, I mugged up the differences between 'Whole Life' and 'Endowment' and all the endless permutations of the company's plans for its clients' futures; I tabulated my prospects, drawing on every source from school friends and the Air Force List (with a couple of really exalted Knights I meant to tackle after practice) to the membership of every major rugger club in the country, and I set out, determined to sell. My first professional appointment was in one of my favourite haunts, the Royal Air Force Club in Piccadilly, and resolution turned to water as the victim turned up on time. We chatted of this and that, swapped increasingly strained reminiscence, until, after the fourth drink and the sixteenth silence, my old buddy-buddy faced me directly and said with ill-feigned bonhomie:

'Now what is it you really want to see me about, Doddy? There's something on your mind and you know I'll help if I possibly can, but for Christ's sake, what is it?'

The gratitude and the blatant lies fairly spurted out of me.

'Well, as a matter of fact there is something. I've only just come to Town, and I was wondering if you could possibly help me find a flat. There must be lots of comings and goings at the Air House, and you might just hear of something?'

Buddy-buddy roared his relief and ordered up doubles.

'As a matter of fact, me old cocker, I probably can find you a place, and quite quickly. But honest to God, boy, the way you've been acting the last hour or so I thought you were going to put the bite on me for some bloody life assurance—sorry, mate, but that's exactly the way you looked and sounded, like one of those wheezy Wing Commanders, all beer and bloody benevolence, with suède shoes and a blazer crammed full of proposal forms already made up in your name. By the way, what *are* you doing these days? There's a rumour around you've joined up with Jimmy Martin; just the sort of damn silly thing you would do—you know no-body's quite clear why you left the Service at all?'

I took the escape-road swiftly and without too much conscious shame, talked easily and with enthusiasm about ejection, and ended up that night better off than I had any right to; okay, so my plans for my new profession had taken a punch under the heart from which they were never to recover, but they were not very real hopes anyway—and the flat he found me in Wimbledon was a delightful apartment in which I lived comfortably for years.

And I did, despite the setback, sell assurance; in fact I sold my first policy only a few days later in a Surrey pub. I sold it to a pleasant young man called Mike Palmer, who had recently quit a promising post in China because the Bank that employed him would not allow him, at his age, to marry the girl of his choice. He later married quite a different girl, but when I first met him he was stoking up for matrimony by selling encyclopaedias door-to-door. We supped our grog one evening, footsore and heartsick after a long day of discouraging endeavour, and bored each other for half-an-hour with phoney eulogies of our respective trades. At last I could stand it no longer.

'Mike, come clean. Just how many of these Morocco-bound miracles have you sold—I mean ever?'

'If you put it that way—none. How about you on insurance?'

'Sweet Jesus, boy, we're running neck and neck. Now Mike ...'

Twenty minutes later I had bought a complete set of an encyclopaedia I never took out of its packing-case. and Mike

Palmer had taken out a Two Thousand Pound Policy in favour of his bride-to-be. Johnny van Haeften, next day, was jubilant:

'I told you so, Doddy—now you're really on the road, and you'll never look back. I knew you had the stuff.'

Mike too was earmarked for early promotion.

I quit, of course, not then but later. After days of sitting in my other, grander Club, gazing at the office from across St. James's Square, ashamed of an impending interview with Johnny in which I would have to confess not only that I had not succeeded but that I had not tried, I blew up completely, disappeared for a week, and came back only to hand in my resignation from a job in which I could never, despite certain natural advantages, have made the grade. One of my warmest memories of Johnny van Haeften is that the relief with which he accepted that resignation was mixed, quite genuinely I think, because we had become friends, with regret.

There followed a brief and unsatisfactory flirtation with the frigid whore of expense-account commerce, and then, mercifully, came the first call from Denham. Martin wanted to see me, at once.

CHAPTER 13

Escape from a V-Bomber

1960

'From what you've told me in the past, Mr. Hay, this is the one that really matters to you,' said Martin. 'I'm going to fire you out of the crew-compartment of a V-Bomber, facing backwards, the way a crewman would have to go in an emergency. All right with you?'

I nodded. Grinning, Jimmy picked up the telephone and called for a number I knew well—Holborn 3434, the Air Ministry. Seconds later, after brusque instructions to the switchboard, the grin developed devilment as well as delight, and his eyes never moved from mine. Then he spoke into the mouthpiece.

'James Martin here. Now see here, Dermot, I want that aeroplane you've been promising me. I've got a young man here in my office all ready to use it. You probably know him, and if you don't you ought to; he used to work for you before coming to me. Doddy Hay—that's right, Doddy, but he's got a fancy set of initials, W.T.H.—I think they stand for What The Hell. Yes, that's the fella—I believe he did use to be a footballer. I thought you must know him.'

Oh God, oh Cranwell, oh commission that once meant so much, oh Jimmy bloody Martin—my veins ran with ice-water, my spine was rigidly erect. There could be only one Dermot on *that* exchange, and what I was hearing was not the sort of conversation customarily directed at the Chief of the Air Staff. I waited petrified for the explosion, the appearance by magic of cohorts of outraged adjutants; I was new, even then, to the ways and weight of James Martin. All that came over the wire was a sibilant murmur, less strident by far than Jimmy's rejoinder;

'All right, then, but see it's no longer. This young fella here is liable to get impatient. I'm trusting you, mind, Dermot, and I don't expect you to let me down.'

Slowly, very slowly, as the 'phone went down, my junior officer's mind unwound from its tension and I relaxed, unbelieving, in my seat.

'That was, I take it, Sir Dermot Boyle?'

'Sure, sure; a nice man, and he remembers you well. He'll keep his promise, never fear, and we'll have that aircraft in no time—a Valiant. Now let me just run through the sequence of ejection for you.'

My first instinct, leaving Denham that evening, was to rush out and tell somebody about it; my second was to do no such thing. This was something more than impending excitement to be savoured, it was a challenge to be considered coldly, clinically, and with qualms. The savour was there all right, the swift surge of adrenalin and the sense of being on the threshold of new experience, of achievement even. But there was awareness of responsibility too, and this new situation, at least for the moment, I wanted to sort out strictly on my own. The qualms, uninvited, came out of their hidey-holes to confront me.

First to contend with would be my friendly old rival, fear. Would I in fact be frightened? Almost certainly—who wouldn't? Would fear be kept under control? Yes, I thought so, on the strength of past experience. What then was there to worry about? For a start, it was many, many months since I had worn a parachute, for with my acceptance into testing my interest in all other forms of parachuting had dropped from me like a snake's skin. The Valiant test had taken a long time, a tragically long time, to set up, and it was now almost two frustrating years since I had signed my contract with Martin-Baker. Perhaps I had been wrong, irresponsible, a cheat even, not to keep myself in practice; no, that was masochistic nonsense. Conventional parachuting was the least of my requirements for this project for which I had been waiting so impatiently, and anyway one doesn't spend years devoted to a game as I had been and then suddenly forget all one has ever learned about its difficulties and skills. Yet was it really as simple, as easily dismissed as that? My body, sure, knew all the tricks, and I had kept myself in good shape, honouring that part of the bargain at least, but supposing lack of recent experience in the air had left me mentally flabby, slow of reaction and irresolute in critical decisions? If that should be so, I was in trouble. On test the Valiant would be flying fast and low; a couple of seconds' hesitation, maybe one even, and I would miss the airfield and the recording cameras entirely, and no explanations or remorse could ever put *that* right. I shuddered; who the hell did I think I was, anyway, to take years of other men's work and dreams in my hands, so confident I wouldn't drop them?

My miseries left me, however, during the long drive home; knowing the problem, I reckoned on balance I had it licked. By the time I reached London I had one other vital question sorted out too—whether to tell Jenny about the impending test and so expose her to the worry of the waiting, or whether to spare her the anxiety and one day come home safe and sound, survivor of a *fait accompli*, with nothing to share but the celebration? Even the daftest of men can sometimes show some insight, and the answer I came up with, fortunately, was the right one.

'Do you realise, you dumb ox,' said my nearest and dearest later that evening, 'that if you hadn't told me about this now, I'd never have known another day's peace, and neither would you? That I'd be worried sick every time you were away for the day or late for dinner, and that I'd make your life as well as my own one long sweet, nagging, doubting hell? And that anyway,' dropping the banter and the assumed exasperation, 'I want to be there with you?'

Both of us, at last, were in business.

* * *

First came the preliminaries, exciting and satisfying in themselves. Another visit to Denham, this time to be weighed and measured first conventionally and then suspended from a meat-hook like something in Smithfield, face-down and ridiculous, in a scientific bid to establish my exact centre of gravity. Yet another visit, with time now running short, to see the newly delivered aircraft and its revolutionary installation; this was the opening whistle, this was when the game began.

It was vast, the Valiant. Stark and silver, so cold and operational, it brought the whole thing home. I walked around it scenting, assessing, stroking, an inquisitive, fascinated cross between a lover and his lass and a dog and his long-buried bone. I was establishing—no whimsy—a *rapport* with the aeroplane of which I would so soon be for all practical purposes an integral but unproven part. I gazed up at the towering steeple of the huge, blade-shaped tail-unit, thrilled to the thought of the thrust, the sheer power that would send me soaring high above it as it rushed towards me at three hundred and fifty miles an hour. I climbed the ladder into the fuselage, averted my eyes, as if *I* should be ashamed, from the two orthodox ejection seats lonely on the loftiness of the bridge, crawled my way back and downwards to the crew-compartment, and stopped as if struck; the engineer by my elbow, understanding, gave a lop-sided, apologetic grin:

'You may be the star of this show, sport, but you've got a supporting cast—and when you leave, you'll leave in a sheet of flame. They've got to have some protection.'

In front of us was not what I had expected, my first sight of the rear-crew quarters, but instead a curving sheet of unpainted metal, raw, blank, naked and new—the blast-screen. Installed, temporarily, for the test, a necessary protective barrier between the familiar and the unknown, it was as arbitrary as barbed wire entanglements and beyond it, appropriately, was No Man's Land —no man's, that is, but mine. I crept around the screen to the side that concerned me. No seat in the centre: that would be placed there, loaded and cocked, at the last possible moment before the off. Just a pair of guide-rails, slender and flimsy, leading upwards out of the gloom to a tiny aperture cut through the skin of the aircraft, many feet above my head.

'Little, isn't it?' said the engineer, looking up.

'It's little.'

'Big enough, though.'

'By how much?'

'Oh,' scanning my shoulders, 'by about an inch either side. Just don't eat too many potatoes the next day or two, and for God's sake, don't take up weight-lifting.'

I met the pilot and I met the crew, officers and men of the Bomber Command Development Unit, and I accepted their good wishes without embarrassment, for this was no pseudo-emotional glad-handing. They were test flyers for the V-Force, and they knew exactly how much was at stake. Serious men, professionals, and if one could fault them at all it would be only for a certain lack of humour characteristic, regrettably, of the truly dedicated. At the end of our first meeting, the skipper, Squadron Leader Ware, brow furrowed in an agony of earnestness, leaned towards me and said gravely:

'You know this thing is so important, I hope to Heaven it works—I really care about the outcome.'

So did I, Squadron Leader, so did I.

I had sorted out with Ware an agreed system of signals; once aboard there would not, could not be any verbal communication, for the cord of an intercom would constitute a lethal hazard; forgotten, secured in its connection, it would break my neck—even remembered it could, in the slipstream, serve efficiently enough as a *garotte*. The choice of signals was entirely mine, limited only by the means of signalling, red lights and green lights in Ware's compartment and in mine, each with a reciprocal button beneath, and I knew exactly what I wanted, what would suit the mood already beginning to creep into me. I wanted warning, but not too much. A long, steady, 'Green' as we committed ourselves to the run-in—three minutes, say, before the action. Then nothing, nothing at all, till five seconds precisely before firing, when I wanted an intermittent 'Green' to which I would reply with a short sharp 'Green' for okay or 'Red' for abort. Then visual silence for two seconds, essential for total concentration and lip-licking, before the final, executive 'Green'. That settled, confirmed, and rehearsed, there was nothing much more to be done; I went home, exhilarated, to wait for the word.

Waiting was a strange emotional experience later to become familiar, almost dominant, in my life. At first it was not a nervy business in the expected, accepted sense, and on the whole it was enjoyable, characterised by eagerness rather than by fear—that came only occasionally and even then, I suspect, it was a mere by-product of other, extraneous, problems. And such fears as I did experience seldom, almost never, concerned either the experimental equipment or what it might do to me, but only my own ability to handle it and whatever emergencies might come my way—my own limitations and possible inadequacies, mental, moral, or physical; slow thinking, momentary cowardice, or just plain butter-fingered ineptitude.

This sort of self-doubting, when it came, could be agonising, deeply damaging, I suspect, for of course it had to be cooped up, fermenting, in the cask; even to discuss such doubts about oneself would be to sow the seeds of them in others, undermining the confidence to which they were entitled and which they needed for their own peace of mind—the belief that the test man could be relied upon absolutely to handle his end of the enterprise calmly, competently, without fuss or fear of foozle. More than that, to talk about an imagined weakness might be to create a real one, through involuntary, sub-conscious, pre-justification of failure. No, it was better on the whole to resist the internal pressures, keep the problem private, and deride only silently the crass conception of total self-confidence and composure.

All this, of course, I was experiencing for the very first time as the hour crept closer for the Valiant test, and more powerful, more memorable by far than the fear was the sheer excitement of anticipation. Idealism may have been the cube of sugar, but this was the drop of L.S.D. It was, and always was, a period of increased awareness, of sharpened and extended perception, of enhanced appreciation of everything around me—my family, my

145

friends, the birds in the trees, a walk down the street, or the music of Brahms. It was the quintessence of life itself, timeless, the best of the whole strange business captured vibrant, selfless, and unspoiled.

The 'phone rang.

'Finningley,' said the voice, cryptic and crisp, 'the day after tomorrow.'

I understood, and we got down to details. Finningley was a Bomber Command aerodrome within cocktail distance of the headquarters from which I had resigned my commission and it was from here, up in Yorkshire, that we would fly; the firing would take place many miles south, over the Martin-Baker airfield at Chalgrove in Oxfordshire. I was to make my way north the following afternoon, spend the night at the take-off airfield, and be ready for action whenever the weather came good. The Martin-Baker ground crew—my *cuadrilla*—would come with me; Jimmy Martin, his executives, and the numberless 'interested' observers, would be at Chalgrove, waiting.

'Well, that just about covers it,' said the voice, 'except—good luck, Doddy.'

It was the first time in that whole conversation the voice had used my name, and I felt suddenly warm and wanted inside.

'Thanks,' I said, 'thanks very much,' and then the 'phone clicked down, breaking all contact, as it seemed, with the outside world. Now, and I knew it, I was on my own.

* * *

My return to the Royal Air Force was as strange and uncomfortable all round as Elliott Carson's to Peyton Place; I was in a familiar community to which I no longer belonged, and though my reception was friendly it smacked of the forced friendliness extended to strangers. And I was a stranger; I had to stifle a surprised protest when I realised that the ground crew were not being accommodated, like myself, in the Officers' Mess, and had to remind myself no, naturally, they wouldn't be—it was not snobbery. Just a straightforward matter of rank and status, and any other arrangement would certainly have caused embarrassment to all concerned, but I had to think that one out where a couple of years earlier I would have taken it for granted.

In the Mess after dinner, to which Jenny had also been invited, the atmosphere was unbearable, and I was puzzled to the point of indignation. No graduate of Dale Carnegie, I had usually managed, none the less, to rub along fairly well with the men I had mixed with, yet here we were, a dozen of us, trapped unhappily in a forest of dead conversational trees, with no-one making any obvious effort at replanting. Just before writing off Finningley as the dullest station in the Royal Air Force, I realised that it was my own presence that had caused the blight. These military men, usually of an evening so sociable, weren't entertaining me, they were *watching* me, and they were watching something else too, their conversation. Throughout that first ghastly half-hour, I realised, through all that stilted small-talk, not once had anyone mentioned the subject uppermost in every mind, the test. These fellows weren't Air Force officers at all—they were warders compelled by courtesy to while out the agony of the last night in the condemned cell. Small wonder the atmosphere was strained: they couldn't even look me in the eye, lest one or other of us should see something he did not want to see.

'You know,' I said chattily to the Wing Commander standing unhappily between Jenny and myself, seeing neither, 'the whole idea tomorrow is to save my neck, not to break it, and I truly believe that is the way it will turn out. But just in case I'm wrong, I would *so* much like to enjoy tonight—d'you think we might possibly have a drink?'

His eyes swung sharply into focus and slowly widened in delight.

'My dear fellow, have a dozen—no, that might be unwise in view of . . . oh God—well anyway, have a double. And your very charming lady; what may I order for you? And you chaps; let's all have a drink. What a perfectly splendid idea—steward!'

'Thank God for that,' said a boyish Flying Officer, turning to Jenny with all the charm and gallantry of youth. 'You know, Mr. Hay here is like a pimple on your girl-friend's nose—you *know* you ought not to look, yet you can't help staring

'Don't worry,' Jenny reassured him, 'I think things are coming to a head,' and from then on the evening was in the bag. An hour later, with no more than a private smile and a murmured goodnight, she drifted off to the W.R.A.F. wing, and soon afterwards I too was ready to quit. Some of the questions had become a mite too searching, and I had found myself once or twice tempted to answer them, to explain. That would have been stupidity indeed; I had still to prove that I could handle the job.

My preparations for bed were meticulous as a bridegroom's. I laid out pyjamas, cool, crisp and uncrumpled as the sheets. After bathing I shaved, after shaving I after-shaved, after that I brushed my teeth, and then, as an after-thought, I washed my hair and bathed again because all this exertion had made me sweat. Clean linen, top to toe, I spread out in readiness for the morning, but one blue hold-all, bulging, I left untouched. That nothing was missing from it I already knew, and the ritual of its unpacking was for tomorrow, tomorrow only, and no sooner. Shades of Twickenham, where the rugger shirt had always been pressed and new, the shorts starched into razor creases, the black boots polished to parade-ground gloss, and their laces, always, virgin white. Vanity? Rubbish—private, personal pride; such details are noticed by no-one but yourself. It's just that, if you really *care* about a game, you don't go on the field in dirty boots. I rolled into bed with cigarettes and a good book handy, prepared to fight out the terrors of the night, and I fell sound asleep five minutes later, with the light on.

* * *

Morning on 1st July 1960, dawned bright and clear, and I knew before quitting the pillows there was no fear of a postponement. No bath on this occasion—too soporific, sybaritic, relaxing, and effete; a shower instead, bouncing, bracing, better suited to the image and, in fairness, to the mood. Breakfast in blissful, sensitive silence, broken only by a youngster's shy, almost inadvertent interjection, 'Christ, sir, I wish I were you—I mean, I hope it goes well—I mean . . . oh hell, you know what I mean. We're all with you, you know.'

'I know; thanks.'

Then, in my room, the private ritual of unpacking the blue hold-all. As a craftsman treasures his tool-kit I loved my parachuting gear. White zippered overalls with the Union Jack emblazoned on the left breast, a legacy from the World Championships; heavy white sports socks to ensure snug fitting of my boots; the boots themselves, that I valued so highly and later had cause to curse—black and shiny, with thick soles studded with huge metal cleats to give just that extra little bite and purchase during fast landings on slippery or uneven terrain; a pair of canvas anklets, painted white, to strap round the meeting point of boots and overalls; a raw silk 'choker', worn throughout the war and by now shamefacedly accepted as a lucky charm; leather inner helmet to fit inside the hard white bone-dome; skin-tight lightweight kid gloves, always carried and never used, for I liked to feel the ripcord and the lift-webs directly in my hands, however cold; lumps of barley-sugar wrapped in Cellophane, cigarettes and matches in a cheap flat tin, available for the very moment after landing; a roll of strong white sticky-tape and a small pair of scissors; a scribble-pad with leg-straps, a stop-watch, and a new, tested, ball-point pen. This was my treasure chest, and it contained one other jewel—a sheath knife, shiny and sharp, to cut through tangled lines—but that really does not count, because for some obscure psychological reason I could never bring myself to wear it; I think it smacked too strongly of Errol Flynn, or perhaps it was simply that having challenged fate, I expected to win.

Half an hour before the staff-car would arrive to carry me down to the aerodrome I began, slowly and methodically, to dress, and at once the strange chemistry of testing started stirring within my mind and body. A fierce, exultant excitement was gradually brought under strict control and directed in a beam of total concentration towards a point not far distant at which nothing would even exist for me, nothing at all, except the job to be done. One cold little maggot of fear was held up, examined, and discarded. Would I really have wanted, have *allowed* any other man to take my place at this moment? Of course not—right then, away with you, and don't come back.

The process, once started, would steadily gather pace, and could not be interrupted, diverted, or checked; extraneous events, noises, thoughts even, were perceptible only dimly, like ships in the distance, and one by one, like ships, they vanished over the horizon of my consciousness. Down at the aerodrome, watching the ground crew swarming over the huge aircraft like ants, to-ing and fro-ing in a business-like frenzy of preparation, I stood apart with Jenny, talking matter-of-factly about our social arrangements for the next few hours while she, equally calm, cut the white sticky-tape into strips and bound them round the wrists of my flying suit, safeguards against the risk of a flapping cuff that might distract or even blind me in the storm of the slipstream. My personal luggage, re-packed, was by her side; soon, when I had been locked away inside the Valiant, she would take it with her own as she flew down to Chalgrove in the Martin-Baker aircraft to await my explosive arrival. The test-plane, its task completed, would merely circle the airfield to scrutinise the outcome and then head for home. We smoked—shared—a last cigarette and discussed what we would have for lunch and where we would go that evening.

'Dinner at Gennaro's, perhaps, and then a show? Or maybe a few drinks first, and then a late supper?'

The questions were left hanging in the air, unanswered, as a shout came from the direction of the Valiant.

'Okay, Doddy—we're ready for you.'

'Don't forget this,' said Jenny, handing me *The Daily Telegraph*, and with one quick, warm peck on the cheek disappeared, quiet, undemonstrative, brave, to handle her own problems while I handled mine.

I stubbed out the cigarette, slipped the butt, as an afterthought, into my pocket, and clambered up into the aircraft with a grin at the boys fussing round me like so many anxious midwives; I squeezed myself into the ejection seat, hauling the lower straps of the parachute forward between my legs. Several pairs of hands at once went to work on the harness, clipping on the leg-restraint lines that would prevent me from parting with my lower extremities when I left, pulling each strap and buckle tight, tighter, tightest till they bit right into me, holding me fast, blending me, almost, into the seat itself. At last, satisfied, I gave the thumbs-up signal and pulled on first my inner helmet and then the bulbous, Man from Mars covering, the bone-dome.

'Hell,' I said immediately, 'I don't like this much.'

'What's the matter?'

'I can't force my head right back—the shape of the back-pad won't allow it. My spine will be bent forward.'

It was true; in this experimental seat there was no deep concavity behind me in which the back of the rigid helmet could nestle.

'Hmm. Well, push as hard back as you can, Doddy, as hard as you possibly can. You should be okay.'

'Well, all right if you say so—but I still don't like it.'

But time was running short now, and as Ware popped his head into my cubby-hole to confirm the details of the programme I stacked the problem away at the back of my mind. Short of calling off the test there was nothing, in any case, I could do about it.

'You're locked in now, I'm afraid, for about forty minutes before we even start to roll,' said Ware. 'That will give your fellows in the Dakota a big enough start to get to Chalgrove ahead of us. Our own flight plan calls for a further thirty-five minutes in the air—I just hope you won't be too uncomfortable.'

'I'll be okay, thanks. I skipped coffee this morning, and I took care of my comfort just before I came on board.'

He smiled. 'I must say you sound pretty cheerful, though I'm damned if I can think why. Anyhow, that just about wraps things up; I'll say cheerio and good luck now, for I shan't be seeing you again. But one of the crew will shove his head round the blast-screen now and again, and if you want to say anything, just scribble a note. You won't be able to hear a spoken word in this aeroplane today, with the door open and that bloody silly little hole of yours up there in the roof. What happens, by the way, if you miss it?'

'I get the most frightful headache and you get a very untidy aeroplane. But I'll try not to miss it; I'll aim very carefully. See you, then, and don't forget those signals—three minutes, five seconds, zero.'

Then came the ground crew to say their brief farewells, looking concerned and leaving me with one final, chilling gesture and the warning sounding sombre in my ears: 'The safety-lock is out now, Doddy—don't pull that handle, for God's sake, until you really mean to. You're sitting on her, and she's alive.'

This was it, then; the ponies were at the post, and I had placed my bet. I shifted gingerly in my seat, half-afraid of igniting the cartridge there and then, and took an inventory of my unfamiliar surroundings, reducing them rapidly to the only three components that counted, the lights in front of me, the blast-screen behind my back, and the little patch of bright blue sky above me; sight of this last triggered off thoughts of the Ballad of Reading Gaol which I dismissed delightedly as quite inappropriate to the occasion —prisoner I might be, but self-immured and not for long, and for me the sky would soon, very soon, be not remote but all around me, and, for one brief moment, mine and mine alone. Another flash of whimsy—the thought that in this, not only the first assisted escape from the crew-compartment of a V-Bomber, but also the first ejection in history made with the parachutist facing the tail of the aircraft, I was doing what as a youngster I had always hated and fought to avoid; sitting with my back to the engine—and then I settled down happily to mental rehearsal.

The signal-pattern I knew by heart; no matter, I went over it again, again, and then again. Now what about something far less simple and at least as important, the action-pattern? The three-minute Green would be the sign to shake my arms and brains around a bit, to make sure that neither had stiffened up, to make a final check of my harness-buckles, to make certain, quite, quite certain, that everything was in fact all right. Half-way through the ensuing pause I would reach up to the firing-handle and loosen it in its housing to ensure a clean, swift action when the time came. At the five-second flicker I would stab the return button—the Green one, please God—and reach up again to the handle, hanging on to it, gripping it hard, fingers firm and elbows forward. After that—well, I knew all too clearly what came after that.

With the firing would come the need for fast, decisive thinking. I must register every detail of a new and strange experience, for I would be the sole custodian of its secrets, and my job was to pass them on. I must decide next whether the experimental seat was working to plan, and act without hesitation if it was not. My parachute should stream five seconds after firing, and if it didn't I would have precious little time to play around. I would already be falling below the test altitude of one thousand feet, and in the event of total failure the ground would be just ten seconds away. Several of these could be written off as useless, for the parachute takes time to develop—and so the difference between life and death would be sorted out in the space of, at best, some six or seven seconds.

There were other contingencies, of course, to consider, failures partial rather than complete, like the one that had almost killed poor Page on his second and final test. I tried to envisage them, to identify in advance their early symptoms, for I knew as sure as shooting there would be no chance of profit or analysis in those that came later, and to work out the best prophylactic treatment for each. I was still busy on this, miming occasionally with my hands, a strong contender, to any casual spectator, for the padded cell, when a crewman poked his head around the blast-screen.

'We'll be off in a couple of minutes. The captain would like to run a test on the signal lights.'

Green flashing, green return; green steady, green return. Red, no flashing, just steady ominous, final and heart-breaking; red, reluctant, defeated, return.

Of the rising whine and tortured scream of the jets I was sharply aware, and the slow trundle out to the runway followed by the swift uncertain acceleration along it was as gut-clutching as ever, but once in the air I abandoned the rehearsal which had, I reckoned, extended my survival chance by perhaps a second and a half, and forced myself to take, as planned, a twenty minute holiday from the test, a mental and emotional cat-nap. I fumbled for my ball-point pen, unfolded *The Daily Telegraph*, and settled down to the crossword. Twenty minutes I allowed myself, and twenty minutes, usually, was sufficient and to spare; today it damned well had to be, for I had promised Jenny the solution, complete, on arrival. The boast had soothed and diverted her in one of her infrequent bad moments, and I wanted to preserve it as something better than a spontaneous flip-trick; I wanted to finish that crossword or bust. I shut out the test completely and got down to work. Exactly seventeen minutes later, unable to suppress a private smirk of sheer self-satisfaction, I capitalled in the final square, patted myself on the back for the erudite, splendid fellow I was, and returned, happy and tingling, to the test.

CHAPTER 14

The Secret Test

1960

The drop was due in just over ten minutes, and I started watching myself closely for signs of excitability or over-tension, suspicious almost when no such signs appeared. My hands were steady and cool; no tell-tale moistness, either, on the upper lip; it looked as if I was going to be all right. I felt almost fraudulent. It couldn't, it shouldn't, surely, be this easy and enjoyable to face up to the unknown with your neck at stake? It wasn't.

Exactly five minutes before the firing, two minutes before the first of Ware's green signals, when I had poised myself for the start of the action, there came a thunderous knocking on the blast-screen behind me. Frightened and furious, I twisted sharply round, almost quartering myself as the harness cut viciously into my shoulders and thighs, to see one of the aircrew reaching round the barrier, pushing something tentatively towards me, like a toddler feeding buns to an elephant—a scrap of paper, a scribbled note, fastened by elastic to a clip-board.

'Sorry. Some of the observers have been delayed. Chalgrove want us to fly around for another hour. It's up to you. Can you cope?'

I looked up into the screwed-up, apologetic face of the messenger, read nothing but pity in his eyes, and even as my spirits dropped to rock-bottom, they bounced right up again, bright and blazing, and I realised in one marvellous, revealing, second of time that this sort of exploratory testing is not a job at all, but a vocation. Who the hell was he feeling sorry for anyway? After that one cold clutch of anti-climax, I was the happiest man in the aeroplane, revelling, actually revelling in the knowledge that I was to be allowed to extend this incomparable experience for sixty precious minutes. I realised that once the test was over, whatever the outcome, it would start to fade from that moment into mere memory, diminishing in intensity as it went; *now*, in the elation of anticipation, now was the time to prize and cherish. Here, on the threshold of a new aviation experience, I was receiving payment in advance for any hazard that experience might entail. In response to my cheerful grin and thumbs-up signal the messenger's eyes widened in sheer incredulity and as he turned away he dropped a hand on my shoulder; he probably imagines to this day he had just seen something brave and admirable.

I turned the *Telegraph* to the sports pages and sucked happily and reflectively on a piece of barley-sugar, substitute for the longed-for cigarette forbidden in Service aircraft. My extra hour passed pleasantly and quickly in reading and rehearsal, with a thought here and there for Jenny, marooned in her anxiety down at Chalgrove—how was she taking the protracted period of waiting? At last came a further message from Wade:

'We are clear to start the run-in ten minutes from now. Ten minutes to the first Green.'

I folded the newspaper carefully, the completed crossword triumphantly upwards to the eye, tucked it away inside my zippered overalls, and turned my mind to total concentration upon the test. At first I forced my eyes to wander around the compartment, afraid that they might become blurred out of focus if directed for too long a period on the lights, dead for a few more moments but mesmeric nonetheless, in their unwinking stare. I shifted slightly in my seat, dangled my arms and flexed my fingers—*My God, this is a long ten minutes*—and suddenly, like a shriek, it was there: G R E E N. I steadied myself for a moment, reached high for the firing-handle only just within reach above my head, and felt a swift, dreadful surge of sheer animal panic rush through me as I found I could not move it; stiff and new, securely bedded down in its housing, it simply would not budge in response to the firm but careful persuasion of my fingers, and for all I knew it might be jammed. I was cold now, cold and scared, but I must be quick, and my decision must be the right one; we were perhaps one and half minutes short of the aerodrome, winding up and over three hundred miles an hour. Should I heave a bit harder on the handle, with the attendant risk of a premature firing that would ruin the whole effect of the test, or should I wait for the signals and pray that one almighty pull would see us through? The second course was tempting—there is nothing to attract one to fiddle with the firing-handle of a live ejection seat—but I decided almost immediately against it. I would work carefully, but I just *had* to know; if this test was going to be a success then it was going to be complete success if that were within my power. That was what I was being paid for.

Sweating, I tightened my grip on the handle and began to haul on it, steadily at first but then, as it still failed to move, in a series of short sharp jerks. It came free suddenly, and for a split second my mind and emotions froze as I waited for the explosion—but no, an ugly moment was safely over, and I had won the race with Ware's Green light. Not by much, though, for almost as soon as my breathing was back to normal came the flickering signal, the sign that we were really and irrevocably in business. I prodded with my finger at the return button and reached up once more and for keeps to the hateful handle, my breath held tight and my eyes fixed unwaveringly on the lights. No thoughts required now—only a Pavlovian pattern of response to a given stimulus, a reaction not only inevitable but just as near instantaneous as I could make it.

G R E E N—Pull—C R A S H: the gun roared out beneath my backside, and there was no room for doubting that it had fired. A shaft of sheer agony seared up my back and into my brain, but we were moving, the seat and I, up through the dark fuselage and into the daylight like an express from a tunnel, and the pain was over in an instant. As I rolled and tumbled in the weightless buffeting of the slipstream I saw the huge tail of the Valiant slice through the sky beneath me and heard the secondary explosion as the drogue-gun fired. Then we were spread out horizontally, parallel to the ground, the seat, myself, and the streaming auxiliary parachutes; I was counting the seconds, and right on time—in fact on 4.9 seconds instead of the estimated 5—the main canopy blossomed open and jerked me, joggling, to a halt. The lift-webs were crossed behind my helmet, forcing my head forward, and by now my upper back felt on fire, but no matter, I'd done it—the new ejection seat was a success and so, by God, was I. I knew without asking that my reaction had been fast, and I could see by looking downwards that we were right over the centre of the air-field; already I could spot James Martin's black Bentley nosing slowly out from the crowd of spectators, following my line of drift. Somewhere down there, too, Jenny would be watching, and I spread-eagled wide with my arms and legs, just once, in a pre-arranged signal that all was well; my back I would worry about later, right now I was very much alive and it was time to clear the twists in my rigging lines and steer in for the land-ing. It was a beauty; a fast side right, my favourite from 'way back, and I was up on my feet and running round my para-chute to collapse it before the first of the ground crew could reach me.

James was up to me in an instant, beaming his congratulations and relief, but abjuring me in the same breath not to say a word to anyone about the test 'until you and me have had a little chat and a nice cup o' tea in the office. I'll arrange for you to give them all a conference afterwards.—It was a lovely shot, Mr. Hay; now come and tell me all about it.'

There was a decision to be made then too, and almost without thinking I made it; there was no need to spoil the occasion, at this stage, by any mention of the injury to my back, for although I was in no doubt that it was an 'injury' and not merely a pain, I also knew what had caused it, and that had no relevance to the problem of escape from a V-Bomber. A modified head-rest anyone could fit: what James Martin had just accomplished and I had just proved was a major break-through in the field of aircrew survival, and no aching back was going to be allowed to spoil it or detract from its importance and essential success. Perched on the edge of a desk in the flight office, dangling my bone-dome and feeling utterly at one with the world, I made my report to the Guv'nor, filling in every detail while it was fresh in my memory, mentioning as if it were funny—but not all *that* funny—my gruesome struggle with the recalcitrant firing-handle and suggesting that in future, for test purposes, I would settle gladly for one sound but second-hand. I was tired, I realised, but it was the blissful exhaustion of a requited lover, and dragging deeply and contentedly on my second cigarette I moved out into the sunlight to meet the Air Force, the Ministry, and the Press.

The first were ecstatic, the second subdued, and the third almost totally absent, represented only by a determined young photographer from the *Daily Express* who, barred from the airfield, had lurked patiently outside its boundaries all morning and who had been rewarded for his pains by the only still photograph in existence of ejected escape from the crew-compartment of a V-Bomber, a picture that made half a page the following day under the unduly optimistic heading 'First Man Out'. That the aviation Press in general were not present was the result of a decision so incomprehensible as to seem sinister, that the test should be classified as 'Secret', as if an ejection seat were a lethal weapon rather than a life-saver. That Whitehall did not stay to celebrate over lunch may have resulted from an awareness even then that for them the success of the test spelled awkward moments and embarrassing questions ahead, questions that could never again be brushed aside with an airy 'impossible' or 'impracticable.' I believe one of the faceless men did actually shake me by the hand, but as congratulation it was both cursory and cool, and I would not recognise him now floating face-uppermost in my soup. Not that I cared at the time—it was in the reaction of the Air Force contingent, two or three Air Marshals and a battery of staff officers from Bomber Command, Bill Stewart and his team from the Institute of Aviation Medicine, that I had the only reward that mattered to me, the inner conviction that everything, the wrecked career, the burning spine, the insecure and unpredictable future, all of it, now and forever, was unquestionably and incomparably worthwhile. As if to confirm that feeling and also, simultaneously, to destroy it, came one appalling moment in front of the camera when Air Marshal Parselle, having posed formally in a handshake, saw fit to emphasise his true feelings without warning by handing me a hearty slap on the back. He is a big, powerful man, the Air Marshal, and I damn near fainted, for it was the fifth, sixth and seventh thoracic vertebrae that had been fractured by the thrust of the seat through my bent back, but somehow I clung to a glassy grin, and the picture is there to prove it.

Reports and formalities over, I was free at last to join Jenny, lingering self-effacingly on the fringe of all the excitement.

'You're hurt. Is it bad?'

'It's not great, but it's okay. But how on earth did you know—they don't, any of them, not even Jimmy.'

'They're so wrapped up in what's happened they haven't even counted your legs. I don't have to; I know your face. You're putting up a good show, but for the last ten minutes you've been white as a sheet, and that grin of yours wouldn't fool a fourteen year old. What happened?'

Over lunch in a little country pub in the lanes beyond Chalgrove I told her; it was no good lying any more, for the pain was setting in hard and horrid, and I knew I should have to do something about it, and soon. Most of the Air Force visitors were still with us, and I kept myself out of their sight during luncheon by pleading a desire only for a drink in the bar adjoining the diningroom, but when the party had at last broken up and the Martin-Baker group, including Jenny and myself, had motored back to Denham, I raised no serious objection when James Martin, aware now that something was amiss, insisted that Eric Stevens, his Project Director, should drive me up to Harley Street for an orthopaedic check-up. That was when I received the confirmation, rather than the news, that some of my vertebrae had crumbled in a series of crush-fractures, and the verdict that my testing career, in surgical opinion, was over.

* * *

A professional training in Physical Education can be a useful asset to a man with a broken back. In between daily visits to the lush environment of the London Clinic for proddings and pushings and pullings I spent hour after hour at home on a tough and progressive battery of rehabilitation exercises, a self-devised programme that would have nobbled a navvy. As a way of life it was both sore and boring, but gradually it began to produce results, and the tedium of the slow-moving weeks was relieved by the awareness of a steady physical improvement, and, more importantly, by the knowledge that the job had been done, the contribution made. Very soon, surely, the wheels of authority must start to turn, and in the V-Bomber Force the whole stage-set of life and survival would be changed into something worthy of decent men. It was a warming, exciting, immensely satisfying thought, and not for one moment was I unhappy or regretful of my decision to play my part in the transformation. I chafed, of course, at the discomfort and the physical restriction, and I bridled resentfully and ungratefully at the well-meant suggestion of a spinal-jacket—what did they think I was, a cripple?—but none of this, deep down, really mattered to me in the least. What did matter was that the job had been done, and that a part of it, small but vital, was mine and mine alone.

Then, like vomit jet-propelled, came the news of the Ministry's decision spread sickeningly across a banner headline in the *Daily Express*:

BOMBER MEN STAY IN PERIL—BY ORDER

I read, not quite believing it, the report.

'The men in the back of Britain's V-Bombers are NOT to be

provided with life-saving ejector seats, although their installation has been proved technically possible.

A new and final Air Ministry decision means that captains and co-pilots must continue to face the awful responsibility of being under orders to leave their three rear-crew friends trapped in a real emergency while they themselves eject to safety.

It is a responsibility which worries some bomber skippers more than the less real and immediate possibility that they might one day be required to drop an H-bomb.

They won new hope after five years of argument in July when the Martin-Baker company, pioneers of ejection systems, successfully fired a man upwards and backwards from a Valiant Bomber.

But, after weeks of questioning about the results of investigations into this experiment, the Air Ministry admitted last night: "In view of the experience and the low accident rate over the five years that the V-Bombers have been in R.A.F. service and of the considerable time, effort, disruption, and cost which would be involved in modifying the aircraft, it has been decided that the provision of ejection seats for rear-crew members cannot be justified".'

'*Cannot be justified.*'

The *Express*, to its credit, picked up the phrase immediately, and in its leader column described the Ministry's decision as 'monstrous.' Perhaps as a result of this publicity, the matter was subsequently raised in the House of Commons, but the Government remained adamant, and the *Express* returned to the attack.

IT'S STILL 'NO' TO THE MEN IN PERIL

'A plea to end the life-and-death dilemma for R.A.F. V-Bomber crews who have to abandon aircraft was turned down in the Commons yesterday.

Mr. Julian Amery, Secretary for Air, said "No" to a demand that A L L crew members should have ejector seats. (This is standard practice on American H-Bombers, but R.A.F. Vulcans and Valiants have only an escape-hatch for rear-crew members.)

Mr. Amery said:

"To have ejector seats for all the crew would involve a large modification programme and the depletion of Bomber Command's front line over a long period."

He was advised that the greatest number of accidents in V-Bombers took place at high altitude, where all the crew had time to escape, but he admitted with a shrug:

"At low level this is not so easy."

Mr. Fred Mulley (Labour, Sheffield Park) asked:

"If it is not possible to make changes in existing aircraft, could it not be done with those now being built?"

Mr. Amery did not reply.'

It was a pity that the Press as a whole did not see fit to continue the fight that the *Express* had started, for a strong wave of public opinion might have compelled Mr. Amery and others to answer questions considerably more searching than that posed by the Member for Sheffield Park. It might even have spared that same politician, Mr. Fred Mulley, from the embarrassment years later of himself refusing publicly to introduce the very reform he had called for so passionately and persistently from the non-executive safety of the Opposition back benches.

When had Martin's plan for universal escape first been submitted? (The answer to that one was, more than four *years* before he had been provided with an aircraft in which to prove it practicable.) On whose authority had it been shelved, and on what grounds? How many V-Bombers had been built since the plan had been put forward? How many more would be built before the V-Force ceased to function operationally? How many rear-crew members had died in accidents where the pilots and co-pilots had survived? How much 'cost and disruption' would have been entailed in the modification of the bombers to include this life-saving device compared to that involved in fitting them out to

163

receive 'Skybolt', the missile that never was? Was the Minister aware that in an emergency, even at high altitude, time was not the only factor affecting a man's chance of survival? Had he ever seen, let alone travelled, the escape route from the crew compartment of a Vulcan and, if so, had he visualised that same journey in full flying kit, under conditions of stress, in an aircraft weaving and twisting out of control at a speed only slightly sub-sonic? Would he be prepared to identify the Air Marshal who had stated that the introduction of ejection seats for rear-crew personnel was not only impracticable but *undesirable*, and would he care to comment on that statement, perhaps the most scurrilous ever uttered by a British officer?

It was left to the *Express*, however, to make one final attempt to force the issue.

Under the bold, challenging headline

VICTOR PILOTS 'CHOSE TO DIE WITH CREW'
NOW ALL V-BOMBER MEN FACE DILEMMA
NO EJECTOR SEATS

their Air Correspondent drew attention to the fact that in a report being prepared for one of Amery's successors as Air Minister, Mr. Peter Thorneycroft, the opinion was being expressed that in the disastrous and unexplained loss of a Victor over the Irish Sea in 1959 the two pilots had died in preference to deserting their three rear-compartment companions. On the subsequent search for the 'black box', the recording instrument that would tell the full story of the mysterious crash, the British Government spent over Two Million Pounds without success—money, as the *Express* pointed out, that had been better spent in providing the facilities that would have obviated the necessity for the search.

Depressed and disillusioned, I drove up to Denham to see James Martin. By now I was writing professionally, at the start of a six-year stint for *The Observer*, and I had some ideas, I think, about blowing the whole disgusting affair wide open from the inside. Soothing, imperturbable, paternal, Martin brought my anger quietly under control.

'Politics is all that matters to politicians, Mr. Hay. Now when did you ever hear of one of them losing face, or losing a vote, by admitting he's made a mistake? Maybe later on one or two o' these fellas may spend a few sleepless nights, but that's their affair, not yours and mine. You forget about recriminations and concentrate on getting that back of yours better—I've got something very tasty bubbling up in the pot, something very important, and you're the man I'd like to sample it for me. That's, of course, if you're still willing?'

'Willing? Barkis isn't in it, and well you know it. What's the recipe?'

James Martin, for all his genius, his dedication and his homespun philosophy, has as strong a sense of the dramatic as the next man. My question hung unanswered in the air for seconds as he tapped his pencil, stared straight into my eyes from across the desk, and finally replied in one word that came rolling off his lips:

'Rockets.'

CHAPTER 15 About Rockets
1960

In those days, in 1960, the very word 'rockets' had a ring to it, and my pulses were racing as I leaned forward to listen to James Martin expounding upon his new project.

'Forget about your disappointment, Mr. Hay.'—I already had—'Except for a few more unfortunate young men all that is already in the past. But you and me, Mr. Hay, we are just about ready to leave the past, skip the present—it's well catered for—and move right into the future. We are going to provide the answer to ejection problems for years and years to come, maybe right through to the end of the era of manned aeroplanes. I'm going to shoot you faster and further than any man has ever been shot before. Now what d'you feel about that?'

'Great. When?'

'Very soon; within a matter of weeks, probably, so if you're thinking about a holiday, now's the time to take it. After that I'll want you on constant stand-by. But first of all you ought to understand clearly what we're doing and why we're doing it. Now what do you consider the moments of maximum hazard in an aeroplane?'

'Take-off, landing, and diving at low altitude.'

'Right. Well, the seats we are making at the moment provide a good answer to all three situations, but "good" isn't good enough. A pilot could escape even during the take-off run, but only if his aeroplane was level and his speed at least a hundred miles an hour to help the parachute blow open, and much the same applies during a landing approach. As for the fellow low down in a dive, his seat is bound to follow the flight-path of the aircraft, downwards that is, during the moments immediately after ejection, so

166

he too is going to be in trouble often for lack of height. No, wait a minute,' said Martin as I started to speak. 'You're going to tell me you know all this already.'

Quite right, I was, though politely, of course.

'But there is more to it than that. You know what V.T.O.L. stands for?'

'Sure. Vertical Take-off and Landing.' The idea was still in its infancy, but I knew, naturally, of its existence.

'Well think, then, Mr. Hay, of what dangers are in store for the pilots of the future. Some of our fastest and most sophisticated aeroplanes won't be using runways at all. At the beginning and end of each flight they'll just be going straight up and down like lifts, and what is the pilot to do in an emergency during either one of those phases?'

'Use his ejection seat, and be damn quick about it, I'd think.'

'Not good enough. These V.T.O.L. aircraft will have a high rate of sinking, and all the gun would do is fire the pilot clear of the cockpit. With nothing solid to push against it wouldn't produce enough upward ejection velocity to throw him to the height where his parachute could develop. And that, mind you, is from an aircraft sinking straight and level. If the nose dropped, as well it might in an emergency, the pilot simply wouldn't stand a chance— he'd be firing himself straight into the ground. Now that is where you and I come into the picture—we're going to change all that before it ever happens.'

James Martin grinned triumphantly. He was more ready than most men to accept the challenge of a complex problem, but he was human enough to feel pleased with himself when he reckoned he had come up with the answer. He proudly led me from the office, drawing a key from his pocket as he walked, and took me on my first visit to the most exciting room I have ever known. Very few men were ever allowed in there; only one or two others besides Martin had a key. This was a secret room, a room for new inventions at an advanced stage of their development, a room to stir the blood. In all the years that followed I never

167

did learn to walk into it without a tingling, shivering sense of expectation.

The one man in there on this first occasion swung round sharply and suspiciously and half-rose from his chair as I came through the door, but he relaxed immediately and smiled as he recognised me and saw the Guv'nor at my elbow. Martin introduced us, saying, 'Show Mr. Hay here what we've been working on. For some queer reason he seems sort of interested.'

With the secretive dust-sheets removed the seat looked grim and impressive in its corner of the shuttered room—no ejection seat can fail to stimulate speculative interest in a man of any imagination, especially if he intends to use it—and yet my first feeling of excitement was diluted by trickles of disappointment and anti-climax.

'Looks just like any other, doesn't it?' said Martin, reading my mind, 'but it isn't. Look here.'

His finger traced the lines of the rocket-tubes, and I listened intently as he described how the seat would still be fired by a gunpowder cartridge but how, after movement had been initiated, the rockets would cut in automatically with their enormous thrust to send the seat and its occupant hurtling hundreds of feet into the air.

'Hundreds?'

'Yes, hundreds; why? does that scare you?'

'No, just impresses me. I had no idea it was possible.'

'It isn't—yet. But it very soon will be, and you're the man who's going to prove it. Think you'll enjoy the experience?'

I chuckled. 'Well, that sort of depends on you, doesn't it? If it works, I reckon I'll enjoy it. What speed and altitude are you thinking of for the test, and what kind of aeroplane?'

Martin hesitated, and the words, when they came, made no sense to me, yet he had never looked less like a man joking.

'No speed, Mr. Hay; no altitude—and no aeroplane.'

Second childhood, obviously.

'That sounds great,' said I, willing to play along with the boss until help arrived. 'I just take off from the ground and fly around for a bit on my own?'

'Doddy,' replied James Martin, using my first name for the first time since I'd known him, 'that is almost exactly what I'm asking you to do, with a little bit of help from me, of course. I want to fire you straight off the middle of the airfield—no aeroplane, just you and the seat. *That* is how powerful the new rocket seat will be, and I want the whole world to know it. You still feel you want to take it on?'

'Sure, if you say it's all right, and if you are happy that I can handle it.'

'Well that,' replied Martin, scrupulously fair as always, 'is the whole point. I'm very happy to have you handle it—that's why I retain you, after all—and I do believe it will work, otherwise I would never ask you to try it out. But I must tell you there are other men, doctors, scientists, and engineers, who don't agree with me. They believe, to put it bluntly, that even if the seat works perfectly that won't mean a thing to the man sitting in it. They don't think the human body will stand up to the thrust—they reckon the rocket will pulp the man on top of it.'

This was straight talking with a vengeance, and I took a cigarette slowly from my pocket and thought about things for a moment, while James Martin sat patiently, placidly, saying nothing more. I thought about the new seat and its implications. In ejection, it seemed, the wheel had come full circle after fourteen years to the point at which Benny Lynch had opened the era of live testing. Unlike the Valiant shot, this projected ride in the rocket seat would be not just a palliative for present ills but preventive medicine against future, predictable, inevitable problems. This, surely, was a project worth while—and more than that, it promised adventure.

I smiled a little ruefully at this thought, cursing my own capacity for seeing both sides of the coinage of motive. It would have been immensely satisfying to see myself, just for once, as a brave and noble creature risking his life for his fellow men. Damn it, I did want to contribute: I thought of my friend Angus, one of the most sensitive, intelligent, warm-hearted and amusing of men, lying dead and broken in a side street of Farnborough, his parachute almost but not quite open, and I thought of others I had known, and I wanted, deep down and fiercely, to play my part in the story of aircrew survival. But I wanted too, to be paid for it. Not in money or in ephemeral fame; both of these come incidentally in a testing career, but neither is a strong enough incentive in itself. There are many easier, more lasting, and more lucrative ways of turning an honest penny, and as for fame, well, a few laudatory articles and dramatic pictures in the Press or Newsreels are scant compensation for the sound and feel of your vertebrae snapping and crumbling in a stabbing sequence of compression fractures. No, the payment I sought in return for my willingness to experiment for high stakes was simply the permission and the opportunity to indulge in it.

Whatever the barrier, I wanted to be the first man through it. There is nothing, I think, to be ashamed of in this attitude—Colonel John Glenn, no less, was on record long before the Space Age as saying to an interviewer of the potential astronauts, 'The man who doesn't want fiercely to be first to go has no place in this (Mercury) program at all'—but nor is there anything to be proud of. The almost compulsive desire to do in real life what other men do only in their Mitty-moments stems, I think, from a trait of character as basic as the colour of one's eyes, and as such it should never be a source of self-satisfaction. Courage comes into it, of course—it would be sheer hypocrisy to suggest otherwise—but it is a sub-division of courage so specialised and essentially egocentric as to look puny in comparison to the quality that enables two parents, for example, to give up the whole of their normal lives to the care and upbringing of a deformed or idiot child. A true test man must, in short, have nerve, self-reliance, and a sense of purpose and responsibility; my point is merely that a man may possess all those qualities, each admirable in itself, and yet not, as a man, be admirable. Like all other breeds we vary one from another, and we all have our weaknesses and our strengths.

One of my strengths was my willingness to put my complete trust
in Jimmy Martin.

'I'll be delighted to make the rocket test, and I don't want a
holiday. I shall be on tap from tomorrow onwards, waiting to hear
from you.'

*   *   *

Another of my strengths, not natural to me but bred from long
years of parachuting in which hours, days, or even weeks might be
spent waiting for the weather, was patience, and patience was
called for in quantity in the period that followed this meeting with
Martin. Not in the first few weeks—they were fine, full of suppressed excitement and the now familiar euphoria; everything in
our daily life had wider dimensions, more fascinating depths, for
Jenny as well as for myself, for by now the whole philosophy of
testing was as integral a part of her existence as it was of my own.
A well-chosen dinner in Soho would send us home singing, a
meeting with friends would disclose in them facets of quite
exceptional charm that we never, for all our affection for them,
had suspected; an occasional anxious nocturnal murmur would be
answered with complete confidence: 'Yes, Jenny, it will be all
right—of course it will,'—and we slept easy and content. We
listened for the telephone, of course, rushed for the morning mail,
but we were looking forward to the news rather than afraid of it.
For the first few weeks; after that it was something less than fun.

After two months I was occasionally moody and fractious, after
three I was low-down, depressed. I felt there was cheating going
on somewhere, and I wasn't sure who was the cheat. Was it Jimmy
Martin, for putting me on a horse and then not letting me ride it,
or was it myself for assuming the thoughts and attitudes of a
character I wasn't, and perhaps would never be? I hadn't talked
around, of course, but one or two close friends had been allowed
to know that something was in the offing, and I felt I could no
longer look them in the eye. They never said anything, never
expressed any doubts, but I started wondering what they were

171

wondering, and that way madness lies. You can take being thought nothing when you think you might perhaps be something, but you can't take being thought a fraud and a poseur when you know you're not. Four months after accepting a twenty-four hour stand-by for the rocket shot I could stand complete silence no longer, telephoned Denham, despising myself for my weakness, and found the first blind spot in a man I admire perhaps more than any other I have known. James Martin, indifferent to the loyalty he commanded, unaware that to be his chosen test parachutist could be the most important achievement of a man's life, was delighted to hear from me, and wondered why I was calling.

I kept my tone casual, and I received an equally unexcited response.

'The rocket shot? Oh sure, sure, that's still on, and perhaps very soon. Just one or two little problems to be ironed out. You'll be hearing from us, Doddy, never fear; just keep yourself fit and available. Now was there anything else on your mind?'

No, there was nothing else on my mind, nothing else at all, and yet even this unsatisfactory and inconclusive conversation was enough to send my spirits soaring. The test was still on, and I was still the man who would make it; I had not been forgotten or quietly replaced, as I had occasionally begun to fear in the depths of a sleepless night. That neither Martin nor any of his aides had seen any reason for speaking to me until there was something positive to say was neither deliberately cruel nor especially insensitive, but merely matter-of-fact. They were concerned solely with their own problems, and they were many. My job would start when theirs had ended; then I would be sent for. Recognising the cold logic of this I accepted it, and it was as well for my mental and emotional equilibrium that I did so, for when the call finally came I had been on stand-by for almost exactly eight months, and I had lost eleven pounds in weight from a physique that carried no surplus fat.

The first summons to Denham was not for the purpose of making the test but simply to watch a preliminary demonstration with an articulated 200 lb dummy occupying my place in the seat. After a talk with Martin in which he promised that we were now within days of the big moment I motored over to Chalgrove for the dress rehearsal and took my stance amongst a cluster of Company executives in the middle of the airfield. They were cheerful and chattering as the dummy was strapped to the seat, the wires attached for the firing by remote control. With everything set the talk subsided, and we watched in silence as Eric Stevens, the project director, swung down his arm in the executive signal.

A button was pressed, and with an ear-splitting bang merging into a roar the gun triggered off the rockets and the ejection seat streaked upwards in a sheet of orange flame, the telescopic gun-barrel falling away from it, expended, as it rose. I was watching fascinated as at about a hundred and fifty feet it seemed to falter; the parachutes paid out hesitantly, uselessly, and flapped crazily like washing in a high wind as the seat and its inanimate occupant came crashing down to gouge a deep and ugly pit out of the surface of the aerodrome.

I didn't want to watch, and I didn't want to talk; I wanted to be alone, and I wanted to be sick. Impossible, of course; I must face the others, hear what they had to say. Search for a cigarette gave me a few brief moments to iron the trembles out of my voice, and it sounded satisfactorily steady as I turned to Harry Elkin, Martin's chief photographer and film-maker.

'You should get some pretty sensational stuff, Harry, if it turns out like that next week.'

'Damn right,' he said cheerily. 'Should make front page in every paper. I'll see Jenny gets a share of the royalties.'

It took time to appreciate that Harry Elkin was not alone in seeming completely unperturbed by the disaster, that Eric Stevens and his staff were going quietly about their business, packing up the damaged seat, the dummy, the parachutes, and the wires and boxes of the firing system, that no-one was paying the slightest attention to me at all. This, I felt, was carrying cold professionalism just a little too far. They might at least have said 'Woops—sorry,' or something to acknowledge my interest in the events of the day. I strolled over to join Stevens.

'Eric, that wasn't a very encouraging performance. What went wrong?'

'Nothing,' he said casually, glancing at me over a busy shoulder, 'why?'

I felt myself growing quietly angry, resentful at being forced into a position of protest when I had been prepared, not without effort, to play things clipped, stoic and cool.

'Because I'm the fellow who's going to be sitting where that damn dummy was, that's why, and because on a shot like that I wouldn't stand a chance, Eric—not a single bloody chance, and you know it. I'm not asking for reassurance and I'm not even sure I'd welcome it, but I would like some explanation of what's going on. Fair enough?'

Eric Stevens, mild, bespectacled, conscientious and benign, looked at me upwards as if he had just been kicked, but the startled hurt in his eyes changed slowly into disbelieving comprehension as he asked, 'D'you mean you didn't *know*, Doddy? Didn't anyone tell you this was an experimental firing with reduced power? The seat could not possibly have reached altitude, and the parachutes were there only to slow down the landing and reduce the damage. God Almighty, laddie, you'll go up almost three times that height with the full charge underneath you, and you'll have all the time in the world—about twenty seconds at least, I should think.'

No, nobody had told me; nobody had felt it necessary to tell me. The incident ended, of course, in merriment all round.

'I must say, Doddy, you did look a little frayed at the edges when she hit the ground, ha, ha,'—but in myself there remained a slight residual sickness, and it was not the nausea of nerves.

CHAPTER 16

The First Rocket Launching
1961

The feeling of cold isolation, of disappointment that the man at the very apex of the action should merit, apparently, such scant consideration, vanished immediately in the charged atmosphere of the conference that followed. The whole hierarchy of the Company was gathered in the Chalgrove flight-office, heads of the various departments batting technical data to and fro across the table like ping-pong balls, Eric Stevens summarising the results of the recent test programme, James Martin himself sitting silent and contemplative like some benevolent Buddha until all the relevant facts and figures had been presented, tabulated, analysed, and found good. Only then did he speak, but his words, to everyone there and especially to myself, were well worth the waiting.

'If Doddy Hay is agreeable,' said James Martin, and I warmed to him at once, 'we shall make the first live rocket shot on Saturday, just four days from now. I see no good reason for waiting until next week as originally planned.' I agreed immediately, and the men around me wondered why I laughed. In all the excitement of the big decision I was the only man present who had noticed at once the unconscious irony of the date selected for this unpredictable leap into the future of flying—1st April 1961.

The meeting broke up in magnificent humour; never before or since did I see the full Martin-Baker team so simmering with excitement, and by the time we had returned to Denham the word of the test had spread through the factory like a prairie-fire. Eric Stevens led me to his office in the main works-building, and as we made our way there heads jerked up from every lathe and press, and a few of the older men stepped out to offer their hands and a gruff 'good luck'. I was happier than I had been for months; there could be no doubting any longer that this whole project was team-work, and the importance of the first test had fired the imagination of every man on the plant. Rockets: three whole years of research and development, of work and of wondering, of dreams discarded and dreams re-born, all narrowing down now towards one tiny moment in time when something would happen that never in history had happened before, when a man would leave the earth under rocket power alone, with no aeroplane, no take-off run, no wings even, to assist his flight. This was to be incomparably the biggest breakthrough since the very start of the ejection story, and even James Martin was moved to uncharacteristic solemnity: 'This will be a great moment for both you and me, Doddy, one that neither of us will ever forget.' I didn't argue.

My first decision was to move up into the area of the airfield on the day before the test, for although I could reach Chalgrove from home in a couple of hours of hard driving I shuddered at the mere thought of changing a wheel by the roadside as the minutes ticked past towards my deadline. Dangerous experimental work should never under any circumstances be hurried—a point I shall return to, with feeling, and it is vital, I believe, that the test man should approach each venture with a mind completely clear of extraneous worries. For testing demands composure, and com-posure, which in such a situation must be induced deliberately and with discipline, may cost all the mental and emotional effort a man can muster; he may find himself with no reserves available for dealing with petty or irrelevant emergencies he had no right or reason to be faced with. With this already in my mind, I booked rooms for Jenny, myself, and a couple of friends in one of my favourite country hotels, the Bull at Gerrards Cross, with the agreement that the other couple would convoy us to the aerodrome in the morning, safeguards against any mechanical misadventure. We dined quite splendidly on lobster and champagne, ordered two bottles held on ice for the following day—one, a token, for early breakfast, the other, a celebration for a return visit some four hours later—and quit early, happy and relaxed after an evening of easy, uninhibited conversation in which the test had figured, off and on, just whenever anyone had seen any reason whatever to mention it. In terms of verbal expenditure it had probably limped home a lame fifth behind politics, music, sport and the latest Fleet Street gossip. This suited me admirably: I was tuned to perfection for the test, neither shy of it nor obsessed by it, and it was good to be in the company of people prepared to take it at my valuation.

* * *

An hour before the firing the aerodrome was already alive. Uniformed officers of many air forces added colour to the throng of executives, scientists, and technicians; air correspondents scribbled busily in their notebooks while newsreel and television camera crews scurried around with their bulky and unwieldy equipment, jostling for vantage points close, but not too close, to the launching site. I recognised several familiar faces and was chatting idly when Martin, swiftly and decisively as any cowboy, cut me out from my herd of family and friends and corralled me in a corner for a final briefing. 'Young Bates will give you a flag-signal when you're clear to go, and then it's up to you; there will be no trouble with the handle this time, for we've tried it and it moves easily. After the shot, talk to me before anyone else, for things will happen very fast, and I'll have some questions I want answered while everything is still crystal clear in your mind. This ride is going to be very different from your last one, and I'll want to know all about the difference. Now away you go and get ready— I must talk to these gentlemen of the Press and the wise men from the Ministry, for if I don't explain exactly what they're going to see they'll never believe the evidence of their own eyes. In fact I'm going to show them a film of a trial shot with the dummy, just to give them some idea of what to expect—we don't want any of them dying of fright when you go up in the air, now do we?'

Like kids at a carnival the spectators were shepherded into the main hangar for their verbal and visual introduction to what was

177

about to happen. It was explained that the rockets, unlike an ejection gun, would function independently of the platform beneath them, and that they would therefore be capable of reaching their maximum height even from a rapidly sinking aircraft. It was explained too that in this new invention the trajectory of the seat would be not only upwards but backwards, a feature setting it importantly apart from any other ejection seat in the world.

'In any rocket-assisted seat ever made,' said Martin to his eager but still sceptical audience, 'the rocket has been attached to the gun, with the result that it has thrown the seat upwards and *forwards* at an angle of about forty-five degrees. From a nose-down emergency near the ground, in other words, the pilot would meet his Maker just that much sooner. In this seat, with the rockets placed independently underneath the pilot's centre of gravity, the effect will be just the opposite. In practical terms, gentlemen, imagine the test you are about to see taking place in absolutely still air; given that condition, in any other rocket system the seat would land three to four hundred feet ahead of the launching-point. With my system it would land two hundred feet behind it. Five or six hundred feet, gentlemen—the difference between life and death.'

While this lecturette was in progress I was in an outer office changing into my flying kit, and I passed the entrance to the hangar just as the first of the spectators came trooping out from the film-show. Jenny gripped my wrist tightly as snatches of their conversation came floating over the morning air.

'Ingenious of course, but it completely ignores the question of human tolerance.'

'It's not a demonstration we're going to see—it's a public execution.'

'Jimmy is really asking for trouble this time.'

'Hay, of course, must be quite, quite mad.'

It was an uncomfortable moment. These speakers were professionals every one in the fields of medicine or aviation and should be supposed, at any rate, to know what they were talking about. Would they perhaps be right in thinking James Martin was over-

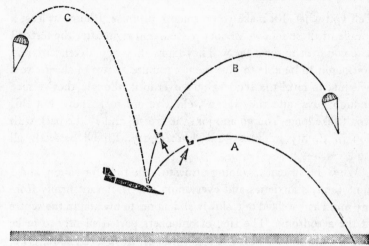

A Trajectory of the seat using an existing type of rocket in which the nozzle is inclined at an angle of approximately 45° to the rear of the seat. This imparts a forward thrust to the seat; ejection from a diving aircraft would result in the seat being driven into the ground before the parachute had time to open.
B Trajectory using the Martin-Baker rocket application which applies a rearward thrust to the seat resulting in the higher trajectory, and thus provides time for the parachute to open.
C The rearward directed trajectory that the seat would follow if ejected from a stationary aircraft.

Three ejection trajectories

optimistic in his assessment of the human frame's capacity to take punishment? They, at any rate, seemed convinced of it and one of them, an aviation doctor I knew well, turned hurriedly back towards the hangar in blatant evasive action as he glanced over and saw me suddenly within earshot. Logic, luckily, stepped in to obviate the agony of protracted speculation. I had no longer any choice of thought or action; I was committed, and so was the girl beside me. From now, more than ever, there simply had to be faith.

'Ignore that rubbish, Jenny. Anything looks dangerous if it's never been done. Never mind about me, just think about Jimmy Martin—he simply can't afford to be wrong, and well he knows it.

The Man in the Hot Seat

Tell you what, I'll make you a solemn promise: I know at least a couple of these fellows we just passed, and right after the test I'll take you over to meet them. They know they were overheard, and you ought to be able to give them a minute or two of sheer sweet hell just to level the score. Don't overdo it, though; they're nice enough guys, and they mean well. I've got to go now, but this won't take long. You go and join the crowd, and I'll be back with you in twenty minutes—and don't worry. I'll be perfectly all right.'

We were, in truth, coming up fast to the time for action, and I shut Jenny's anxieties and everything else irrelevant firmly from my mind as I walked out, slowly and alone, to my seat in the centre of the aerodrome. The ring of onlookers parted silently to make way for me and I had my first glimpse of the test rig, stark, grim, and black, lodged securely in the gaunt iron framework of the little launching-pad, the whole contraption bearing a faintly disturbing resemblance to the electric chair, straps, buckles, and all. The reporters and the cameramen closed in on me now, and not even Martin's eloquence could hold them back as they pressed for pictures and 'quotes'. I heard his exasperated 'Give the boy a chance now, for God's sake, will you?' but in fact his concern for my concentration was unnecessary; I was perfectly happy and totally relaxed, for these men were not interfering, could not interfere with my actual conduct of the test. For simple safety they would have to move far back from me before the count-down could be started, and I was content in the meantime to answer their questions and accept their cigarettes. I believe, though it shames me now to confess it, I was quite gratified by my capacity under the circumstances to talk confidently and cheerfully about the impending experiment and so to fire the first salvo against the arguments of the pessimists. I had lined myself up on Jimmy Martin's side, and until the test was over his critics were the friendly enemy.

With the clearing of the casuals from the firing area and the start of the buckling-down process the excitement quickened inside me and the tiny knot of tension grew tighter. I was not yet alone; the *cuadrilla* were still with me, securing and hauling in on my harness straps, Martin was standing beside me quietly talking of nothing very much, like a mother at bedtime; a couple of determined cameramen, movie and still, poked their lenses under official elbows in an attempt to capture the atmosphere of the final moments, and one or two privileged outsiders—Bill Stewart from the Institute of Aviation Medicine, Bill Bedford, chief test pilot of Hawkers—followed with rapt professional interest every detail of the setting-up process. Then, at last, it was all over. The last strap was tightened, the safety-pin removed from the rocket-assembly; Martin waved the other men imperiously away, patted me on the helmet, and walked off, leaving me with nothing in view but the impending explosion and the tiny figure of Arthur Bates a hundred yards ahead of me, holding over his head the yellow flag that would tell me when I was clear to fire. I looked to each side of the seat to ensure that no-one had lingered within the danger zone, waved to young Arthur to signify my readiness, reached up for the firing handle, and stared steadily at the upraised pennant.

Arthur was slow to start it moving, slow enough for him to receive his final orders from Control, slow enough for me to thrill through all my intense concentration to the magical magnetism of the utterly unknown, of the 'first time ever,' now, after all the long months of waiting, only a few short seconds away from me. Even when the flag began its inexorable arc towards the ground its travel was unhurried, and as I tightened my grip on the firing handle I had time for one quick flash of wondering what would happen when I heaved down on it. Then the tip of Arthur's flag-stick touched the ground, and wondering became suddenly a thing of the past. I jerked both hands swiftly, savagely, right down to my chest, pulling the trigger and simultaneously dragging the canvas face-blind down over my head, protection against blinding during the first wild seconds of an ejection.

Nothing happened. Nothing at all. In total darkness and in total silence I sat there, drained and unbelieving—the rocket seat had failed. Shock, at such a moment, could be a relief from unwilling consciousness, but shock was a luxury I could not afford. This was not something that had happened, it was something that was happening, and to me—action, or at least coherent thought, was imperative, and on my decisions might depend my life. Just one sick thought delayed the onset of logical analysis; my mind flashed back to the failure I had watched only a few days previously on this same aerodrome, and to the explanation of it that had been offered and unhesitatingly accepted. These men, surely, could never have been lying to me for the sake of the programme? I thought of Dumbo Willans's words so long ago, 'never trust the boffins, Doddy,' and I forced the memory from my mind—it was not, could not be possible, not of men like these, my friends. With all the calm I could muster I began working out the possibilities, the real, practical chances.

The shot could be a total failure; all right, a sickening disappointment, but I was safe. But I did not know that, and had no way of finding out. The rockets might be smouldering a few inches beneath me and might at any second ignite. I could sit still and wait, but if I did, would they fire, or merely explode? If they fired, but not to full effect, what chance would I have of kicking myself out of the seat with enough altitude for my parachute to open? Maybe two seconds' worth, if I was lucky. I could of course start unbuckling myself now, ready to make a run for it, but supposing the seat then fired? If I was half-in half-out when that happened my body would be broken to bits; if I had scrambled just clear I would be incinerated in the flames of the launching. Either way, no chance, an ugly end, the shame, at best, of having bolted. I decided to stay with the seat and worked one hand away from the firing handle and on to the manual over-ride, ready to pull the ripcord the very second I reached the apex of whatever flight was coming. The waiting lasted well over a minute, the longest eighty seconds of my life, before an arm was thrust around me from behind and Eric Stevens's voice sounded strained and strangulated in my ear; 'All right, Doddy, you can climb out. She won't go off.'

What followed is on the record, though it has never been published, of every air correspondent who was present that day. I mention it now not with any sense of vanity or pride but because knowledge of this whole incident can no longer after seven years cause hurt or embarrassment to anyone, and because my own reaction to it at the time illustrates better than anything I have ever experienced the essential outlook of the true test man within my own definition of the term. To understand its significance one must accept that I had been badly scared, more frightened perhaps than ever before in my life.

'Eric,' I said, taking command of the conversation immediately, 'tell me simply and quickly what went wrong; no frills, just facts.'

'The head of the gun wasn't screwed down far enough. The firing-pin couldn't reach the cartridge. That's all.'

'Now tell me just one other thing. Can we have another go and be sure of firing, and if so, how long before we do it?'

'Yes, Doddy, we can do it if you're sure you're willing. It would take about fifteen to twenty minutes to set up again.'

'Is that an absolute promise, Eric?' He nodded. 'Right, then, you go and set it up, and tell the Guv'nor I'll be all right for it. I'm going over to talk to these boys.'

Martin and a few of his senior associates were standing in a group apart, about a hundred yards to the left of the seat as I had been sitting in it. I waved to him once and turned in the opposite direction, to my right, where all the other spectators, including the Press and the photographers, were lined up, watching and speculating. I strolled over, removing my helmet and lighting a cigarette as I walked, working out my act and wondering if I could carry it off. Straight away came the obvious first question, fired at me by the aviation correspondent of one of the national dailies: 'What's going on, Doddy? What went wrong?'

My surprise showed clearly, my smile was sweet and innocent. 'Nothing wrong—went smooth as cream.'

'Sure,' came the answer, 'exciting, too. Now what was it all about?'

Another expression of innocence, but more emphatic this time, almost daring my questioner to challenge me. 'You don't mean you thought that was going to be the firing, surely? D'you seriously expect me to tackle a shot like that without a dummy run? Not on your life, boy—you'll see the real thing in a few minutes, when they've loaded the seat and re-packed the handle.'

They accepted it; there was little else they could do, with me standing there in front of them and the nearest Martin-Baker man two hundred yards away across the aerodrome and clearly not receptive to interrogation. Ten minutes later, after a quick remark of reassurance to Jenny, I wandered back to the middle of the field, buckling on my bone-dome as I went, and took my place once again in the ejection seat. The incident was over; not one newspaper printed a word about the initial failure to fire, and the only reference to it I ever heard came years later in a London pub when one of the most experienced air correspondents in England smiled at me over a beer and remarked conversationally, 'You didn't fool us that day at Chalgrove, Doddy—not all of us, anyway. But we reckoned if you could play it that way, the least we could do was to play it with you. I'll tell you this, though: if anything had gone wrong the second time, we'd have crucified your boss.'

Nothing, however, did go wrong; nothing in my whole life has ever gone better. As the yellow flag swung down for the second time that morning I pulled down on the firing handle and the gun roared out beneath me. A swift acceleration, and then came the rockets with their fantastic, unthinkable thrust, not a punch, but a push, as if some giant's hand had scooped me suddenly up into the clouds. A conventional ejection seat gives an altitude of about seventy feet. I was past that height almost before I had started, a twenty-foot streak of orange flame blazing out from two inches behind my ankles, and at a hundred and twenty feet the seat turned completely upside down. I had cleared

184

myself by now from the face-blind, and there followed the most extraordinary split second of my life, a fantastic, flashing image that will never be repeated. I was climbing, feet first, on the crest of the rockets, a total reversal of all that my past parachuting experience had trained me to expect. Instead of green fields there was cloud, instead of dropping gently away from it I was rushing upwards towards it, promising, so it seemed, to pierce the sky. The sensation, unbelievably thrilling, was also almost grotesque as if, stretching one's arm suddenly forward, one saw the biceps and deltoids at the far end and the finger-tips attached to one's shoulder.

At two hundred feet the drogue-gun fired, the parachute began to pay out, and the men on the ground gazed spell-bound at a phenomenon never seen before or since that day, except on the one occasion on which I myself repeated the Zero-Zero performance. For such was the power of those rockets that I was still soaring boots first towards the heavens, dragging an open parachute beneath me in my climb. But for the braking-effect of the huge nylon canopy I might, from the feel of it, have been the first man into orbit, a slightly more significant breakthrough achieved by Yuri Gagarin just eleven days after my maiden rocket flight.

Unlike the great Gagarin, however, I know when to stop, and as I reached the crest of the ride I swung across the sky in a gigantic cartwheel while the seat fell away from me to bury itself in the ground with a shattering 'clunk' that made me uncommonly glad we had parted company. There was no time for self-congratulation, however, for there was still work to be done. Buckled beneath my backside was the dinghy-pack normally worn by pilots, and I had previously determined that as a point of parachuting pride, and also to prove that the rocket-shot had not impaired my speed of reaction, I would release it before reaching the ground. A rapid look around me established my line of drift, and I immediately abandoned my grasp on the lift-webs, gave the spread-eagle signal to those below, and reached around behind me for the dinghy attachments. With seconds only to spare I

185

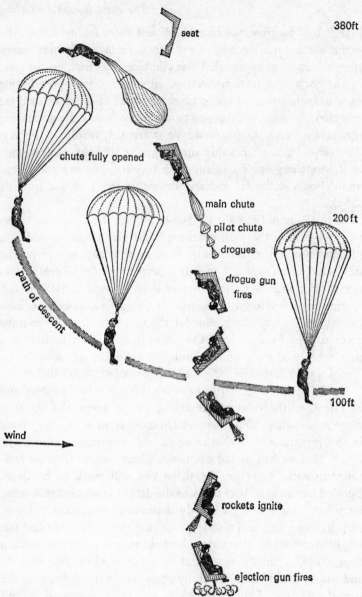

380ft

seat

chute fully opened

main chute

pilot chute

drogues

200ft

path of descent

drogue gun
fires

100ft

wind

rockets ignite

ejection gun fires

The zero-zero test

managed to unfasten them, drop the dinghy from a few feet up, reach for the lift-webs, and steer in for a comfortable, uncluttered landing. The rocket-shot, as records later showed, had reached, despite the braking-power of the parachute, three hundred and eighty feet, more than five times the height of any previous ejection, and that it had done so without in any way damaging the test subject was obvious for all to see. The entire flight, from take-off to touchdown, had occupied exactly nineteen seconds, but those seconds had changed the whole future of aircrew survival. Jimmy Martin, once again, had proved his point.

CHAPTER 17

Disaster at Le Bourget

The next hour or two passed in blissful confusion. After a triumphant de-briefing in the flight office came press and television interviews in which I was able to report total success in every phase of the experiment, a claim that was virtually self-evident simply because I was standing there in a fit condition to make it. Most significant by far of the test data was my report that the rockets, for all their frightening power, had provided me with a ride infinitely smoother than the jolting upthrust of an ejection in a conventional cartridge-propelled seat; Bill Stewart's medicos, after rummaging through my vertebrae as if hunting for bargains in a basement sale, confirmed with almost rueful approval that there was no evidence of any new damage to my injured spine. All this, and the palpable delight not only of the Martin-Baker faction but of every single witness to the flight, added up within myself to a feeling of supreme physical and mental well-being such as I had never experienced before, a *joie-de-vivre* enhanced, if that were possible, when Jenny and I returned to our hotel. 'No disrespect, sir,' said the barman, twirling our champagne in its ice-bucket with professional *panache*, 'but you look as if you've been up to something this morning,' a remark that caused the bride of my bosom to sneeze suddenly into her glass before murmuring happily, 'You can say that again, sport, in spades.'

The wine of celebration has never tasted better, nor conversation flowed more easily from our lips. Our exhilaration was at its height, and the slow winding-down process of reaction and of return to normal life had yet to begin. The key moments of that morning were still fresh and vibrant in our minds as we filled in

188

the gaps in each other's knowledge and understanding of all that had taken place. We were two partners exploring the instinctive conventions of our complementary play and we were coming to know one another better, as persons, in the process.

Only once, after a short and thoughtful silence, did Jenny seem to be standing apart from our understanding, and her voice sounded almost like a stranger's:

'Tell me just one thing. How *could* you go through it all again after that ghastly start? Weren't you frightened?'

No matter how close the relationship, it seems, no-one ever quite sees the problems of testing through the eyes of the test man himself. I tried, as best I could, to explain.

'Sure, I was terrified, but only during the misfire. After that the rough stuff was over, and I knew I could handle the rest. It was like facing up to a sprint final in track-shoes after winning your heat in army boots; I was absolutely confident about the only factor I'd ever really doubted—myself. So the second shot, you see, in one way was easier than the first.'

Jenny smiled, a warm, slow smile. 'All right, shirker, since you've had things so easy, you can do the rest of the driving. Me, I'm exhausted, so how about taking me home?'

*　　*　　*

'Amazing Rocket Bale-Out,' said the *News of the World* across its front page. 'Whoosh Goes the Pilot to Safety,' said the *Sunday Express*; the whole of the national press gave handsome coverage to the test, and when Jenny and I called into The Crooked Billet at Beckenham for our customary Sunday lunch-time snifter we found ourselves at the centre of a splendid impromptu party. Enjoyable at first, it became both over-bibulous and embarrassing as more and more total strangers began to join the happy throng, and that evening we opted for the greater anonymity of a corner table in Gennaro's, that admirable eating-place in Soho. The effort was in vain; the *maître* greeted us effusively, the waiter grinned 'careful sir,' as he held my chair, and we watched him whispering as he threaded his way amongst the tables. Before we were half-way through the minestrone the heads had begun to turn, and with the spaghetti came the first of the congratulatory, kind, but embarrassing enquirers. It was then that inspiration struck, and Jenny blinked as I placed my final order: 'Coffee, cognac, and two seats, if you can get them, on the next plane to Scotland.'

We hit Glasgow around midnight, kitted ourselves out next morning at a multiple store, hired a car and headed north to the country where I had spent my boyhood. Aberdeen with its great wide avenues flanked by green trees and glittering granite mansions, its Caledonian Hotel where the cocktail-barman remarked, 'Hello, sir, I've not seen you for a while,' so spanning a gap of some twelve years; my old school with its tall turrets, its nostalgic team-photographs on the walls, and the statue of its most romantic former pupil, Lord Byron; then out into Royal Deeside, wandering far past Balmoral to the Linn o' Dee and to the foothills of the Cairngorms, those craggy, magnificent mountains I had climbed so often in the days before the war; over the Devil's Elbow, where we stood in sunshine between ten-foot snow-drifts, and down to low-lying, lovely Pitlochry—for ten days we sauntered through the splendours of a British Spring, staying at last with one of my greatest friends, Dr. Ewan Douglas, and his wife in their charming home outside Edinburgh. With Ewan, a vast raw-boned Highlander, British hammer-throwing champion, Olympic athlete and Scottish rugger international, I had travelled Europe in our playing days; kilted, he had piped and I had danced our way from Paris to Perpignan, stirred up a Caledonian Conga in the waterfront stews of Marseilles—now, in the gentler ambience of Edinburgh's Apéritif Grill, we re-lived our indiscretions in reminiscence while our wives smiled tolerantly and talked sense; this was the unwinding from the tensions of the rocket test, and a happier holiday I have never known.

For what followed I had only myself to blame. After all my years in the Air Force, I flouted the very first rule of *la vie militaire*

—I volunteered. I had been back in London only a few days when I learned that James Martin meant to put the rocket seat on public display during the international Air Show at Le Bourget in June and that the plan was to make two firings—with the dummy in the chair. This I could not take, not in *my* seat. I pleaded, I persuaded, and at last I won, carrying the day, I believe, with my deliberate attack upon the weak spot in the Guv'nor's aversion to live testing. 'A dummy shot has no impact whatsoever. People who don't want to be convinced will simply ask why you are not prepared to risk putting a man in the seat; and if you say you already have done, they'll ask what went wrong, what is stopping you from doing the same again.' James gave in, and at the end of May Jenny and I set out with the rest of the Martin-Baker party for Paris.

'Enjoy yourself, but keep out of the way,' were my instructions on arrival three days before the first firing. With more than sixty journalists and countless 'representatives' visiting Paris from the other side of the Curtain, Martin was afraid, I believe, I might in some way be 'got at.' The seat was to be seen in action, but its details were still very much under wraps of secrecy. My orders, then, seemed reasonable enough, if a trifle melodramatic, but in the event they were to prove disastrous.

The firing was to take place this time not from the ground but from the platform of a truck, which would be driven into place shortly before the launching. On the afternoon of 2nd June, far out on the perimeter of the airfield, I climbed aboard the lorry, standing hat in hand beside the rocket seat as we crawled our way round towards the firing point. Reaching it, I stared in sheer disbelief; the take-off had been planned, in my absence and without consultation, for a spot less than thirty yards from the main runway. I protested vehemently, and was hushed like a fractious child. No, we could not move back, for the French authorities were unwilling to allow the rocket flames any closer to a line of helicopters parked behind us; no, we could not select another site, and would I please stop making difficulties, because it was almost time to fire? I was still standing, helmet unfastened, beside the seat.

'How long have I got?'

'Two and a half minutes exactly. Now for God's sake, Doddy, hurry up. There's a low fly-past of fighters coming immediately after you, and you've got to be out of the air before they arrive.'

'Thanks. I'd rather like that, too. But this is bloody ridiculous; it just isn't safe.'

I was in the ejection seat now, feverishly buckling up my helmet and harness straps, but there was still one vital question to be asked, and answered. I still like to believe that the answer was a genuine, unintentional error.

'What is the wind speed and direction?'

'Five knots and straight down parallel with the runway. You'll be all right. Now off you go, boy—there's the signal.'

Sweating, swearing, totally unprepared, I watched the yellow flag sweep downwards and, against all my judgment, I pulled the firing handle. From the moment I reached the crest of the ride I knew I was in trouble. Already the grass was disappearing fast, a thin green ribbon sliding away between me and the vast, hostile spread of the runway. The wind, moreover, was far above five knots, and it was not carrying me safely down the field; instead of blowing down the runway it was streaming across it, and worse than that it was moving across it not directly but diagonally. Up my right-hand lift-web I swarmed like a monkey, trying to drag myself back, but before the canopy had even started to react I was already over the concrete. I changed my tactics, hoping to pull myself clear across it to a fast landing on the far side. Useless: the wind has a power of its own against which technique is impotent. I was drifting fast down the runway and on it, I now knew, I would make my landfall. I was angry, but not frightened. I had taken hard arrivals before, and I was confident of both my skill and my resilience—a bruise or two, maybe, but what the hell. I had forgotten just one little detail—my boots.

As I swept in fast along the concrete the metal cleats skidded wildly in a shower of sparks, technique fragmented, and with a horrible, crunching snap my left leg shot up between my shoulder-blades; my parachute, still full of air, was dragging me roughly along the runway, and waves of sickness washed over me as I bumped struggling, striving to collapse it and to haul myself at least to a sitting position. The pain was appalling—an impacted fracture of tibia and fibula, with splinters like squashed celery driving deep into the ankle—yet rising over everything, even then, was the anger. Anger at my own thoughtlessness over the boots, anger that the very first failure in four hundred jumps should occur, of all places, at the most important air show in the world, anger above all that I had let myself be pressured into an action I had known from the outset to be ill-considered to the point of cynical, selfish stupidity.

A test man, especially one whose loyalty has been proven, should never be made the subject of moral blackmail. His should be the final word on any project, and it should be made easy for him, moreover, to request or even to demand a postponement or a cancellation. His is the life at stake and he, after all, is the expert in this final stage of the programme. He puts his total trust in the designer; if he in turn is not to be trusted, if there exists the slightest suspicion, even the fear, that he may abuse his power of veto, then he should be relieved of his responsibilities—but he should never, I submit, be expected to exceed them, under conditions of danger, to ease another man's administrative embarrassment.

The immediate aftermath of the accident was a tragi-comic nightmare. Being driven out to the extremities of the airfield I managed to muster a resigned smile at an anxious-looking Bill Bedford, who was himself to come to grief at Le Bourget just two years later, ejecting from the Hawker Jump-Jet with only seconds to spare; lying on the grass I listened without protest, though in dazed disbelief, to James Martin declining on my behalf a morphine injection and an airlift by helicopter to hospital, suggesting that 'a couple of aspirin should do the trick; he's tough.' Later, though, there was that same James Martin sitting solicitous in the back of a lorry, feeding me cigarettes as I gritted my teeth to maintain silence through the jumping, jarring ordeal over the miles of cobbled *pavé* separating Le Bourget from the city centre, while a swarthy French private did his muscular best to hold my leg at rest as we swerved and faltered, to a screeching of brakes, amongst the demented Dauphines swarming and rushing like lemmings hell-bent on self-destruction. And then, dear God, the British Military Hospital, and the little house-surgeon, pink, fresh-faced, and seemingly straight from school, who rotated my foot busily and interminably as if stirring stiff porridge, mindless of the audible crackling of the crepitus and of the fact that, left at rest, it was pointing the wrong way round. Asked through stiff lips to desist on the grounds that the discomfort seemed, by any standards, excessive, he departed in a cherubic huff, and it was not until two hours later, and then on my own insistence, that he arranged for the elementary assistance of an X-ray.

'My God,' said young Schweizer, gazing fascinated at the wet plates, 'we've really done ourselves a mischief here, haven't we, old chap?' and plastered me from instep to waist-line before slipping into my shoulder the belated needle of relief. Even then my problems were anything but over, for by next day the pressure on my leg was almost unbearable, my toes were swollen into purple plums, and the nails showed sickly white. Back in London forty-eight hours later after a surrealistic switchback of doping and near-delirium I lay in hospital while one of the finest orthopaedic surgeons in the country, stripping off the plaster in favour of another, half the size and differently angled, remarked grimly, 'That one, my lad, would have left you lame.'

Our visit to Paris had fallen some way short of the romantic. On arrival I had decided to leave all sight-seeing and jollification until after the two planned shots had taken place, when I had intended that Jenny and I should stay on in France for a couple of weeks. After the accident, out of the Military Hospital and returned to our hotel, I had made one attempt to rescue something from the wreckage, sallying out on crutches in search of luncheon, but when my exquisite Tournedos Rossini had been merely nibbled, and wild strawberries pushed aside untasted, Jenny called firmly for a taxi, and in truth I had neither will nor wish to argue; I was whipped, and I knew it. From then on my programme was syringe-induced sleep when I could get it and squirming discomfort when I could not.

At last came the flight back to England, my leg in one seat and my body in another, and a ride through London's fog to the room waiting for me in the University College Hospital, where James Martin had himself been treated after his terrible experience with the gypsies, the attack that had almost cost him his life. I was in poor shape on arrival, craving only Seconal and sleep, and my first clear memory of that admirable infirmary, where I received every possible consideration, is of a charge-nurse, next morning, poking a timorous, tentative head around the door to whisper 'I'm sorry to bother you, Mr. Hay, but it's about the details you gave for your pro-forma last night. Are you really a Zen Buddhist by religion? And is your next-of-kin honestly your Auntie Nellie McCulloch, of doubtful morality and no fixed abode? I've got to know before we get it all typed out.' Reassured, the little nurse went happily away, bearing my apologies, and even Matron admitted later it had perhaps been tactless to greet a patient so palpably immobile, late at night, with the trappings of hospital administration.

The weeks in hospital passed busily enough, with television and a daily stream of visitors to relieve the tedium, with books to be reviewed for *The Observer* and articles to be written that had been mouldering for months on the mental shelf. Later, back home again, came the aching boredom of twice-daily remedial sessions but also, as compensation, the partial mobility of life on crutches. After five months these were discarded in favour of sticks, and by January 1962 I was once again walking unaided, though with a heavy limp. Until one very important evening.

We were sitting, several hundred of us, evening-dressed in the ballroom of the Dorchester Hotel, a grateful gathering met to

195

honour James Martin and to celebrate the saving of the Five
Hundredth Life in his ejection seat. The aristocracy of the air was
here; after dinner Marshal of the Royal Air Force Lord Tedder
spoke for the Guests; Bill Bedford, by now Britain's leading test
pilot, spoke for the Five Hundred, many of whom were present
with their wives; all the way from America, specially for this
occasion, had come the legendary Leslie Irvin, inventor of the
modern parachute; there was scarcely a man in the room who had
not experienced adventure the hard way. After the speeches came
the dancing, with Jenny and myself trapped immobile by my
injury. A message was passed over inviting us to join James Martin
and the principal guests and enquiring after the progress of my
recovery. I glanced over to where he was sitting with Lord Tedder
and Leslie Irvin, and at that exact moment the orchestra swung
into the opening bars of the Gay Gordons. It could have been a
cue; I took Jenny by the hand—'Let's show him, shall we?'

She shook her head incredulously. 'We can't possibly. You'll
fall.'

'In front of this crowd? I wouldn't dare. Come on.'

'Doddy, you can't, you mustn't. You'll never forgive yourself if
you go down and take me with you. You'd hate it, you know you
would.'

I looked again at Martin. 'Calculated risk. Come on; we'll be
all right. Please.'

We took the floor slowly, carefully, counted the beat, and
began. A man can walk with his partner in the Gay Gordons, or
he can dance it properly with Scottish steps; I could feel Jenny
trembling slightly as I led her into the sequence we had danced
together a hundred times or more. There was a terrifying lurch
as I made the first 'reverse' of the pattern, a quick clutching as I
turned too slowly to keep time with the music and a faltering
amounting almost to a stagger as I struggled to catch up with it
again, and then, somehow, we were safely through the first
movement, into the second, and dancing as a Scottish couple
should. Down the line we went, past James Martin's table where

he stood up for us, beaming hugely and beckoning with a paternal paw. We completed one more movement, retired without pushing our luck, and walked over to greet the Guv'nor: my ankle was throbbing and pulsing, and by next morning it had swollen into a fiery football, but the laboured limping was gone, and for good— the leg still crackles in damp weather, and occasionally it has let me down, but I travel on an even keel.

'Come and meet these gentlemen, now,' said James Martin, taking Jenny by the arm. 'I've just been telling them how glad I am to see Doddy looking so sprightly, for between you and me I don't think it will be all that long before I have another little job for him. What's that, my dear?' he added, and in truth my wife's reply had been almost inaudible. I, however, had picked it up, just two words between tight lips. 'Calculated risk.'

CHAPTER 18

The Ultimate Test

1962-1963

James Martin's plan, outlined to me several days later, was simplicity itself. Having proved the rocket seat at one end of the scale of performance, he now wanted to prove it at the other. My test shots at Zero Altitude—Zero Speed, the only ones ever made, had provided the answer to escape from conventional aircraft at low level and from V.T.O.L. aeroplanes during their hovering or lifting movements. All such military aircraft, however, must by their very nature fly fast as well as low, and disaster can strike them in any phase of their flight. We hoped to prove the new seat effective under all conditions, and the ideal proof was obvious: a new world record for high-speed ejection. Martin was confident that both the seat and the parachute assembly would stand up to the strain and function efficiently; the unknown factor that must be determined was the old familiar unpredictable, incalculable—human tolerance.

'What are we going for in terms of speed and altitude?'

Martin looked at me long and steadily. 'Seven hundred miles an hour—at sea level.'

I thought about this and shivered, partly from excitement but not entirely. Sea level, where the air is dense and speed is really speed. Seven hundred miles an hour, scratching the surface of the Sound Barrier. I tried to visualise the battering and the buffeting to be borne in such a slipstream, the forces I would meet face-forwards when thrown into them, exposed, as if into a concrete wall, the shuddering drag of almost instant deceleration. I imagined myself, a tiny figure, tossed into all this like a cork into the Atlantic, and for a moment the prospect appalled me; not so much the actual physical danger of it, but rather its sheer immeasurable

198

magnitude. Who was I to think of challenging powers like this, almost challenging Nature itself? Yet in the question, of course, lay also the answer; as a challenge it was irresistible, and my decision was never in doubt.

'Will I need any protection?'

'From the wind, d'you mean? Well yes and no. It will be an open seat like the one you're used to, not a capsule or anything fancy like that. You'll get a hammering of course, there's no denying that, but I reckon you'll be all right. The deceleration will be pretty severe, but not so bad you can't take it: Stapp has proved that.'

This last remark could have been a psychological boomerang. Certainly I knew of Colonel Stapp, one of the greatest test men of all time, who on America's rocket sleds had subjected himself over and over again to horrifying high-speed runs terminating with awesome finality when the sled hit the water-barrier at the end of the line. But I knew also what Colonel Stapp had suffered on some of these rides, not least the agony, mental no less than physical, of the long long wait for knowledge as to whether the total blindness that had struck him would be permanent. That I admired this man and his achievements could be taken for granted —but to cite him in answer to an enquiry as to personal safety was an act of confidence indeed; to admire such a man is not necessarily to wish to emulate him. If the remark, however, was a gamble, it was also a winner, and the Guv'nor had the grace both to grin and to decline when I suggested borrowing one of the Colonel's sled-runs for our experiment. 'No, the area around there is not suitable for parachuting, and I'd like to get you down safe after shooting you up. We can't have you breaking your leg again, now can we?' *Touché*—honours even.

'Seriously, though,' he went on, 'you will need a special sort of protection, and there's a couple of things I'd like you to have a look at.' I followed him, fascinated now and eager to hear more, to the little room where I had first seen the original rocket seat. From a cupboard he produced a rigid helmet with a screen that completely enclosed the face, and motioned to me to put it on and to take my place in an ejection seat in the middle of the room. I sat down, buckled myself in as directed, and had my helmet connected by slim steel cables to the seat behind me.

'There's no charge in the chair,' said Martin, 'or I wouldn't be standing where I am, but I want you to pull the firing-handle anyway.' Strangely, it took nerve and a deliberate effort to obey him. When I did, my head was at once dragged hard back into the padded concavity behind it. I tried, in response to instructions, to force myself forward, and found the movement quite impossible; I was fixed, spine erect, in a perfect position for ejection. 'That's your first protection, Doddy. No unholy gale blowing into your eyes and mouth to blind you or swell you up like a football, and no more broken backs. But we've got more to think about than that, this time. Leg restraint we already have, to stop you chopping them off, but have you thought yet what would happen to your arms if you ejected at round about the speed of sound?'

I admitted that, in the short time since such a suggestion had been made to me, I had not. 'They'd be flung wide apart,' James said cheerfully, 'just about torn out at the roots, and you'd be split clean up the middle like a porker in a butcher's shop. Wide open.'

I hastily re-swallowed my rising lunch. 'You've got something in mind to prevent it, I suppose? I feel I'd almost have to insist on that.'

'Sure,' said my master, and I waited for a description of some highly complex protective barrier between me and disembowelment. 'I'll fix you up with a sort of pair of handcuffs to hold your wrists together, and you can fire the seat from the emergency handle between your knees. Then, don't you see, when the slip-stream hits you your arms just can't fly apart—they'll both be swung round to one side—it may stretch you a bit, but it won't split you, I promise.'

'Thanks,' I managed faintly, 'that really is a load off my mind. When do we go?'

'Ah now, that really is a problem. You see, it's all a matter of finding a suitable aircraft. The only one available that's fast enough is the Hunter, and in that the pilot and the passenger sit side by side, so if you went out on the rocket seat you'd burn him to a crisp. The only way we could do it would be if you and he went out simultaneously, and he might not fancy that—anyway I'm sure the Ministry wouldn't, for it's their aeroplane, and Hunters come pretty expensive. But I'll give some thought to where we can borrow a suitable fighter in the seven hundred miles an hour class, with the seats placed one behind the other, and when I find one I'll let you know.'

And so, once again, I went home to wait. That was in January 1962. In July I again visited Denham but came away with no news more definite than that the project was still very much alive and that mine, most certainly, would be the privilege of making the just-sub-sonic shot.

The waiting, though, can be a variable delight. When it flourishes in the mind in the form of anticipation, that is fine; one hugs the secret promise of new excitement, thrills to the thought that positive living is not yet over, that one still has some contribution to offer, that one's failings and weaknesses may yet be balanced out, voluntarily and in full. But such anticipation requires at least a few crumbs of factual nourishment, and as the year 1962 passed into history, and the first months of 1963 went by with no further word of the awaited test, the prospect would occasionally turn rancid, and I would begin to wonder if I were not wasting and wishing my life away in some strange sort of half-existence. I was working, of course, working quite hard and quite successfully in my capacity as a journalist, with my stuff being syndicated all over the world, and socially I seemed busy enough, but always there was this essential part of me withdrawn from real living, lurking, as it were, in the wings. Thoughts of the high-speed shot, consciousness of what was coming—one day, any day, tomorrow if the 'phone should ring—began to intrude too often into the pattern of my daily life, preventing my proper involvement in all that was happening around me. Surrounded by a happy marriage, a few good friends, and congenial work with congenial colleagues I was often, far too often, absolutely alone and without the means of communication. The pressure was beginning to build up.

After eighteen months of waiting, on 24th July 1963, came Jimmy Martin's letter: 'It may well be that we shall ask you to do the high-speed shot in the very near future, and Eric will get in touch with you when we are ready.' This was it; all the introspective misery evaporated, all the doubts and withdrawals disappeared, denied in retrospect their very existence. The message had come by post, not by telephone or by wire; there was time, obviously, for a party, and a party we had—and paradoxically we were both, my wife and I, suddenly and completely relaxed.

And then we waited, and we waited, and we waited. For months: on mental, physical, and emotional stand-by. I lost a few pounds, and I lost a few friends. A man who doesn't answer when you speak to him makes a poor companion, and one who sometimes answers sharply for no reason makes a worse one; the black moods came only occasionally, but they came, and of course I could offer only an apology, never an explanation—the impending test was Company, not public, business. Where I had been tuned up I was now only keyed up, and still there was no word from Denham; I was feeling the first mild fever of a situation that was later to become almost an illness.

It was late October when the word came through, warning me that the shot was scheduled for the following week. The excitement was there at once, almost crackling in its fierce intensity, but this time I was also wary, and for a long time I stayed seated at the desk in my study debating whether to pass the news to Jenny immediately or to wait until the test was quite indisputably a going concern. The strain of past uncertainty had been more severe, if anything, on her than upon myself, and she of course drew no thrill or satisfaction from either the anticipation or the performance; I was reluctant to expose her to the punishment of several days of mounting tension while there remained the slightest chance of their culminating in yet another postponement.

Waiting seemed the best idea, but in fact my decision was unimportant, for the whole question was resolved for me in an hour or two of pure Mack Sennett that followed later in the day. In the afternoon came the second 'phone-call, telling me that the date of the test had been advanced and asking me to travel up to Denham next morning for weighing and measuring. An hour afterwards came another message telling me not to bother; a works employee had been found whose height and weight exactly matched my own, and he would be used in establishing the setting of the seat, so saving me a long and unnecessary double journey. This suited me admirably; dusk was already drawing in and I settled down to my interrupted work, a lengthy article for an overseas magazine. After a couple of paragraphs I swore fluently and with feeling when the telephone on my desk buzzed once more into infuriating life.

'Eric here, Doddy. I'm sorry to bother you, and I know it's rather short notice, but how do you feel about coming up here tomorrow after all?'

'Sure, that'll be easy enough, but why? Are the measurements not working out?'

'No, they're all right.' There was a barely perceptible pause and then, in tones of slight but unmistakable embarrassment, 'The fact is, we'd like you to do the test. The Guv'nor reckons everything is ready, and the weather forecast looks good.'

Rather short notice; less than twenty hours of warning after more than twenty months of waiting. Half dazed and half delighted, I wandered through to the kitchen, where my wife was stirring something at the stove; 'Is that anything very special?'

'No, just some soup. Why?'

'Well, that's good. Switch it off—I'm taking you out to dinner.'

'Nice man. But what's it all about—I thought you wanted to finish that article?'

'Not tonight, Josephine. Now you go and change and I'll tell you all about it. I have, my sweet, some rather startling news for you.'

* * *

I did not know it that night as we sipped our wine and ruminated on the strangeness of the situation, wondering if other couples could ever enjoy life quite so much without such moments as these, but the startling had barely started. The first real shock came when I entered the Denham office in the morning; amid all the alarms and excursions of the previous day I had omitted, almost incredibly, to ask one vital question. I asked it now: 'What aircraft are we using?' and I sat down bewildered as James Martin answered without batting the proverbial eyelid, 'The Meteor.'

'The Meteor? But that can't do anything like seven hundred miles an hour at sea level—or is this some mystery marque I've never heard of?'

'Doddy,' said James, 'forget about the high-speed shot for the moment. That can wait, at least for another few weeks. This one concerns a question that *must* be answered, and I want the answer now.' My disappointment and sickening sense of let-down must, I imagine, have momentarily shown through, for he hurried on with greater emphasis, jabbing his fore-finger with quite uncharacteristic urgency on the desk between us. 'This, I tell you, is vital—more important than the fast run, at least as important as any test you've done, including, believe it or not, the original rocket shot.'

Fascinated in spite of myself, grudgingly almost, I accepted the fact that I was not, after all, to be exposed that day to the experience I had been awaiting, half magnetised half frightened, for very close on two years, and immediately came the next, faith-testing, surprise. 'What exactly is it,' I asked, 'that you want me to try out or find out?'

He puffed slowly on his cigarette, handing one across to me as he spoke. 'Well now, that's rather a tricky point. Obviously you have a right to know, and I'll tell you what it's all about if you

204

really want me to—but the truth is, I'd rather not. You're a good test man—you've got integrity and you've got courage, and I'm not insulting you—but things may happen very very fast today, and what I want from you is an account of what really happens, not of what, half-consciously, you may have been expecting to happen. It isn't always easy to separate the two. A great deal, more than you could imagine, hangs on this shot today: it isn't often, I tell you, that I don't know the answers in advance. Now what do you say about it—will you do the test on these terms? It's entirely up to you.'

It wasn't, of course, after that speech; I was either up to my chosen job, or I was not. It takes over an hour to motor from Denham to the airfield at Chalgrove, and all the way there I was wondering what lay in store for me. Fortunately for my frame of mind, my guesswork carried me nowhere near to the truth.

* * *

The Meteor was standing out on the tarmac, stark, grey, cold and potent, like some aerial torpedo. Behind the front cockpit the steel-and-Perspex canopy had been cut away to facilitate my departure, and I was standing on a ladder, peering into my armour-plated compartment in the rear, memorising its lay-out, when I was joined by the Company's chief pilot, Squadron Leader Fifield, O.B.E., A.F.C., a man of immense and varied aviation experience. Fifield, before my day, had made the first-ever ejection from an aircraft travelling along the runway, and I was happy to have as my partner in this new experiment a man who understood, from within, both the attractions and the tensions of testing.

'Tell me, Doddy,' he began, 'how do you feel really about this particular little outing?' and for a moment I was tempted to the point of dishonesty to let him carry on, innocently divulging the exact nature and purpose of the test. A bargain, however, had been agreed, and I cut in at once: 'Just give me the speed and altitude, Fifi, and then let's go over the signals-pattern,' before taking the sting out of my abruptness by explaining what had passed between me and the Guv'nor. Fifield whistled quietly and raised a quizzical eyebrow: 'Okay, if you say so, but frankly, speed and altitude don't mean a damn thing this time. We'll come over the airfield at around two thousand feet and three hundred knots—nice and comfy, nothing to worry about either way. But are you sure . . .?'

'I'm sure. Let's sort out the signals.'

I had given a good deal of not over-comfortable thought during the previous few hours to this vitally important question of timing and visual communication. At first the answer had seemed simple enough, a mere repetition of the programme I had agreed with Squadron Leader Ware for the rearward-facing ejection from the Valiant three and a half years before, but it was at that very point of reasoning that the first doubts and hesitations had begun to creep in. Three and a half years, when past one's physical peak, is a very long time in an active profession. I was now forty-one, and much of my time since the Valiant test had been spent in inactivity enforced by my injuries. Was I right, or even justified, I wondered, in assuming that my speed of reaction would be the same as before? I wondered, too, about my mental attitude towards this new test. I was not afraid of it, but I was, beyond question, curious about it; might not that curiosity, that built-in feeling of under-standable doubt, prompt some tiny hesitation when the moment came for action? It would be safer, perhaps, to incorporate in the signals-pattern some means of compensating, in terms of time, for any such failings; that might take a little thinking out but it could, undoubtedly, be done.

Staring this thought in the face I made up my mind with complete finality: it could be done, but it would not be done. If I had lost confidence in my own ability to handle this job as well as any other man in the world could handle it, regardless of his age, his make-up, or his history, then only one course, in honesty, was open to me—I could not compromise, but I could quit. Had I lost confidence? No, I had not; I was being asked, goddamit, to carry out the task I was trained for, not to run a four-minute mile. I settled with Fifield for the signals as before—three minutes, five seconds. Go.

Jimmy Martin was waiting for us by the time we had sorted out the system, but this time there was no last-minute briefing, just a hand-shake, a slap on the shoulder, and 'Good luck.' There was no carnival atmosphere, either, on the airfield; no invited visitors, no ranking officers, no pressmen, no cameras turning but the Company's own, placed with practised accuracy to record every visible detail of the test. There was no ceremony, no air of suppressed excitement; this was business, cold, hard, clinical, and grey. The ground crew wore, not their smart white Paris Air Show overalls, but sports jackets, sweaters and slacks. No Ministry official was in attendance nor, more regrettably, was any doctor. No inner helmet, essential for the close-fitting of the bone-drome, had been brought to me as promised, from Denham; I borrowed one of Fifield's and apologised as I cut away the potentially-lethal intercom plug with a hacksaw. 'Forget it,' said my pilot, 'you're more than welcome. Now if you're ready, I reckon we ought to be off and get it over with.' That, on reflection, was the attitude prevailing over the whole of the aerodrome that autumn day. Just how many of the men present were in on the secret of the test I have never known, for the simple reason that I have never asked.

I at least, though, was happy, unbelievably happy, as I clambered into the rear compartment of the Meteor, flexed my mental and emotional muscles, and helped the crew to adjust my harness and buckles; one needs no side-shows, no spectators, no extraneous excitements at all, to make a situation like this one come to life. Speed, danger, qualitative introspection, and the unknown, each has its own fascination, and beneath—or above?—all this was the quickening pulse of certainty that the job ahead of me had a purpose and that of that job and of that purpose I was to be, for the next few vital minutes, the central, the human, the living part; not, by any means, the only part, but the heart of the thing.

The take-off run had its awkward moments. Never fond of wearing goggles, and prepared to act upon my allergy, I found myself mildly in trouble; the wind whistling into the open cockpit brought tears to my eyes, and before the wheels had left the tarmac I was blind and frightened. Supposing, dear God, my eyes should go on watering and I should be unable to read the signal lights? My parachuting experience should have taught me better than that; once clear of the runway and the acceleration the weeping ended immediately and by the time the aircraft had reached altitude I had come to terms with my surroundings and was tucked happily in behind the bulkhead, comfortably enough and completely in control. Which was as well, for on this sortie there was no hanging about whatever; our climb swept us swiftly around Oxfordshire, as Fifield levelled off I set myself for what was coming, and within minutes saw the first green light, bright and dramatic, announcing that the run was good. The firing-handle came loose from its housing with obliging smoothness, and I was quite astonishingly composed as I sat waiting, hands held high, for the five second signal; my God, I thought, this business is becoming *routine*. I enjoyed perhaps one minute of amusement at the thought of being probably the only man in history to feel blasé about an impending ejection from a high-performance aircraft and then, in one split, excruciating second, I learned the nonsense of my indifference.

First came the warning and then came the 'Go.' I yanked down hard on the handle, thrilled to the first smooth surge of movement, and then screamed silently, because no breath was there, as the rockets exploded beneath me and I was catapulted, high and twisting sideways, far out of the cockpit of the aircraft. I felt, I *knew*, my body was broken, and I cared nothing of what might lie ahead of me; I only wanted everything to end, and at once. Even the realisation that my parachute had opened safely seemed unimportant. I could not look up to see it; my arms, like my legs, were dangling helplessly and useless, and no effort of will could drag them up to the lift-webs where they belonged. I tried, God

208

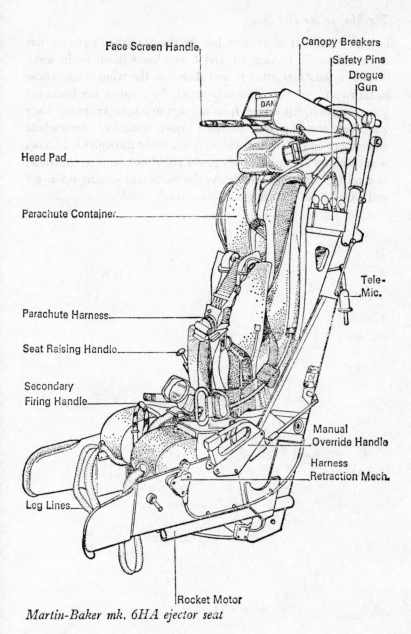

Face Screen Handle

Canopy Breakers

Safety Pins

Drogue
Gun

Head Pad

Parachute Container

Tele-
Mic.

Parachute Harness

Seat Raising Handle

Secondary
Firing Handle

Manual
Override Handle

Harness
Retraction Mech.

Leg Lines

Rocket Motor

Martin-Baker mk. 6HA ejector seat

how I tried, but there was left in them neither strength nor control; I would be slapped, and I now knew it, on to the aerodrome in whatever attitude and direction the wind might chose to throw me, yet still I scarcely cared. Everything, my back, my guts, my groin, felt wrong; from my toes to my fingertips my body was screaming in protest though I myself was silent. Somewhere down there on the ground was my wife, going through God knows what, waiting for the all-safe signal I could not manage, this time, to send her, and now, suddenly, the earth was coming up at me and I could not lift a finger to ward it off.

CHAPTER 19 Recovery

1963

The crash of the landing made no difference to me; it was merely a continuation, not an event in itself. The ground crew, running white-faced and urgent across the airfield, collapsed my billowing parachute and hauled me out of the harness and then with the onset, I imagine, of shock, a vast numbness began to draw slowly, like a blanket, over my grateful body. The black Bentley came gliding up beside us and I was lifted into, at my own request, the front passenger seat; I knew instinctively, somehow, that I must not lie down. I felt I had to hold myself firmly, physically, together, and later I was to find out I had been right. Some sort of smile through the window for Jenny, standing shaken beside the hangar, and then we were in the flight office, with Jimmy Martin murmuring, 'No discussion here. I want you to ride back with me; the others will look after your little girl.' Even as he spoke we were joined by Fifield, grinning, who gave me without knowing it perhaps the greatest satisfaction of my parachuting career. 'By God, boy,' said he, 'you didn't wait long, did you? We damn near undershot the airfield.' With the exquisite tact and understanding of a man who knows what flying is all about he had, as he put it, 'allowed a little bit of leeway on the timing—thought you might be a bit rusty after all these years,' and my speed of reaction had proved his courtesy and consideration unnecessary. This time my smile was genuine; 'Thanks, Fifi, it was a nice thought,' and he will never know how much I meant it. And then I was out of the flight office, back into the big black Bentley.

James Martin spoke not one single word for half an hour, thirty minutes of shared and silent agony that brought me closer to this man than I had ever been before, closer than I have been to any

211

man except my own father. For the first time I understood fully and deeply the true burden of responsibility that he had borne. For mile after mile he stared unwaveringly ahead of him, driving fast and superbly despite his nearly eighty years, giving not so much as a glance in my direction; he was, I feel certain, afraid. I in my turn said nothing; I was content to wait.

'I was wrong, of course,' were the words when at last they came. 'You've been hurt badly, very badly, and I'm sorry. But now I know what I had to know, and no-one else will ever be hurt that way again. This test was necessary, Doddy Hay.' The strange mode of address had an indefinable ring to it that meant much to me, that seemed to ease the pain as he continued. 'I want you to believe that, for you have the right to believe it, and I want you to understand just why it was necessary.'

Slumped in my seat, on fire from head to foot, I listened, and it all made sense. In a tandem aircraft, a machine with one cockpit placed behind the other, the rocket seat, for all its power and efficiency, had one total and obviously unacceptable drawback that would prevent its introduction into squadron service. If, in an emergency, the man in the front cockpit should be first to fire himself to safety, his companion behind him would be incinerated in the flames of the ejection—the same argument, in short, that had prevented me from making the high-speed shot from the Hunter. The Hunter, however, was an aeroplane of the past and the present; James Martin, as always, had his eyes on the future.

There were several ways in which it might have proved possible to obviate the danger, among them the insertion of some form of baffle-plate or shield, or the linking of the two firing-mechanisms to ensure that only simultaneous ejection of both passengers would be possible. The simplest and cleanest of all solutions, however, would be to delay the onset of the rocket power just long enough for the aircraft underneath it, and its remaining occupant, to have passed beyond the zone of danger. This was precisely what James Martin had had in mind when planning the test. The mere firing of the gun-cartridge to initiate the seat's movement would not, as he knew, endanger the man in the seat behind; the potential killer was the huge sheet of flame that accompanies the cutting-in of the rockets. Now if that cutting-in could be delayed by even a fraction of a second, then the man on the rockets would be clear of the aeroplane, and the man left in the aeroplane would be clear of the rockets. Simple, but between the idea's conception and its adoption had stood one question that had to be answered.

To effect the necessary delay it was essential to separate the action of the rocket from the action of the gun, a negation, in one sense, of the very principle on which the success of the original rocket shot had been based. It was with misgivings that James had deserted this principle—I remembered his words to me earlier that day, 'It isn't often, I tell you, that I don't know the answers in advance'—but the separation he had planned had been so minimal, a mere one-sixteenth of a second, that he had considered it a justifiable risk. He had believed, in fact, that the effect on the man riding the seat would be so slight as to be virtually unnoticeable, and this, of course, and nothing more sinister, had been his reason for asking me to undertake the test without knowing what was in store for me. 'I knew you were the only man who could make comparisons, Doddy, and I wanted to be quite sure whether there were in fact any comparisons to make.'

Well, now he knew, and later, when all the scientific data had been analysed, James Martin was to write to me, 'The effect was like an atom bomb going off beneath your backside; you were, in effect, almost coming *down* on to the rockets as they fired.'

On our return to Denham the plan was that I should be shipped off once again to hospital, but this time I dug my heels in; I wanted one place only, and that was home. Medical opinion and treatment could wait. I was prepared, in fact determined, to follow in the first place sheer animal instinct. I still did not feel, could not think, like a human being. I was not yet sure whether I was going to live, not yet convinced I even wanted to: I knew what I wanted and needed, and it was not then a doctor, however skilled. James demurred, I insisted, and we compromised. In return for my promise to submit to medical examination within forty-eight hours he provided Jenny and myself with a Company driver, one of my own ground crew, the broad and burly George. And George did more than drive. After a ride I wish to God I could forget, with every bump in the road an injury and with Jenny biting her lips till the blood ran, he picked me up bodily, carried me up three flights of stairs, and spread me gently on the bed, muttering 'Jesus Christ, Doddy, we've really done it to you this time.'

And it was so. When Jenny had undressed me the evidence of the rockets' thrust was there, quite horribly, to be seen. My legs and arms were puffed and swollen into mottled purple; my belly, once rippled and rigid, was swinging down almost to my knees like some obscene and pendulous sack of frog-spawn, the muscles in and all around it ripped, slack, and useless like ruptured elastic. My wife stood at my bedside, shocked and embarrassed—on my behalf—into near-tearful silence. Laughter, for both of us, was the only possible antidote. 'Jenny,' I whispered, 'call the doctor, but for God's sake no reporters. I think I'm pregnant.'

* * *

Our family medico was appalled by my appearance and puzzled, understandably, by my refusal to account for it, but he could recognise a clear case for the hypodermic when he saw one, and the day, in murmurs and faint moanings, passed into a deep and dreamless night. The orthopod, not at all puzzled, two days later, because he had been brought into consultation by James Martin, brandished the X-ray plates and remarked, with a delightful informality not normally associated with the great names of Harley Street, 'I must tell you, Mr. Hay, if you will forgive my being personal, that you have a most singularly tatty spine. Some day— I trust in the far far future—it really should pass to the medical profession.' I promised to consider the matter and asked for his

214

opinion on subjects of more immediate concern. 'Well, no more of this nonsense, under any circumstances,' was his uncompromising answer, 'and I shall say as much in my report to Mr. Martin,' but I talked him out of it.

For the first few weeks after the accident I made no serious attempt at physical rehabilitation; merely to climb the stairs to my flat was exercise enough, and with damage now in the lumbar as well as the thoracic region of my spine I was in no state to carry out any gymnastic activity, however gentle. But in December came word from James Martin that he would like me to carry out another test before the end of January, when Eric Stevens was due to make an important visit to introduce the rocket to the United States. This time, James promised, there would be no 'atomic explosion,' and he went on to say that he wished me to make the test only if and when I had recovered from the effects of the previous one.

This new and unexpected development posed its problems. I had not even vaguely recovered, and could walk for no more than a minute or two at a time without resting; sitting down, conversely, I had to be constantly changing my position to acquire an acceptable degree of comfort. My back had suffered damage which never could, never will, be effectively repaired, and the muscles around my middle were still stretched, painful, and flabby. And so something had to be done. I wrote to Denham saying I was confident I would be fully fit within the time allotted, and then I went to work.

Restoring the muscle-tone to a reasonable standard of strength and elasticity was comparatively simple, requiring only an intensive course of exercises I knew well from earlier days and would already have been carrying out had they not been both boring and extremely uncomfortable. The problem of my back, though, was a different matter, one that defeated me for days until I suddenly hit upon an idea as simple as the safety-pin. I removed the foam-rubber cushion from my wooden typing chair and sat down on the solid seat; then, taking my weight on my hands, I lifted myself

215

perhaps half an inch and let go. A pain like a hot poker shot straight up into my skull and so set the standard for the weeks to follow. Every half hour of every day I would plug away for a few minutes at this one exercise, gradually increasing the force of contact, and whilst it may have done nothing to improve the condition of my spine it did enable me to build up a progressive tolerance of the jolting. By Christmas I could drop myself quite heavily from a full three inches and I was feeling well pleased with my progress until my wife, all unwittingly, took the wind clean out of my sails.

'Must you go on doing this to yourself?' she said one morning, her voice full of concern as she walked into my study. 'I can't bear to see it. Dammit, darling, you wince even when you sit down normally.' As the implication of her words sank in I realised, full of sudden despair, that my programme was leading me precisely nowhere. Soon, I knew, I must pay a visit to Denham to discuss the test, and if James Martin saw me in physical difficulties, that would be the end of the matter. He was perfectly capable of compelling me to sit down hard, just to see my reactions, and if I gave any sign of either pain or reluctance he would read the message and would never, I knew, allow me to make the shot. For an hour or two I was completely dejected, ready almost to give up my musical-chairs programme completely, and then came my macabre, Black Comedy, brainwave.

'What on earth has happened to the mirror from the hall? asked Jenny, wandering through the flat to announce that lunch was ready. 'I've borrowed it. Watch this.' The long Chinese-carved mirror was propped on its end in my study, directly opposite my chair. I sat down, wreathed my well-worn features in my best imitation of a relaxed but engaging grin, and bobbed sharply up and down again, twice, staring steadily into the mirror throughout the entire performance. 'The smile slipped a bit the second bounce,' I admitted, 'but I'm getting the hang of it,' and sure enough, by the middle of January I had added one more eccentricity to my already extensive inventory—if anything hurt me I automatically smiled. Pavlov would have been proud to own me; so, come to think of it, might Barnum and Bailey. But one day, just once, I looked up to find my wife watching me, quite silently, and weeping.

Epilogue

At this time, the news that the next test had been postponed came as almost pure relief, undiluted by frustration, for I knew that it would be weeks or even months before I could hope to approach anything like a satisfactory state of fitness. I also began to realise to what extent the human frame is—not unimportant, never, never that—but subservient to and dependent upon something quite separate, what one really *is*.

I saw that I, whose whole life had been one of activity, whose principal enjoyments and whose successes, such as they had been, had come almost entirely in the field of the physical, from rugby football to the Cresta Run, was not only prepared but determined to hazard my whole physical future. I was putting at risk my body's efficiency, comfort, and capacity for enjoyment—perhaps its very existence—for the sake of something my mind had decided I should do, for something I believed to be fundamentally good, and necessary. There was no craving, I realised, for the excitements of the aerodrome and the thrills of the flight, but only a demand from within for the fulfilment of what I had set myself to contribute—the advancement of aircrew survival, the one field in which I had anything positive and of value to offer.

The inactivity was not easy but I was helped by the almost daily affirmation of my work's value and importance. One could scarcely pick up a newspaper without reading 'Aircraft crashes—pilot ejects to safety.'

Then I heard that following a detailed analysis of the shot that had come so close to killing me, the design of the rocket pack had been modified and its only fault eliminated. On 14th September 1964 the rocket seat, fitted to a prototype aircraft, flown by

George Bright, had saved his life, as described in the prologue. The new rocket-pack, beyond question, was in business and here to stay, and the need for further testing had clearly disappeared.

From now on, the Martin-Baker story marched steadily forward from one triumph to the next. In the Birthday Honours List of 1965 the Guv'nor, to the delight of airmen and their families all over the world, received the accolade and became Sir James Martin, so receiving his just recognition and incidentally allowing me the luxury of sending a telegram: 'Congratulations. Looking forward to my first day's work for a Knight.' A few months later another huge and grateful gathering met for dinner at the Dorchester Hotel, this time to celebrate the saving of the Thousandth Life in the seat Sir James had created. (Three years later yet another such dinner was to be held, this time to signify the hoisting of the total to Two Thousand.)

The rocket seat was in 1965 installed in aircraft of the United States Navy and two years later came an incident of immense and, within context, almost final significance; the West German Government, appalled by the mounting losses of the Starfighter aircraft with which their Air Force was equipped—in sixty-six crashes thirty-seven pilots had died—reversed its previous policy in the face of public demand and ruled that its aeroplanes should henceforth be fitted with the Martin-Baker rocket seat.

The writing was on the wall. I telephoned for an appointment and set out on the last of my many visits to Denham. Sir James Martin, Jimmy Martin, the Guv'nor, confirmed what was in my mind: 'The days of live testing are over for us, Doddy, and I'll appoint no successor to you. We have proved everything there is to prove, for a great many years to come.'

We shook hands on it, and left it at that.